THE LAST MILE
IN ENDING
EXTREME POVERTY

THE LAST MILE
IN ENDING
EXTREME POVERTY

LAURENCE CHANDY
HIROSHI KATO
HOMI KHARAS
Editors

BROOKINGS INSTITUTION PRESS
Washington, D.C.

Library of Congress Cataloging-in-Publication data

The last mile in ending extreme poverty / Laurence Chandy, Hiroshi Kato, and Homi
Kharas, editors. — 1st Edition.
    pages cm
Includes bibliographical references and index.
    Summary: "Examines through new evidence, ideas, and solutions how to implement
three central changes that could lead to the eradication of extreme poverty in the world:
breaking cycles of conflict, supporting inclusive growth, and managing shocks and risks"
— Provided by publisher.
    ISBN 978-0-8157-2633-3 (pbk. : alk. paper) — ISBN 978-0-8157-2634-0 (e-book)
    1. Poverty. 2. Economic policy. 3. Economic development—Social aspects.
4. Risk management. I. Chandy, Laurence, editor. II. Kato, Hiroshi, 1926– editor.
III. Kharas, Homi J., 1954– editor.

    HC79.P6L355 2015
    339.4'6—dc23   2015006125

9 8 7 6 5 4 3 2 1

Typeset in Adobe Garamond

Composition by Cynthia Stock
Silver Spring, Maryland

Contents

Part II. Creating Jobs

Part III. Building Resilience

    Raj M. Desai

11 The Two Fragilities:
    Vulnerability to Conflict, Environmental Stress, and
    Their Interactions as Challenges to Ending Poverty   328
    Stephen C. Smith

12 Toward Community Resilience:
    The Role of Social Capital after Disasters   369
    Go Shimada

    Contributors   399

    Index   401

Acknowledgments

This volume is the outcome of an eighteen-month collaborative project between the Brookings Institution and the Japan International Cooperation Agency Research Institute (JICA-RI).

Earlier drafts of the volume's chapters were discussed at a two-day workshop held in Washington, D.C., in January 2014. The editors are grateful to the following individuals who attended the workshop and provided feedback on those drafts: Manish Bapna, Kathleen Beegle, Gero Carletto, Lindsay Coates, Margaret Enis Spears, Beth Ferris, Abigail Friedman, Alan Gelb, Margaret Grosh, Dean Jolliffe, Bob Lamb, Terra Lawson-Remer, Uma Lele, Johannes Linn, Margaret McMillan, Nigel Purvis, Steve Radelet, Amadou Sy, Alex Thier, Chris Tinning, and Caroline Wadhams.

The editors would also like to thank Noam Unger and Vera Songwe for reviewing the entire volume, Madelyn Swift for proofreading and overseeing the preparation of the final manuscript, and Eileen Hughes, Valentina Kalk, and Janet Walker from Brookings Institution Press.

Brookings is grateful to JICA for its financial and intellectual support of this project. Brookings recognizes that the value it provides is in its absolute commitment to quality, independence, and impact. Activities supported by its donors reflect this commitment, and the analysis and recommendations contained in this volume are not determined or influenced by any donation. The chapters reflect the views of the authors and not the official position of any specific organization.

1

From a Billion to Zero:
Three Key Ingredients to End Extreme Poverty

LAURENCE CHANDY, HIROSHI KATO, AND HOMI KHARAS

On January 20, 1949, in the first-ever televised U.S. presidential inauguration, President Harry Truman stood on the steps of the Capitol and foretold of a better world, one of international order and justice and greater freedom, rid of the scourge of poverty:

> More than half the people of the world are living in conditions approaching misery. Their food is inadequate. They are victims of disease. Their economic life is primitive and stagnant. Their poverty is a handicap and a threat both to them and to more prosperous areas. For the first time in history, humanity possesses the knowledge and the skill to relieve the suffering of these people.

More than sixty years later, the idea of a poverty-free world continues to capture the imagination of world leaders as well as lesser mortals. President Barack Obama, Truman's eleventh successor, had this to say in his 2013 State of the Union address:

> We also know that progress in the most impoverished parts of our world enriches us all—not only because it creates new markets, more stable order in certain regions of the world, but also because it's the right thing to do. In many places, people live on little more than a dollar a day. So the United States will join with our allies to eradicate such extreme poverty

in the next two decades by connecting more people to the global economy; by empowering women; by giving our young and brightest minds new opportunities to serve and helping communities to feed, and power, and educate themselves; by saving the world's children from preventable deaths; and by realizing the promise of an AIDS-free generation, which is within our reach.

Each of these two proclamations is inspiring on its own. Yet taken together, they cannot help but appear naïve. The elusiveness of the goal over so many years suggests that however well-meant, its pursuit may ultimately be futile.[1] Is achieving an end to poverty really possible?

If we think about poverty as a relative concept, then almost certainly it is not. Living standards among people vary greatly within every country, so the have-nots, as much as the haves, are a feature of every society. Many countries set national poverty lines in explicitly relative terms to capture this kind of disadvantage. For instance, the OECD club of rich economies tracks the share of each country's population that lives on less than half the income earned by the person in the middle of distribution (the median). Even in the OECD's most egalitarian countries, such as Denmark and Iceland, poverty by this measure remains prevalent. Since living standards vary much more between countries than within countries, global poverty, measured in relative terms, would appear even harder to eliminate.

If instead we think of poverty as an absolute concept, then its persistence should be less certain and its eradication more readily imaginable. Many countries set national poverty lines in absolute terms that reflect the cost of meeting certain basic needs. As any one of these countries grows richer, one can reasonably expect poverty by this measure to continuously fall as the needs of an increasing share of its population are fulfilled. Yet with rising living standards come changing social norms regarding what constitutes basic needs. Absolute poverty lines are consequently revised upward, ensuring that the goal of poverty elimination remains out of reach. (To be clear, this is a good thing, since it implies that the minimum standards by which people are expected to live are higher.) In this way, poverty lines defined in absolute terms usually still engender a relative concept of poverty.

Figure 1-1 illustrates this phenomenon. The richer countries are, the higher they set their poverty line—and the poorer they are, the lower their poverty line. It is notable, however, that this relationship does not hold in countries where the average income falls below a very meager level—around $3 to $4 a day, or a little over $1,000 a year. The poverty lines in those countries tend to gravitate

---

1. We credit Owen Barder for pointing out the historical precedents of these proclamations.

Figure 1-1. *Increase in Poverty Lines with Rise in Living Standards, Selected Countries*[a]

Daily poverty line per capita[b]

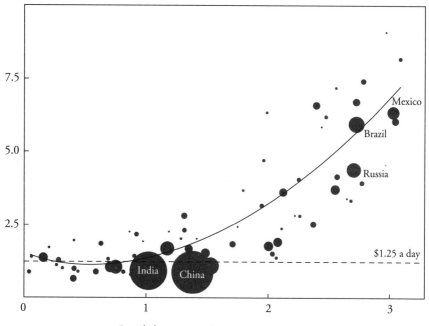

Log daily consumption per capita, 2005

Source: Authors' calculations based on data from Ravallion, Chen, and Sangraula (2009).
a. Bubble size represents relative size of country populations.
b. In 2005 purchasing power parity dollars.

around a similar mark. This discontinuity provides the basis for defining a truly absolute concept of poverty: the $1.25 a day poverty line that is used to measure extreme poverty globally.

The extreme poverty line corresponds to the average value of national poverty lines in the world's poorest countries and so avoids concerns about relative welfare or subjective judgments about who might be considered poor in any given society. Poverty has many dimensions, including poor health, unsafe drinking water, and lack of education, personal safety, and human rights—along with other, intangible elements that deny people a life of dignity. But its most fundamental element concerns the ability of families to have enough food and resources to survive and to think and plan beyond their short-term survival.

Under this most parsimonious definition, the end of poverty becomes a more reasonable proposition. Figure 1-2 illustrates the declining share of the world

Figure 1-2. *Global Extreme Poverty Rate, 1820–2010*[a]

Global extreme poverty rate

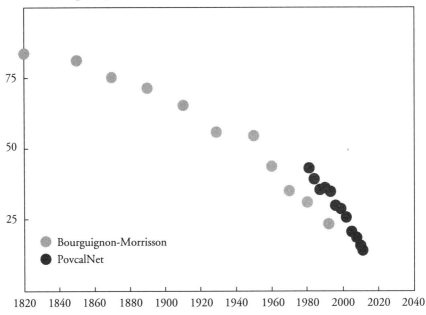

Source: Bourguignon and Morrisson (2002) and World Bank, "PovcalNet: An Online Analysis Tool for Global Poverty Monitoring" (http://iresearch.worldbank.org/PovcalNet/index.htm).
a. In contrast to official survey-based poverty measures, Bourguinon and Morrisson's poverty measures are based on national account estimates of income. To allow for comparison, Bourguinon and Morrisson anchor their results to the prevailing official global poverty estimate for 1992, which employed a poverty line of $1 a day (1985 purchasing power parity). The poverty line for PovcalNet poverty estimates is defined as $1.25 a day (2005 purchasing power parity).

population living on under $1.25 a day over time. This figure combines official estimates from the World Bank beginning in 1981 with admittedly shakier historical data constructed by François Bourguignon and Christian Morrisson that extend back to the Industrial Revolution in 1820. The pattern of observations shows that the rate of progress has remained relatively constant throughout the past 200 years. Some commentators point to a possible acceleration in the mid-twentieth century and to another at the start of the twenty-first century, but the overall picture is one of slow, gradual change: for two centuries the poverty rate has declined, on average, by just less than 0.5 percentage point a year. This trend seems humdrum in its monotony and its palpable lack of speed. Yet the story that it implies is all the more spectacular.

In the early 1800s, fewer than one in five people lived above the meager $1.25 threshold. In 2010, fewer than one in five people lived below it. This remarkable transition—from a world where destitution was virtually ubiquitous to one where only pockets of acute deprivation remain—suggests that the end of a long journey in extreme poverty eradication could be nearing. In 2011 (the most recent year for which we have global data), about 1 billion people lived in extreme poverty, or 14 percent of the world's population. Extending the trend from the past two centuries just a short distance into the future implies that the end of extreme poverty could soon be upon us. It is this inference that provides the empirical foundation for the global movement to eliminate extreme poverty by 2030. In 2015, this goal will likely be enshrined in an agreement between member states of the United Nations as one of the Sustainable Development Goals for 2030.

To be sure, it would be absurd to claim that an end to extreme poverty means an end to all deprivation and hardship in the world. Rather, it describes a world where the most egregious forms of destitution are consigned to history, where people no longer live so precariously that they fret about the source of their next meal or face a perpetual threat to their survival. Nor does the end of extreme poverty mark the end of global development—the end of the beginning may be a more accurate description. Nevertheless, it would be churlish to downplay its significance were this goal to be achieved: the end of extreme poverty would represent a key milestone in human progress.

We believe that the end of extreme poverty is achievable, but simply extrapolating from the historical trend of the global poverty rate is problematic. That's because the global poverty problem—its sources and solutions—is constantly evolving. In other words, the last mile in ending extreme poverty looks different from the miles already traveled. In this book we attempt to explain why—and how the last mile might successfully be completed.

We argue that ending extreme poverty requires peace, jobs, and resilience. These are issues that have been largely overlooked by so-called development experts and on which cutting-edge knowledge is blunt and for which best-practice solutions feel decidedly underwhelming. To make our case, we must shift our perspective beyond the global poverty rate to consider the trajectory of individual countries. In the remainder of this chapter, all references to "poverty" refer to extreme, monetary poverty, unless we state otherwise. We are acutely aware that the two are not the same, but we drop the prefixes for the sake of brevity.

Country Paths

The incremental, even-paced record of poverty reduction at the global level can give the impression that individual countries have followed a correspondingly uniform path—albeit from different starting points, with poorer countries beginning further back. That clearly has not been the case historically. The global poverty trajectory illustrated in figure 1-2 can be thought of as a middle road, with individual countries veering off wildly in different directions. Take just the past two decades: 1990 to 2010. In this period, the global poverty rate fell from 36.1 percent to 16.3 percent.[2] Success has been celebrated—the first Millennium Development Goal to halve global poverty was achieved seven years ahead of schedule. Yet of the developing countries for which there are data, two-thirds matched or exceeded the global record in percentage terms while one-third lagged behind. This twenty-year stretch contains cases of supercharged development (Indonesia, Vietnam), arrested development (Kenya, Madagascar), and development in reverse (Côte d'Ivoire, Bolivia), each reflected in the poverty rates reported from national surveys of household living standards. If the global poverty rate's historical regularity is cause for optimism that the end of extreme poverty is in sight, the record of individual countries offers a more ambivalent view.

On one hand, the star performers of the past twenty years serve as a reminder that sustained rapid poverty reduction is indeed possible, so that entire societies can be transformed in the space of a single generation. Given its sheer size, China is the most compelling example of this. What the world achieved in the space of 200 years—the reversal from fewer than one in five people living above $1.25 to fewer than one in five living below that threshold—China managed in little more than twenty years. The experience of China and other trailblazers provides a historical precedent for countries to sustain a rate of poverty reduction of 2.5 percentage points a year over decades—five times the speed of the global average over the past two centuries. If we assume conservatively that this is the maximum sustainable rate of poverty reduction, ending extreme poverty by 2030 would be a mathematical possibility virtually everywhere. The only exceptions would be a dozen or so small countries where poverty rates remained above 50 percent in 2010. Moreover, with a stronger concentration of global knowledge, skills, and resources devoted to helping those countries, it is not unreasonable to argue that they too could end extreme poverty.

On the other hand, the large number of countries that have made little or no inroads in reducing poverty over the past twenty years highlights the complexity of the task ahead. Take Côte d'Ivoire as an example. In the late 1980s, its extreme poverty rate stood at less than 10 percent and the country was widely admired for the capacity and professionalism of its government.[3] The

---

2. More commonly reported is the poverty rate for the developing world, which fell from 43.4 percent to 19.2 percent over the same period.
3. Van de Walle (2001).

subsequent two decades saw a macroeconomic crisis snowball into a deep and prolonged economic contraction, bringing with it rising poverty, falling school enrollment, and rising child malnutrition. Highly charged political competition inflamed ethnic tension and social unrest, culminating in a military coup in 1999 and two subsequent civil wars between the north and south.[4] According to the most recent survey of living standards, conducted in 2008 before the second civil war, the extreme poverty rate had risen to 35 percent. Côte d'Ivoire serves as a reminder that there is nothing inevitable about poverty reduction. The goal of ending extreme poverty in Côte d'Ivoire has morphed from a reasonable proposition only a generation ago to a herculean task today.

Côte d'Ivoire's reversal is tragic, but in terms of global poverty aggregates, it represents no more than a rounding error. It stands in contrast to China's takeoff, which has driven global poverty aggregates downward over the past two decades. The reason is obvious: China's population is sixty-eight times that of Côte d'Ivoire. More generally, global progress in fighting poverty has been judged by the average performance of developing countries. That allowed better performing countries—especially larger ones—to compensate for lagging ones. In the last mile, this rule no longer holds. It is not enough for most countries or a few big countries to perform well. There must be progress everywhere, without exception. The last mile requires not just good progress on average, but progress that leaves no one behind. That means progress is measured not by average performance but by the weakest performance, making the goal to end extreme poverty much more exacting than the earlier goal to halve global poverty—even though the numbers of people to be lifted out of poverty are similar.

Expressed another way, in the last mile every country must be on a short trajectory to end poverty. This is especially daunting for countries with high poverty rates today and a weak record of progress. Their trajectories to reach the zero mark by 2030 are especially steep and require the biggest turnarounds in performance. If any country deviates from its zero-poverty trajectory, the last mile will remain unfinished.

What holds true for countries is true for smaller units of analysis. The levels of and changes in national poverty rates inevitably conceal differences between subnational regions. Living standards in the coastal provinces of China rival those of advanced countries, but there are tens of millions of people living in extreme poverty in the hinterland. Côte d'Ivoire's conflict has left the country's northern population especially impoverished. The record of the last decade shows that rising prosperity within developing countries has, on average, been broadly shared but that this masks widening distributions in some economies

---

4. Cogneau, Houngbedji, and Mesplé-Somps (2014).

whose poor have been shortchanged.[5] Some fear that the Western phenomenon whereby a rising share of national income is captured by the richest 1 percent of the population could spread to the developing world. The last mile demands improving living standards not just across all countries but across all regions within countries and all households within those regions. No country, region, or household can be left behind.

In *The Great Escape*, Angus Deaton describes how the discovery and spread of technologies that underpin the development process necessarily result in imbalanced progress across people and places. Global poverty reduction has historically been characterized by that imbalance. In the last mile, the imbalance must be at least partially rectified, so that people everywhere see their living standards raised above the extreme poverty threshold.

Table 1-1 classifies the billion people living in extreme poverty according to two characteristics of the countries in which they live: the recent record of progress in reducing poverty and the poverty rate today.[6] This illustrates how fast countries are traveling and how far they have to go to reach the 2030 goal. The twenty-four countries in the top-left quadrant, which combine a high prevalence of poverty with a dismal record of progress over the past decade, give the goal its sternest test and must be a focus of any serious effort to understand what its achievement requires.[7] People in these countries face the greatest risk of being left behind.

However, an escape from extreme poverty for the nearly three-quarters of a billion people in the other three categories remains far from ensured. A particular concern is that countries may find it harder to maintain the same rate of poverty reduction as poverty levels approach zero. Since concentrations of people are typically thinner at the ends of the income spectrum, countrywide gains in income typically deliver less poverty reduction once poverty numbers reach low levels. Marginalized and remote communities can be hard to reach and can remain disconnected even if income growth at the country level is strong and sustained. Market and local governance failures or discrimination and exclusion

5. World Bank (2014b).

6. In countries with high poverty rates, more than 20 percent of the population lived on less than $1.25 a day in 2011; in countries with low poverty rates, less than 20 percent lived on $1.25. Slow- or no-progress countries saw poverty rates fall by less than 10 percent between 2002 and 2011; fast-progress countries saw poverty rates fall by at least 10 percent during that period. All country poverty estimates are based on official global poverty estimates produced by the World Bank, available on PovcalNet (http://iresearch.worldbank.org/PovcalNet/index.htm). PovcalNet assumes that the few countries with no data have the same poverty rate as the regional average. The record of progress for these countries is based on an informed guess.

7. The twenty-four countries are Afghanistan, Benin, Burundi, Cameroon, Central African Republic, Comoros, Democratic Republic of Congo, Côte d'Ivoire, Eritrea, Guinea-Bissau, Kenya, Liberia, Madagascar, Mauritania, Nigeria, Sao Tome and Principe, Sierra Leone, Somalia, South Sudan, Swaziland, Timor-Leste, Togo, Zambia, and Zimbabwe.

Table 1-1. *Country Prospects for Ending Poverty*[a]

	High poverty rate	Low poverty rate
Slow/no progress	265 million people in 24 countries	7 million people in 6 countries
Fast progress	520 million people in 22 countries	208 million people in 38 countries

Source: Authors' calculations based on World Bank. "PovcalNet: An Online Analysis Tool for Global Poverty Monitoring" (http://iresearch.worldbank.org/PovcalNet/index.htm).

a. See footnote 6 in text for details.

can create pockets of poverty in lagging subnational regions or among particular population groups. These groups face a real risk of being left behind. Although table 1-1 shows that at present there are only a few small countries with low poverty rates that show slow or no progress, the risk remains that others that have enjoyed fast rates of poverty reduction in the past will find it difficult to sustain that pace over their last mile.

Framing the Problem

For countries with a poor record in fighting poverty, the most immediate problem would appear to be getting on a zero-poverty trajectory in the first place because the factors that undermined past poverty reduction efforts may persist and thwart future progress. The idea that poverty is "sticky" is usually described in terms of poverty traps, in which poverty is a self-reinforcing equilibrium state. Poverty traps are used to explain the persistence of poverty in many of the most popular books on global poverty from the last decade, including Jeffrey Sachs's *The End of Poverty* and Paul Collier's *The Bottom Billion*. Thankfully, the empirical evidence for such traps is limited.[8] Canonical models that purport to explain poverty's self-reinforcing properties—such as the low-savings/low-capital trap and the malnourishment/low-productivity trap—seem to occur rarely in the real world, if at all.

Where Sachs and Collier are unquestionably right, however, is in their conclusion that poverty will not disappear of its own accord, especially in countries where it has been consistently high. A change in circumstances (such as the end of conflict in Cambodia) or policies (such as China's household responsibility system) or a well-crafted intervention (such as Brazil's Bolsa Família cash transfer program) is required to trigger a turning point in the quest to end poverty. The results of such changes, which usually are followed by subsequent changes

---

8. Kraay and McKenzie (2014). For recent research that purports to find evidence that poverty traps do exist, see Dercon and Christiaensen (2011) and Marenya and Barrett (2009).

in circumstances, policies, and interventions, can be dramatic. It therefore is prudent to focus attention on what circumstances, policies, and interventions can bring about positive change. We reject as foolhardy and dangerous the cynical view that government actions or aid cannot accomplish anything at all.

History is littered with examples of dramatic turnarounds in the fortunes of poor countries. Countries are readily written off as a lost cause, only to later prove that assessment spectacularly wrong. Max Weber, the pioneer of sociology, hypothesized in his 1915 book, *The Religion of China,* that the country's poverty was attributable to Confucian values, specifically the belief that individuals should adjust to the world's constraints. Weber saw that belief as incompatible with the tenets of capitalism—most prominently, entrepreneurship and innovation—which suggest that the world is something to be shaped. Gunnar Myrdal, a Nobel Laureate in economics, argued in his 1968 three-part volume, *The Asian Drama,* that India's economic takeoff was unlikely because of the country's traditional power structures, which could not enforce the discipline needed to implement development plans.

Bearing those cases in mind, we see no reason why extreme poverty cannot be eliminated by 2030 in any country. But conversely, there is no basis for assuming that poverty will end without positive changes in circumstances, policies, and interventions in each case.

Economic growth has, of course, been the main engine of mass poverty reduction in the past; the pursuit of poverty reduction has therefore been synonymous with the quest for growth. Historically, that search proved elusive in many developing countries. But since the 1990s, it has gradually become more successful. As illustrated in figure 1-3, more developing countries are recording sustained and rapid economic growth; consequently, fewer are seeing their economies shrink. Expressed another way, the last two decades have seen the fastest and most broad-based growth in developing countries, ever. That is why so many of the world's remaining poor live in countries with a strong recent record of poverty reduction, as shown in table 1-1.

This trend is a boon for the prospect of completing the last mile. Yet given the depth of poverty that exists in the world's poorest countries, it is not enough. These countries require full-fledged growth miracles that span decades; thankfully, those miracles are becoming more common. In 2007, the Growth Commission could identify only thirteen miracles—defined as average growth of 7 percent or more for at least twenty-five years—since 1950. They include many of the best-known and most studied examples of rapid development, such as Botswana, China, Japan, Korea, and Singapore. If the International Monetary Fund's growth projections until 2019 hold true, an astonishing sixteen more miracles could be added by that time, including in some of the world's poorest countries, such as Ethiopia, Laos, Liberia, Mozambique, and Rwanda.

Figure 1-3. *Dispersion in Average Rates of GDP per Capita Growth across Developing Countries*

Percent of countries

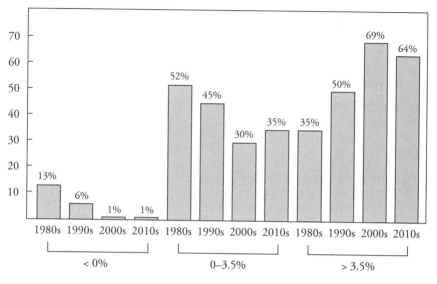

Source: Calculations based on data from International Monetary Fund (2014).

Despite that good news, we remain convinced that it will take more than growth strategies alone to finish the last mile. There will be places where growth fails to take off, where growth is only sporadic, and where the benefits of growth are unequally shared. That is why analyses of the future trajectory of global poverty view the completion of the last mile as a challenge even under the most optimistic growth scenarios.[9] Equatorial Guinea, which features among the sixteen potential new entries to the Growth Commission's miracle list, provides an arresting example of how in extreme circumstances, citizens can be almost entirely cut off from the benefits of growth. While lifting the constraints to growth must remain a focus of poverty reduction efforts, this book's focus is on three other ingredients that are needed to promote fast and sustained poverty reduction in many of today's poorest countries: peace, jobs, and resilience.

The absence of these ingredients is not a trap in the classical sense. Steady improvements in poverty reduction are possible without them. But neither is their absence simply a symptom of poverty: these ingredients are needed to

9. Bluhm, de Crombrugghe, and Szirmai (2015), Chandy, Ledlie, and Penciakova (2013), and World Bank (2014b).

Figure 1-4. *The Three Ingredients for Ending Poverty*

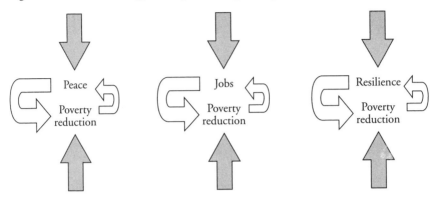

Source: Adapted from Blattman (2014).

accelerate and sustain the pace of poverty reduction; without them all, poverty is unlikely to end by 2030. We also believe that the standard toolkit of development economics has been of limited effectiveness in supplying these ingredients, which reflects the complexity of the problems that they engender and our limited understanding of them. The purpose of this book is both to expose and to begin to address these gaps in our knowledge.

Figure 1-4 illustrates the interdependence of these ingredients and poverty reduction. The circular arrows show that causation runs in both directions. Peace, jobs, and resilience promote poverty reduction, while poverty reduction promotes peace, jobs, and resilience. Crucially, the former effect outweighs the latter, as conveyed by the size of the circular arrows. In other words, reducing poverty improves the prospects for peace, jobs, and resilience only marginally, so antipoverty programs, illustrated by the upward facing arrows, will struggle to create a virtuous circle of poverty reduction by themselves. The last mile also requires investing in actions that directly seek to foster peace, jobs, and resilience, illustrated by the downward-facing arrows.

In the section that follows, we examine each of these ingredients and its relationship to poverty reduction. We treat the three ingredients separately, while recognizing that there are important links between them.

Peace

It is well established empirically that poor societies are less peaceful societies, given their greater propensity for armed conflict.[10] There are multiple mechanisms through which poverty can undermine the foundations of peace. Poverty

10. Fearon (2010).

can act as a direct trigger for conflict when resource scarcity creates competition between population groups, especially for basic needs such as food and land. Poverty can also create conditions in which peace is less likely, both by lowering the opportunity cost of violence for those with limited economic opportunities and by contributing to the weakness or absence of institutions that could mediate tensions.

Important though these mechanisms are, the impact of a society's stability on poverty is undoubtedly greater. Conflicts lead to the destruction of assets, both physical and human, that underpin productivity. They create uncertainty, which shortens people's time horizons and alters incentives in a way that stifles investment. These effects can endure long after a conflict ceases and peace is restored. Assets are slow to rebuild, and the high probability of a recurrence of conflict means that behavior is slow to revert to normal. This is borne out in surveys of entrepreneurs working in conflict-affected states. After controlling for a country's level of income, analysis shows that firms in these settings start smaller and grow more slowly, are less likely to upgrade products and services, and have less access to credit.[11]

Macroeconomic evidence is equally persuasive. Conflict is one of a small number of factors that have consistently been found to explain decelerations in economic growth. It is important to note, however, that the cessation of conflict is not a significant determinant of immediate accelerations of growth.[12] Countries need more than a window of stability to lay the foundations for poverty reduction and development; they need a guarantee of long-term peace and security.

Recent years have seen growing recognition in the global development community of this interdependence, enshrined in the mantra "no peace without development, no development without peace." But it is one thing to agree that peace and development should be addressed simultaneously; it is another to agree on how to do that. Exacerbating the challenge is the recognition that interventions relied on to secure peace remain limited and their impact blunt. International peacekeeping scores very well on measures of cost effectiveness but there are well-documented instances of failure. Increasingly the onus is on brokering inclusive political settlements to definitively end conflicts, although questions abound as to precisely how they can be achieved. Institutions that provide security, justice, and jobs are seen as critical pillars for forging trust and stability, but they take generations to build.[13]

As learning on how to secure and sustain peace advances slowly, the nature of modern war evolves apace. Until recently, the most talked about trend in conflict had been the sharp reduction in the number of concurrent conflicts around

11. Speakman and Rysova (2015).
12. Easterly and others (1993); Jones and Olken (2008); Pritchett and others (2013).
13. World Bank (2011).

Figure 1-5. *Extreme Poverty in Fragile and Stable Countries, 1990–2030*[a]

Number of people in extreme poverty (millions)

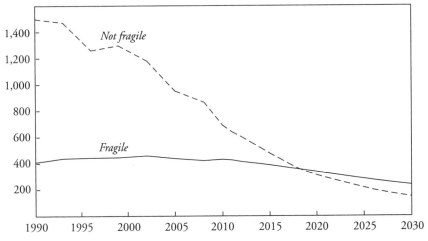

Source: Chandy, Ledlie, and Penciakova (2013).
a. Poverty data up to 2010 are official estimates; data after 2010 are projections.

the world, most notably the drop in civil wars. As a result of the end of the cold war, the number of active civil wars dropped from fifty or so to around thirty. But just as analysts began to believe that there was a secular trend toward peace, the pattern disappeared. The dominant narrative today is that conflicts are, on average, becoming more complex and protracted; that they have a greater impact on civilians, whose protection and rights are difficult to uphold; and that they involve more opportunistic actors who have less interest in agreeing to a settlement and less desire to govern.

It should come as no surprise that conflict is a dominant feature among the countries that are losing the battle against extreme poverty. Of the twenty-four countries identified in table 1-1 as combining high poverty rates with dismal records of poverty reduction, thirteen had hosted UN or regional peacekeeping missions in the last decade. Over that period, only three of the twenty-four—Benin, Swaziland, and Zambia—did not at some point meet the OECD DAC classification criteria for state fragility. Global poverty is becoming more concentrated in these countries: in 1990, one in five poor people in the world lived in a fragile state; two in five do so today. Baseline projections from one study show that share rising above 50 percent in 2018 and reaching nearly two-thirds by 2030 (figure 1-5).[14]

14. Chandy, Ledlie, and Penciakova (2013).

Conflict should not be considered a national affliction alone. Several countries that have low poverty rates and impressive records of poverty reduction have withstood long-standing subnational conflicts, such as the Naxalite guerilla movement in India's Red Corridor, the Moro rebellion in the Philippines, and until recently, the twenty-year rebellion by Joseph Kony's Lord's Resistance Army in Northern Uganda. These conflicts have remained relatively contained and have not prevented development from taking off elsewhere in each country. But the affected regions lag behind economically, creating pockets of poverty that inhabitants cannot escape.

Jobs

In a recent study, researchers at the World Bank analyzed over a dozen countries that recorded a large decrease in poverty over the past decade.[15] Their purpose was to identify the sources of additional household income that brought about an escape from poverty. In most cases, the dominant factor was an increase in the labor income of households, as illustrated in figure 1-6. A closer study of a subset of countries found that increased labor productivity, as opposed to increased hours worked, was the principal cause of income growth.[16] Understanding what factors enable people living in poverty to find productive work would therefore appear to offer some insight into how to complete the last mile.

Productive work for the poor typically means either wage-paying occupations; contractual agreements that incorporate workers into value chains; or raising yields on smallholder farms. Those who are unable to find such work are rarely unemployed in the sense that they are idle; instead, they are heavily underemployed, working in informal occupations in markets that are insufficiently integrated, or they are self-employed. In geographic areas where residents have little purchasing power and minimal connection to neighboring markets, people must scrape by on their own, often relying on natural resources for their livelihood, whether by farming without fertilizer or irrigation, foraging in forests, or fishing in rivers and coastal waters. As a result of population growth and the degradation of the environment, those resources are increasingly under stress and less capable of supporting decent livelihoods.

Poverty itself can be a hindrance to productive employment. The meager purchasing power of poor communities creates few opportunities for selling goods and services domestically, thereby reducing the demand for labor. In its severest form, poverty can result in the malnourishment of workers, which erodes their productivity. However, the dominant direction of causation runs

15. Azevedo and others (2013).
16. Inchauste and others (2012).

Figure 1-6. *Contributions to the Decline in $1.25-a-Day Poverty since 2000, Selected Countries*

Annual poverty reduction (percentage points)

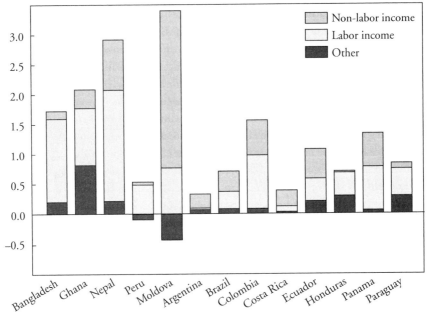

Source: Authors' calculations based on Azevedo and others (2013).

in the opposite direction. A move toward productive employment can mean a dramatic increase in household income and an overnight escape from poverty.

The centrality of productive jobs to both poverty reduction and the broader development agenda is increasingly recognized, as evidenced by the 2013 *World Development Report* and the emphasis on jobs in early iterations of the 2030 Sustainable Development Goals. However, it has proven difficult to translate diagnoses into actionable policies. For instance, there remains a lively debate over which sector provides the strongest basis for exiting poverty and sustaining development. Wage-paying jobs—or at least those with connections to the rest of the economy—can be found in many sectors: agriculture, nonfarm rural employment, manufacturing, and services. The traditional policy toolkit for supporting job creation contains prescriptions that have proven difficult to implement effectively (for instance, industrial policy and public works programs) or that are of doubtful effectiveness in affecting marginalized groups (for instance, easing business regulations).

Among the constraints to the promotion of productive jobs is the absence of any significant change in the structure of most of the world's poor economies, especially those in sub-Saharan Africa, despite the fact that many have recorded impressive rates of growth over the past decade. Structural transformation is a catalyst both for raising labor productivity and for enabling poor workers to switch occupations. Another constraint is the chronic underinvestment in the networks that connect people to markets.[17] It is self-evident that businesses and the people that they hire are more productive when they have access to electricity, water, transportation, communication, and financial services. But the high fixed costs of constructing the infrastructure behind those networks preclude their diffusion, especially in small, often landlocked, economies that dominate the last mile. Incomplete networks can account for the vast within-country differences in income observed in many economies—in Latin America, for instance, between-municipality differences in labor income within countries have been found to be twice as large as between-country differences.[18]

Resilience

There is a tendency to think of movement across a poverty line as being a one-way street, but in reality, households can easily slip backward. Longitudinal surveys of living standards typically show a high degree of "churn" around the poverty line. For instance, one study of Malawi found that 35 percent of all households fell into poverty while 38 percent moved out of poverty over a ten-year period.[19] Similar risks of backsliding exist for regions and countries: as discussed earlier, Côte d'Ivoire was held up as a model African economy in the 1980s before entering a protracted political and economic crisis.

Resilience—the mitigation of shocks and their effects—is critical to preserving progress against poverty and to completing the last mile. Shocks come in various forms. At the household level, they include illness, loss of a job, or stolen assets. At the community or regional level, poor harvests or natural disasters can have devastating consequences. At the country level, commodity price swings and political turmoil are major sources of instability. Cross-border shocks such as outbreaks of infectious diseases present a unique set of challenges. Resilience to these shocks entails a combination of risk reduction, risk sharing, better preparation, and effective response and recovery.

Poverty itself is an important driver of vulnerability and the absence of resilience. Poor people live in places that lack effective institutions to provide resilience. They have no access to formal coping mechanisms, such as credit

17. Hausmann (2014).
18. Acemoglu and Dell (2010).
19. Narayan, Pritchett, and Kapoor (2009).

and insurance markets: only 23 percent of adults living on less than $2 a day report having an account at a formal financial institution.[20] Informal insurance mechanisms such as group or kin-based arrangements can quickly break down when entire communities are affected.[21] Weak or bad governance in many poor countries means that public goods that can act as a critical defense against shocks for the poor—infrastructure, regulation, access to information—are too often underprovided.

Conversely, vulnerability to shocks is a powerful cause of poverty. Shocks can mean not just the drying up of an income stream for a household but the destruction of wealth, the buildup of debt, and the erosion of future earning potential. Families may sell productive assets such as livestock in a desperate effort to survive a drop in income and maintain a subsistence rate of consumption. Even temporary shocks can therefore have permanent negative effects on living standards that can cross generations when nutrition and children's schooling are affected. For instance, ten years after droughts hit communities in Ethiopia and Tanzania in the 1990s, the consumption levels of poor households remained 17 to 40 percent below pre-disaster levels.[22]

While poor people are the least resilient, risks remain considerable at income levels that far exceed the poverty line. One study of Chile, Mexico, and Peru found that while the probability of backsliding into poverty during a five-year period decreased as incomes rose further from the poverty line, it remained significant (above 10 percent) even when incomes stood at twice the poverty line (figure 1-7).[23] That demonstrates the importance of boosting resilience if poverty is to be eradicated. There is growing recognition of the importance of this issue in the global development community. Cost-benefit analyses have shown many risk management interventions to be highly effective, although those interventions remain underused.[24] One notable success has been the spread of social safety net programs across the developing world. However, their coverage remains thinnest in the poorest countries. In low-income countries, less than 10 percent of the population is covered.[25] When it comes to mitigating the effects of shocks, speed has proven a particular challenge. A study of East Africa found that the cost of a drought to households living in extreme poverty increases from $0 to $50 per household if the response is delayed by four months after harvest but rises sharply to $1,300 if support is delayed by six

20. Global Findex (2014).
21. Morduch (1999).
22. Carter and others (2005); Beegle, Dehejia, and Gatti (2006).
23. López-Calva and Ortiz-Juárez (2014). National poverty lines in the three countries range between $4 and $5 a day in 2005 purchasing power parity. For evidence of similar dynamics in Nigeria using a poverty line close to the global $1.25 threshold, see Corral, Molini and Oseni (2015).
24. World Bank (2014a).
25. Gentilini and others (2014).

Figure 1-7. *Vulnerability to Falling into Poverty*

Probability of falling into poverty based on national poverty lines (percent)[b]

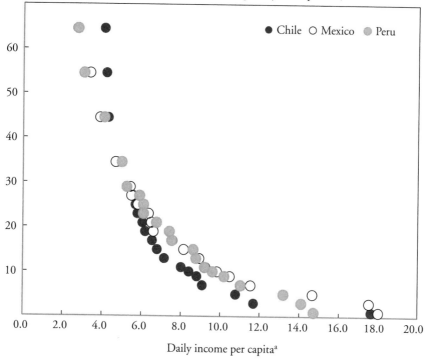

Daily income per capita[a]

Source: López-Calva and Ortiz-Juárez (2015).
a. In 2005 purchasing power parity (PPP) dollars.
b. National poverty rates in the three countries range between $4 and $5 a day in 2005 PPP.

months or more due to the impact on children and distress sales of livestock and other property.[26]

Moreover, the changing nature of risks means that the resilience agenda is constantly evolving. For instance, over the past two decades, maternal health risks and the frequency of economic recessions have subsided in all regions. Meanwhile, rates of reported crime have risen in Latin America and sub-Saharan Africa. Arguably the most alarming trend in risks is the increased reports of natural disasters. There are currently about 800 natural disasters each year, affecting 200 million people, or approximately double the number reported twenty years ago.[27] One-fifth of the affected people have to leave their homes, becoming internally displaced.[28] The Intergovernmental Panel on Climate Change

26. Clarke and Vargas Hill (2013).
27. Relief Web (2014).
28. Ferris (2010).

predicts that the frequency of natural disasters is likely to increase further as a consequence of global warming.

Crafting Solutions

The previous discussion argues that peace, jobs, and resilience are critical ingredients in completing the last mile, that completion demands actions that extend beyond traditional poverty reduction efforts, and that existing approaches to supply these ingredients have not had enough impact and reflect insufficient understanding of the issues entailed.

To explore these issues further, we brought together a group of leading experts, including both practitioners and academics, and asked them to think about what can be done to secure peace, create jobs, and strengthen resilience for the world's poorest people. Their answers are contained in the eleven chapters that follow. These chapters do not offer comprehensive solutions nor are they wholly prescriptive. In some cases, their aim is simply to better understand the problem. In that respect, they help to define an agenda for the current generation of development analysts and practitioners. In other cases, they offer bold proposals that deserve serious consideration and scrutiny. Common to all chapters is the recognition that past experiences, both good and bad, are replete with lessons. Poor countries have a great deal to learn from each other—as do the panoply of organizations that make up the global development community. As a collection, these chapters represent an important step in closing the knowledge gap that defines the last mile.

Securing Peace

Bruce Jones begins in chapter 2 by assessing the global community's capability of sustaining peace. Jones argues that with respect to the short-term goal of intervening in and ending conflicts, the international system deserves more credit than it normally receives. He notes the significant role that it has played in reducing the number of conflicts since the end of the cold war, citing the actions of the UN Security Council, regional and national actors, and the plethora of mediators, peacekeepers, and observers. While the success rate of its efforts appears meager in absolute terms—mediation efforts fail roughly three-quarters of the time while peacekeeping operations fail roughly half the time—measured against the counterfactual of ongoing conflict, their value comes into focus.

Jones's chapter is devoted for the most part to the broader goal of establishing long-term peace in states that have experienced conflict. He begins by highlighting the importance of forging strong political settlements or pacts between elites—a process that he describes as an essential interim step between postconflict stabilization and longer-term institution building. Such settlements provide a medium-term guarantee of stability and a means for extending the time horizon of citizens and elites so that longer-term planning can begin. Jones argues that we remain very much at the bottom of the learning curve in terms of understanding what makes for an enduring political settlement. One salient factor on which there is reasonable evidence is the degree to which settlements are inclusive and so bring together key warring factions. Open competition and full inclusion can foster factionalism and have potentially destabilizing effects, so a balanced, "inclusive-enough" approach to which elites subscribe may be preferred.

Jones then turns to the longer-term challenge of building credible political and security institutions in developing countries to serve as stress buffers when countries inevitably incur shocks and societal or political pressures. These institutions offer the best chance of ending cycles of conflict. This is where the international system comes in for Jones's most withering criticism. The international system's weakness here owes less to the paucity of technical expertise and more to the absence of a dedicated organization or agency to impart that expertise. No part of the existing international architecture is devoted to helping states engage in political development, foster credible security institutions, or build the instruments of the rule of law. The solution, Jones insists, is to stop castigating the security, humanitarian, and development communities for failing to build bridges to each other and instead to build a coherent architecture to fill the gap between those communities.

One of the most striking new elements of national development strategies in many countries over the past fifteen years has been the inclusion of state building as an overarching goal, defined by the OECD as "an effort to strengthen the capacity and legitimacy of state institutions to consolidate effective, legitimate, and resilient states." This objective has been enthusiastically promoted within parts of the development community as an essential antidote to fragility and conflict. In chapter 3, Ryutaro Murotani and Yoichi Mine grapple with the practical challenges that donors have faced in designing and implementing state building programs.

The authors begin by identifying an inherent tension in the theory of state building: that the ability of the *central* state to earn legitimacy depends on its demonstrated capacity to deliver services *locally*. This mechanism for fostering trust in the state seems plausible so long as citizens view the different levels of the state as being one and the same. But if central and local institutions are viewed as distinct—which seems especially likely in countries where the central state is weak, information flows are limited, and society is fragmented—then the mechanism would appear to break down.

Murotani and Mine show how donors have struggled to resolve this tension and in so doing may have exacerbated it instead. Donor efforts to support state building have tended to be concentrated on the central state and have consequently been criticized for lack of visibility outside national capitals and for failing to alter the most obvious aspects of government performance: access to and quality of services delivered to beneficiaries. Furthermore, a focus on strengthening the central state has drawn skilled personnel away from local-level institutions, especially in countries where the size of the overall skill pool is limited.

The authors argue persuasively that donor engagement in fragile states should be geared toward bridging the gap between state institution building and improvement of local livelihoods. They suggest three ways in which that can be achieved: strengthening the capacity of subnational institutions to deliver services; raising the accountability of local institutions by promoting participation and establishing feedback mechanisms; and promoting inclusive partnerships between national and local levels of government by ensuring that subnational units are treated equally.

The authors demonstrate this approach through three case studies. Afghanistan's community-driven development initiative, the National Solidarity Program, demonstrates that improved trust and institutional development at the village level do not automatically "trickle up" to the provincial and federal level. In Northern Uganda, the expulsion of the Lord's Resistance Army provided an opportunity to address long-standing horizontal inequalities through capacity building of subnational institutions and participation of returning displaced people. Finally, finding an appropriate mechanism of cooperation between the Bangsamoro autonomous government and the national government provided the basis for successful completion of peace negotiations in the Mindanao region of the Philippines.

In chapter 4 Alastair McKechnie and Marcus Manuel examine the role of external assistance in reducing poverty in fragile and conflict-affected environments. In these countries, aid remains a dominant source of funds; therefore, how it is used is of critical importance. Foreign direct investment is either altogether absent or limited to the extractive sector; domestic revenues are growing but more slowly than elsewhere and from a modest base; and remittances feature prominently in only a few countries. Therefore, while in other settings donors are looking for new ways to be useful, in fragile states the debate is over how to address a multitude of critical needs with limited resources.

Recent experience demonstrates just how hard it is to balance those needs. McKechnie and Manuel juxtapose the postconflict experience of Afghanistan and Sierra Leone to show how easily progress on different fronts can become imbalanced. In Afghanistan, large amounts of quickly disbursed aid helped drive significant development gains, but the sustainability of those gains stands in jeopardy given the failure to improve the security and political environment. In Sierra Leone, personal security and a successful political transition represent hard-won goals, but inadequate donor funding has slowed the pace of economic rehabilitation and hence increased the threats to longer-term peace.

The establishment of the g7+ in 2008—a coalition of self-identifying fragile states—has sought to resolve these issues. Its purpose has been to encourage fragile states to share their experiences and to advocate reforms in the way that the international community engages in conflict-affected environments. A "New Deal," endorsed by g7+ members and most donors, was agreed on in 2011 and is now being rolled out in eight pilot countries. McKechnie and Manuel strongly welcome the g7+ leadership and the core elements of the New Deal. But they're withering in their criticism of donors' behavior since the agreement was signed, and with a few notable exceptions they see little sign of broad substantial change.

The authors identify three areas where reforms to external assistance are most urgently needed and could transform its impact. The first is a top-to-bottom refocusing of resource allocation. They argue for a shift in resources within donors from security to aid and development spending; in aid allocations across countries from richer, more stable countries to fragile states; and in aid allocations within those countries to peacekeeping and state-building objectives, specifically law enforcement, the judicial system, job creation, and infrastructure. Second, they advocate a shift to aid delivery that embodies principles of effectiveness—using country systems, better risk management, faster delivery, and fostering institutions—that today receive only lip service. Finally, the authors propose a New Deal for the private sector in fragile states that envisions a country-driven approach to private sector development, one in which stakeholders agree to reforms through a mutual accountability agreement.

From a purely arithmetic point of view, ending extreme poverty in many of the world's fragile and conflict-affected states within a generation appears a daunting challenge. As already demonstrated, many of these countries have very high poverty rates, a persistently poor track record in reducing poverty, or both. But, as Gary Milante argues in chapter 5, the goal is more complicated than mere numbers convey. He characterizes development in countries affected by violence and war as a "wicked problem," meaning that there are no definitively right or wrong solutions in those settings. The application of development blueprints and paradigmatic models is likely to prove unworkable and possibly even harmful. A rejection of such models does not imply a rejection of all historical experience, however. On the contrary, Milante suggests that as fragile states seek to identify their own paths toward ending poverty, the trajectories of other countries over the past generation—whose record against poverty has been mapped through hundreds of household surveys—provide a valuable source of information from which to draw lessons. The experiences of other countries are best understood as heuristics. They can serve as touchstones when there is an opportunity to benefit from similar programs, waypoints when a country finds itself on a similar positive path, and warning signs when a country is on a similar but undesirable path.

To put this idea into practice, Milante develops a new methodology, which he calls the "thousand paths" approach. Starting with a particular country of interest, he runs a simulation exploring a range of possible futures, each consisting of a sequence of relevant historical spells of poverty reduction drawn from other countries that have been hypothetically threaded together into a chain. The relevance of each spell to the country of interest is determined by the degree to which the two share common features, captured in a collection of variables. The simulations are re-run a thousand times, during which the weights applied to the variables are randomized to generate new threads composed of different historical spells. The spells that are repeatedly drawn from the simulations are then explored to produce lessons for the country of interest.

The results of this approach are original and compelling. They reveal what the Democratic Republic of Congo can learn from Cambodia's agricultural productivity gains in the 2000s, what Yemen might garner from Ecuador's use of oil revenues to finance social assistance programs in the 2000s, and how Nepal might avoid Tanzania's mistakes in land reforms in the 1990s and 2000s. Milante recommends deeper dives into these and other cases studies and proposes knowledge exchanges involving policymakers and advisers who participated in those experiences as a way of using these results to assist leaders of fragile states tasked with navigating an uncertain future.

Creating Jobs

Approximately 80 percent of the world's extremely poor people live in rural areas and 60 percent work in agriculture. Those striking statistics suggest a critical role for agricultural development in the last mile. In chapter 6, John McArthur looks at how this role can be played most effectively. The volume of donor assistance to agriculture has doubled since 2006, although it remains at only half of its peak in the mid-1980s. In addition, new multilateral initiatives and national investor roundtables are seeking to mobilize and direct private capital in ways that include poor people in agricultural value chains.

McArthur begins by parsing a pivotal debate in development economics: is poverty elimination best achieved by boosting the incomes of farmers where they already work or by creating higher-wage, off-farm jobs for them? He notes the general equilibrium effects triggered by agricultural development, identifying three routes through which agricultural productivity can support poverty reduction: by directly raising the income of farmers; by freeing up labor for nonfarm jobs; and by raising the competitiveness of an economy by reducing food prices. These potential effects help to explain the significant role attributed to agricultural development in the empirical literature. Left unresolved is the question of the sufficiency of agricultural development for aggregate growth and poverty reduction and its implications for public investment decisions, in which trade-offs are paramount. This issue becomes more complicated once it is acknowledged that the relevance of agricultural development to poverty reduction differs according to an economy's characteristics and the depth of the poverty being addressed.

Indeed, the hazards of drawing generalizations from one country to another extend beyond the question of agriculture's role in poverty reduction to the potential for and constraints to agricultural development. McArthur demonstrates the extent to which the agricultural sector varies across economies with respect to their location in global markets, their current mix of crops, and their agricultural potential. Each crop has its own physical yield profile, market price, and responsiveness to inputs. Farm success depends on access to high-yielding seeds, water, nutrients, and reliable markets for buying inputs and selling outputs. That adds up to a vast number of moving parts that need to be controlled for in order to conduct a rigorous comparative analysis.

Alongside this tremendous country-specific variation some common challenges remain. For instance, among the world's poorest economies, employment is especially concentrated in agriculture, yields are persistently low and linked with negligible use of inputs, and low input use is partly explained by the cost of inputs and the difficulty of accessing them. McArthur identifies multiple priorities that can serve to boost agricultural productivity in these settings, including investment in transport infrastructure, subsidized inputs for the poor, warehousing, pooled sales, climate insurance, pooled credit facilities, and research on disease-resistant seed varieties. So despite the need for case specificity, the components of a broad agenda to reduce poverty through agricultural development are already largely known—the challenge is to tailor them to each economy's circumstances and bring them to scale.

One of the clearest takeaways from analyses of the future trajectory of global poverty is the pivotal role that Africa will play. It is not just that poverty in Africa is deeper and more prevalent than in other regions. Sufficient economic growth should, in theory, be able to overcome that, and many African economies have demonstrated a capacity for sustained growth over the past decade or more. An additional challenge is the failure of economic growth to convert into significant poverty reduction on the continent. In chapter 7, John Page argues that Africa's structural pattern of growth is partly responsible for that failure.

As economies develop, the allocation of capital and labor to different sectors and the contribution of those sectors to overall output typically shift. That transformation represents an important source of growth in itself if it entails a shift from lower- to higher-productivity activities. Africa's economies have the potential for significant structural change as the productivity of different sectors varies widely and most of the continent's labor force is engaged in its least productive sector: agriculture. As noted earlier, however, such a transformation has failed to come about.

One consequence of that failure is the meager scale of Africa's manufacturing sector, whose share of the continent's output has remained unchanged for forty years. This stands in stark contrast to the output of the tiger economies of Asia, whose textile and electronics factories are enduring symbols of their dynamic growth. Page notes a small shift in Africa's economic structure since 2000, but rather than marking a delayed start to the continent's industrialization, it signals a movement of labor into trade and distribution services. These sectors have only marginally higher productivity than agriculture, and their productivity has fallen with the entry of new workers. That leads Page to conclude that the structural changes observed represent a symptom of poverty rather than a source of poverty reduction. He presents both cross-country evidence and country-level simulations to argue that Africa's performance in reducing poverty would have been better had the region started its structural transformation earlier and had it experienced more robust growth of manufacturing and other sectors that yield high value added per worker.

Page offers a two-pronged strategy for raising the poverty dividend from Africa's growth. The first part builds on McArthur's recommendations in chapter 6 to boost the productivity of the continent's least productive and most labor-intensive sector, agriculture. The second part is to develop an industrial strategy that can deliver the continent's much-needed structural transformation. It is important to note that this strategy can be used to support not just manufacturing but agro-industry and tradable services. Page describes the latter as "industries without smokestacks," given their job-creating potential and their responsiveness to the same interventions: infrastructure and skills development, improved trade logistics and border procedures, and development of special economic zones.

Governance is fundamentally about choices and trade-offs, and navigating them successfully is a challenge both for the governments of developing countries and for the donor governments that assist them. In fragile states, the challenge is especially acute. The problems that underlie fragility—poverty, weak governance, ethnic fragmentation—are intertwined, and the combination of fast-unfolding events and goals with markedly different time frames means that the best choices and the valuation of trade-offs need to be regularly reassessed. In chapter 8, Shane Evans and Michael Carnahan explore these issues in the context of a renewed focus on the imperative of job creation and private sector–led development in fragile states. They focus on small island states where small domestic markets, long distances to global markets, and vulnerability to external shocks make it especially difficult to build a thriving and dynamic private sector.

The authors identify three foundations of economic growth in fragile states. The first is peace and stability. There is a complicated feedback loop here since certain patterns of economic growth can exacerbate the drivers of conflict, such as competition for scarce resources. The second foundation is investments in productivity and participation. The latter may include the reintegration of combatants and displaced people into the labor market so that growth does not entrench the marginalization of excluded groups. The third foundation is policy and institutional development to support the two other foundations, which may entail unwinding short-termist, unsustainable, and distortionary policies that served governments during a prior conflict.

Evans and Carnahan explain the difficulty that developing country governments and donor agencies face in allocating their efforts and resources across these three domains. An attempt to sequence rather than distribute efforts emerges as a sensible strategy, even though any sequencing can easily be superseded by changing circumstances. The authors propose an initial emphasis on peace and stability followed by a gradual shift toward productivity and participation over the medium to long term, with policy and institutional strengthening embedded throughout. The corollary of this sequence for developing country governments entails initially channeling a disproportionately large share of government expenditures through the recurrent budget and then transitioning toward devoting a greater share to the development (or capital) budget. Through an analysis of Australian aid and partner governments' public expenditures, the authors find some evidence of this stylized pattern in the postconflict transitions under way in the Solomon Islands and Timor-Leste respectively. Both countries find themselves in the difficult transition between focusing on peace and stability and increasing productivity and participation.

"Inclusive growth" may be a relatively new term, but it has deep roots in the literature on growth with equity that arose from East Asia's development experience. In chapter 9, Akio Hosono draws lessons from the Asian experience for sub-Saharan Africa. He begins by highlighting the importance of policies and a physical environment that support efficient growth. Much has been written about the former, much less about the latter. Hosono emphasizes basic infrastructure for energy and transport, sometimes in economic development corridors, along with "inclusive finance" to provide credit to agricultural producers and to small and medium-size firms.

He goes on to identify three strategies for inclusive growth. In each case, he draws on case studies from Africa to show how East and South Asian strategies can be adapted and implemented in different settings. The first strategy, of increasing staple crop productivity, points to the importance of staples produced and consumed by the poor. In South Asia, the initial wave of the Green Revolution increased wheat yields in the northwest and delta regions of India, but it was the second wave, which focused on rice, that had a transformative impact on poverty. In the case of Tanzania, rice yields of six tons per hectare (thrice the national average) have already been reached with improved farming techniques and irrigation.

The second strategy concerns diversifying agriculture to include higher-value crops and strengthening the agro-industry value chain. Thailand made this an explicit strategy in its economic development plans in the mid-1980s. A similar approach has since been taken by Kenya that has served not only to create productive jobs but to stem the trend of deforestation through use of small-holder horticulture and new farm forestry models. The third strategy—support for light manufacturing—is inextricably associated with East Asia's rise. Hosono adds a twist by emphasizing the links that light manufacturing can have with the development of agriculture. This approach is currently being attempted by Ethiopia.

Building Resilience

What can the history of social policy reform in rich countries teach us about the role of social protection in completing the last mile? This question is explored by Raj Desai in chapter 10, which focuses on the political feasibility of designing and sustaining poverty-reducing welfare programs. He submits that social protection is likely to play a significant part in eliminating global poverty. The end of extreme poverty in today's rich countries, where poverty rates fell from single digits to zero, coincided with the creation of large welfare states in the post–World War II era. Welfare programs had a transformative impact, lifting the living standards of the destitute while establishing a social floor that protected all members of society. Many of today's middle-income countries appear to be at a similar stage of development, in which social protection is needed to tackle remaining pockets of extreme poverty.

One of the salient features in the creation of welfare states in today's rich countries was the support of the middle class as well as the organized working class, which together represented an unassailable political alliance. The durability of welfare programs and institutions is attributed to the buy-in of the middle class, the principal source of public financing through tax revenues. Achieving that buy-in had implications for program design: at their inception, welfare programs in today's rich countries had broad or universal coverage so that the middle class itself was not excluded from their benefits.

Many of today's developing countries are in the midst of establishing their own social protection programs. But the pattern that they have tended to follow is different from that in rich countries, a difference that can be explained largely by context. In today's developing countries, labor tends to be less organized and have less bargaining strength; much of the labor force remains in the informal sector and thus is excluded from formal contributory welfare schemes; and public policy preferences have shifted toward targeting particular populations to achieve efficiency and value for money.

The upshot is that the reverse dynamic appears to be playing out: instead of middle class buy-in resulting in broader and more comprehensive social protection programs in developed countries, targeted and fragmented programs are inhibiting middle-class support for social protection in developing countries. Through a simple benchmark exercise, Desai shows that Asian states are lagging well behind today's rich countries in their development of social protection: India today is already richer than Germany was when it introduced social insurance for all workers in the late 1880s; Indonesia is richer than the United States was in 1935, when the Social Security Act was passed; and China is richer than Britain was in 1948, when the National Health service was introduced. Desai infers that the last mile in poverty reduction is more likely to be achieved and sustained through universal social policies that garner broader political support by including the nonpoor as beneficiaries. That is especially true in fragile states, where targeting may exacerbate social tensions, whereas universality can support the goals of nation building and social cohesion. This approach goes against the targeting paradigm championed by the donor community.

Across the multitude of development indexes that rank countries, it is common to see the usual suspects bunched at one end or the other. That holds true for indexes of state weakness and of vulnerability to negative effects of climate change. In chapter 11, Stephen Smith explores the interactions between these two types of fragility, which are especially important given the challenge that both pose for poverty reduction and the increasing environmental fragility anticipated over the next fifteen years as a result of climate change and other forms of environmental degradation. The chapter gives thirty-five examples from across the developing world that bring home the immediacy of these issues and discusses ongoing efforts to manage them effectively.

The causality running from climate change to conflict predominantly concerns the externalities of climate adaptation strategies. Large-scale migration and accelerated exploitation of natural resources by individuals and communities act as stressors that lead to heightened risks of conflict. This dynamic is exemplified by experiences in Bangladesh, Kenya, Nigeria, Sudan, and Uganda. Poorly conceived adaptation strategies pursued by governments, such as interest group–dominated management of environmental resources, can likewise lead to violence and war.

Moreover, violent conflict can lead to accelerated environmental degradation. This time the key channel is the breakdown or distortion of governance. Smith explores examples from Afghanistan, Nepal, the Democratic Republic of Congo, and Sierra Leone.

Smith examines policy options for facilitating peaceful adaptation to environmental change, halting the more egregious instances of domestic environmental damage, and securing the livelihoods of populations affected by environmental degradation. He describes the tension between supporting autonomous adaptation and planned adaptation, especially in fragile and poorly governed environments. For the donor community, that balancing act is reflected in efforts to strengthen state capacity while protecting citizens and strengthening citizens' resilience. Smith persuasively argues that just as the two fragilities can create a vicious cycle, there are likely to be significant mutual benefits to governments and donors in taking an integrated approach to addressing the two issues.

What role can social capital play in building the resilience of communities to natural disasters? That is the question investigated by Go Shimada in chapter 12. Interest in the role of social capital has arisen partly from necessity: with natural disasters becoming more frequent, poor countries being most at risk, and the poorest members of those countries facing the greatest vulnerability, autonomous solutions that center on the actions of poor people themselves arguably offer the best chance of success. Shimada views social capital as the most viable—and perhaps only—social safety net available to the extremely poor during a crisis. That is partly a function of the typically weak states within which extremely poor populations live, where formal safety nets are undeveloped. But more important is the resilience of social capital itself. In the immediate aftermath of a natural disaster, the functioning of institutions and markets can quickly break down. For that reason, social capital is especially relied on during emergencies, when social networks and norms of reciprocity and trust become core components of survival strategies.

Shimada makes a helpful distinction between what he describes as the recovery and reconstruction phases that follow a disaster, each of which is key to demonstrating resilience. The recovery phase concerns the restoration of the basic functions of society. In the reconstruction phase, the goal is to create a new and vibrant economy, recognizing that the pre-disaster state can never be fully reproduced. Shimada argues that social capital has an important role to play during both phases. During the recovery phase, social capital supports mutual assistance and collective action and ultimately encourages community members to return to disaster-hit areas. During the reconstruction phase, social capital can catalyze job matching and help businesses to rebuild. Drawing on examples from JICA aid programs, Shimada argues that there are many opportunities for promoting social capital through disaster prevention and relief efforts and that they should be seized. The preparation of hazard maps and community-based recovery projects offer some promising lessons to inform the design of future programming.

Conclusion: Push-Pull Engines for the Last Mile

The most efficient way of propelling a long train forward is to employ multiple engines, positioned strategically along its length. Typically, the engine(s) at the front "pulls" about two-thirds of the weight, while the rear engine(s) "pushes" the remaining one-third. This structure of "distributed power" reduces friction losses. The process of economic development and poverty reduction can be thought of in a similar way. Economic growth and the policies that support it provide the bulk of the force that pulls people toward higher living standards. But simultaneous efforts are needed to push those people and places that are left behind. The chapters in this book focus on where the push needs to occur if the last mile in ending extreme poverty is to be completed. They address common problems that serve as a drag on poverty reduction. In each case, the potential for overcoming the problem through general growth-enhancing policies seems to be insufficient. Additional actions to solve these problems are needed.

The goals of securing peace, creating jobs, and building resilience have tended to evade straightforward solutions and technocratic learning. As a result, today's toolkit of strategies and interventions remains inadequate and incomplete. While the proposals presented in this book fall short of providing complete guidance to developing countries and the broader global development community, they begin to address those deficiencies.

The future trajectory of global poverty remains impossible to predict, but our understanding of what it will take to navigate the last mile is growing. The challenge for the global community is to expand and act on that knowledge so that the goal of achieving a poverty-free world by 2030 is achieved.

References

Acemoglu, Daron, and Melissa Dell. 2010. "Productivity Differences between and within Countries." *American Economic Journal: Macroeconomics* 2, no.1: 169–88.

Azevedo, Joao Pedro, and others. 2013. "Is Labor Income Responsible for Poverty Reduction? A Decomposition Approach." Policy Research Working Paper 6414. Washington: World Bank.

Beegle, Kathleen, Rajeev H. Dehejia, and Roberta Gatti. 2006. "Child Labor and Agricultural Shocks." *Journal of Development Economics* 81, no.1: 80–96.

Blattman, Chris. 2014. "Poverty and Violence: The Micro-Level Evidence" (http://chrisblattman.com/files/2014/06/USAID-CMM-June-2014-Speaking-notes.pdf).

Bluhm, Richard, Denis de Crombrugghe, and Adam Szirmai. 2015. "Poor Trends: The Pace of Poverty Reduction after the Millennium Development Agenda." In *Growth Is Dead, Long Live Growth: The Quality of Economic Growth and Why It Matters*, edited by Lawrence Haddad, Hiroshi Kato, and Nicolas Meisel. JICA Research Institute.

Bourguignon, Francois, and Christian Morrisson. 2002. "Inequality among World Citizens: 1820–1992." *American Economic Review* 92, no. 4: 727–44.

Carter, Michael R., and others. 2005. "The Long-Term Impacts of Short-Term Shocks: Poverty Traps and Environmental Disasters in Ethiopia and Honduras." *Basis Brief* 28 (May). Collaborative Research Support Program, Department of Agricultural and Applied Economics, University of Wisconsin, Madison (http://crsps.net/wp-content/downloads/BASIS/Inventoried%202.24/13-2005-2-56.pdf).

Chandy, Laurence, Natasha Ledlie, and Veronika Penciakova. 2013. "The Final Countdown: Prospects for Ending Extreme Poverty by 2030." Global Views Policy Paper 2013-04. Brookings.

Clarke, Daniel J., and Ruth Vargas Hill. 2013. "Cost-Benefit Analysis of the African Risk Capacity Facility." International Food Policy Research Institute (www.ifpri.org/publication/cost-benefit-analysis-african-risk-capacity-facility).

Cogneau, Denis, Kenneth Houngbedji, and Sandrine Mesplé-Somps. 2014. "The Fall of the Elephant. Two Decades of Poverty Increase in Côte d'Ivoire (1988–2008)." Working Paper 2014/144. United Nations University.

Corral, Paul, Vasco Molini, and Gbemisola Oseni. 2015. "No Condition Is Permanent: Middle Class in Nigeria in the Last Decade." Policy Research Working Paper 7214. Washington: World Bank.

Dercon, Stefan, and Luc Christiaensen. 2011. "Consumption Risk, Technology Adoption, and Poverty Traps: Evidence from Ethiopia." *Journal of Development Economics* 96, no. 2: 159–73.

Easterly, William, and others. 1993. "Good Policy or Good Luck? Country Growth Performance and Temporary Shocks." *Journal of Monetary Economics* 32, no. 3: 459–83.

Fearon, James D. 2010. "Governance and Civil War Onset." World Development Report 2011 Background Paper. Washington: World Bank (http://web.worldbank.org/archive/website01306/web/pdf/wdr%20background%20paper_fearon_0.pdf).

Ferris, Elizabeth. 2010. "Natural Disasters, Conflict, and Human Rights: Tracing the Connections" (http://www.brookings.edu/research/speeches/2010/03/03-natural-disasters-ferris).

Gentilini, Ugo, Maddalena Honorati, and Ruslan Yemtsov. 2014. *The State of Social Safety Nets 2014.* Washington: World Bank Group.

Global Findex. 2014. Washington: World Bank (http://econ.worldbank.org/WBSITE/EXTERNAL/EXTDEC/EXTRESEARCH/EXTPROGRAMS/EXTFINRES/EXTGLOBALFIN/0,,contentMDK:23172730~pagePK:64168182~piPK:64168060~theSitePK:8519639,00.html).

Hausmann, Ricardo. 2014. "The Economics of Inclusion." *Project Syndicate* (www.project-syndicate.org/commentary/inclusiveness-key-strategy-for-growth-by-ricardo-hausmann-2014-11).

Inchauste, Gabriela, and others. 2012. "What Is Behind the Decline in Poverty since 2000? Evidence from Bangladesh, Peru and Thailand." Policy Research Working Paper 6199. Washington: World Bank.

International Monetary Fund. 2014. *World Economic Outlook.* Washington (October).

Jones, Benjamin F., and Benjamin A. Olken. 2008. "The Anatomy of Start-Stop Growth." *Review of Economics and Statistics* 90, no. 3: 582–87.

Kraay, Aart, and David McKenzie. 2014. "Do Poverty Traps Exist? Assessing the Evidence." *Journal of Economic Perspectives* 28, no. 3: 127–48.

López-Calva, Luis F., and Eduardo Ortiz-Juárez. 2015. "A Vulnerability Approach to the Definition of the Middle Class." *Journal of Economic Inequality* 12, no. 1 (March): 23–47.

Marenya, Paswel P., and Christopher B. Barrett. 2009. "Soil Quality and Fertilizer Use Rates among Smallholder Farmers in Western Kenya." *Agricultural Economics* 40, no. 5: 561–72.

Morduch, Jonathan. 1999. "The Microfinance Promise." *Journal of Economic Literature* 37, no. 4: 1569–614.

Narayan, Deepa, Lant Pritchett, and Soumya Kapoor. 2009. *Moving Out of Poverty: Success from the Bottom Up (Volume 2).* World Bank Publications.

Pritchett, Lant, and others. 2014. "Trillions Gained and Lost: Estimating the Magnitude of Growth Episodes." Harvard University, Center for International Development.

Ravallion, Martin, Shaohua Chen, and Prem Sangraula. 2009. "Dollar a Day Revisited." *World Bank Economic Review* 23, no. 2: 163–84 (http://wber.oxfordjournals.org/content/23/2/163.full.pdf+html).

Relief Web. 2014. "Loss Events Worldwide: 1980–2013." Munich, Germany (www.munichre.com/site/wrap/get/documents_E-736590296/mram/assetpool.munichreamerica.wrap/PDF/2013/1980_2013_events.pdf).

Speakman, John, and Annoula Rysova. 2015. "The Small Entrepreneur in Fragile and Conflict-Affected Situations." Washington: World Bank.

Van de Walle, Nicolas. 2001. *African Economies and the Politics of Permanent Crisis: 1979–1999.* Cambridge University Press.

World Bank. 2011. *World Development Report 2011: Conflict, Security, and Development.* Washington.

World Bank. 2014a. *World Development Report 2014: Risk and Opportunity—Managing Risk for Development.* Washington.

World Bank. 2014b. *Global Monitoring Report 2014–15: Ending Poverty and Sharing Prosperity.* Washington.

PART I

Securing Peace

2

No Development without Peace: Laying the Political and Security Foundations

BRUCE JONES

I n November 2012 a newly formed rebel movement, known as Seleka, began fighting in the northern and central regions of the Central African Republic (CAR), quickly scoring victories and holding territory. In March 2013 they overran the capital, Bangui, and seized power, suspending the constitution and dissolving parliament. By August 2013 the UN secretary general was warning that CAR had suffered a total breakdown of law and order.[1] In October 2013 the UN Security Council approved the deployment of a United Nations peace-keeping mission to reinforce an existing African Union mission on the ground.

Characteristically slow to arrive, the UN forces were not yet on the ground when new rounds of fighting broke out in November 2013. Unlike the fighting a year earlier, this round pitted Selaka versus anti-Seleka militias and had a distinctly sectarian tinge, with rival Muslim and Christian militias targeting civilians. By December several hundred people had been reported killed, but this was probably a serious underestimate, as access to the countryside was sharply limited. In December, France deployed troops into CAR to help quell the fighting, and the U.S. Air Force began airlifting Rwandan and other troops into CAR to reinforce the African Union mission.

---

1. For an account of the unfolding of violent rebellion in the Central African Republic in late 2013, see International Crisis Group (2013a).

This was neither CAR's first bout of violence nor the first time international peacekeeping forces had been deployed into the country to quell violence of one form or another. Indeed, the timeline of CAR since independence is a sad tale of coups, countercoups, dissolved parliaments, French forces, and UN/AU/EU forces, interspersed with very brief bouts of semi-stability. In the 1970s CAR was led—to use a euphemistic term—by the notorious Jean-Bedel Bokassa, who ruled the country he renamed the Central African Empire like a character out of a William Boyd novel, replete with rumors that he fed his political opponents to crocodiles.[2] Unlike many other African states, its territory was not the site of a cold war-era proxy battle, but it was mired in low-level violence through much of that period. Then, as the cold war refocused international priorities, CAR like many other African states came under intense pressure from France and other donor governments to form political parties and hold elections. Moderately free elections were held in 1993, ending twelve years of military rule. The winner of those elections, Ange-Felix Patassa, was re-elected in 1999. International development actors began efforts at reform. But things began to erode. A coup attempt against President Patassa was suppressed in 2001 in part through the assistance of Libyan and Chadian troops. But then Patassa was ousted in 2003 by forces loyal to former army chief of staff Francois Bozize, and the situation descended back into violent instability.

A new chance for peace came in 2007, when the government and a series of rebel groups signed a peace accord. The UN authorized a peacekeeping force to help implement the peace agreement. Peace talks continued with holdout rebel forces, and concluded in December 2008. A reasonably stable peace held among the internal forces. The UN established a Peacebuilding Office—which straddles traditional political engagement and traditional development action—and CAR came onto the agenda of the UN's Peacebuilding Commission.

But CAR is not lucky in its neighborhood, and in February 2009 Ugandan Lord's Resistance Army rebels entered into CAR. French troops helped chase out the LRA, later with help from the African Union. The situation continued to be one of low-level instability in parallel with halting efforts to restore parliament, renew the constitution, and hold new elections. Still, by May 2010 the Security Council (also preoccupied with fights on many fronts) judged the situation to be stable enough to withdraw the UN force. The Peacebuilding Office stayed on (UN 2012). In January 2011 presidential and parliamentary elections were held, under the UN's watch, and Bozize won another term. In August 2012 the last holdout rebel force signed the peace agreement with the government.[3]

---

2. For an account of the self-styled Emperor Bokassa's brutal rule, see Titley (1997).

3. For an account of the effort to establish some degree of political stability, see International Crisis Group (2013b).

All this held for exactly six months. Throughout this period, the international development community continued to press for and monitor progress against the Millennium Development Goals, reporting regularly on improvement. It is hard to know how to react to those reports. The earlier reports reflect the norm of the time and make for slightly Orwellian reading—in the introductory chapter to the 2004 report a mere paragraph refers to political crises, all but ignoring sustained violence in the country (Republique Centrafricaine 2004). By 2010 reality had begun to penetrate even UN political correctness, and the report does focus on the violence, the peace process, and the challenge of governance (Republique Centrafricaine 2010).

The analysis of the underlying economic realities is largely unchanged, and the statistics are grim. In 2013 CAR occupied the 180th spot on the UN's Human Development Index. In the 1990s, by measures like child mortality and women dying in childbirth, CAR was moving in reverse. Take child mortality (one of the more reliably monitored indicators, even in situations of instability): having declined from 212 per 1,000 in 1988 to 157 in 1995, the situation had deteriorated, with child deaths per 1,000 rising to 194 by 2000. The 2010 account of progress on the MDGs is sobering. Of the twelve goals or subgoals against which progress is measured, the government and the UN team writing the 2010 report assigned a mark of "probable" that CAR would meet *one* of them—from a base of 74 percent in 2003, the proportion of the country without access to potable water had declined to 65 percent, meaning that it was within the realm of the possible that it would hit the MDG target of 40 percent by 2015. But the assessment of "probable" here is a heartily optimistic one and, given recent events, likely now out of reach. Two other targets were judged to be "possible"—enrollment of children in primary school and prevalence of malaria. On the other nine targets, the CAR UN team gave a clear, frank assessment of the likelihood of hitting the MDGs by 2015: "impossible" (Republique Centrafricaine 2010).

Joseph Stalin is commonly reported to have once quipped that "one death is a tragedy; one million is a statistic."[4] In the global scheme of development and progress against poverty, the acute, crushing, and frequently violent poverty of CAR's 4 million people may only be a minor part of the statistics, but it's also a tragedy. And it's a tragedy that's being replicated, at greater or lesser degrees of intensity, in a further thirty-plus countries that currently host roughly a third

4. There's no written record of this; but McCollough's biography of Truman cites a biography of Stalin by Anton Antonov-Ovseyenko, who in turn refers to an exchange between Churchill and Stalin in the famous Tehran conference. According to McCollough, the more precise rendering is, "When one man dies it is a tragedy, when thousands die it's statistics." See McCollough (1992).

of the world's poorest people.[5] While poverty is declining in many places, the poor are increasingly clustered in others. As stable low-income countries make progress, and middle-income countries improve their rates of poverty reduction, the world's absolute poor will be increasingly concentrated in fragile states. Under more than one scenario, by 2025, 60–70 percent of the global poor will be located in forty-five fragile states (Edward and Sumner 2013; Chandy and Gertz 2011). Even if progress in middle-income countries slows, still by 2015 roughly half of the world's absolute poor will live in fragile states.[6]

The Challenge Ahead

To say that the situation in CAR poses a challenge for the international development project is an understatement. Quite apart from a weak economic base and appalling human development conditions, CAR exhibits a series of features any one of which would complicate development: abusive leadership, poor governance, weak institutions, repeated violence, subregional conflict, and cross-border violence. The fact is, though, that these features are common across the world's so-called fragile states (still a poorly defined, categorically confused term).[7]

The development project, at least at the official level, relies on globalist language and universal standards. In the UN debate about what will replace the Millennium Development Goals when that project reaches an end in 2015, the concept of universal goals will be taken even farther forward—despite ongoing negotiations on just about every aspect of what those goals should cover (or whether there should even be goals). The one thing every government at the UN seems to agree on is that the normative framework for post-2015 should have universality as its starting point. There are good moral and political reasons for that. But the concept of universality clouds a basic reality, which is that the development challenge is rapidly diverging into two fundamentally different projects. In large swathes of the previously poor world, reasonable governance, sustained growth during much of the past decade, and steady declines in poverty mean that many low-income or low middle-income countries now face challenges that have primarily to do with economic and fiscal strategy, global economic governance, national resource mobilization

5. Exactly what percentage of the world's absolute poor live in conflict-affected states is debated, with estimates ranging as high as 70 percent if the statistic includes the poor living in conflict-affected subnational areas of middle-income countries, especially India.

6. Depends on definition and boundaries of list; for OECD figures used here, see DAC (2012).

7. For a discussion of the terminological and categorical confusion that applies to the concept of fragility, see in particular Patrick (2011). Simply put, any category that includes both North Korea and Central African Republic is self-evidently flawed.

and allocation, targeting investments in human development, and managing energy growth under conditions of mounting climate pressure. In these states, the emerging concept of actually eradicating extreme poverty in a generation is an ambitious but conceptually achievable—and powerfully ennobling—goal. In another set of states, beset by weak institutions and recurrent violence, it's an abstraction.

This book focuses on poverty eradication, and that involves a necessary focus on the second set of states—for lack of a better term, the world's fragile states, where weak institutions, recurrent violence, regional insecurity, acute poverty, and severe human underdevelopment intersect. And this chapter in turn focuses on one particular subset of the challenges, and one of the most difficult: restoring some form of peaceful political process and some degree of stability as foundations for broader development. Over the long term, as more and more research shows us, it is stable political institutions that are foundational to economic development (Acemoglu and Robinson 2012; North, Wallis, and Weingast 2009; Fukuyama 2004). But the pathway to effective political institutions can be long, tortured, and fraught with risks of relapse into conflict or war.

This chapter makes the following basic arguments. First, that there's an interim step between the narrow business of postconflict stabilization and the more ambitious business of building effective institutions—that is, forging political settlements, or pacts, between elites, pacts that can maintain some degree of stability even in the absence of robust institutions. Second, that there's reasonable evidence to suggest that a major determinant of whether political settlements will hold or relapse into violence is how inclusive they are—an issue we need to understand with greater granularity. Third, then, when it comes to the longer term job of building credible political and security institutions, international efforts are in their infancy. For all the flaws of the development practice, there is a body of technical expertise on the practice of building economic, financial, and social institutions. But when it comes to the political and security institutions on which those ultimately must rest, the international system faces a major void.

In making these arguments, I infer that if there is no progress in levels of acute violence and poor governance in fragile states, there will be sharp limits on progress either in economic growth or poverty reduction (though some progress against human development indicators could be possible). Of course, some states with limited conflict have been able to make some progress against development goals; but large-scale conflict is a major drag both on growth and on achieving development objectives (World Bank 2011). It is clear that at some level weak governance and recurrent exposure to violence is a challenge for development. It does *not* follow, however, that it is necessarily a challenge for development agencies, either those of governments or the multilateral system.

None of these, as yet, can credibly be argued to be well suited to the job of helping states navigate a long and frequently violent process of forging more resilient or responsive political and security institutions. And many development actors have semirecognized this: they acknowledge that the growing concentration of the world's poor in fragile and conflict-affected states means that the global development project can no longer ignore the question of violence and political governance; they also acknowledge that "partners" should take on the tough part of that challenge, namely political governance and security institutions.

Here's the problem: there are no partners. The plain fact of the matter is, there is no part of the international system, with rare and highly limited exceptions, that's actually geared to this challenge. The international political and security architecture has done a better job than it's often credited for in helping to reduce levels of outright war. But there's almost no part of that architecture that's geared to the challenge of helping states engage in political development or the articulation of credible and sustainable security institutions, or the instruments or attitudes of the rule of law. And so if the broad notion that the international system should not abandon people to states of protracted poverty and insecurity is to be sustained, we need new answers to the question of not only how international systems can help with the challenge of fragile states but also about who these actors are.

And Yet, Peace Happens:
The International System for Responding to Conflict

The November 2013 return to violence in CAR, which happened while the international human rights community was starting to gear up for the twentieth anniversary of the Rwandan genocide, generated many comparisons between the CAR violence and that earlier brutal event. Many in the activist community argued or intimated that the UN and the international community had largely failed to learn the lessons of Rwanda and that international efforts to contain or mitigate violence against civilians still fell far short of what is needed (Goldberg 2014).[8] There were disturbing echoes in the brutality of the violence and the hateful rhetoric that accompanied it. And in one of those moments when history laughs at us, CAR joined the UN Security Council in January 2014, just as Rwanda had been in on the UNSC twenty years earlier, when the UN was avoiding a debate over how to respond to warnings there of impending genocide.[9]

8. Also see Savita Pawnday, Twitter post, January 14, 2014, 12:59 p.m. (https://twitter.com/savita_pawnday).
9. On the question of how much progress the UN has or has not made in dealing with genocide, see Elliasson (2014).

While no serious analyst would question the notion that more could be done to improve the international response to conflict or to improve the protection of civilians against internal violence, the notion that little or nothing has improved since Rwanda is facile. That's true even in CAR, bad as things are. In Rwanda, a UN peacekeeping presence already on the ground when genocidal violence broke out *withdrew* in the face of the fighting, which began in April 1994. Genocide had engulfed the entire country before a French military contingent deployed into western Rwanda in a late and limited bid to halt the killings. In CAR it was a matter of days, not months, before a French military contingent was deployed in to help stabilize the situation. In Rwanda, the U.S. military refused to have its equipment used by potential African troop contributors to a UN force; in CAR, the U.S. air force is flying African troop contributors in to rapidly reinforce an African Union mission there (Roulo 2013). No less than six international missions have been deployed to CAR over the past half decade to help quell the fighting, and as I draft this, the European Union looks set to deploy a force to prevent further deterioration. In Rwanda roughly 800,000 people were killed in the genocide; in CAR, international estimates so far are of roughly 1,000 people killed (*BBC News* 2013). The real number is surely higher, but it does not begin to approach the scale of Rwanda.

And this is characteristic of broader trends. For the past twenty-five years, national, international, and regional actors (in that order of importance) have applied themselves to the challenge of bringing long-running civil wars to an end. The UN Security Council did so extensively; since the end of the cold war, the UNSC has acted in more than sixty cases to authorize mediators, peacekeepers, observers, and police to help national actors bring civil wars to an end. Alongside this, the UN Secretariat and UN agencies as well as the World Bank, NGOs, and Western aid donors deployed a legion of disarmament teams, humanitarian teams, and postconflict reconstruction teams to aid the effort. Regional organizations and later NATO also added their capacities (Jones 2007).

It used to be, in the conflict resolution literature, that there were two dominant narratives about how wars could end. One on the one hand, simply, one side could win: there was a substantial body of thought that argued that stable peace only came through one-sided victory (Luttwak 1999). Another scenario was that the parties to a conflict could reach what was known as a "mutually hurting stalemate," and from this point of exhaustion—and having reached the conclusion that they could not win outright victory by military means—the parties would then be amenable to some form of mediated solution (Zartman 2000).

The explosion of international mediation efforts after the cold war created a third option. And the time that elapsed between when wars started and when wars ended began to shrink. Some civil wars in Africa had run more or less from independence until the end of the cold war (for example in Mozambique and Angola) and only reached a negotiated outcome some thirty years after their start. But in Burundi, Sierra Leone, Liberia, Bosnia, and elsewhere peace agreements were being reached within three to four years of the outbreak of violence.

Why should international mediation and peacekeeping succeed, even if only sometimes? If the earlier understanding was that a government or a rebel force had to reach the exhausting conclusion that they could not win outright victory by force alone before mediation had a chance to succeed, why, in the post–cold war era, have international mediators seemed to be able to bring parties to the table faster than cold war precedent would suggest? There's surprisingly little examination of this question, but we can reason the following. Mediators, having probed the parties' attitudes, gleaned some sense of their dynamics and potential red lines, and with a lot of trial and error can put on the table a package of power-sharing and wealth-sharing measures long before that package would be attainable through attrition and exhaustion. Once they do so, fighters are confronted by the following calculation: they can continue to fight, in the hope or estimate that they could secure an ultimate one-sided victory; but they also have to estimate the odds that they could continue to fight for years and either lose or, more likely, end up in some form of stalemate. Or they can short-circuit the effort and accept the package. The appeal of the mediators' package rises if also on offer is some form of international guarantee. Stedman (2002) among others stresses that "guarantees" from the international community are pretty thin. But in the case of a rebel leader looking at whether to accept a mediated deal, the willingness of the international system to deploy forces into the country to provide physical protection of elites, at least for a few years, may have its attractions. In other words, an international mediator may be able to offer a shorter route to the place that the parties would ultimately reach through exhaustion and stalemate. And there are demonstration effects: as more and more cases of mediation and peacekeeping are undertaken, the more it's believable for parties to a conflict that peacekeepers would indeed arrive, would indeed protect them, and would indeed stick around at least for a few years.

Despite this logic, the blunt fact is that much of international mediation and peacekeeping since the end of the cold war has failed. Over the past twenty years, mediation efforts have failed roughly three-quarters of the times that they've been tried. Peacekeeping operations fail—that is, the country reverts to violence—roughly half the time that missions are deployed (Fortna 2008). That's a lot. But the fact is that during the cold war, we fueled rather than fought civil wars. When you shift from adding to a problem to trying to help solve it, even a three-quarters failure rate actually represents one-quarter progress on where you were before. And so, slowly, as international mediation efforts continued and international peacekeepers continued to be deployed, at ever larger scale, the

Figure 2-1. *Battle-Related Deaths in Civil Wars, 1990–2011*

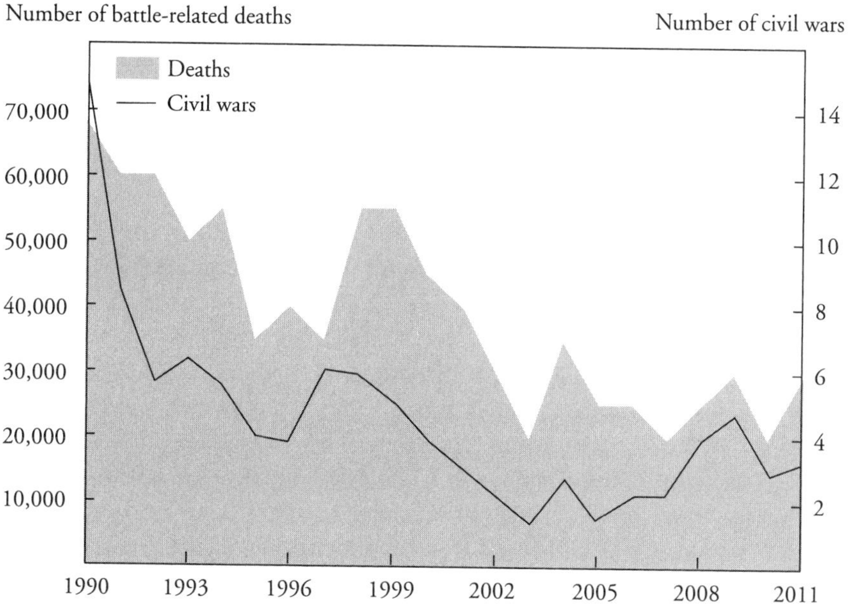

Number of battle-related deaths   Number of civil wars

Source: Mack (2012).

number of civil wars that ended and stayed ended began to outstrip the number of new wars that started (Fortna 2008). The net effect of this was that the total number of civil wars in the world slowly but steadily declined. In the period from 1991 to 1992, there were twenty-one active major civil wars—fifty-one when minor wars are included. Minor wars are defined as having at least twenty-five battle deaths a year; major wars are defined as having a thousand battle deaths a year (Mack 2012; also see figure 2-1). By 2008 the number of major wars had fallen to the low single digits; of minor wars, the number had fallen from fifty-one to thirty-one (Mack 2010). Death tolls fell sharply as well, as did the number of countries at war: in 1992, 21 percent of the world's countries were at war; in 2012, that percentage was down to 13 percent.[10]

The implications of all this for contemporary development can be understood in two distinct ways. First, civil wars themselves are not, at least not primarily, a development challenge. It matters to make this point, because when the issue

10. Did international peacekeeping actually contribute to this? The evidence suggests, yes. Increasingly the research literature on peacekeeping suggests that it played a substantial role in contributing to declining levels of violence. See Fortna (2008); Walter (2002); World Bank (2011).

of the relationship between conflict and development is raised, it's often stressed that the job of responding to conflict and war properly belongs with the Security Council and regional organizations, not the development community; and that is absolutely true. And when we look at the on-again, off-again international response to CAR, while I argue that the response is better, by a long measure, than that which occurred in Rwanda, it's clear that there's room for major improvement. Any case in which six or more peacekeeping operations have to be deployed in the course of a decade is a case in which international peacekeeping isn't getting the job done. So it's a reality that if the international security architecture doesn't continue to improve its efforts in helping bring wars to a stable end, that will sharply limit the prospects for development in states where violence recurs.

Second, despite its weaknesses, the continued operation and expansion of international conflict management efforts have contributed to the fact that a growing number of countries—in 2013, roughly twenty of them—have escaped the acute phase of civil war and managed to get through the early phase of post-conflict recovery. From Mozambique to Ethiopia to Bosnia to Timor-Leste to Rwanda and arguably to Sierra Leone, Liberia, and Angola, the acute violence of the recent past has receded. But these states face a new challenge. This has been described as "development under the shadow of violence" (Jones and Elgin-Cossart 2011). The most recent bout of fighting may have receded, but the threat of renewed war remains: distrust between parties lingers long after the fighting stops. Indeed, as civil wars in richer states have come to an end, among the poorer states the risk that they will experience new bouts of war is increasing. Of new civil wars in the early 2000s, 90 percent were in countries that had experienced a prior civil war (compared to 67 percent in the previous decade, 62 percent in the 1980s, and 57 percent in the 1970s; see World Bank 2011).

Why Does Peace Fail?

The large-scale ramping up of international efforts to mitigate internal violence has helped produce a steady decline in war. But the fact is, in places like CAR, such efforts often fail to sustain the peace. Why? To understand this phenomenon, it helps to turn for a moment to the broader debate about the causes of internal war.[11]

11. For a brief moment after the end of the cold war, there was an effort to see whether the dynamics of internal war corresponded to the causal dynamics of international war; see Snyder and Jervis (1999). That effort shed some light on one aspect of causation—security dilemmas—but it also illustrated the limits of an approach that lumps internal wars with interstate wars. That's even more relevant to the present day, when interstate war is a slightly growing phenomenon, while internal wars continue to decline.

First, and critically, violence should not be assumed an irrational response: for many actors in many settings, violence is a rational choice of strategy (Tilly 1975, 2003, 2008; Weede and Muller 1998; Kaufmann 2005). Some in the economics profession think of violence and war as intrinsically irrational and look for explanations (Blattman and Miguel 2010; Burnham and Peterson 2014). The political science profession starts from a different logic. It is, for example, perfectly rational to adopt a violent posture if you believe that you or your identity group may be subject to violence by an opposing group; such calculations can be an important motivator for group violence (de Figueiredo and Weingast 1999).

Moreover, every subgroup is aware that every other subgroup is making similar calculations, and so risk avoidance may suggest moving first to pick up weapons and organize for self-defense, a move that will seem threatening to another group, causing them also to organize for war (Snyder and Jervis 1999; Walter 1997). History is replete with examples of wars that start as one group moves to defend themselves from a possible attack by the state or another group, causing the state or the opposing group in turn to move toward violence. This kind of "security dilemma" can contribute to the outbreak of war, including internal war, where the state is too weak to guarantee security or to suppress incipient rebellion (Walter 1999, 2002). Leaders may also start wars to improve their political position in a postwar settlement or to gain access to territory where natural resources can be looted. In taking such steps, leaders rarely risk violent death: it is foot soldiers, not generals or rebel commanders, who die in wars.

Second, in a given setting, any one of a number of factors can motivate political leaders or opportunists to pursue a violent strategy. Those factors can be political in basis: the exclusion of an ethnic or religious or territorial group from the trappings of power can create powerful motivations to challenge the existing order, including through violence (Hartzell and Hoddie 2003; Rothchild 1997; Hartzell and Rothchild 1997; Hartzell, Hoddie, and Rothchild 2001). They can be security oriented: minority groups can fear, or actually experience, persecution or oppression and turn to arms to redress the situation (de Figueireda and Weingast 1999; Walter 2004; Posen 1993). External security factors—including the threat of invasion and spillover factors like cross-border militants, equipment, resources, criminal networks, finances, and refugees—can also trigger violence (Brown 1996; Gomez and Christensen 2010; Gleditsch 2007; Fearon and Laitin 2003; Saleyhan and Gleditsch 2006; Saleyhan 2008; Collier and others 2003; Craft and Smaldone 2002). Motives can also be economic: if marginal groups are blocked from accessing a state's budget and the private sector is limited and controlled, powerful economic incentives exist to challenge the existing order, and these are amplified when the state has significant natural resources (Collier and Hoeffler 2004; Berdal and Malone 2000; Ross 2004; Humphreys

2005). The calculations and motivations that trigger war are usually internal, but they can be amplified, manipulated, supported, or restrained by regional and external dynamics (Fearon and Laitin 2004; Auty 2001; de Soysa 2000; Svensson 2000). A lot of recent quantitative scholarship has searched for single-variable explanations for war (rain, inequality, mountains, economic incentives), but efforts to find single-variable causes of internal war have not been broadly successful.

Third, weak institutions are unable to provide peaceful and durable resolution to these stress factors, and thus they create the conditions whereby violence is a rational choice for pursuing claims. The causal mechanism for this is clear: where political and accountability institutions are strong, challenges to the existing order can often be accommodated through political dialogue, legal action, nonviolent civil strife, or similar. But where institutions are weak, lack of confidence in the ability of institutions to resolve claims increases the incentives for violence, while a calculation that weak security services are unlikely to be able to repress opposition decreases the obstacles to rebellion. In a study for the World Bank, Fearon (2010b) found that weak financial, administrative, and coercive capacities are a better predictor of the onset of civil war and extreme violence than poverty or other economic measures—or than political grievances or ethnic inclusion. Weak institutions are the necessary condition, not the sufficient condition: a trigger is needed.

The research literature is weak on two additional factors that practitioners consistently find to be strongly relevant to war and peace dynamics: legitimacy and leadership. Legitimacy is a complex issue, poorly understood in the research literature on conflict and development, yet evidently important to the political dynamics of states. An important part of the research agenda on conflict and development is to gain a better understanding of the dynamics of legitimacy—including, vitally, non-Western forms of legitimacy, such as revolutionary legitimacy and embedded historical legitimacy (Jones and Chandran 2008)—and the way legitimacy plays into causes of conflict and of recovery. Leadership, too, is given weak treatment in the research literature, but few if any practitioner accounts of conflict dynamics do not give it a major role. A better understanding of leadership—and in particular of the kinds of social dynamics that facilitate certain forms of leadership—will matter a lot to better understandings of the business of forging stability after war.

The causes of any *specific* war emerge from this complex mix of motivations, regional/international dynamics, weak institutions, and leadership/legitimacy issues. In one way, this is an unsatisfying outcome: it would be far more reassuring to find a single cause to explain fragility and war. Common sense, though, tells us that phenomena as complex as war and fragility should have complex causes and that these should vary considerably from case to case—and that is what the science increasingly tells us too.[12] If the onset of war is a fairly complex problem, the fact that wars continue, that they recur, that fragility is endemic—this is a rather simple problem. Simple analytically—but not at all simple to solve. It's a story in three parts.

First, whatever set of factors engendered conflict in the first place is likely to remain and intensify with violence. If security fears triggered violence, the reality of conflict exacerbates and confirms those fears (Stedman 1996; Brown 1996; Fearon and Laitin 2003; Walter 1999; Snyder and Jervis 1999). If political or ethnic discrimination motivates violence, acts of war intensify a sense of difference and enmity (Horowitz 1985, 1998; Huntington 1997; Walter 1997; Kaufman 2006). If economic factors are to blame, they are likely to worsen—violence often provides opportunities for predatory entrepreneurship, and it can be hard to convince people that they can profit as much from peace as from predation, though they often can (Berdal and Malone 2000; Collier and Hoeffler 2004; Herbst 2000).

Second, whatever else has happened, at least two sizable portions of the population will have proven to one another that they are willing to use violence to deny the other their claims or demands or rights. Even once a cease-fire or peace agreement has been reached, rational analysis by the other side tells them that it's possible—not certain, but *possible*—that their former opponents could at any point return to violence (Powell 2006; Posen 1993; Walter 1999; Fearon 1995). (And violence amplifies irrational views, often through acts of brutality that reinforce perceptions of ancient enmity and atavistic hatreds; see Kalyvas 2003.) Each side knows this about the other. The rational decision for both sides is thus to retain the option to return to violence—and in many cases, the rational decision is to take violent action preemptively (Kaufman 1996; Walter 1999, 2004; de Figueireda and Weingast 1999; Posen 1993). This "commitment gap" or "trust deficit" is a powerful explanation for why many cease-fires or peace agreements fail (Fortna 2004).

Third, whatever the quality of institutions before violence, they are likely to be worse after it. Institutions fail to maintain political relations. Security institutions fail to provide security and prey on the populace. Leaders and officials flee or are killed. Physical damage may also be extensive. Since weak institutions are a strong indicator of conflict onset, the deleterious effect of violence on institutions becomes a negative cycle (Walter 2010).

And just in case this wasn't already complicated enough, a further factor in postconflict settings is organized crime. Protracted episodes of internal violence

---

12. There is a literature that looks to complex causes of war. Exemplars include Stedman (1996); Brown (1996); Fearon (1995). More recent quantitative literature includes Fearon and Laitin (2003); Vreeland (2008); Collier and Hoeffler (2009); Hegre, Ostby, and Raleigh (2009).

often create opportunities for armed groups to engage in illicit commercial activity, sometimes to fund rebellion, sometimes as a side activity (Muggah 2005). The end of violence and the elaboration of a political agreement that includes the leaders of a rebellion may not constitute sufficient incentive for them to end their illicit commercial activity, or subgroups that do not profit deeply from the settlement may break away. Moreover, weak but nevertheless semistable political settlements may create conditions conducive to organized crime—organized criminal groups may avoid all-out war but take advantage of weak security structures and fluid political conditions to penetrate postconflict settings—for example, as in Guinea-Bissau. (It should be stressed that evidence about organized crime is sharply limited and the knowledge base about the relationship between organized crime and conflict is in its infancy.)[13]

In short, once a country with weak institutions has gone down the route of internal violence, sustained exit is hard. The challenge is to create arrangements in which potential combatants see their interests in participating in stable, positive-sum arrangements, rather than returning to war for negative-sum gains. From a game-theoretic perspective, opponents in a civil war are in a form of single-iteration prisoners' dilemma game, for which there's no reward for cooperation; the challenge is to move them into a repeated prisoners' dilemma game, for which there is at least a potential reward for cooperation. And this, of course, is the function of institutions.

But you don't move from war to institutions overnight. Where institutions were strong before a war, it may be possible to move back into institutional arrangements with some form of power-sharing deal attached to them, or some set of international guarantees about inclusion. (That, in sum, is the story line of how war was ended in Bosnia.) But where institutions are very weak, as they are in many low-income states that have experienced violence, an interim step is needed (Prichett and de Weijer 2010). The interim step is structured political settlements.

In the Short Term: Political Settlements as a First Step

Over the long run, the most successful economic states have developed "open access" orders—that is, formal institutions that limit the role of informal agreements among elites in regulating the affairs of the state and that provide for rule-based access to administration for all (North, Wallis, and Weingast 2009). These institutions are not a guarantee of conflict avoidance: Yugoslavia had fairly developed institutions before the unraveling of the Soviet Union created

---

13. For a review of the literature, see Kavanagh (2011).

centrifugal forces stronger than the centripetal forces of the state institutions, ripping it apart with extreme violence. Stronger institutions, though, mean the ability to withstand stronger political, economic, and security pressures, or stresses, on the state, both internal and external.

Here, of course, we encounter a Catch-22, for when states have weak institutions and have experienced violence, they encounter a powerful trust deficit, and that trust deficit is a major obstacle to building institutions. But there are pathways out of fragility. States that have successfully exited violence and begun a process of development have often started with strong political settlements, or elite pacts (OECD 2011; Licklider 1995; Hartzell and Hoddie 2003). These have sometimes taken the form of peace agreements; sometimes they are simply informal understandings between elites about the rules of the political game and the division of economic spoils (Walter 2004, 2009; Licklider 1995; Wagner 1993). They are, in short, informal protoinstitutions. They are, by definition, primarily about elites and thus dependent on elite relationships and only secondarily address the needs of broader populations.

The research provides preliminary evidence of the positive effects of power-sharing regimes on the duration of peace (Hartzell and Hoddie 2003). But empirical evidence on the potential adverse effects of such agreements in ethnically divided societies, or when power is given to former armed groups, is still limited to case studies of varying rigor (Simonsen 2005; Samuels and von Einsiedel 2004; Horowitz 1985; on the opposite side, López-Pintor 2006; see also Tull and Mehler 2005; De Zeeuw 2008). That political settlements matter is clear; but we are only beginning to know much about the *shape* of political settlements that do or don't endure. For all of the literature on the causes of war, there is a paucity of literature on successful recovery.[14] This is unsurprising: it is only now that there is a generation of post–cold war cases of civil war that have ended conflict and sustained peace for more than a decade. This creates an important opportunity to shift the research focus.

One important element is the political settlement that follows a particular episode of conflict—that is, in essence, an agreement among elites about the allocation and distribution of power in the aftermath of violence. Scholarship shows that there's an important relationship between contested power-sharing arrangements and conflict relapse, and between elite pacts and stability (see Walter 2004, 2009; Licklider 1995; Wagner 1993; Hartzell and Hoddie 2007;

---

14. There is a broad literature on peace building; but little of it is methodologically rigorous in its treatment of causation. Important exceptions include Doyle and Sambanis (2000, 2006); Cousens and Kumar (2001); Oberschall (2007). There is good reason for the lack so far of rigorous treatment of successful exit: until recently, there was not a sufficient body of cases where enough time has elapsed to form confident judgments about continued stability.

Lindemann 2010). But what, exactly, is a political settlement? There are two quite distinct ways of thinking about political settlements. One approach is oriented toward informal, long-running dynamics between political actors, especially elites. Another is focused on specific, often formal renegotiations of political arrangements through power-sharing deals, constitutional conferences, peace agreements, and the like. Each approach has its merits in substantive terms.

In what follows, I take a "peace agreements plus" approach—in other words, a substantial focus of the analysis of political settlements is on peace agreements *and their implementation* (which sometimes differs substantially from paper agreements), but I use the term also to cover other discrete episodes of political renegotiation among elites. Power-sharing arrangements negotiated after limited episodes of political violence (as in Kenya in 2008 and Yemen in 2011) or after mass public demonstrations (as in Lebanon after the Cedar Revolution) share important characteristics with postwar settlements, as do leadership changes and shifts in the balance of power that follow political assassinations (as in Pakistan after the assassination of Benazir Bhutto) and the death of prominent leaders (as with the renegotiation of power distribution arrangements in South Sudan following the death of John Garang). The use of strategic appointments by government elites to bring in former opponents is particularly relevant to political settlements in cases of one-sided military victory (Rwanda, Nicaragua).

Others have focused on longer-running processes. Among the broadest definitions in use is that of the DfID: "the expression of a common understanding, usually forged between elites, about how power is organised and exercised" (UK 2010). That builds on a prior definition by Whaites, whose fuller discussion of the concept provides a useful grounding: "The structures of the state are determined by an underlying political settlement; 'the forging of a common understanding, usually among elites, that their interests or beliefs are served by a particular way of organising political power.' A political settlement may survive for centuries, but within that time decision-making power is likely to transfer among elite groups as individual governments come and go" (Whaites 2008).

This brings us to the second question: Is the settlement (and the question of how inclusive the settlement is) just about elites or also about wider social groupings? Here too there is a definitional debate, with some scholars and practitioners focusing on elites and others on wider state-society relations. A widely cited study that takes a more explicitly broad view of elite/social relations is that of Di John and Putzel (2009), whose definition also reflects a long historical process by which state-society relations are forged, challenged, and reforged, sometimes through violence: "The balance or distribution of power between contending social groups and classes, on which any state is based." Similarly, Fritz and Rocha Menocal (2007) treat political settlements as "the expression of a negotiated agreement . . . binding together state and society and providing the necessary legitimacy for those who govern over those who are ruled." The distinction between narrow and broad concepts of political settlement is often elided.

Here it is important to note that the literature on political settlements relates to a wider literature on "elite pacts," a literature that focuses on the relationships between elites after periods of turmoil. Weingast (1997) defines elite pacts as "agreements among competing (and often warring) elites that initiate a transition to democracy." Higley and Burton (1998) refer to "elite settlements" as "sudden, deliberate, and lasting compromises of core disputes among political elites. . . . After settlements, elite persons and groups continue to be affiliated with conflicting parties, movements, and beliefs, but they share a consensus about government institutions and the codes and rules of political competition." O'Donnell and Schmitter (1986) and Przeworski (1991) argue that elite pacts represent both formal agreements and informal arrangements to limit competition. *Elite pacts* is a concept that runs throughout the state-building process and is not necessarily linked to violence. Political settlements forged in the wake of violence, or to prevent it, should be seen as a distinct subset of elite pacts.

Of course, elite pacts and broader social compacts are not entirely distinct phenomena, as most citizen participation in political discourse happens through a variety of forms of political representatives or other elites. So elite inclusion may carry with it broader forms of citizen participation or at least broader group recognition so that their interests are reflected in a given settlement. Was the appointment of Hutu elites to significant district government positions by the Tutsi-dominated RPF, in postgenocide Rwanda, an act of elite inclusion or an act of reassurance to the broader Hutu population (McDoom 2010)? Surely both.

Whaites (2008), reviewing the elite pacting and state-building literature, reaches similar conclusions. He argues, "Elites are prominent within the literature on state building, but elites can rarely take social constituencies for granted; they must maintain an ability to organise, persuade, command or inspire. Wider societies are not bystanders in political settlements or state building." I largely agree; but note that there are sometimes a subset of elites, particularly economic elites, that are largely abstracted from broader social groupings and who may well be able to profit and reinforce their position by reference only to economic deals with the state and external actors, freeing them to broadly ignore local social dynamics.

Moreover, we know less than we should about the different patterns of elite/social relationships within the context of violence. There is an important agenda here of marrying the research literature on how elites emerge, and what forms of social mobilization facilitate which kinds of leadership, with the specific circumstances of violence. One important critique of both the *2011 World Development Report* and much of the recent OECD work on state building is that it does too little to elucidate the relationship between elites and broader social groupings, to understand thereby the extent to which elite pacts or other versions of elite settlements actually represent broader political forces or are abstracted from them. It would be helpful, for example, to adapt the work by Khan (1996, 1998) on the differences between patron-client relationships in advanced democracies and developing countries to the specific circumstances of violence in fragile states; and to elaborate initial work by Gauri and others (2007) on the ways different social dynamics (including across generations) shape which elites gain prominence.

Finally, policy research increasingly highlights the importance of *inclusion* for sustained peace and development. DfID's peace-building and state-building framework (UK 2010) states:

> Political settlements define how political and economic power is organized. Exclusionary settlements are more likely to lead to instability. Supporting inclusive settlements means understanding the incentives of the elites and identifying when and how to empower different actors to push for a broader settlement. Peace processes provide windows of opportunity to reshape existing settlements, but may not address underlying power dynamics. Support to democratic and political processes can help promote more inclusive decision-making.

How strong is the empirical evidence for these arguments? It is worth noting that the OECD has reached similar conclusions. Its policy studies have concluded that "the overarching priority of state building must be a form of political governance and the articulation of a set of political processes or accountability mechanisms through which the state and society reconcile their expectations of one another" (Jones and Chandran 2008). And also that "for a state to be perceived as legitimate, it is crucial that a political process exists that creates space for debate and dialogue among power elites and includes all major political forces" (Papagianni 2008). These claims draw on a growing body of literature that applies state-building theory and the history of contested state building to the contemporary experience of fragile states (Fukuyama 2004; Ghani and Lockhart 2008; Chesterman, Ignatieff, and Thakur 2005; Call 2008; Brinkerhoff 2007; Barnett 2006; Patrick 2011; Rice, Pascual, and Graff 2010; Keating and Knight 2004). Studies of state building in Papua New Guinea and Indonesia by Francis Fukuyama (Fukuyama 2004, 2007), and comparative studies by Ashraf Ghani and Clare Lockhart (Ghani and Lockhart 2008) have been particularly influential in this regard. The OECD also argues that "the participation of the public in the state-building process may also contribute to the legitimacy of the state" (Papagianni 2008), but the evidence for this is less developed. Studies also find evidence that points to elite inclusion as the main factor driving ethnic strife and civil war, because failure to include elites from other groups incentivizes them to foment rebellion (Lindemann 2008). And three recent mixed-method studies find more empirical evidence pointing to inclusion as an important factor in escaping cycles of violence and poverty.

The idea that "'inclusive-enough" settlements matter for recovery is a central conclusion of the *2011 World Development Report*. As the report began its inquiry, the team turned its attention to a question that has until late received little attention in the conflict literature: What is it that has allowed some postconflict states to *not* relapse? In other words, why does peace endure in some settings? The focus in the literature has been on the predominance of relapse; less attention has been paid to the question of the causal mechanisms that allow some postconflict societies to weather the inevitable bumps in the road of implementation of peace agreements or postvictory settlements.

To focus attention on the question, the World Bank commissioned in-depth case studies of older cases (Germany, France, and Poland after WWII; the U.S. post–Civil War), more recent cases like Rwanda, and multiple case studies comparing successful cases of exit (Vietnam, Rwanda, South Africa, Mozambique, and Cambodia) (see World Bank 2010; McDoom 2010; Roque and others 2010). (These studies were peer-reviewed by the World Bank's Development Economics research team as well as by panels of external scholars.) The comparison of exit pathways threw up a series of interesting conclusions:

—The initial form of settlement heavily shapes the pathways via which a country emerges from violent conflict, but it does not ultimately determine the outcomes in terms of political and institutional formation/configuration and regime type.

—The existence of substantial differences within nations (ethnic and economic inequalities) has not prevented the maintenance of stability. In fact, in the case countries, poverty and marginalized groups have been conspicuously used or actively managed using regime maintenance and state-society relations mechanisms, to the extent that they form a plausible part of overall consolidation.

—In the medium term, in all cases, a dominant party emerged that was able to reinvent itself as inclusive or democratic while it consolidated the regime through deepening hegemony, executive capability, and privileged patron-client networks.

Particularly notable about these conclusions is that they held even in cases of successful exits, where war had ended through one-sided military victory. In all but one of those cases, the victorious party had reached out to oppositional forces and offered them some form of participation or inclusion in governing processes, often through strategic appointments. This was a potentially important corrective to a line of argument that has run in the civil war literature since the end of the cold war, namely the "give war a chance" argument (Luttwak 1999.) One of the strong findings in the literature has been that wars that end through military victory are less likely to relapse into conflict than wars that end through negotiated settlement. The presumed causal mechanism here is that defeated opponents cannot muster the political or military capacity to challenge ongoing government and that, having once failed, they cannot convince enough followers to back a second attempt.

A comparative study of successful exits suggests a third mechanism: that those who might have led a second or second-stage rebellion were brought in or bought into the ruling coalition or otherwise into the machinery and spoils of government. Thus defeated "communities" were reassured that their interests would not be neglected under the postconflict governing arrangements. The appointment by the victorious Rwandan People's Front of key Hutu figures to positions as governors of important Rwandan provinces is an example of such confidence-building terms (McDoom 2010).

To examine this further, I reviewed all cases of civil war conclusion since the end of the cold war. That examination looked at every case of internal or civil conflict extant by 1989, or that started afterward, and coded against a wide range of criteria. For those that ended, I looked for evidence of either deliberate inclusion, or lack thereof, ranging from full-blown power sharing to the use of strategic appointments to bring in opposition leaders. That examination found that, of cases that had ended through one-sided military victory, all but one fell into one of two categories: the victorious party had engaged in some form of inclusion to the opposition forces, and the settlement had endured; or the victorious party had not been inclusive, and the settlement had collapsed back into a new round of conflict (World Bank 2011).

In parallel to the *World Development Report*, Call (2012) conducted a study to address why peace fails or why, following civil wars, countries experience a resurgence of violence.[15] In seeking to find causal patterns as to why civil wars ended, Call uses three parallel methodologies: a quantitative analysis, an in-depth case study of Liberia, and structured smaller case studies of another fourteen cases of recurrence. He finds that "one factor seems to play a more common causal role in civil war recurrence than others. This central finding is that *political exclusion*, rather than economic or social factors, plays the decisive role in most cases of civil war recurrence: Political exclusion acts as a trigger

---

15. At the time of the design of this study, Call was a CIC nonresident fellow; he conducted the Nepal case study for the adjacent country study and contributed through discussion and written inputs to the initial phase of research and thinking about this preliminary concept study.

for renewed armed conflict. Conversely, *political inclusion*, including but not limited to power-sharing agreements, is highly correlated with consolidation of peace" (Call 2012).

Call is worth quoting at length:

> Political exclusion here refers to processes rather than substantive policy outcomes. It refers to participation in political or policy processes: the opportunity either to compete in the electoral arena or to enjoy representation in appointed state offices. Political processes signify both the potential and the actual exercise of power, and thus they provide a means of attaining desired ends. Chief among these ends is security for the group and its adherents or associated populations. As such, participation in the security forces (military or police) is an especially important arena of state inclusionary or exclusionary behavior affecting the likelihood of subsequent violent conflict. It is especially perilous for postconflict regimes to violate expectations about the ability of formerly armed and mobilized social groups to participate in the policing and defense of their own country or territory.
>
> Second, political exclusion is contextually defined rather than measured by a single objective standard of participation. . . . That is, exclusion refers here not to a globally applicable objective level of political participation but to subjective perceptions among former warring factions about whether the state engages in exclusion based on prior understandings that emerged from prior war termination. . . . And these expectations are often heavily shaped by peace agreements, which serve as an initial indicator of minimal expectations. However, expectations are also shaped by promises by one party to others and by initial practices that are subsequently changed. Actions that may not be formally proscribed in an agreement can constitute a violation of expected inclusionary behavior, such as firing or persecuting a number of members of one or more parties associated with the prior war. Such a definition complicates, but also enriches, cross-national comparisons.

Call (2012) also links inclusion and exclusion to state legitimacy. Vertical legitimacy he defines as "the broad set of appropriateness of the state and its functioning" and horizontal legitimacy as "the extent to which various social groups 'accept and tolerate each other.'" He argues that horizontal legitimacy in particular is affected by exclusion, as it is predicated on the inclusion of at least the key groups (through their leadership or elites) in any contested environment.

In addition to this evidence, the Political Instability Task Force—formerly known as the State Failure Task Force—adds to the argument. The PITF was a CIA-funded study designed to identify factors that increase vulnerability to political instability. The task force considered failure as political crises: revolutionary wars, ethnic wars, adverse or disruptive regime transitions, and genocides or politicides. The model employed 117 cases of failure, each matched to two control cases that appeared similar two years before onset but did not experience crisis in the succeeding five years. Through a combination of statistical logistic regression and neural network analyses, the project analyzed 600 variables related to demographic, economic, political, and environmental conditions in a state. From this, the task force found that four variables could explain over 80 percent of all cases of state failure: regime type, determined by executive recruitment and the competitiveness of participation; infant mortality, as an indirect measure of the quality of life; conflict-ridden neighborhood, for whether a state has four or more bordering states with major armed conflict; and state-led discrimination, reflecting political or economic discrimination against minorities.

Two features of these findings are particularly important to the concept of political settlements. First, the PITF found surprisingly strong results attached to measures of factionalism, which create "extraordinarily high" risks of instability in situations of open competition (Bates and others 2010). Both partial democracies and partial autocracies, based on a measurement of two variables in the Polity IV data set, are about thirty times more likely to experience instability than full autocracies and democracies. Within this, factionalism is most common in new democracies, where "party systems are weak and political participation is more likely to flow through networks rooted in traditional identities or other parochial interests" (Bates and others 2005). Though factionalism exists in autocracies, the strength of its predicting influence is largely based on the presence of open competition (Epstein and others 2006). Second, political and economic discrimination—determined by the Minorities at Risk Project's codings—is strongly linked to instability. Systematic discrimination is found to be particularly important in models of ethnic war, though it also strengthens the global model (Gurr, Woodward, and Marshall 2005).

The findings on factionalism, open competition, and discrimination highlight important tensions between stability and inclusion in political settlements. The finding on discrimination's link to political instability, particularly in ethnic wars, is strong evidence for the importance of inclusion. On the other hand, the link between factionalism, open competition, and instability highlights the importance of "inclusive-enough" political settlements and confidence building: open competition and full inclusion have potentially destabilizing effects in the absence of interim steps to decrease factionalism.

Elite pacts have been particularly emphasized in two related literatures: one on the implementation of peace agreements, the other on the stability of democratic regimes. Hartzell and Hoddie (2003) use regression analysis to show that power sharing supports lasting peace following episodes of violence. Schneckener (2002), considering cases of power sharing in European countries over time, highlights that political elites and the institutional arrangements they develop are critical to avoiding a breakdown of peace agreements. Rothchild (2002) argues that pacts are "dependent upon the maintenance of balanced elite power and a preparedness to resolve conflicts among pact members through ongoing bargaining encounters." Elite settlements have also been used to explain both regime transitions and democratic stability.[16]

In this regard, it is important to note that the *World Development Report 2011* also incorporated the notion that some forms of exclusion not only may not threaten political stability, they may be necessary for stability. This argument draws on a line of literature about "spoilers" and similar dynamics. For example, Nilsson (2008) argues that strategic exclusion of actors outside peace agreements will not *necessarily* disrupt peace. Lanz (2011) argues for a framework to determine who should be included in peace processes, depending on whether their inclusion would augment the peace process and would be consistent with the values of international actors. Hartzell and Hoddie (2003) argue that power sharing is most effective when peace agreements address power sharing across multiple political, territorial, military, or economic dimensions. Rothchild and Roeder (2005) argue against explicit power sharing in ethnically divided countries, since "these institutions frequently shape political processes so that there are greater incentives to act in ways that threaten democracy and the peace."

Of course, there are cases where groups or powerful individuals within groups actively resist participation in a settlement—actors that Stedman (1997) describes as "spoilers." The presence of spoilers in a conflict complicates the search for an inclusive settlement—one reason the *World Development Report 2011* focuses on the notion of "inclusive enough" settlements. Stedman also argues that spoilers who continue to fight do not always undermine peace, depending on the strategies employed by those seeking peace. In other words, there is a relationship between the degree of exclusion and the capacity of the

---

16. Lijphart (1969) explains the roots of stable democracies in deeply divided societies as a function of "consociationalism": "The leaders of the rival subcultures may engage in competitive behavior, and thus further aggravate mutual tensions and political instability, but they may also make deliberate efforts to counteract the immobilizing and unstabilizing effects of cultural fragmentation." Building on this, Lustick (1997) later argued that stability rested on two elite dynamics: either consociationalism or control, in which one group used its relative power to maintain peace. In consociational democracies, stability rests on elite willingness for cooperation. Diamond (1994) explains: "Elites choose democracy instrumentally because they perceive that the costs of attempting to suppress their political opponents exceed the costs of tolerating them" (and engaging them in constitutionally regulated competition). O'Donnell and Schmitter (1986) focus on elite processes to explain how transitions to democracy and subsequent democratic consolidation occur.

state (sometimes supplemented by the UN or other peacekeepers) to combat recalcitrant forces. This is an important side note: whereas the provision of external security forces for peace implementation (that is, peacekeeping) has traditionally been viewed as having an impartial function relative to the political settlement, increasingly UN peacekeepers have been mandated to "extend state authority," including by helping the state to demobilize or even defeat recalcitrant or rebelling forces (Jones, Gowan, and Sherman 2009). The presence of such external security assistance obviously alters the equation for state actors as to the degree of exclusion they can get away with.

There is also an initial literature on the ways in which elite pacts and their renegotiation are also related to patterns in organized crime. Some of this relates to postconflict cases; for example, Guatemala is a case where organized crime has emerged as a massive source of instability for the state in the period after the settlement of the long-running civil war there (Gavigan 2009). Guinea-Bissau is another example. However, the relationship between organized crime and political settlements is not limited to postconflict cases. For example, some analyses of the upsurge in violence in Mexico point to a triggering event being the challenge, posed by the first election of a non-PRI government in 2000, to the existing political settlement developed under successive PRI governments whereby organized criminal networks were largely left alone in exchange for corrupt flows to government officials and electoral and financial support to the government. Organized criminal groups reacted negatively against the proposed change and went on the warpath against the state, resulting in a massive spike in homicide deaths in the ensuring years. (For an account of the dynamics of democratization and organized crime in Mexico, see in particular O'Neil 2012.)

The emphasis on inclusion in political settlements aligns with a greater emphasis on inclusive institutions in the literature on new institutional economics. That literature starts with the assertion that institutions are the fundamental cause of long-run growth (Acemoglu, Johnson, and Robinson 2004; Rodrik, Subramanian, and Trebbi 2002; Weingast 1995; Przeworski 1991). Recent applications of that literature to state failure emphasize inclusion. For example Acemoglu and Robinson (2012), in arguing that the fundamental difference between rich and poor countries relates to the inclusivity of their political institutions, also find that the presence of extractive or inclusive institutions creates a self-reinforcing cycle and propose that, by creating incentives for outside actors to become part of the elite, an extractive state is more likely to suffer from infighting and civil war. Similarly, North, Wallis, and Weingast (2009) argue that limited access orders—where institutions and organizations are controlled by a narrow elite and defined by interpersonal relationships—are more violence prone than states that have impersonal institutions. They show a "virtuous circle," which discourages violence in open-access orders, predicated on citizens' belief in equality and inclusion; the channeling of dissent through political avenues; and the costs imposed on any organization that attempts to limit access. While these studies are not specifically focused on fragile states, they point to broad conclusions about the role of inclusion that reinforces the initial findings cited above.

What about the Long Term?
The Long Process of Building Political and Security Institutions

When we move from political settlements to building institutions, we encounter an important lacuna, both in applied knowledge and in practice. Development actors have studied institution building but have largely neglected political and security institutions. Political and security actors have long engaged in providing or understanding short-term security gaps (such as wars and peacekeeping operations) but have largely neglected true institution building. Only a small body of political science has studied the development of political and security institutions, mostly in comparative and historical perspective, and we've only begun to apply the conclusions of that study to the contemporary experience of fragile states (to which the findings of earlier developments may or may not be relevant; see Moore 1958, 1966; Huntington 1965; Moe 1990). Yet the development of political (accountable, representative), justice, and security institutions is fundamental to long-term, sustained recovery from war and to the prevention of relapse.

There's substantial normative resistance to this agenda. This comes first from parts of the development community itself, which still see the issues that arise in fragile states—issues that are necessarily political and that stray heavily into the security terrain—as being outside the development framework. There's political pressure on development agencies to avoid going too deeply into this question. This comes from nonfragile developing countries, many of which (justly) fear that there will be a continuing shift in the prioritization of resources away from reasonably successful lower middle-income countries toward fragile states, where there's a greater concentration of the absolute poor. (This gets expressed, among other ways, in a debate over whether international development should concentrate simply on the absolute poor, defined as incomes below $1.25 a day, or rather on a wider bandwidth of poverty, at least up to $2.00 a day.)

The resistance comes also from powerful middle-income countries, including the emerging powers, which are cautious about the agenda, in part because several of them have ongoing subregional conflicts or experience high levels of organized crime, and do not wish to be tarred with an international brush on these issues. There are, arguably, mandate problems too; for example the World Bank ruled that direct financing of national police structures constitutes a violation of the IBRD's apolitical charter. (Though, weirdly, the far more contentious issue of community policing can be financed.) The notion that providing law and order is a more political function than economic bargaining (the bread and butter of World Bank work) is bizarre, even laughable. The Bank does not agree.

Still, the sheer fact of where the absolute poor are, combined with mounting political advocacy from fragile states themselves, is likely to continue to create pressure for a deepening of the normative space for dealing with issues of fragility and conflict as part of the development agenda. Then there are the problems of modalities. Aid projects are often of short duration, and financing and strategic frameworks for engagement are generally applied in three-to-five-year increments. Finding processes that yield meaningful institutional reform in these short engagement periods is unusual, and when an engagement period ends, the strategy is often revised. Multiyear funding is insufficient. As a result, the consistent, predictable support for institution building that is needed is not the norm.

Moreover, there's the additional challenge of volatile aid flows. Fluctuations in aid have negative effects in their own right, and practitioners have observed the negative impacts that aid volatility has on recipient states' deficits. Without steady assistance, governments are left with uncertain budget outlooks, introducing yet another element of difficulty into planning their expenditures (Kharas, Makino, and Jung 2011). Fragile and semistable situations are the ones most in need of reliable assistance, given the need to guard against backsliding and reform setbacks. Yet volatility in aid flows is worse for fragile and conflict-affected states than for other recipients. By some estimates, this volatility is more than twice that of aid to other states. The costs of this volatility are only magnified by their effect on already-weak institutions, as opposed to functioning institutions in other aid recipients. Recent work on the topic shows that the impact of volatility in net official development assistance flows on economic performance for weak states was double that for other states (Kharas 2008). The estimated decrease in efficiency is 2.5 percent of GDP in fragile and conflict-affected states (World Bank 2011).

And the gaps are not found just in development agencies. There are also serious problems about long-term support to interim security—as the story of CAR's multiple authorized peacekeeping operations suggests, we need to be thinking about longer-term engagement in the provision of security or of over-the-horizon security for states facing the risk of relapse into conflict. This is a critical part of the agenda, but it is undertheorized, underexplored, and uncosted. A simple step would be do to some detailed costing of various alternatives, partially to counteract the argument that sustained security engagement is simply too expensive: it may be; but it may be less expensive than paying the costs of response to a relapse into conflict, and that's to say nothing of the economic effects on neighbors. But there's been little work on long-term security provision.

We do now have, though, a set of important cases from which it would be possible to draw lessons about alternative modalities for longer-term support. In Bosnia, the UN, the EU, and NATO have retained various forms of light political and security support arrangements for almost twenty years. In Somalia, a radically different case, there was important innovation by the UN and the World Bank in developing new techniques for financing the recurrent costs of national armed services. In Burundi, a long-term partnership between the national authorities and the Dutch government—on the basis of a sustained partnership between the Dutch development and security departments—has shown promising results. A detailed, lessons-learned, exercise, ideally conducted jointly by development and security actors, could inform policy development.

In addition, the international policy community has increasingly focused on the importance of the rule of law—both as part of what causes instability and as important elements of recovery strategy. There's good long-term logic to this, but there are deep gaps in our understanding of what works in the shorter term, absent robust institutions. We lack, for example, a solid understanding of the relationship between political settlements and judicial/accountability processes (Kalyvas 2006; Collier 1999). Under what conditions do tentative political settlements support the development of justice/accountability mechanisms? Under what conditions can justice/accountability mechanisms survive even in the absence of strong political support? Under what conditions can justice/accountability mechanisms actually drive political reform? Deeper understanding of such questions is essential to understanding where and when policy engagement aimed at support to justice/accountability mechanisms can actually succeed.

But all of this ignores what is arguably the most critical question, which is about gaps in trust, gaps in confidence, and the challenge these gaps pose to institution building (Collier 2011; Stedman 2001; Walter 2010). The argument is that a lack of confidence in the future action of other parties constitutes a major barrier to cooperation, and thus to institution building, and that real institution building can only begin after some basic restoration of confidence or the use of commitment technologies to overcome trust dilemmas. If this is right, it should constitute a major new starting point for how to think about policy intervention in fragile states. But first, the conclusions must be challenged, tested, and refined. Essential research questions include the following:

—If violence produces a confidence barrier to cooperation/development, how long does that effect last?

—Does it have different lengths of endurance in different sectors (that is, does economic risk taking recover more quickly than political/security risk taking?).

—What set of factors drives elite/popular decisionmaking to rebalance between risk avoidance (because of a confidence gap) and risk taking?

—What roles do economic opportunity/need play? Family/household pressures? Regional/global factors? Security guarantees?

—How much does national mobilization matter?

—Can national projects unify a population and restore some degree of trust among elites?

And then, external actors need to look at what they can do to help overcome some of these commitment gaps. By analogy to the financial sector, what post-violence societies need are a set of commitment technologies—third-party tools that the various elites involved in contesting the course of a settlement can refer to and rely on in choosing to make the choice, to take the risk, of betting on new institutional arrangements for long-term growth. In a study I found five examples of things that outsiders can do to nudge, or in one case shove, things in the right direction (Jones, Elgin-Cossart, and Esberg 2012). They can

—Provide direct support to government and use policy engagement to try to persuade government elites to adopt an inclusion agenda. The theory of change in this case is simply that national authorities may be more susceptible to engaged policy argument from reliable partners than they are from intrusive outsiders. This approach has been used, for example, in Nepal by Western donors seeking to support an inclusive peace process, peace implementation, and elections. The evidence from Ethiopia, Pakistan, Rwanda, and other places where this approach has been used is mixed.

—Provide support to opposition groups and civil society actors, to increase their ability to make their own claims for inclusion in the political settlement. This approach has been used at various times, with varying degrees of success, from Tanzania during its democratic transition (relative success) to Nepal after elections (mixed results) to Serbia (relative success).

—Help create normative space by investing in research or public debate around issues of inclusion. Topics that have been the subject of internationally supported debate include minority rights, women's rights, and decentralization. The theory of change here is about increasing domestic pressure on established elites. As yet there's not a sufficient track record to evaluate the success of such strategies.

—Engage in direct mediation between parties (often through diplomatic rather than developmental arms of government), or financial and capacity-building support to national mediation or dialogue processes. Mediation fails roughly three out of every four times it is attempted; but a 75 percent failure rate is also a 25 percent success rate, and mediation strategies—unlike peacekeeping strategies or war strategies—can be repeated frequently at low cost.

—Peacekeeping operations increasingly undertake "extension of state authority" activities designed to help an elected or otherwise (internationally) legitimate government weaken the military challenge posed by excluded actors. That changes the underlying realities in which the above strategies may then play out.

And then there are more coercive strategies designed to compel government elites to adopt more inclusive strategies, or forgo specific exclusive or abusive policies. This can involve military action, ideally authorized by the UN. In addition, economic and aid actors may impose a range of penalties or sanctions to try to induce inclusive behavior or, more commonly, to attempt to stave off specific exclusion strategies.

Finally, we should not exclude from the analysis options like transitional authorities (as were imposed in Timor-Leste, Kosovo, and Eastern Slavonia); and longer-term arrangements for shared sovereignty (as in Bosnia). These arrangements are unpopular, replete with challenges, and have been met with widespread criticism about neoimperial attitudes and the like (Chesterman 2005). But we would be unwise to rule them out a priori, not least because in each of these cases and even arguably Cambodia they've been moderately successful—certainly by comparison to other modes of international engagement.

Conclusion

Of course, because something is a problem doesn't mean it has a solution; and it certainly doesn't mean it has an international solution. It's possible that outsiders can't do much to help states forge political settlements. But that's not a conclusion we should yet reach with certainty. Certainly there's no need to overlearn from recent cases like Afghanistan and Iraq—no need to overlearn from the extraordinary arrogance of NATO and the overall incompetence of the effort. There are examples of more savvy, more sensitive, and above all more humble efforts—in Mozambique, in Sierra Leone, arguably in Liberia, even in Timor-Leste—and there are lessons to learn.

This is a challenge for the development community and the security community, both. It's going to require moving past tried and tired divisions of labor between political, security, and development actors and beyond exhausted approaches to coordination. Fifteen years of learning lessons on this issue make it unequivocally clear that only genuinely unified operations can deliver the combination of physical and economic security that states are going to need to make the sustained transition from war and poverty to peace and development. These are intrinsically interlinked transitions, and each will fail without progress on the other. There are really only two options as to how to go about this: build on what exists, or build from scratch.

Build on What Exists

The first, most obvious, and most likely approach is to build with existing tools and instruments, most of them located within the UN and the World Bank, but linking also to regional organizations. The existing tools are not trivial, despite the critique of performance above. They include the office of rule of law and security institutions at the UN Department for Peacekeeping Operations and the global rule of law center at the UN Development Program (now, somewhat usefully, colocated); the office on rule of law in the secretary general's office (a kind of normative coordinating entity, albeit one with few if any powers); the High Commissioner for Human Rights; and the World Bank's Global Center on Conflict, Security and Development.

However, the track record on reform of these entities has been slow and disappointing. At the UN, more than fifteen years of continuous efforts to cajole the UNDP into a more concerted focus on conflict has produced modest results. In its most recent reform bid, soft launched in 2013, the UNDP administrator Helen Clark stressed that conflict would go from being a subtheme of UNDP's work to a central one, but insiders and observers alike were confused by the adjoining proposals, which downgraded the existing conflict-focused unit, with no corollary recruitment effort to replace core UNDP staff with staff having greater experience in conflict or political and security institutions. The UNDP has been losing donor funds and donor confidence at a steady rate, and it is too early to say whether this round of proposed reforms will be enough to reverse that tide. But absent a more dramatic change to personnel, funding, and policy, it's hard to see how reform of the UNDP can be more than a piece of this particular puzzle.

At the World Bank there was an initial burst of reform enthusiasm that followed the *World Development Report 2011*. This resulted, notably, in the establishment of the Global Center for Conflict, Security and Development in Nairobi (colloquially known as "the Hub"), designed as a one-stop policy shop on conflict and fragility issues. But like the UNDP conflict bureau that preceded it, the Hub was given no authority over resources in fragile states, nor hiring, nor evaluation. The track record of global advisory services shows that they can be useful sources of support to country programs that are seeking to deepen their conflict expertise, but they cannot drive deeper change. Moreover, there have been partial reversals. In the (extraordinarily complicated, opaque, and apparently mismanaged) reform proposals developed by the new Bank president Jim Kim, conflict issues did not arise as one of the major pillars of the Bank, but these were treated as a form of cross-cutting issue, and the early hires by Kim did not include the position dealing with conflict issues (see "Restructuring Hell" 2014; Northam 2014).

More worrying still, after several years of effort to generate flexibility in the Bank's legal office, the most recent legal rulings take a very narrow view of what it is that the Bank can do in political and legal institution building.

Efforts to link the work of the Bank and the UN have also been similarly slow and underwhelming. Years and years of donor efforts in New York and Washington during the early 2000s made almost no progress on this score. Whatever modest progress has been made can be attributed to the accidental fact of the shared Korean heritage of the two institution heads. The two took a trip together to Central Africa, where Kim pledged additional support for development initiatives undertaken in the context of peace implementation overseen by the UN. But officials in both institutions readily acknowledge that this chief-executive-to-chief-executive coordination has not filtered down even to the very senior working level, let alone to the staff level, and no mechanism has been put in place to achieve that goal.

Hence, my recurrent interest in the second option, which is to recognize that these two, large, important institutions are not fit for this particular purpose and, like all large bureaucracies, are extraordinarily resistant to deep change. And thus, to starting fresh.

Build from Scratch

To really begin anew, a new structure would be needed. This could be a hybrid, part NGO, part formal institution. Although it also could be another UN agency within the UN Secretariat, the risks are that it would replicate some of the existing flaws of UN structures. Third, it could be a hybrid entity composed of hived-off parts of the World Bank and the UN: the Bank's Hub merged with DPKO's Office of Rule of Law and Security Institutions and UNDP's Global Center, all fused into one new, separate entity.

If an official model is needed, one choice is the successful aspects of a UN High Commission. The UN High Commissioner for Refugees has been one of the most effective UN bodies over many years, and for good reasons. The membership structure is self-selecting: it's not universal but rather is confined to governments that have signed and implemented the UN Convention on Refugees, which not all governments have. This means that rather than constantly debating core principles within the governance structure, the governance structure reinforces both the core mandate of the institution and creates a form of peer pressure for continued compliance by those same governments. The management structure is useful too. Because high commissions are structurally part of the UN Secretariat, their heads are appointed by the secretary general and thus escape some of the horse-trading and race-to-the-bottom modes that sometimes characterizes appointments by intergovernmental bodies. Further, high commissions are not managed by the UN's budget, human resource, or administrative arms; they have their own, far more efficient, far more operational, administrative vehicles.

So one idea might be to establish a high commissioner for the rule of law, or something similar, with a focus on institution building for political, security, and justice institutions. This would not in fact have to be built from scratch, because there's a body of talent, experience, and expertise already resident at the Bank, the UN, regional institutions, and donor governments that could form the core of any new institution designed to tackle this thorny problem. The experiences and experiential knowledge of Bank staff in Afghanistan and Libya, by UN staff in the Democratic Republic of Congo and Tunisia and Jamaica, by USAID staff in Egypt and Iraq, by Dutch SSR teams in Burundi—these form the necessary core that any new institution would need. Unlike existing high commissions, an effective body should seek to replicate something of the research culture of the World Bank (unlike the antievidence culture of the UN). The scholarly expertise that resides in such centers as Stanford's Center for Democracy, Development and the Rule of Law and in research centers in South Africa, the UK, Brazil, and points in between could be brought to bear, either through in-house capacities or through structured, long-term engagement with outside bodies (which might be more effective).

This would not be starting with a blank slate, but it would be a fresh start. And there's little doubt that a fresh start is needed if we're going to succeed in going the last mile in helping states build the institutions they need—political, security, justice—to escape the trap of recurrent violence and fragility by becoming resilient.

For almost twenty years, the debate among development and humanitarian actors has been about bridging the gap between humanitarian relief and long-term development. It's a fairly sorry tale of repeated trial and error without anywhere near sufficient learning—a story of turf wars and tortured concepts, of a long-running "pass the buck" game among development agencies, but also of humanitarian actors, peacekeepers, and donors. It's time to do better—time to stop trying to bridge the gap—and instead, to fill it.

References

Acemoglu, Daron, Simon Johnson, and James Robinson. 2004. "Institutions as the Fundamental Cause of Long-Run Growth." Cambridge, Mass.: National Bureau of Economic Research.

Acemoglu, Daron, and James A. Robinson. 2012. *Why Nations Fail.* Crown Business.

Auty, Richard. 2001. "The Political Economy of Resource-Driven Growth." *European Economic Review* 45, no. 4-6.

Barnett, Michael. 2006. "Building a Republican Peace: Stabilizing States after War." *International Security* 30, no. 4.

Bates, Robert H., Jack A. Goldstone, David L. Epstein, Ted Robert Gurr, Michael B. Lustik, Monty G. Marshall, Jay Ulfelder, and Mark Woodward. 2005. "A Global Model for Forecasting Political Instability." Paper prepared for the American Political Science Association, September 1–4. Washington.

———. 2010. "A Global Model for Forecasting Political Instability." *American Journal of Political Science* 54, no. 1: 190–208.

BBC News. 2013. "CAR Death Toll Much Higher than Thought, Says Amnesty." December 19.

Berdal, Mats, and David M. Malone, eds. 2000. *Greed and Grievance: Economic Agendas in Civil War.* Lynne Rienner.

Blattman, Christopher, and Edward Miguel. 2010. "Civil War." *Journal of Economic Literature* 48, no. 1: 3–57.

Brinkerhoff, Derick, ed. 2007. *Governance in Post-Conflict Societies: Rebuilding Fragile States.* Routledge.

Brown, Michael, ed. 1996. *The International Dimensions of Internal Conflict.* MIT Press.

Burnham, Mike, and Shannon Peterson. 2014. "The Moral Foundations of Nationalism and Ethnic Conflict." *Georgetown Security Studies Review* (June).

Call, Charles, ed. 2008. *Building States to Build Peace.* Lynne Rienner.

———. 2012. *Why Peace Fails: The Causes and Prevention of Civil War Recurrence.* Georgetown University Press.

Chandy, Laurence, and Geoffrey Gertz. 2011. "Poverty in Numbers: The Changing State of Global Poverty from 2005 to 2015." Brookings Institution, January.

Chesterman, Simon. 2005. *You the People.* Oxford University Press.

Chesterman, Simon, Michael Ignatieff, and Ramesh Thakur. 2005. *Making States Work: State Failure and the Crisis of Governance.* United Nations University Press.

Collier, Jane F. 1999. "Models of Indigenous Justice in Chiapas, Mexico: A Comparison of State and Zinacanteco Visions." *Political and Legal Anthropology Review* 22, no. 1.

Collier, Paul. 2011. "State-Building: Job Creation, Investment Promotion, and the Provision of Basic Services." *PRISM* 2, no. 4.

Collier, Paul, and Anke Hoeffler. 2004. "Greed and Grievance in Civil War." *Oxford Economic Papers* 56, no. 4: 563–95.

———. 2009. "Beyond Greed and Grievance: Feasibility and Civil War." *Oxford Economic Papers* 61: 1–27.

Collier, Paul, and others. 2003. *Breaking the Conflict Trap: Civil War and Development Policy.* World Bank.

Cousens, Elizabeth M., and Chetan Kumar. 2001. *Peacebuilding as Politics: Cultivating Peace in Fragile Societies.* Lynne Rienner.

Craft, Cassady, and Joseph P. Smaldone. 2002. "The Arms Trade and the Incidence of Political Violence in Sub-Saharan Africa, 1967–1997." *Journal of Peace Research* 39, no. 6: 693–710.

DAC (International Network on Conflict and Fragility). 2012. "Fragile States 2013: Resource Flows and Trends in a Shifting World." OECD.

de Figueiredo, Rui J. P., and Barry R. Weingast. 1999. "The Rationality of Fear: Political Opportunism and Ethnic Conflict." In *Civil Wars, Insecurity and Intervention*, edited by Barbara Walter and Jack Snyder. Columbia University Press.

de Soysa, Indra. 2000. "The Resource Curse: Are Civil Wars Driven by Rapacity or Paucity?" In *Greed and Grievance: Economic Agendas in Civil Wars*, edited by Mats Berdal and David Malone. Lynne Rienner.

De Zeeuw, Jeroen. 2008. *From Soldiers to Politicians: Transforming Rebel Movements after Civil War.* Boulder: Lynne Rienner.

Diamond, Larry. 1994. "Introduction: Political Culture and Democracy." In *Political Culture and Democracy in Developing Countries*, edited by Larry Diamond. Boulder: Lynne Rienner.

Di John, Jonathan, and James Putzel. 2009. "Political Settlements." Governance and Social Development Resources Center (www.gsdrc.orgdocs/open/eirs7.pdf).

Doyle, Michael W., and Nicholas Sambanis. 2000. "International Peacebuilding: A Theoretical and Quantitative Analysis." *American Political Science Review* 94, no. 4: 779–801.

———. 2006. *Making War and Building Peace: United Nations Peace Operations.* Princeton University Press.

Edward, Peter, and Andy Sumner. 2013. "The Future of Global Poverty in a Multi-Speed World: New Estimates of Scale and Location, 2010–2030." Working Paper 327. Center for Global Development.

Elliasson, Jan. 2014. "Deputy Secretary-General's Remarks at Event on the Rwandan Genocide," January 15 (www.un.org/sg/dsg/statements/index.asp?nid=481).

Epstein, David, Robert Bates, Jack Goldstone, Ida Kristensen, and Sharun O'Halloran. 2006. "Democratic Transitions." *American Journal of Political Science* 50, no. 3.

Fearon, James. 1995. "Rationalist Explanations for War." *International Organization* 49, no. 3: 379–414.

———. 2010a. "Civil War Onset." Background paper for *World Development Report 2011.* Washington: World Bank.

———. 2010b. "Governance and Civil War Onset." Background paper for *World Development Report 2011.* Washington: World Bank.

Fearon, James, and David Laitin. 2003. "Ethnicity, Insurgency, and Civil War." *American Political Science Review* 97, no. 1: 75–90.

———. 2004. "Why Do Some Civil Wars Last So Much Longer than Others?" *Journal of Peace Research* 41, no. 3: 275–302.

Fortna, Virginia Page. 2004. *Peace Time: Cease-Fire Agreements and the Durability of Peace.* Princeton University Press.

———. 2008. *Does Peacekeeping Work? Shaping Belligerents' Choices after Civil War.* Princeton University Press.

Fritz, Verena, and Alina Rocha Menocal. 2007. *Understanding State-Building from a Political Economy Perspective.* ODI.

Fukuyama, Francis. 2004. "The Imperative of State-Building." *Journal of Democracy* 15, no. 2.

———. 2007. "Governance Reform in Papua New Guinea." Working Paper. Washington: World Bank.

Gauri, Varun, Jean Fares, Emmanuel Jimenez, Elizabeth King, Mattias Lundberg, David McKenzie, Mamta Murthi, and Cristobal Ridao-Cano. 2007. *World Development Report 2007: Development and the Next Generation.* Washington: World Bank.

Gavigan, Patrick. 2009. "Organized Crime, Illicit Power Structures and Guatemala's Threatened Peace Process." *International Peacekeeping* 16, no. 1: 62–76.

Ghani, Ashraf, and Clare Lockhart. 2008. *Fixing Failed States: A Framework for Rebuilding a Fractured World.* Oxford University Press.

Gleditsch, Kristian Skrede. 2007. "Transnational Dimensions of Civil War." *Journal of Peace Research* 44, no. 3: 293–309.

Goldberg, Mark Leon. 2014. "Has the International Community Gotten Better at Stopping Genocide?" UN Dispatch blog, January 17 (http://www.undispatch.com/has-the-international-community-gotten-better-at-stopping-genocide/).

Gomez, Margarita P., and Asger Christensen. 2010. "The Impacts of Refugees on Neighboring Countries: A Development Challenge." Background paper for *World Development Report 2011*. Washington: World Bank.

Gurr, Ted Robert, Mark Woodward, and Monty G. Marshall. 2005. "Forecasting Instability: Are Ethnic Wars and Muslim Countries Different?" A Political Instability Task Force paper prepared for the American Political Science Association, September 1-4. Washington.

Hartzell, Caroline, and Matthew Hoddie. 2003. "Institutionalizing Peace: Power Sharing and Post-Civil War Conflict Management." *American Journal of Political Science* 47, no. 2: 318–32.

———. 2007. *Crafting Peace: Power-Sharing Institutions and the Negotiated Settlement of Civil Wars*. Pennsylvania State University Press.

Hartzell, Caroline, Matthew Hoddie, and Donald Rothchild. 2001. "Stabilizing the Peace after Civil War: An Investigation of Some Key Variables." *International Organization* 55: 183–208.

Hartzell, Caroline, and Donald Rothchild. 1997. "Political Pacts as Negotiated Agreements: Comparing Ethnic and Non-Ethnic Cases." *International Negotiation* 2, no. 1: 147–71.

Hegre, Havard, Gudrin Ostby, and Clionadh Raleigh. 2009. "Poverty and Civil War Events: A Disaggregated Study of Liberia." *Journal of Conflict Resolution* 53, no. 4: 598–623.

Herbst, Jeffrey. 2000. "Economic Incentives, Natural Resources and Conflict in Africa." *Journal of African Economies* 9: 270–94.

Higley, John, and Michael Burton. 1998. "Elite Settlements and the Taming of Politics." *Government and Opposition* 33, no. 1: 98–115.

Horowitz, Donald L. 1985. *Ethnic Groups in Conflict*. University of California Press.

———. 1998. "Structure and Strategy in Ethnic Conflict: A Few Steps toward Synthesis." World Bank.

Humphreys, MacArtan. 2005. "Natural Resources, Conflict, and Conflict Resolution." *Journal of Conflict Resolution* 49, no. 1: 508–37.

Huntington, Samuel. 1965. "Political Development and Political Decay." *World Politics* 17, no. 3.

———. 1997. *The Clash of Civilizations and the Remaking of World Order*. Touchstone.

International Crisis Group. 2013a. "Central African Republic: Better Late than Never." Africa Briefing 96.

———. 2013b. "Central African Republic: Priorities of the Transition." Africa Report 203.

Jones, Bruce, ed. 2007. *Annual Review of Global Peace Operations 2007*. Lynne Rienner.

Jones, Bruce, and Rahul Chandran. 2008. *From Fragility to Resilience: Concepts and Dilemmas of Statebuilding in Fragile States*. OECD.

Jones, Bruce, and Molly Elgin-Cossart. 2011. "Development under the Shadow of Violence: A Knowledge Agenda for Policy." Geneva: IDRC/DfID/AFD.

Jones, Bruce, Molly Elgin-Cossart, and Jane Esberg. 2012. "Pathways out of Fragility: The Case for a Research Agenda on Inclusive Political Settlements in Fragile States." Center on International Cooperation, New York University.

Jones, Bruce, Richard Gowan, and Jake Sherman. 2009. *Building on Brahimi: Peacekeeping in an Era of Strategic Uncertainty*. NYU Center on International Cooperation.

Kalyvas, Stathis N. 2003. "The Ontology of 'Political Violence': Action and Identity in Civil Wars." *Perspectives on Politics* 1, no. 3: 475–94.

———. 2006. *The Logic of Violence in Civil War*. Cambridge University Press.

Kaufman, Stuart J. 1996. "Spiraling to Ethnic War: Elites, Masses, and Moscow in Moldova's Civil War." *International Security* 21, no. 2: 108–38.

———. 2006. "Escaping the Symbolic Politics Trap: Reconciliation Initiatives and Conflict Resolution in Ethnic Wars." *Journal of Peace Research* 43, no. 2: 201–18.

Kaufmann, Chaim. 1998. "What Is the Offense/Defense Balance and Can We Measure It?" *International Security* 22, no. 4.

———. 2005. "Rational Choice and Progress in the Study of Ethnic Conflict: A Review Essay." *Security Studies* 14, no. 1: 178–207.

Kavanagh, Camino. 2011. "State Capture and Organized Crime or Capture of Organized Crime by the State." Background paper. New York University Center on International Cooperation (www.cic.nyu.edu/peacebuilding/docs/Lima percent20Seminar percent-20Background percent20Paper.pdf).

Keating, Tom, and W. Andy Knight, eds. 2004. *Building Sustainable Peace.* United Nations University Press.

Khan, Mushtaq. 1996. "A Typology of Corrupt Transactions in Developing Countries." *IDS Bulletin* 27, no. 2: 12–21.

———. 1998. "Patron-Client Networks and the Economic Effects of Corruption." *European Journal of Development Research* 10, no. 1: 15–39.

Kharas, Homi. 2008. "Measuring the Cost of Aid Volatility." Wolfensohn Center for Development Working Paper 3/20. Brookings Institution.

Kharas, Homi, Koji Makino, and Woojin Jung, eds. 2011. *Catalyzing Development: A New Vision for Aid.* Brookings Institution Press.

Lanz, David. 2011. "Who Gets a Seat at the Table? A Framework for Understanding the Dynamics of Inclusion and Exclusion in Peace Negotiations." *International Negotiation* 16, no. 2: 275–95.

Licklider, Roy. 1995. "The Consequences of Negotiated Settlements in Civil Wars, 1945–1993." *American Political Science Review* 89, no. 3: 681–90.

Lijphart, Arend. 1969. "Consociational Democracy." *World Politics* 21, no. 2: 207–25.

Lindemann, Stefan. 2008. "Do Inclusive Elite Bargains Matter? A Research Framework for Understanding the Causes of Civil War in Sub-Saharan Africa." Discussion paper. Governance and Social Development Resource Center.

———. 2010. "Inclusive Elite Bargains and the Dilemmas of Unproductive Peace: Evidence from Zambia." Governance and Social Development Resource Center.

López-Pintor, Rafael. 2006. "Post-Conflict Elections and Ethnic Divides Measures to Encourage Participation." *Electoral Insight*, December.

Lustick, Ian. 1997. "Lijphart, Lakatos, and Consociationalism." *World Politics* 50, no. 1: 88–117.

Luttwak, Edward. 1999. "Give War a Chance." *Foreign Affairs* 78, no. 4: 36–44.

Mack, Andrew. 2010. "Human Security Report 2009/2010." Vancouver: Human Security Press.

———. 2012. "Human Security Report 2012." Vancouver: Human Security Press.

Malan, Mark, and Fiona McFarlane. 1998. "Crisis and Response in the Central African Republic: A New Trend in African Peacekeeping?" *African Security Review* 7, no. 2: 48–58.

McCollough, David. 1992. *Truman.* Simon and Schuster.

McDoom, Omar. 2011. "Rwanda's Exit Pathway from Violence: A Strategic Assessment." Background paper for *World Development Report 2011*. Washington: World Bank.

Moe, Terry. 1990. "Political Institutions: The Neglected Side of the Story." *Journal of Law, Economics, and Organization* 6, special issue.

Moore, W. Barrington. 1958. *Social Origins of Dictatorship and Democracy: Lord and Peasant in the Making of the Modern World.* New York: Beacon.

———. 1966. *Political Power and Social Theory, Six Studies.* Harvard University Press.

Muggah, Robert. 2005. "No Magic Bullet: A Critical Perspective on Disarmament, Demobilization, and Reintegration (DDR), and Weapons Reduction in Post-Conflict Contexts." *International Journal of Commonwealth Affairs* 94.

Nilsson, Desirée. 2008. "Partial Peace: Rebel Groups Inside and Outside Civil War Settlements." Conflict Transitions Working Paper 19. Development Research Group, Macroeconomics and Growth Team. Washington: World Bank.

North, Douglas, John Joseph Wallis, and Barry Weingast. 2009. *Violence and Social Orders.* Cambridge University Press.

Northam, Jackie. 2014. "The World Bank Gets an Overhaul—and Not Everyone's Happy." NPR, March 13 (www.npr.org/blogs/parallels/2014/03/13/289819931/the-world-bank-gets-an-overhaul-and-not-everyones-happy).

Oberschall, Anthony. 2007. *Conflict and Peace Building in Divided Societies: Responses to Ethnic Violence.* Routledge.

O'Donnell, Guillermo, and Philip Schmitter. 1986. *Transitions from Authoritarian Rule.* Johns Hopkins University Press.

OECD (Organization for Economic Cooperation and Development). 2011. *International Engagement in Fragile States: Can't We Do Better?*

O'Neil, Shannon. 2012. "Refocusing U.S.-Mexico Security Cooperation." Policy Innovation Memorandum 27. New York: Council on Foreign Relations.

Papagianni, Katia. 2008. "Participation and State Legitimation." In *Building States to Build Peace,* edited by Charles T. Call and Vanessa Wyeth. Boulder, Colo.: Lynne Rienner.

Patrick, Stewart. 2011. *Weak Links: Fragile States, Global Threats, and International Security.* Oxford University Press.

Posen, Barry R. 1993. "The Security Dilemma and Ethnic Conflict." *Survival* 35, no. 1: 27–47.

Powell, Robert. 2006. "War as a Commitment Problem." *International Organization* 60, no. 1: 169–203.

Prichett, Lant, and Frauke de Weijer. 2010. "Fragile States: Stuck in a Capability Trap." Background paper for *World Development Report 2011.* Washington: World Bank.

Przeworski, Adam. 1991. *Democracy and the Market.* Cambridge University Press.

Republique Centrafricaine. 2004. "Objectifs du millenaire pour le developpement." Septembre.

———. 2010. "Objectifs du millenaire pour le developpement." Septembre.

"Restructuring Hell at the World Bank." 2014. Editorial. *Financial Times,* April 9.

Rice, Susan, Carlos Pascual, and Corinne Graff. 2010. *Confronting Poverty: Weak States and U.S. National Security.* Brookings Institution Press.

Rodrik, Dani, Arvind Subramanian, and Francesco Trebbi. 2002. "Institutions Rule: The Primacy of Institutions over Geography and Integration in Economic Development." Working Paper. National Bureau of Economic Research (www.nber.org/papers/w9305).

Roque, Paula Cristina, Judy Smith-Höhn, Paul-Simon Handy, and David Craig. 2010. "Exit Pathways: South Africa, Mozambique, Vietnam, Cambodia, Rwanda." Background paper for *World Development Report 2011.* Washington: World Bank.

Ross, Michael L. 2004. "How Do Natural Resources Influence Civil War? Evidence from Thirteen Cases." *International Organization* 58: 35–67.

Rothchild, Donald. 1997. "Ethnic Bargaining and the Management of Intense Conflict." *International Negotiation* 2, no.1: 1–20.

———. 2002. "Settlement Terms and Postagreement Stability." In *Ending Civil Wars: The Implementation of Peace Agreements*, edited by Stephen John Stedman, Donald Rothchild, and Elizabeth M. Cousens. Lynne Rienner.

Rothchild, Donald, and Philip G. Roeder. 2005. *Sustainable Peace: Power and Democracy after Civil War.* Cornell University Press.

Roulo, Claudette. 2013. "U.S. Supports Peacekeeping Efforts in Central African Republic." American Forces Press Service, December 11.

Saleyhan, Idean. 2008. "No Shelter Here: Rebel Sanctuaries and International Conflict." *Journal of Politics* 70, no. 1: 54–66.

Saleyhan, Idean, and Kristian Skrede Gleditsch. 2006. "Refugees and the Spread of Civil War." *International Organization* 60, no. 2: 335–68.

Samuels, Kirsti, and Sebastien von Einsiedel. 2004. "The Future of UN State-Building: Strategic and Operational Challenges and the Legacy of Iraq." Policy report. International Peace Academy,

Schneckener, Ulrich. 2002. "Making Power-Sharing Work: Lessons from Successes and Failures in Ethnic Conflict Regulation." *Journal of Peace Research* 39, no. 2.

Simonsen, Sven Gunnar. 2005. "Addressing Ethnic Divisions in Post-Conflict Institution-Building: Lessons from Recent Cases." *Security Dialogue* 36, no. 3.

Snyder, Jack, and Robert Jervis. 1999. "Civil War and the Security Dilemma." In *Civil Wars, Insecurity and Intervention*, edited by Barbara Walter and Jack Snyder. Columbia University Press.

Stedman, Stephen John. 1996. "Mediation and Negotiation in Internal Conflicts." In *International Dimensions of Internal Conflicts*, edited by Michael Brown. MIT Press.

———. 1997. "Spoiler Problems in Peace Processes." *International Security* 22, no. 2.

———. 2001. "Implementing Peace Agreements in Civil Wars: Lessons and Recommendations for Policymakers." Policy paper. Peace Implementation. International Peace Academy, and Center for International Security and Cooperation. Stanford University.

———. 2002. "Strategy and Transitional Authority." In *Ending Civil Wars: The Implementation of Peace Agreements*, edited by Stephen John Stedman, Donald Rothchild, and Elizabath Cousens. Lynne Rienner.

Svensson, Jan. 2000. "Foreign Aid and Rent-Seeking." *Journal of International Economics* 51: 437–61.

Tilly, Charles. 1975. *The Formation of National States in Western Europe.* Princeton University Press.

———. 2003. *The Politics of Collective Violence.* Cambridge University Press.

———. 2008. *Contentious Performances.* Cambridge University Press.

Titley, Brian. 1997. *Dark Age: The Political Odyssey of Emperor Bokassa.* McGill-Queen's University Press.

Tull, Denis, and Andreas Mehler. 2005. "The Hidden Costs of Power-Sharing: Reproducing Insurgent Violence in Africa." *African Affairs* 104, no. 416.

UK (Department for International Development). 2010. "Building Peaceful States and Societies." DfID practice paper.

UN (United Nations Peacebuilding Support Office). 2012. "2012 Annual Report."

Vreeland, James. 2008. "The Effect of Political Regime on Civil War." *Journal of Conflict Resolution* 52, no. 1: 401–25.

Wagner, Robert Harrison. 1993. "The Causes of Peace." In *Stopping the Killing: How Civil Wars End*, edited by Roy Licklider. New York University Press.

Walter, Barbara F. 1997. "The Critical Barrier to Civil War Settlement." *International Organization* 51: 335–64.

———. 1999. "Designing Transitions from Civil War: Demobilization, Democratization and Commitments to Peace." *International Security* 24, no. 1: 127–55.

———. 2002. *Committing to Peace: The Successful Settlement of Civil War.* Princeton University Press.

———. 2004. "Does Conflict Beget Conflict? Explaining Recurring Civil War." *Journal of Peace Research* 41, no. 3: 371–88.

———. 2009. "Bargaining Failures and Civil War." *Annual Review of Political Science* 12 (June): 243–61.

———. 2010. "Conflict Relapse and the Sustainability of Post-Conflict Peace." Background paper for *World Development Report 2011*. Washington: World Bank.

Weede, Erich, and Edward N. Muller. 1998. "Rebellion, Violence, and Revolution: A Rational Choice Perspective." *Journal of Peace Research* 35, no. 1: 43–59.

Weingast, Barry R. 1995. "The Economic Role of Political Institutions." *Journal of Law, Economics and Organization* 11, no. 1: 1–31.

———. 1997. "The Political Foundations of Democracy and the Rule of Law." *American Political Science Review* 91, no. 2: 245–63.

Whaites, Alan. 2008. "States in Development: Understanding State-Building." DfID Working Paper. Government and Social Development Group, Policy and Research Division, UK Department for International Development.

World Bank. 2010. "Out of Defeat: Germany, France, and Poland post-WWII." Background paper for *World Development Report 2011*. Washington: World Bank.

———. 2011. *World Development Report 2011: Conflict, Security, and Development.*

Zartman, I. William. 2000. "Ripeness: The Hurting Stalemate and Beyond." In *International Conflict Resolution after the Cold War*, edited by Paul C.Stern and Daniel Druckman. National Academies Press.

3

Bridging State and Local Communities in Fragile States: Subnational Institutions as a Strategic Focus to Restore State Legitimacy

RYUTARO MUROTANI AND YOICHI MINE

E xtreme poverty will persist in fragile states for a long time to come, even beyond 2015, the target year for the Millennium Development Goals (MDGs). As Gertz and Chandy (2011) point out, fragile states, in contrast to many developing countries, have not succeeded in reducing poverty significantly despite efforts to meet the MDGs. Chandy, Ledlie, and Penciakova (2013) predict that the percentage of the world's poor living in fragile states will rise from one-third (as it currently stands) to one-half by 2018, and to nearly two-thirds by 2030. Given that nearly 1.5 billion people presently live in countries affected by fragility, conflict, or large-scale, organized, criminal violence, it is imperative that policymakers and development and peace-building practitioners address the question of fragility as effectively as possible. In order to run the last mile successfully, the issue of fragility must be tackled head-on.

While the exact definition of a fragile state varies according to the organizations and scholars involved, it is commonly understood that the risk of armed conflict is high in countries categorized as being fragile and also that the occurrence and recurrence of violent conflict hamper development in those countries. In 2011, the World Bank (2011) indicated that no fragile or low-income country affected by armed conflict has been able to achieve a single MDG. The World Bank also identifies the negative impact of violence on such development outcomes as nutrition, primary school enrollment, infant mortality, maternal mortality, and access to water and sanitation.

Though violent conflict has for a long time been recognized as an impediment to development, the efforts of the international community have not always been successful in bringing peace and development to fragile states. Since the early 1990s, the United Nations has actively provided peace-building support to postconflict societies, while bilateral donors have also increased their assistance to those countries. It appears that the modalities of engagement by the UN and by donors are now changing, with new priorities emerging. For example, UN missions tend to be longer than before, and more emphasis is now on state building as a path to long-term stability. Despite the fact that state building has been central to UN efforts for nearly a decade, satisfactory outcomes have not always followed. This is partly because state building and peace building are inherently long-term processes. But another problem is that the governments of fragile states, as well as international efforts to engage with these governments, have largely failed to earn the trust and confidence of the citizens of these fragile states.

This chapter reviews the international debate on state building in fragile states and identifies the gap between the concept of state building and the realities on the ground, more specifically the gap between institution building at the national level and improvement in lives at the local level that could help the state win the trust of local communities.

To examine this gap, this chapter presents case studies of three fragile situations: Afghanistan, northern Uganda, and Mindanao in the Philippines. The chapter draws lessons from the engagement of donors in these fragile situations. The discussion describes a benevolent cycle, in which state-building efforts at the national level are translated into socioeconomic development at the local level, which in turn strengthens the legitimacy of the national government in the eyes of the people.

The chapter ends with an examination of the lessons learned from the case studies as well as their relevance from the perspective of human security.

State Building: The Concept and International Efforts

The nexus of conflict and development is not a new item on the international agenda. After the end of the cold war, donors started to engage actively in postconflict peace building. Witnessing the recurrence of conflicts caused by the lack of political mechanisms to reduce instabilities, the international community began to pay greater attention to the importance of building effective public institutions. As donors increased their engagement in postconflict countries, they found the concept of good governance, and its realization, to be of particular importance in fragile states. Such understanding on the part of donors was reinforced by 9/11 and its aftermath, which compelled donor governments to realize that security threats could spill over from weakly governed countries into developed ones. In the mid-2000s, various books and articles gave full weight to state institutions and used the concept of state building as the key to fixing fragile states and reducing the risk of violent conflict (see Fukuyama 2005; Chesterman 2004; Fearon and Laitin 2004; Krasner and Pascual 2005; Ghani and Lockhart 2008; Paris and Sisk 2009).

The Development Assistance Committee of the Organization for Economic Cooperation and Development (OECD/DAC) is one of the major forums in which donors discuss policy options to engage with fragile states in a better way. In December 2008 the OECD/DAC created the International Network on Conflict and Fragility (INCAF) by bringing together the Fragile States Group (FSG) and the Network on Conflict, Peace and Development Cooperation (CPDC). This merger was premised on a common understanding that fragility, defined as the lack of capable and legitimate state institutions, should be squarely addressed to prevent future violent conflict. The INCAF was to create policy guidance on state building in fragile states (see for example, OECD 2011). Within this organization, state building is understood to be an effort to strengthen the capacity and legitimacy of state institutions to consolidate effective, legitimate, and resilient states (OECD 2007, 2008a).

Since the early 2000s, although the number of armed conflicts has been in decline, the new pattern of violent conflict has started to present a tough obstacle to state-building endeavors. Although countrywide civil wars have in recent years been less frequent, the fact remains that, during the same period, many armed conflicts have been fought at the subnational level or near state borders. In Africa, as Straus (2012) points out, a war is typically a small-scale insurgency, fought in peripheral areas of a country or across multiple state territories, and involves insurgents and factions who are usually unable to maintain control over a significant part of the national territory or to capture state capitals. Alarmingly, this new type of conflict is on the rise in Africa. Today, violent conflicts in Africa often involve transnational, nonstate actors such as al-Shabaab, AQIM (al-Qaeda in the Islamic Maghreb), the FDLR (Forces démocratiques de libération du Rwanda, or Democratic Forces for the Liberation of Rwanda), and the LRA (Lord's Resistance Army). For the moment, large-scale violent conflict is not likely in Asia. However, the region is also faced with a variety of subnational conflicts (Parks, Colletta, and Oppenheim 2013). In regard to Latin America, where countries classified as being fragile are very few, the World Bank (2011) highlights the significance of criminal violence and organized crime. Threats to citizen security are also of grave concern in some countries in the region.

This phenomenon of a multitude of small-scale insurgencies persisting at state peripheries is observable around the world. This new pattern of violent conflict reaffirms the urgent necessity of state building in fragile states and underscores the effort needed to spread its benefits to local communities, including those in remote areas. Fundamentally, the problem needs to be resolved by building capable and legitimate state institutions that will make basic public services, including public safety, accessible everywhere, even in areas distant from the capital. If state public institutions lack the capacity to maintain public order, transnational criminal actors could gain a footing. But the government may be able to reduce support for these groups by building trust among local people. This necessitates having in place not only political and social mechanisms for citizens to articulate their needs but also effective systems of service delivery to respond to these expectations. However, practical ways of building an "effective, legitimate, and resilient state" (OECD 2008a) are yet to be specified.

Implementation of the New Deal by Fragile States and Donors

The activities of INCAF, which have been instrumental in enhancing donors' common understanding of the nature of challenges in fragile states, must be matched by efforts from local people and their leaders. As state building is inherently an endogenous process, it can be achieved only when ownership of the process by local people is respected by all stakeholders. To this end, leaders of fragile states have formed a group, the g7+, and have increased their active engagement in dialogue with their donors so as to design better international engagement in support of state building in their countries. The g7+, now consisting of eighteen fragile states, contributed to the creation of the New Deal to overcome fragility, signed at the Busan High Level Forum in 2011.[1] The discussion among g7+ countries led to agreements on the Peacebuilding and Statebuilding Goals (PSGs) that would help them monitor their progress toward peace and development. Additionally, the New Deal resulted from the dialogues between the g7+ and the donors.[2]

The New Deal is a major initiative toward implementing the OECD/DAC's ideas to improve the impact of their operations on state-building processes in fragile states. It was designed through the International Dialogue on Peacebuilding and Statebuilding among the g7+ governments, civil society, and DAC donors and is based on an unambiguous emphasis on national ownership. After

1. The eighteen member states are Afghanistan, Burundi, the Central African Republic, Chad, Comoros, Côte d'Ivoire, the Democratic Republic of Congo (DRC), Guinea, Guinea-Bissau, Haiti, Liberia, Papua New Guinea, Sierra Leone, Solomon Islands, Somalia, South Sudan, Timor-Leste, and Togo. For details of the g7+, visit www.g7plus.org/.

2. The Peacebuilding and Statebuilding Goals (PSGs) are legitimate politics, security, justice, economic foundations, and revenues and services. The five measures to support a country-led and country-owned transition out of fragility are fragility assessment, one vision and one plan, a compact, use of goals to monitor and support political dialogue and leadership (these are gathered under the acronym FOCUS). The five operating principles are transparency, risk sharing, the use and strengthening of country systems, strengthening capacities, and timely and predictable aid (these are gathered under the acronym TRUST).

its inauguration at the Busan High Level Forum, the International Dialogue set forth guidelines for putting New Deal principles into practice. The governments of fragile states have intensified their efforts to conduct fragility assessments, so as to create a common understanding of what the bottlenecks to state building and peace building are. Several countries, including Timor-Leste, the Democratic Republic of Congo (DRC), and South Sudan, have conducted participatory workshops, inviting government officials, civil society representatives, and local people to raise a shared awareness of their circumstances and to identify priorities. The results of the fragility assessment exercise were to serve as a basis for an agreement on a compact between the donors and the governments of fragile states, which would address the most pressing issues for overcoming fragility.

However, despite the strong initiatives undertaken by these governments, their activities have yet to improve people's everyday lives. Although a consensus was reached between national governments and donors as to priority areas and the ways to approach them, those initiatives have not succeeded in delivering benefits to ordinary citizens. Efforts have been made to improve the framework in which national governments and donors work together, but it may take a long time to make a difference in people's lives at the local level. It must be also noted that institution building at the national level does not automatically translate into improvement in local people's lives.

The international effort to support state building has often been criticized for this lack of visible impact on the ground. Critics blame the imposition of state institutions "from above" and credit the effort of mainstreaming voices "from below" (see for example Hilhorst, Christoplos, and Van Der Haar 2010). They also emphasize the centrality to improvement in people's livelihood of postconflict peace building as well as the ways in which local people and communities perceive it (Richmond 2009; Shanmugaratnam 2008). Given the paucity of skilled administrators and financial resources, an overemphasis on the building of state institutions may have had the unintended consequence of leaving the development of institutions and economic activities at the local level behind. It is only when local people realize the benefits of institution building at the local level that the state gains legitimacy in their eyes. For this reason, the successful delivery of basic public services aimed at improving lives at the local level is of paramount importance.

Subnational Public Institutions as a Focus

Given the problems of distrust identified in the previous section, the engagement of donors in fragile states should be geared toward the effort to bridge the gap between state institution building and improvement in the lives of the general population. To this end, we argue that building capable subnational public institutions is the way to help the state to garner the trust of local communities.

Even in postconflict environments, where the legitimacy of the national government is not widely accepted, contributions by the national government to the well-being of local people are appreciated. Subnational institutions, which have direct and regular contact with local populations, are the key mechanisms for the state to consolidate its legitimacy.

Conflict-affected states often lack the capacity to provide basic public services. The problem is compounded by the fact that international support for institution building tends to concentrate on national rather than local institutions. The general shortage of human resources and the lack of state capacity in fragile states make it painstaking and time consuming to consolidate the entire system of public service delivery. However, both national and subnational institutions need to be capable of effectively delivering services to people at the local level. While organizations in the capital play an indispensable role in making national strategies and in guiding the entire process, it is subnational public organizations that directly influence the lives of people through the delivery of public services. Ordinary citizens are regularly in touch with those subnational institutions, and such experiences shape their image of the government. The extent to which these subnational institutions are capable and responsive affects every aspect of people's daily life, and shapes their impression of, and attitude toward, the national government. Capacity development of subnational institutions, as the primary interface of the government with citizens, is therefore critically important. Having said that, what is in question is not so much the determination of the relative advantage of national and subnational institutions. Rather the emphasis should be on looking for an appropriate combination, role sharing, and harmonization of the activities of those institutions. The aim is bridging the gap rather than replacing national institutions with other systems.

Subnational institutions can be the juncture at which institution building at the national level is translated into improved livelihoods at the local level. Violent conflict can easily change people's attitude and destroy their trust in the government overnight. In some postconflict countries, people have not received any public support from the state for more than a decade due to the devastation caused by violence. In order to make service delivery effective in such difficult circumstances, the government needs to listen to the voices of the people and to respond to their demands in an effective manner. The OECD/DAC report on service delivery in fragile states (OECD 2008b) also recognizes the nexus between service delivery and fragility, emphasizing the reciprocal relationship between service delivery and state legitimacy.[3] The more capacity a state has to

3. While the lack of service-delivery capacity weakens people's trust in the state, the development of state capacity is difficult in unstable areas. Takeuchi, Murotani, and Tsunekawa (2011) examine the difficulties of capacity development in areas where state legitimacy is extremely weak in the eyes of the people. They call this vicious cycle "the capacity trap."

deliver public services, the more legitimacy it will build. Yet the less legitimate the state, the more challenging it is to deliver services effectively.

Bridging the Gap between Institution Building at the National Level and Livelihood Improvement at the Local Level

As discussed in the previous section, in order to overcome fragility and appropriately manage conflict risks, fragile states must be able to fill the gap between institution building at the national level and livelihood improvement of the general population. International support for fragile states should not be limited to either of the two ends but should aim to bridge this gap. To translate state institution building into improvement in the quality of everyday life, the capacity of subnational public institutions needs to be enhanced, an accountability mechanism should be in place, and inclusive development encompassing all parts of the country should be put on track. Each of these three challenges requires collaborative efforts from different levels of public institutions, and the support of donors should be geared toward these efforts.

The case studies that follow examine the engagement of donors in public service delivery and livelihood improvement in local communities in fragile and conflict-affected situations. As mentioned, the case studies are Afghanistan, northern Uganda, and Mindanao in the Philippines. All three of these cases illustrate the way international engagement has improved the everyday lives of people and has, to varying degrees, strengthened the trust of people in the national government. These cases highlight improvements in the following three areas as being the key to addressing the gaps in question: capacity (strengthening subnational institutions for service delivery), accountability (consolidating feedback mechanisms through local participation), and inclusiveness (promoting partnership between the national and the local governments).

Improving Capacity

Expanding the capacity of subnational institutions is indispensable as a means of reaching out to those who are left behind. This is particularly so where the national government cannot meet the local population's demands and expectations. In order to increase efficiency in service delivery, the national government is required to relegate a significant number of its tasks to subnational public institutions in the principal-agent framework (Fukuyama 2005). Moreover, given that violent conflict tends to break out in remote areas of fragile states, it is critically important to improve the quality of service delivery in areas distant from the capital, where the capacity of local institutions tends to be weak. Their capacity to deliver services largely depends on the effectiveness of administrative organizations in charge of local service delivery. A major hindrance to effective delivery is weak institutional capacity and a paucity of human resources at the local level. The high demand for competent public officers in fragile states is hard to meet. Qualified civil servants tend to be concentrated in capital cities, thus limiting the potential for the capacity development of subnational institutions. Although contracting out service delivery to private companies or to NGOs can be an effective solution, such a practice runs the risk that people will lose trust in the national government, particularly where they see private companies and NGOs as primary providers of those services. Donors' assistance in expanding the capacity of local public institutions can make a difference in fixing such a problem.

Improving Accountability

Local people are not just passive recipients of public services but the principal actors in institutional transformation. These people must be empowered to actively engage in the decisionmaking processes that hold policymakers accountable. OECD (2008b) recognizes the importance of accountability mechanisms: "Governments everywhere deliver services effectively when there is *accountability* between citizens and their leaders." This holds true especially for fragile states in which violence has destroyed or weakened communication mechanisms between citizens and the government. In fragile situations it is important to build a system of democratic feedback that covers villages and small towns as well as big cities. Community-driven development and participatory planning at the local level can be an effective tool for creating such institutional arrangements. The participation of local people in the making and remaking of accountability mechanisms within subnational institutions is expected to contribute not only to the efficiency of service delivery but also to the development of democratic feedback across the multiple tiers of government, thereby consolidating state legitimacy. As described by Bryce in the spirit of Tocqueville, the best school of democracy is the practice of local self-government (Bryce 1920; Tocqueville 1836). This is the plain truth applicable to any political community that desires to be democratic.

Improving Inclusiveness

In delivering public services throughout the country, the national government should treat all subnational institutions impartially. While subnational institutions are in a better position to respond quickly to local demands, the national government has the indispensable role of providing an overall framework of inclusive development across the country and of allocating resources for service delivery in an equitable way. In fragile states the relationship between the national government and subnational institutions is often complicated by horizontal inequalities (HIs): socioeconomic, political, and cultural status inequalities between identity groups defined in terms of ethnicity, race, religion, language, culture, and region. In some cases, people in subnational regions fought against the central government, calling for autonomy and even secession. HIs fuel the grievances of disadvantaged groups and generate fear within privileged groups, affecting which measures are used to address those inequalities (Gurr 1970; Stewart 2008). In such situations, an effective partnership between the central government and subnational groups can be achieved through a political compact based on power sharing and decentralization (Mine and others 2013). Promoting inclusive partnerships between the national government and local governments provides the stable conditions in which public services can reach every part of the country without alienating major stakeholders.[4]

Case Studies

The following case studies highlight the significance of the three challenges described in the preceding section. They provide lessons learned from fragile states where donors have worked to fill the gap between the national and the local levels. All of these countries (Afghanistan, Uganda, and the Philippines) have experienced violent conflict that jeopardized development in substantial parts of the country. Given the lingering distrust of the local population toward the central government, effective public service delivery is a key to restoring state legitimacy in the eyes of people living in conflict-affected areas. In this endeavor, the three challenges outlined above must be consistently addressed.

Afghanistan

Since the fall of the Taliban regime in Afghanistan in 2001, various state institutions have been established. Throughout this time donors have firmly stood behind the initiative of the Afghan government to improve people's livelihoods. The new government was elected first through the Emergency Loya Jirga (Grand Council) in 2002 and later by a series of national elections. The new constitution of Afghanistan was eventually enacted in 2004. Running parallel to this process of state institution building, the assistance of donors in the reconstruction process has succeeded in delivering electricity, roads, education, health services, and other social services to the local people and communities. While physical insecurity and uncertainty about the outcomes of negotiations with the Taliban remain serious concerns, improvement in the lives of the local population has been identified as the task that should be implemented before anything else.

---

4. Regardless of gender, generation, occupation, region, ethnicity, and other attributes, all people should be part of inclusive development. In this chapter we pay special attention to inequalities between regional groups based on the fact that geographic divides and center-periphery tensions have been a major roadblock to peace building in fragile states.

Although the new constitution calls for a strong centralized state with a four-tier government structure, the history of Afghanistan abounds with failed attempts at centralization. Throughout its history, traditional local institutions maintained their relative autonomy, and state institutions have been unsuccessful in extending their influence to the local level. The existence of an illicit drug economy and undemocratic warlords has made it even more difficult to strengthen state institutions (Murotani and others 2010; Takeuchi, Murotani, and Tsunekawa 2011). Despite some progress, such as the introduction of the new constitution, the holding of elections, and improving the public financial management system of the central government, it is still very hard to improve the lives of the local population, especially in remote areas of the country.

Under such circumstances, the World Bank and many other donors support a community-driven development program called the National Solidarity Program (NSP), which aims to improve the living conditions of local people by enhancing the capacity and accountability of local institutions to reach out to the rural population. The program encourages local communities to create their own Community Development Councils (CDCs) as tools of participatory decisionmaking. These councils, elected through secret ballot, at least formally establish a democratic accountability mechanism. Also, with the support of the national government and donors, CDCs have expanded their capacity to deliver basic public services. Each CDC can utilize block grants provided under the supervision of the Ministry of Rural Rehabilitation and Development (MRRD). These grants work to improve the lives of local people through, for example, the building and rehabilitation of roads, irrigation canals, schools, and clinics. By August 2013 more than 30,000 communities had elected their CDCs and received financial support from the NSP.[5]

Based on a randomized controlled trial, the impact evaluation of the NSP program confirms the positive impact of the program on the capacity of CDCs to bring basic services to the local population, while it also identifies a number of shortcomings (Beath, Christia, and Enikolopov 2013). The evaluation finds robust evidence that the NSP had a substantial impact on villagers' access to drinking water and electricity. The perceptions of the villagers over the economy also improved, which may be attributable to the fact that drinking water and electricity are central matters of concern in their everyday lives. However, the evaluation finds little evidence of the economic impact of infrastructure development, such as irrigation and roads.

---

5. The NSP was first introduced by the MRRD and the World Bank in June 2002, as a component of the Emergency Community Empowerment and Public Works Program (Murotani and others 2010). As for the number of CDCs and their activities, see www.nspafghanistan.org/.

The impact of the program on accountability also seems to be mixed. The same analysis reveals a positive and durable impact on women's empowerment in terms of openness to their participation in local governance, their actual participation, improved access of women to counseling, the inter-village mobility of women, school attendance by girls, and women's access to medical services. However, the impact on local governance does not seem to have been long lasting. Key local governance services, such as dispute mediation and notarization, largely disappeared when donors left upon the completion of NSP-funded activities. Despite strong evidence that the NSP improved people's general perception toward the government, such impact was not durable, and the evaluation of the quality of local governance has even fallen.

The findings of the weak connection between the impact on people's lives and local governance coincide with the results of the national opinion survey conducted by the Asia Foundation (Hopkins 2013); the linkage between the betterment of local living conditions and people's perceptions of the quality of national development is still weak in Afghanistan. While the percentage of people who think the country is going in the right direction has been increasing since 2008 (from 38 percent in 2008 to 57 percent in 2013), "reconstruction/rebuilding" is now the biggest reason (32 percent) for such a positive rating. During this five-year period, the percentage of people who chose "good security" as a reason for a positive perception of development sharply dropped from 44 percent in 2009 to 24 percent in 2013. In contrast, "reconstruction" was chosen consistently throughout the period. On the other hand, "unemployment" and "poor economy" were selected as being among the four biggest problems faced by the country, which may suggest a lack of improvement in objective economic performance. With regard to the level of trust in government institutions, the CDCs have always been among the most trusted organizations (61 percent in 2007, rising to 68 percent in 2013), while the provincial government, the provincial parliament, and the government ministries have been losing confidence among the people. Apparently, the expanded capacity of the CDCs to deliver public services won people's trust at the local level. However, the trust people put in the CDCs has not yet been translated into confidence in state institutions. Despite the effort of the MRRD at the national level to implement the NSP and assist the CDCs to function, a gap remains between trust in the CDCs and the legitimacy of the state.

Overall, the NSP has had a positive impact on people's well-being at the local level, but its linkage with the broader state-building processes seems to have remained relatively weak. In particular, people's trust in the CDC does not reach beyond the local communities to the state institutions. This indicates a failure to link the national and the local governments in an inclusive way. In fact, CDCs are too small to be linked to the provincial or the national government, particularly given the estimate that there would need to be more than 40,000 CDCs to cover the entire territory of Afghanistan. Initially introduced by the Inter-Communal Rural Development Project (IRDP) of the Japan International Cooperation Agency (JICA), and then followed by the NSP cluster model pilot project, an attempt was made to consolidate three to five CDCs into one Cluster CDC.[6] This was intended to strengthen the linkage between the villages and the larger units of the subnational government. Although neither CDCs nor Cluster CDCs have been officially recognized as local administrative units, this attempt at clustering might yet push the state-building effort one step further by making local public institutions accountable to ordinary Afghans (Takeuchi, Murotani, and Tsunekawa 2011).

Afghanistan faces various challenges at the national level. Insecurity and corruption are said to be the two biggest problems pointed out by the general public (Hopkins 2013). The outcome of reconciliation negotiations with the Taliban is a significant concern and may fundamentally change the framework of state building. However, policies at the national level cannot be designed without taking into consideration their linkage with the reality at the local level. The effort by the NSP suggests that the formation of CDCs had a positive impact at least in the lives of the local population. Nevertheless, to make the impact sustainable, such an effort must be connected with a broader state-building endeavor.

Northern Uganda

Since the 1980s the northern region of Uganda has suffered a protracted and violent conflict, which is said to have forced more than 2 million people into internal displacement. While a series of negotiations between the government of Uganda and the largest rebel group, the Lord's Resistance Army (LRA), took place between 2006 and 2008, these did not bear fruit. Rather, the LRA's pullout from Uganda to the DRC around 2009 ended the civil war, which had lasted more than two decades. Upon the fading of the conflict, millions of internally displaced persons (IDPs) started to return from camps to their original villages. Together with various humanitarian and development agencies, JICA offered the support needed to meet the immediate needs of the returnees. At the same time, it assisted the capacity development of subnational institutions, which had broken down during the conflict.

---

6. Funded by the World Bank Japan Social Development Fund (JSDF), the pilot project was introduced in the second phase of the NSP.

The capacity development of subnational institutions in northern Uganda thus had to begin from scratch. As public services were delivered solely inside the IDP camps during the years of conflict, subnational institutions were almost nonexistent when the IDPs moved from the camps to their original villages in 2009–10. Recognizing the lack of capacity in those institutions, JICA helped the Ugandan national government to respond to the immediate demands of the former IDPs and to simultaneously design a plan for the future. Together with the Ugandan government, JICA first formulated a blueprint for community development and road networks in the Amuru district (later divided into the Amuru and Nwoya districts) in the Acholi subregion. These projects provided for the construction of two bridges and supported agricultural development, thereby boosting commercial transportation, stabilizing and increasing the income of farmers, and promoting cotton cultivation for export (JICA 2013). At the same time, the project aimed at laying the foundations for the delivery of social services. As local governments were not equipped even with basic facilities, such as city halls and offices, the projects provided office buildings and multipurpose assembly halls, which were used for a variety of public events, such as public meetings, training courses, music festivals, and cooking contests. As a result of these projects, the capacity of civil servants working in the local governments has been strengthened (JICA 2012).

Improved service delivery by enhanced local government capacity was expected to nurture trust in the local government among the people and, eventually, to realize participatory accountability. Given that local people did not receive any public services from their local government for many years, it was vitally important for the local government to be seen to improve the lives of the people. For historic reasons, people in the north were skeptical of the national government and perceived it to be controlled by southerners. In this context, subnational institutions needed to enhance people's trust in the entire government structure. For that purpose, the Amuru and Nwoya district governments organized various public events that were meant to foster an affinity among local residents, particularly women's groups. They also worked closely with returnees in designing subprojects as a way of ensuring that people's trust in local government officials would be enhanced through collaborative work (JICA 2012). These trust-building actions were envisaged as the first step toward bringing the people and the government closer and to establishing an accountability mechanism. It was hoped that this would eventually lead to the state's legitimacy.

While the short-term needs of the returnees appear to have been met up to this point, the challenge of long-term inclusive institution building is daunting, and a more harmonized combination between various levels of governments is yet to be achieved. For the purpose of building inclusive institutions, the capacity development of subnational institutions should be matched by decentralization by the government of Uganda. The national government has implemented a vigorous decentralization policy since the 1990s. Today this national decentralization policy forms a framework for various activities by local governments. Since 2011, in cooperation with the Ministry of Local Government (MoLG), JICA has facilitated coordination between local and national governments. As its first step, JICA aimed to clarify the roles and authority of the different tiers of the government in order to establish a system of resource transfer from the central government to local governments. JICA has also invited officials from both the MoLG and district governments to training programs in Japan. These programs have enhanced mutual understanding by providing a forum for constructive discussions between the parties (JICA 2013). Such mutual understanding is necessary to drive the partnership forward and to promote inclusive development.

Despite these efforts, challenges still remain. The weak capacity of subnational institutions is only one part of the problem, and it appears that the national policy to promote inclusive development has not been effective enough. The state of human development in northern Uganda still lags seriously behind the rest of the country. In 2009–10 the poverty rate of the region was 46.2 percent, a very high figure compared with 10.7 percent in central Uganda and the 24.5 percent national average. In an opinion survey conducted by the JICA Research Institute (JICA-RI) in towns in the northern, central, and western parts of the country, about 90 percent of respondents shared the view that the north had been the area least favored by the government (Sasaoka and Nyang'oro 2013). Decentralization and an effective partnership between the national and local governments should be promoted to address the real and perceived inequalities between northerners and the rest of the country, thereby enhancing mutual confidence nationwide.

Mindanao (Philippines)

Mindanao, one of the poorest regions in the Philippines, has long been affected by prolonged and violent conflict. In 1996 the Moro National Liberation Front (MNLF) signed a peace agreement with the government of the Philippines and started to work with a unit of the national system of governance, the Autonomous Region of Muslim Mindanao (ARMM). However, another Muslim group called the Moro Islamic Liberation Front (MILF) continued to rebel against the government with intermittent cease-fires and peace negotiations. The subnational governance structure has been one of the major concerns of the MILF. During the recent peace process, however, international assistance demonstrated that there were successful examples of community development that both sides could accept as models for future collaboration. In the October 2012 framework agreement for peace, the MILF and the government of the Philippines committed themselves to a peaceful transition toward the enlargement of the Muslim autonomous region and the possible renaming of the region to Bangsamoro (the land of the Moro people). On March 27, 2014, the two parties signed the Comprehensive Agreement on the Bangsamoro, thus paving the way for the establishment of the new Bangsamoro government in 2016. In searching for an appropriate framework for subnational governance, three aspects have always been important for both the government and the MILF, namely the capacity of subnational institutions; accountability within, and people's reciprocal trust of, the institutions; and an inclusive partnership between central and subnational institutions. In relation to each of these aspects, international donors have supported both sides in finding a better arrangement.

Despite the demand for improving socioeconomic development in the region, the newly created ARMM government lacked the capacity to deliver public services. The autonomous government was faced with several obstacles, such as the shortage of staff with administrative skills and the ambiguous scope of administrative responsibilities. JICA's ARMM Human Capacity Development Project supported capacity development for middle-level managers aimed at streamlining administrative orders and establishing a personnel information system (JICA 2013). Unlike other donors, Japan also implemented its projects through another channel, namely the Bangsamoro Development Agency (BDA). The BDA was an ad hoc organization based on the cease-fire agreement between the government and the MILF, yet strongly influenced by the MILF (Murotani and others 2010). However, the national government was willing to allow the BDA to function as a counterpart to donor agencies, including JICA (Ishikawa 2013). As a result, initiatives to support the capacity development of the BDA were launched much earlier than the signing of the framework agreement, and this preparatory process enabled BDA actors to prepare themselves to be a future autonomous government.

Community development projects provided opportunities for local citizens to engage with local governments, as well as with other people in the same area, enhancing the accountability of local institutions and nurturing mutual trust between the people and the government. Japan initiated community development projects under the auspices of the Japan Bangsamoro Initiatives for Reconstruction and Development (J-BIRD), which encouraged villagers to participate in the planning and implementation of community development projects, such as the construction of roads and schools, and consequently fostering a spirit of cooperation and mutual confidence among competing groups. In some villages, Christians and Muslims who were hostile toward each other had the chance to work together for their mutual benefit; for example, managing postharvest facilities as cooperative ventures. These opportunities enabled people and the governments to understand in what ways they can work together to improve their own lives (Murotani and others 2010).

Although the framework for a better partnership between the central and subnational governments should be agreed upon by Filipino stakeholders, external actors can still facilitate dialogue between various stakeholders. In the case of the recent Mindanao peace process, Universiti Sains Malaysia and JICA co-organized a series of Consolidation for Peace (COP) seminars to encourage various actors to communicate with each other. Through these seminars, stakeholders from both sides, at all levels of government and civil society, were able to exchange views and to learn what the other side wished to do (Ishikawa 2013). JICA's community development programs also provided opportunities for participating parties to meet frequently and learn about each other. To achieve meaningful results for the residents, officials from the central and local governments, on the one hand, and the officials from MILF's BDA, on the other, were compelled to work together. This cooperation resulted in the mutual confidence of all major stakeholders (Tsunekawa and Murotani 2014). Both parties were able to understand what the other side envisioned for the inclusive development of the country. Such mutual understanding was essential to the eventual peace agreement.

The Japanese government and JICA got involved in the Mindanao peace process at an early stage, enabling them to learn lessons from the capacity development and community development projects as well as the COP seminars. Those lessons showed practical ways in which the central government, subnational institutions, and local people could work collectively to improve the well-being of local communities. They provided local stakeholders with a clear picture of how the newly agreed-upon government structure could function to the benefit of local everyday lives and a more inclusive national development. These activities not only strengthened state capacity and legitimacy but also facilitated the agreement by local stakeholders on their framework for subnational governance, which later materialized as the Comprehensive Agreement on the Bangsamoro.

Conclusion

The case studies in this chapter illustrate possible ways in which the capacity development of subnational institutions enhances the quality of public service delivery, which then strengthens the legitimacy of the state. Since subnational institution building should be connected to broader state-building endeavors, the case studies underscore the three key challenges in bridging the gap between state building at the national level and improved well-being at the local level. The three challenges are to expand the subnational capacity for service delivery, to consolidate accountability mechanisms through local participation, and to promote inclusive development through equitable partnerships between national and local governments. Strengthening the linkage among the multiple tiers of the government in all three aspects is expected to enhance capacity, accountability, and inclusiveness in the entire governance structure, and eventually give rise to a capable, legitimate, and resilient state in the middle of fragile situations.

Historical experiences and local contexts vary from one country to another. As unique features in each fragile state significantly affect the ways in which people look at national and subnational institutions, careful attention should be paid to local contexts when designing policy frameworks for state building. To strengthen the coordinated functions of national and subnational institutions, the weakest link between the capital and local communities should be identified and bridged. In the case of Afghanistan, the link in bringing local voices upward beyond the CDCs is still very weak. In Uganda, multiple inequalities between the north and the rest of the country remain serious. In the Philippines, the coordination between the Bangsamoro autonomous government and the national government was crucial to the successful peace negotiations in Mindanao. Finding a leverage point and addressing it will facilitate the process of state building through public service delivery and open up a way of breaking through the last mile of global poverty.

In their efforts to tackle these challenges, the concept of human security may be helpful for policymakers when reconciling national priorities and local realities. *Human Security Now* (CHS 2003), the final report of the Commission on Human Security (CHS) co-chaired by Sadako Ogata and Amartya Sen, reaffirms the significance of combining top-down protection with bottom-up empowerment as an effective measure for operationalizing human security. When the state is not capable of providing protection to its citizens, as is often the case for fragile states, empowered individuals and communities should play the principal role in ensuring their own security. Then, instead of the ailing national government, donors are expected to provide short-term protection to vulnerable people and to finance efforts to empower them. In fragile situations, public goods need not be provided exclusively by the state but rather can be provided effectively by a number of actors.

However, as indicated by Ogata (CHS 2003), human security and state security do not negate but complement each other. In the longer term, public services to improve people's lives can only be provided in a sustainable way through the coordinating agency of multiple tiers of government. Moreover, the national government is expected to play a critical role in scaling up local innovations and spreading them to other areas. Casting the dynamic interactions of protection and empowerment into the realm of national governance, donors can play a considerable role in helping to strengthen the capable, accountable, and equitable linkages between the national and local governments in fragile situations, by combining the top-down and bottom-up approaches. Such a concerted effort will contribute to the ultimate aim of securing the survival, livelihood, and dignity of individuals and communities in fragile states.

References

Beath, Andrew, Fotini Christia, and Ruben Enikolopov. 2013. "Randomized Impact Evaluation of Afghanistan's National Solidarity Programme: Final Report." Kabul: World Bank, July 1.

Bryce, James. 1920. *Modern Democracies.* New York: Macmillan.

Chandy, Laurence, Natasha Ledlie, and Veronika Penciakova. 2013. "The Final Countdown: Prospects for Ending Extreme Poverty by 2030." Policy Brief 2013-04. Brookings Institution, April.

Chesterman, Simon. 2004. *You, the People: The United Nations, Transitional Administrations, and State Building.* Oxford University Press.

CHS (Commission on Human Security). 2003. *Human Security Now.* New York.

Fearon, James D., and David D. Laitin. 2004. "Neotrusteeship and the Problem of Weak States." *International Security* 28, no. 4: 5–43.

Fukuyama, Francis. 2005. *State Building: Governance and World Order in the Twenty-First Century.* London: Profile Books.

Gertz, Geoffrey, and Laurence Chandy. 2011. "Two Trends in Global Poverty." Brookings Institution, May.

Ghani, Ashraf, and Clare Lockhart. 2008. *Fixing Failed States: A Framework for Rebuilding a Fractured World.* Oxford University Press.

Gurr, Ted Robert. 1970. *Why Men Rebel.* Princeton University Press.

Hilhorst, Dorothea, Ian Christoplos, and Gemma Van Der Haar. 2010. "Reconstruction 'From Below': A New Magic Bullet or Shooting from the Hip?" *Third World Quarterly* 31, no. 7: 1107–24.

Hopkins, Nancy, ed. 2013. *Afghanistan 2013: A Survey of the Afghan People.* San Francisco: Asia Foundation.

Ishikawa, Sachiko. 2013. "Peacebuilding and Human Security in Japan's Official Development Assistance (ODA): The Development and Transformation of JICA's Peacebuilding Assistance." Ph.D. dissertation, Universiti Sains Malaysia.

JICA. 2012. "Livelihood and Employment Promotion in Conflict Affected Countries: Final Report Executive Summary."

———. 2013. "Effective Approaches for Mobilizing Resources and Enhancing Government's Functions to Execute Services in Conflict-Affected States." Presentation Material for the Working Group on Lessons Learned of the UN Peace-Building Commission, July 10.

Krasner, Stephen D., and Carlos Pascual. 2005. "Addressing State Failure." *Foreign Affairs* 84, no. 4: 153–63.

Mine, Yoichi, Frances Stewart, Sakiko Fukuda-Parr, and Thandika Mkandawire, eds. 2013. *Preventing Violent Conflict in Africa: Inequalities, Perceptions and Institutions.* Basingstoke, UK: Palgrave Macmillan.

Murotani, Ryutaro, Eiji Wakamatsu, Tomonori Kikuchi, Masafumi Nagaishi, and Naoyuki Ochiai. 2010. "State-Building in Fragile Situations: Japanese Aid Experiences in Cambodia, Afghanistan, and Mindanao." JICA-RI Working Paper 5. Tokyo: JICA Research Institute.

OECD. 2007. "Principles for Good International Engagement in Fragile States and Situations." Paris.

———. 2008a. "Concepts and Dilemmas of State Building in Fragile Situations." Paris.

———. 2008b. "Service Delivery in Fragile Situations: Key Concepts, Findings and Lessons."OECD/DAC discussion paper. Paris.

———. 2011. "Supporting Statebuilding in Situations of Conflict and Fragility: Policy Guidance." DAC Guidelines and Reference Series. Paris.

Paris, Roland, and Timothy D. Sisk. 2009. *The Dilemmas of Statebuilding: Confronting the Contradictions of Postwar Peace Operations.* London: Routledge.

Parks, Thomas, Nat Colletta, and Ben Oppenheim, eds. 2013. *The Contested Corners of Asia: Subnational Conflict and International Development Assistance.* San Francisco: Asia Foundation.

Richmond, Oliver P. 2009. "Becoming Liberal, Unbecoming Liberalism: Liberal-Local Hybridity via the Everyday as a Response to the Paradoxes of Liberal Peacebuilding." *Journal of Intervention and Statebuilding* 3, no. 3: 324–44.

Sasaoka, Yuichi, and Julius E. Nyang'oro. 2013. "Is Ethnic Autonomy Compatible with a Unitary State? The Case of Uganda and Tanzania." In *Preventing Violent Conflict in Africa: Inequalities, Perceptions and Institutions,* edited by Yoichi Mine, Frances Stewart, Sakiko Fukuda-Parr, and Thandika Mkandawire. Basingstoke, UK: Palgrave Macmillan.

Shanmugaratnam, Nadarajah. 2008. "Civil War, Peace Processes, and Livelihoods." In *Between War and Peace in Sudan and Sri Lanka*, edited by Nadarajah Shanmugaratnam. Oxford, UK: James Currey.

Stewart, Frances. 2008. *Horizontal Inequalities and Conflict: Understanding Group Violence in Multiethnic Societies.* Basingstoke, UK: Palgrave Macmillan.

Straus, Scott. 2012. "Wars Do End! Changing Patterns of Political Violence in Sub-Saharan Africa." *African Affairs* 111, no. 443: 179–201.

Takeuchi, Shinichi, Ryutaro Murotani, and Keiichi Tsunekawa. 2011. "Capacity Traps and Legitimacy Traps: Development Assistance and State Building in Fragile Situations." In *Catalyzing Development: A New Vision for Aid*, edited by Homi Kharas, Koji Makino, and Woojin Jung. Brookings Institution Press.

Tocqueville, Alexis de. 1836. *Democracy in America.* Translated by Henry Reeve. London: Saunders and Otley.

Tsunekawa, Keiichi, and Ryutaro Murotani. 2014. "Working for Human Security: JICA's Experiences." In *Post-Conflict Development in East Asia,* edited by Brendan M. Howe. Farnham, UK: Ashgate.

World Bank. 2011. *World Development Report 2011: Conflict, Security, and Development.* Washington.

4

Peace Building and State Building in Fragile States: External Support That Works

ALASTAIR McKECHNIE AND MARCUS MANUEL

While there is no internationally agreed definition of a fragile state or an agreed list of fragile states, there is an emerging consensus of what constitutes fragility and why development is so difficult in fragile settings. Most of human history has been characterized by the threat of armed violence and chaos (North and others 2013), although the risk of politically motivated violence that affects civil order in industrialized countries is now small. More recent examples show how civil conflict, sometimes in countries that appear stable and on a development trajectory, sets back development and destroys not only past investment but also institutions that took decades to build. Armed violence spills across borders and can have regional or global consequences, as shown by the events unleashed by the Soviet invasion of Afghanistan in 1978 and the U.S. invasion of Iraq in 2003. A "typical" civil war costs the country and its neighbors US$64 billion (Collier 2007). To put this in perspective, Official Development Assistance (ODA) in 2010 to all fragile states was US$50 billion, UN peacekeeping costs around US$7 billion a year, and U.S. military spending in Afghanistan alone was about US$88 billion in fiscal year 2010.[1] Conflict is associated with terrorism, trafficking, narcotics, and organized crime, and these affect countries beyond the zone of war. Peace is a global public good.

---

1. For ODA flows to fragile states see OECD (2013a). For UN peacekeeping expenditure, see www.un.org/en/peacekeeping/operations/financing.shtml. And for U.S. expenditure in Afghanistan, see Livingston and O'Hanlon (2012).

State fragility is essentially the breakdown in relations between the state and society caused by institutional failure. The state can no longer deliver basic services, establish and enforce laws so as to protect human dignity and property, and reinforce a shared national identity. Within the development policy community there is a consensus that building institutions that are legitimate, that balance different interests, and that deliver services effectively underpins and defines development (Acemoglu and Robinson 2012; Fukuyama 2011). Institutional development is at the heart of the transition from fragility to resilience; this is an endogenous process, which outsiders can influence but not control, since each country finds its own arrangements that fit its circumstances. Institutional diversity and hybrid traditional-modern frameworks are the norm, even in OECD countries.[2]

The record of international assistance in helping countries transition from fragility to resilience is mixed. Some countries have used external support to substantially reduce the risk of armed violence; these include Mozambique, Timor-Leste, Sierra Leone, Rwanda, and Uganda. These countries have also made considerable progress in reducing poverty, creating capable institutions, and promoting investment and growth. At the other extreme are low-income countries whose situations are more uncertain despite considerable foreign development, security and political assistance, and natural resource revenues; these include Afghanistan, South Sudan, Haiti, and the Democratic Republic of Congo (DRC). Other low-income fragile states, such as Central African Republic (CAR) and Guinea-Bissau, have been largely ignored by the international community and are sometimes considered to be aid orphans. In addition, localized pockets of fragility exist in otherwise functioning countries like India, Nigeria, Thailand, and Philippines, pockets that are sometimes neglected by the central government, which may see the problem as one of security. Similarly, apparently stable middle-income countries in the Americas, the Balkans, central Europe, central Asia, and the Middle East may be at risk from political chaos and armed insurrection or from the organized criminal violence that often follows. These countries may have access to resources but be unable to resolve group inequalities and injustices that can lead to violence.

Foreign Aid and Fragile States

Foreign aid remains the largest source of financing for fragile states, but this aid is fragmented, volatile, poorly concentrated on low-income countries, and is vulnerable to conflict. Aid to fragile states did not change much during 2005–10. According to the OECD, it reached US$50 billion in 2010—representing

2. OECD countries have a range of constitutional arrangements that includes states based on rational legality, constitutional monarchies without written constitutions, states with centralized political order, and states that are highly decentralized.

38 percent of net ODA from all donors, slightly more than remittances and nearly twice as much as foreign direct investment (FDI) in those countries. However, aid flows have been biased upward by a few costly interventions by the international community, especially in Afghanistan, DRC, Haiti, and Palestine; ODA to fragile states in 2000 was only $12 billion, and half of that went to only seven countries (OECD/DAC 2013a).[3] This concentration of aid results in some fragile states having very high levels of per capita aid. Excluding countries with less than a million population, only eight out of forty fragile states on the OECD list (Palestine, Liberia, DRC, Haiti, Timor-Leste, Afghanistan, Georgia, and Bosnia Herzegovina) received aid per capita above the average of US$129 in 2010, sometimes substantially so (Palestine US$631, Liberia US$355), and only three of the eight countries were low income (figure 4-1).

Aid flows have been volatile such that every fragile state received at least one aid shock during the decade 2000–10. Shock is defined as a change of more than 15 percent in aid per capita from one year to another. Donor funding tends to be large after a crisis or at the end of hostilities but declines shortly thereafter, even though it takes at least twenty years to build basic institutions in a fragile state (World Bank 2011a). Despite the Accra Agenda for Action, which commits donors to decrease aid fragmentation by increasing complementarity and division of labor, some recipient countries still have many small donors; Afghanistan had thirty-seven donors in 2010, of which twenty-seven were "nonsignificant."[4] Such fragmentation exacerbates the coordination problem and increases transaction costs for the recipient government, unless funds are pooled in a multidonor trust fund or similar arrangement.

Fragile states are perceived as risky places for foreign aid, but these perceptions are often not well founded. The performance of World Bank projects in fragile states is little different from its projects in nonfragile states, and this is also the case for other aid agencies (World Bank 2013a; Chandy 2011). While the countries on the bottom of Transparency International's Corruption Perceptions Index are mostly fragile states, the risks of putting aid through government budget systems can be largely mitigated (McKechnie and Davies 2013). This paradox may be due to the nature of corruption, which can involve abuse of power, theft of state property, and the diversion of revenues before they enter government accounts. Funds, including foreign aid, that have entered the

3. Country aid flows are for 2010. The seven countries are Afghanistan, Ethiopia, Democratic Republic of Congo, Haiti, Pakistan, Palestine, and Iraq. The OECD list of fragile states differs from other lists, such as the harmonized list used by multilateral development banks, and includes middle-income countries. About half of the aid going to Haiti is for humanitarian purposes.

4. The OECD (2010b) defines aid as significant when the donor is among the largest development partners that together account for at least 90 percent of the volume of the country's aid, or if the donor provides more than its global share of aid to the country. Aid from a donor is "nonsignificant" when these criteria do not apply.

Figure 4-1. *Foreign Assistance per 1,000 Population to Fragile States, 2010*

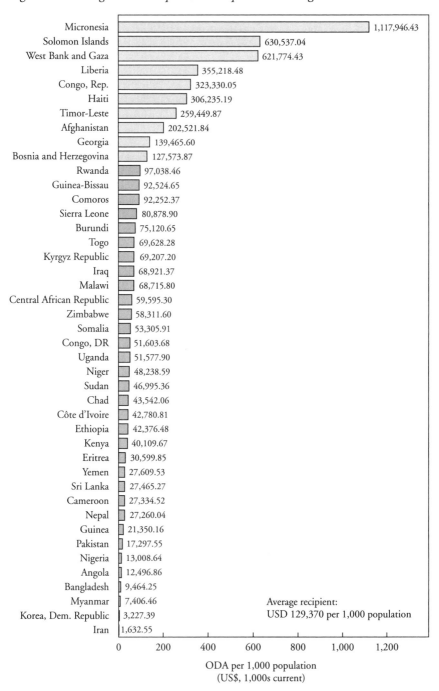

ODA per 1,000 population
(US$, 1,000s current)

Source: OECD (2012).

government treasury can be difficult to misuse, particularly when these funds are protected by financial management systems established with outside assistance.

Case Study: Afghanistan

Afghanistan is an example of the interdependence of security, politics, development, and the failure of the international system to work in a coherent and coordinated manner. Considerable development has taken place nevertheless; school enrollment between 2001 and 2011 increased from less than 1 million, to more than 8 million, the proportion of girls increasing from zero to about one-third; and child and maternal mortality fell by more than 60 percent.[5] In 2009 there were about 19 million telephone subscribers in a country of 30 million people, compared to only 57,000 subscribers in 2001. Other areas of success include national highways and community development. By 2010, 22,000 community councils had been elected through secret ballot and had prepared 50,000 projects financed by $700 million in block grants. In addition, most urban areas now receive continuous electric power supply.

Innovative approaches to aid contributed to this rapid development progress. Pooling donor funds through the short-term Afghan Interim Authority Fund got money moving in the first year; the Afghanistan Reconstruction Trust Fund (ARTF) then took over.[6] Also critical was accelerating procurement by the extended use of fast-track emergency procurement procedures.[7] In addition, deliberate early investments in building local procurement and fiduciary capacity were important (Manuel and others 2012).[8] These are examples of what Collier (2010) calls the need for "investing in investing."[9]

5. The mortality of children under five fell from 257 per thousand live births in 2003 to 97 in 2010; maternal mortality fell from 1,600 per thousand live births in 2002 to 330 in 2012.

6. One of the key innovations that enabled the ARTF to provide such rapid, flexible support was the process of managing fiduciary risk while building government capacity. As with the earlier Holst Fund in Palestine, ARTF reimbursed the government for recurrent expenditures only after an external agent had audited them. Many of the innovations are still being drawn upon (for example, the USAID's new fixed amount reimbursement agreements, which provide many of the benefits of budget support but with much tighter control of fiduciary risks).

7. The World Bank applied "emergency" procedures, originally intended for managing the immediate aftermath of natural disaster, for at least nine years. USAID also used the flexibility allowed within its rules "where overriding foreign policy considerations are invoked." Development partners accepted the need to run greater risks (for example, by accepting a heavy reliance on sole-source procurements).

8. Manuel and others (2012) argue that establishing governmental procurement capacity was a significant factor in rapid implementation in Afghanistan. One of the innovations in Afghanistan was separating direct provision of procurement services and capacity-building assistance, recognizing that short-term demands for services crowd out the development of longer-term capacity.

9. The title of chapter 7 of Collier (2010) is "Investing in Investing." where he makes the case for allocating more funds to public investment, particularly in countries that export natural resources, providing that parallel reforms in public financial management can raise the ability of the economy to manage such investment.

Development of public institutions has been mixed, but on balance there has been substantial progress since 2002. The finance ministry and central bank developed quickly, and Afghanistan scores well against select Public Expenditure Fiduciary Assessment indicators. Many ministries have developed the capacity to deliver services, even if this has meant a high proportion of contract staff in senior positions. Subnational governance has been less successful due to unrealistic initial expectations, externally driven models of governance, security-driven compromises in appointments of governors and funding, patronage networks, and the lack of a coherent strategy shared by Afghanistan and its partners.[10]

These development gains are dependent on improvement in those political, security, and governance areas where success has been elusive. International assistance to Afghanistan has tended to create parallel structures that bypassed Afghan institutions. On one track, aid from multilateral financial institutions and ARTF financed budget items, mainly through country systems, and was responsible for many of the development achievements noted above. On the other track, politicians and bureaucrats sitting in partner capitals prepared strategies that were changed almost yearly with little consultation or ownership by Afghans, despite formal commitments to the contrary, such as the Afghanistan Compact in 2006.[11]

For many years there were three foreign military commands operating simultaneously in Afghanistan pursuing goals ranging from antiterrorism, to counterinsurgency, to peacekeeping. The immediate personal security interests of Afghans were given less attention, and inadequate efforts to improve a police force that was often predatory did not strengthen the reputation of the state. More than two-thirds of civilian aid bypassed government systems; in some cases ministers were not aware of donor activities in their sector. These parallel systems retarded the development of Afghan institutions by shifting accountability and responsibility for service delivery from government to foreign actors and denying the government opportunities for learning by doing. Parallel systems also led to fragmentation of bilateral aid into small projects, which typically failed to achieve scale, were not sustainable in operation, and represented low value for the money. International firms contracted by donors often undertook such parallel activities; these firms established a chain of subcontractors, which complicated coordination, accountability, and management of quality.

10. This and the preceding paragraph are based on information in World Bank project reports and databases. See Cowper-Coles (2012) for an insider account of the problems in implementing a coherent strategy in Afghanistan.

11. See Manuel, McKechnie, and others (2012) for detailed analysis of why implementation of this compact fell far short of its ambitions. Failure to focus, prioritize, and set intermediate targets to measure progress were key issues. See also Cowper-Coles (2012) for a diplomatic perspective.

Other bilateral aid was delivered through international NGOs and UN agencies, with little transparency about amounts reaching Afghanistan and the results achieved.

Large amounts of foreign assistance chasing short-term results through parallel systems led to considerable waste and a high proportion of funds going either to firms domiciled outside of Afghanistan or to local firms with good political connections. This, coupled with shoddy workmanship and with projects not owned by Afghans, led many Afghans to perceive large-scale corruption, even if this was mostly waste. Rather than building the Afghan state and strengthening legitimate authority, bilateral international civil and military assistance managed to undermine both.[12] While the impact of development assistance on security may be overrated (Fishbein and Wilder 2012), it is clear that development requires a reasonably benign security environment, which in turn depends on legitimate governance. Even when distributing funds to local power holders in the interests of short-term security might seem justified, these payments might create dependencies and entitlements that are unsustainable and that undermine governance. A coordinated, Afghan-owned strategy incorporating the three policy communities was elusive in Afghanistan, as neither the Afghan government itself, nor its main bilateral partners, nor the multilateral institutions could produce the leadership or joint decisionmaking that could prepare and implement an integrated strategy. Facing similar uncoordinated chaos in Malaya in 1951, a noted British general wrote a memo of masterful brevity: "We must have a plan. Secondly we must have a man. When we have a plan and a man, we shall succeed: not otherwise."[13]

Afghanistan demonstrates that foreign aid delivered through country systems with country ownership can deliver results that transform the lives of millions of people. Afghanistan also shows that providing aid beyond the absorptive capacity of the country is associated with waste and corruption and undermines legitimate authority. Aid can provide an environment for peace and stability to thrive, but Afghanistan shows that aid cannot buy peace. In the first two years after the demise of the Taliban government Afghanistan had men (and women) with plans and the capacity to implement them. The same could not be said for its international partners.

---

12. Based on Ghani and Lockhart (2008); reports by the Special Inspector General for Afghanistan Reconstruction (SIGAR); and conversations of one of the authors with Afghan ministers and lead partners responsible for assistance to Afghanistan.

13. Note from Field Marshal Bernard Montgomery to British Colonial Secretary Oliver Lyttleton, quoted in Nagl (2002). Given the role that women have increasingly played in postconflict reconstruction—most visibly by Liberian President Ellen Johnson Sirleaf—Montgomery would perhaps have drafted his memo more inclusively today.

Case Study: Sierra Leone

Sierra Leone is regarded as an example of successful engagement by external actors. While the recent Ebola crisis has had an enormous impact on the country, certainly in terms of security and politics there has been much greater progress than in Afghanistan. In 1999 Sierra Leone was mired in a grim conflict fueled by blood diamonds and fought by child soldiers. Now, fifteen years later, the UN peacekeepers are long gone, children are in school, and elections have delivered a peaceful change of government. Sierra Leonean troops are now helping to keep the peace in Somalia.

The UN's peacekeeping success and the broader reform in the UK-led security sector are relatively well known. And some of the key lessons from the reform echo those from many sectors in other fragile states. Getting the right people on the ground and taking action is more valuable than extensive and time-consuming planning. National ownership and a capable national team are both critical but very hard to achieve and maintain (Albrecht and Jackson 2009).

The complex, complementary story of the support of the UK government—the degree of political commitment, the extent of engagement, and the recognition that it would take at least ten years—is less known. Aid was part of the story. The UK made an unusual, formal, ten-year overarching aid partnership commitment. By limiting the number of countries it worked in, the UK was able to mobilize much greater support to Sierra Leone than anywhere else (on a per capita basis). The UK also recognized the need to take risks, and it started providing budget support at a very early stage that comprised an unusually high proportion of the total aid provided. To limit the risks of budget support the UK made only one-year specific commitments, making it difficult for the Sierra Leone government to plan in the medium term. Increasing predictability would have increased the risk to the UK but would also have increased the development impact.[14]

Behind the general success, though, there is a much more concerning story about how slow progress has been in other areas, such as rebuilding the civil service (Srivastava and Larizza 2012) and rehabilitating economic infrastructure. Indeed, even now there are only 1,000 kilometers of paved roads, and only 20 percent of the population is within 2 kilometers of an all-season road (compared to 30 percent for all low-income fragile states). Part of the issue is funding. The European Commission focused on one of the key regional roads back in 2002,

14. This analysis is based in part on the experience of one of the authors in the mid-2000s as DfID's West Africa regional director and chair of the UK government's Africa conflict prevention pool, which funded Ministry of Defence support to the Sierra Leone army. See Manuel and others (2012) for more details on the aid issues.

but due to lack of funding it had to do this in two phases. Even now, as the World Bank noted recently (Pushak and Foster 2011), at current rates of spending it will take another fifteen years just to rehabilitate the road network.

But part of the issue was the capacity of aid agencies. Only the European Commission had sector staff present in Freetown, and even they struggled with contracting issues. The contract for the 2002 road project terminated in 2007 due to lack of progress. Overall, only sixty kilometers of core class A roads were rehabilitated each year between 2005 and 2010, just half the planned amount. Rehabilitation of the power sector has also taken years. Only in 2009 was a modest fifty megawatts added to capacity. Even with this addition, only 5 percent of the population has access to electricity (a third of the proportion in other low-income fragile states), and power outages are four times more common than in other low-income fragile states.[15] The cost of the hydropower dam was US$200 million, less than 10 percent of the cost of the UN peacekeeping mission but more than the resources allocated to Sierra Leone by either the AfDB or the World Bank over the same period.

New Deal for Fragile States

In 2008 several fragile states, recognizing that they shared common concerns about how external actors were trying to support them, formed a new group, the g7+. The group's two aims are to share experiences and to advocate reforms of the way the international community engages with conflict-affected states. Fifteen of the twenty members of the group share two characteristics: they are on the UN list of least developed countries and they have benefited from a UN or regional peacekeeping mission.[16] There is also considerable overlap between this criterion and the list of slow-progress, high-poverty countries in the introductory chapter of this book. Nearly all members of both groups are included in the World Bank and OECD lists of fragile states.

At the OECD-sponsored Busan High Level Forum on Aid Effectiveness in November 2011, the g7+ group and development partners agreed on a "New Deal" that would shape future external support to fragile states. The New Deal for Engagement in Fragile States was subsequently formally endorsed by the g7+

---

15. It would be interesting to research whether the use in Sierra Leone of the innovative approaches to procurement in Afghanistan would have made a difference.

16. The fifteen g7+ members where UN or regional peacekeeping/peace-building missions have been deployed are Afghanistan, Burundi, Central African Republic, Chad, Comoros, Democratic Republic of Congo, Guinea-Bissau, Guinea, Haiti, Liberia, Sierra Leone, Solomon Islands, Somalia, South Sudan, and Timor-Leste. The other five g7+ members are Côte d'Ivoire, Papua New Guinea, Sao Tome and Principe, Togo, and Yemen.

and by more than twenty-five multilateral and bilateral development partners.[17] The New Deal acknowledges that the previous ways of working needed
improvement and that transitioning out of fragility involves a long political process requiring country leadership and ownership. International partners had too
often bypassed national interests and actors, providing aid in overly technocratic
ways, and supported short-term results at the expense of their long-term sustainability. Three fundamental breakthroughs were agreed in the New Deal: the
group's priorities, who should be in the lead, and how governments and donors
should work together.

First, priority setting would be based on five peace-building and state-building goals (PSGs), the foundation for progress toward reaching the Millennium
Development Goals (MDGs). The first of the PSGs is legitimate politics—the
need to foster inclusive political settlements and to tackle conflict resolution.
The second PSG is to establish people's security. These first two goals alone
imply a radical reprioritization of transitional partner effort, which too often
regards politics and security as "too difficult" and to be avoided in favor of easier
areas, such as education and health.[18] As the tragic events in South Sudan have
shown, the failure to resolve fundamental issues of political settlement undermines all other work.

Second, fragile states must be in the lead beginning with an initial fragility
assessment and continuing through a plan for transitioning out of fragility. This
is a radical shift from individual agencies making their own assessments and
plans. In the past, the UN would often lead in assessments and planning, coordinating other development partners, and working with the government, but
the final document would still be a UN document. This shift mirrors a similar
change in assessment and planning processes in non-fragile states that occurred
with the debt process for heavily indebted poor countries (HIPC). Under HIPC,
governments wrote their own national poverty reduction plans, replacing previous memoranda of economic policy that were all too often drafted in Washington by the IMF and the World Bank and then negotiated with the country.

Third, better modalities were agreed on for more effective joint efforts by
the government and its partners. For example, agreement on priority actions
would be formally expressed in country-partner compacts. Compacts would
also include such changes as making more use of country systems, strengthening

---

17. As of April 2014 the development partners that had signed are all of the G-7 countries, all
Benelux and Nordic countries, Australia, Austria, Canada, Ireland, Japan, New Zealand, Portugal,
Republic of Korea, and Switzerland, as well as the EU, all members of the UN Development Group
(including WFP, UNICEF, UNDP), the World Bank, the African Development Bank, the Asian
Development Bank, and the OECD.

18. The three other peace-building and state-building goals focus on justice, jobs, and managing
resources.

country institutional capacity, and increasing the speed, predictability, and transparency of aid. Many of the changes are politically challenging for development partners, and it remains to be seen how much their performance will change and whether they are prepared for performance to be measured.

As the New Deal was agreed at the Busan High Level Forum on Aid Effectiveness, it naturally focused on the roles of governments and donors. But since then there has been increasing interest in improving the private sector's engagement in fragile states. If each g7+ country applied all the individual g7+ best practices on specific World Bank Doing Business indicators, then the g7+ would score as highly as Australia.[19] This not only shows the potential for lesson learning within the g7+ group but also underlines how much more is needed to build private sector engagement.

Nearly three years after the New Deal was originally agreed there has been some progress,[20] especially in the eight pilot countries.[21] Six full fragile assessments have been completed in the DRC, Liberia, Sierra Leone, South Sudan, Comoros, and Timor-Leste. A "light" fragility assessment has been done in Somalia. The Central African Republic had started preparation, but the process was interrupted by renewed conflict. A fragility study has been launched in Afghanistan, and plans for assessments are under discussion in Guinea-Bissau and Togo. The South Sudan experience has revealed the challenges of conducting a country-led fragility assessment. This assessment rated political legitimacy issues as the least cause for concern and was carried out before political power-sharing arrangements unraveled in mid-2013, which led to renewed conflict. In addition three country compacts are in place in Afghanistan, Sierra Leone, and Somalia. Compact discussions are under way in two more countries: the Democratic Republic of Congo and Liberia. Another compact was about to be signed in South Sudan when the process was interrupted by renewed conflict. Two countries have significantly more aid that uses country systems. In Timor-Leste, Australia has started to use budget support, and in Somalia, Norway established a mechanism to fund government salaries.

However, the most striking conclusion from the experience of the New Deal is the limited change in donor behavior. For example, in South Sudan donors have continued to support MDG-based programs, and there has not been a reallocation of resources toward the key peace-building and state-building

19. This prediction was made by a speaker at the April 2013 seminar on private sector development in fragile states, which was sponsored by the g7+ and the World Bank.
20. See International Dialogue on Peace-Building and State-Building (2014) for latest position. All figures are based on the progress review published in October 2014.
21. There were seven pilots when the New Deal was agreed in Busan: Afghanistan, the Central African Republic, the Democratic Republic of Congo, Liberia, Sierra Leone, South Sudan, and Timor-Leste. Somalia was added soon after.

Box 4-1. *Roads in South Sudan*

When Southern Sudan's peace agreement was signed in 2005, the country had one paved road. It was just 100 meters long in a country the size of France. During the wet season the rough tracks that connect the country together and with neighboring countries turn to mud. A small group of South Sudanese and local donors devised a long-term plan to build a national road network of around 5,000 kilometers. On one level, this was a grand plan. It would have cost around US$5 billion. But on another level it was a modest plan. It would have still left the country with the lowest paved-road density in the world: half that of Niger and one-tenth that of Kenya.

What happened to that vision? Over the next nine years only one major paved long-distance road has materialized. It is just 200 kilometers long. Why was only one road built? One reason was clearly critical: the cost of building roads is very high, and only the largest aid agencies had the resources to finance road construction. So this very practical nation-building step was not prioritized. And the nine-year-old vision of thousands of kilometers of roads joining up a new nation has been replaced by the nightmare of militias tearing a fractured country apart. More aid and more roads by themselves would not have solved the problems in South Sudan. Other constraints, such as managing corruption around construction contracts and allocating oil revenues for investment, were also issues that the compact might have given more attention.

The solution to the country's problems is fundamentally a political one, and this can only come from South Sudan itself. But too few new roads certainly made the political problems much harder to manage.

issue—the marginalization of many parts of the country—despite this being identified as such in a joint government-donor evaluation in 2010. One example of this lack of reallocation of resources is the failure to deliver on the planned national road network, which would have integrated regions of the country and provided political as well as economic benefits (see box 4-1).

More generally, there has been little progress in implementing the five TRUST principles for donor engagement: Transparency, Risk sharing, Use and strengthen country systems, Strengthen capacities, and Timely and predictable aid. There has been some progress at the global and country levels on increasing transparency but there is little evidence that this is making it any easier for governments to access information in a way that helps their budget planning processes. Risk management commitments made at high-level forums have not been translated into significant changes in-country. Some donors have made significant progress on the use of country systems—with the introduction of new instruments by the United States, the European Community, and Norway. But many more donors have failed to deliver any significant improvements, and overall progress lags behind commitments. Strengthening capacities in ways that deepen country institutions while implementing investment and services has also been difficult for donors to implement. There are no examples of codes of conduct on remuneration of national staff and little evidence of a reduction in the number of project implementation units. And finally, there is no evidence that donors are adopting new mechanisms to provide development aid (as opposed to humanitarian aid) in a more timely and predictable manner.

In short, although the fragile states made a significant political commitment to the New Deal in moving forward on nationwide fragility consultations on implementing the TRUST principles, the lack of action by donors (with some impressive exceptions in a few areas) is striking. It is not yet clear whether this is just a case of development partners taking longer to implement the New Deal than originally planned or whether their commitment to the New Deal has changed.

The mixed experience of international engagement with fragile states during the past fifteen years shows three sets of issues still unresolved. These concern aid flows, aid practices, and private sector engagement.

Aid Flows

Misallocation of Security and Development Resources

Spending on military and peacekeeping far exceeds spending on investment in development. UN peacekeeping is relatively cheap compared to national military expenditure in fragile states; UN peacekeeping in fiscal year 2013–14 was only US$7.54 billion to support 118,600 personnel in sixteen peacekeeping missions, or US$63,574 per person (OECD 2013). Bilateral spending on security in fragile states is much higher. For Afghanistan alone the security budget in fiscal year 2011 was US$114 billion, which amounts to US$1.3 million per military personnel.[22] By contrast, the U.S. budget for civilian activities (through the State Department and USAID) in Afghanistan was only US$4.1 billion (Belasco 2011, table 3). In the largest seventeen OECD donor countries in 2012 military expenditures were nearly nine times greater than their development assistance (table 4-1). The United States is an outlier, accounting for 64 percent of the military expenditure of the seventeen countries and 25 percent of official development assistance. Without the United States, the ratio of military expenditure to ODA would be 4:3.

---

22. The bipartisan Congressional Research Service puts the operational cost per military person at US$667,000, since other costs, such as procurement of equipment and contributions to financing the Afghan security forces, are also included in the defense budget.

Table 4-1. *Official Development Assistance (ODA) and Military Expenditures of the Largest OECD/DAC Donors, 2012*

US$ million except as indicated

Country	ODA	Military expenditure	Military expenditure/ ODA ratio
Australia	5,403	26,158	4.84
Austria	1,106	3,188	2.88
Belgium	2,315	5,171	2.23
Canada	5,650	20,379	3.61
Finland	1,320	3,072	2.33
France	12,028	60,058	4.99
Germany	12,939	46,488	3.59
Italy	2,737	33,746	12.33
Japan	10,605	59,564	5.62
Korea	1,597	31,660	19.82
Netherlands	5,523	10,596	1.92
Norway	4,753	7,143	1.50
Spain	2,037	13,918	6.83
Sweden	5,240	6,239	1.19
Switzerland	3,045	4,591	1.51
United Kingdom	13,892	58,500	4.21
United States	30,824	684,780	22.22
Total or average	121,014	1,075,251	8.89

Source: OECD (2013b); SIPRI (2014); authors' calculations.

Countries such as Korea can justify their military expenditure in terms of their existential threats. But U.S. politicians argue that their security expenditures relative to European countries is for protecting global commons such as seaways and space. Nevertheless, since countries with large military expenditures also provide expeditionary forces to developing countries, the question arises whether a marginal dollar spent on development would contribute more to their security, both short term and long term, than its being spent on their militaries. This is before considering whether the global disparity in military expenditure results in much Western investment in hardware becoming stranded. Since public appetite for foreign deployment of troops diminished following the Iraq and Afghanistan wars, NATO countries and their partners may have to shift military resources from forces abroad that are increasingly constrained politically, including in UN peacekeeping missions, to the immediate defense of their own territories, where other threats may be emerging. Although the impact of development alone on security may be less than proponents of development argue, incremental resources spent on development can achieve both security and development goals, particularly when activities in all three areas are coordinated and coherent.[23] Development activities need to be part of an integrated peace-building approach, which includes diplomacy and security assistance among such security organizations as the UN, the African Union, and NATO. Fragile states have their own legitimate security needs, not least because they are at risk of violence and chaos. Assistance in building their police and armed forces will be needed, and this provides an opportunity for them to create a professional security sector under civilian control. Moving beyond 2015, we see a need for a more integrated approach to peace building, diplomacy, security, and development and for striking the right balance between expenditures on security and development.

Misallocation of Aid across Developing Countries

Recovering from a conflict is costly; postconflict countries normally lack the resources to recover, particularly the poorest countries that are just beginning recovery.[24] Global aid allocations, however, do not reflect this need. Aid often goes disproportionately to richer countries, and little allowance is made for whether a country has been affected by conflict. Since most conflict-affected countries are also low-income countries, this group loses out on both counts.

This misallocation of aid is obscured by the standard OECD aid analysis, which focuses on aid per capita. Given that the post-2015 challenge is elimination of extreme poverty, it is helpful to examine aid allocations in terms of aid provided per person living in extreme poverty (less than US$1.25 a day). Low-income countries receive US$122 a year of long-term development aid

---

23. There is an extensive literature on the causes of civil war. Papers by Collier and Hoeffler (1998, 2004), which emphasize economic explanations of civil war, sparked a debate about the roles of "greed and grievance" (Cramer 2002). Analysis of insurgencies by Berman and others (2010) and Berman, Shapiro, and Felter (2011) indicate that insurgencies tend not to be driven by relative poverty and that conventional economic development instruments may have little short-term impact on violence. Fishbein and Wilder (2012) show, based on research in Afghanistan, that aid alone cannot address political drivers of conflict and, while perhaps producing short-term tactical security benefits, can actually be counterproductive if too much is spent too quickly.

24. Afghanistan and Sierra Leone tax/GDP ratios in the early 2000s were around 5 percent. While there was very rapid growth—in part due to strong support from development partners and from the development of natural resources—it has taken ten years for the ratios to rise to the more normal levels of around 15 percent. The federal government share of Somalia's tax revenue is just US$50 million.

Figure 4-2. *Allocation of Aid Relative to the Prevalence of Extreme Poverty*

US$ (aid per person living in extreme poverty)

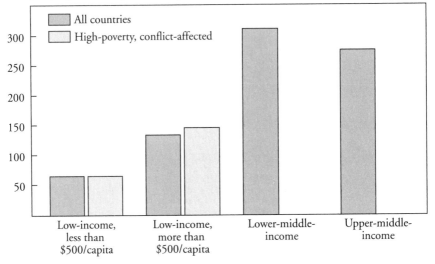

Source: Authors' calculations using OECD/DAC and World Bank data.

per person living in extreme poverty.[25] Middle-income countries, which are not typically affected by conflict, receive nearly three times more than that—on average, US$310 per person living in extreme poverty. No preference is given to conflict-affected states. The average for the most needy group of countries—high-poverty and conflict-affected countries—is just US$123 per person living in extreme poverty.

The misallocation is even starker for the very poorest counties—those with an income of less than US$500 per capita per year, half the per capita threshold for low-income countries. For this poorest group, the average amount of aid is just US$66 per person living in extreme poverty (figure 4-2). The Central African Republic is an example of a very low-income, conflict-affected aid orphan. The country currently receives US$66 of aid per person living in extreme poverty. This is a third of the average for all countries.

25. Aid figures cited refer to the OECD definition of country-programmable aid, which is aid that can be programmed by the government for spending in the country and so excludes debt relief, humanitarian aid, and aid spent in the donor country (such as support for students attending university in the donor country). Figures used are for 2011 and cover ninety-one low- and middle-income countries. Countries with populations of less than half a million are excluded to avoid the figures being distorted by high per capita allocations in small states. Figures are medians to avoid distortion by outliers.

Misallocation of Aid within Fragile States

The g7+ governments complain that aid does not flow to their priorities, particularly to police and justice or to infrastructure and employment. Furthermore, aid is typically poorly coordinated among partners and with government priorities.

Regarding the underfunding of police and justice, there is a glaring gap between assistance to build an effective military and the international effort to support police, justice, and prisons. The Millennium Development Goals have pushed foreign aid toward investments that directly reduce poverty, such as education and health. This had led to underinvestment in the foundations for the MDGs in fragile states—peace-building and state-building goals (PSGs). Policing is fundamental to security (the second PSG) which, together with the judiciary and corrections, is central to an effective justice system (the third PSG). Policing, and to some extent justice, is inherently transaction intensive, involving many thousands of interactions with the population. It also requires decisions based on unclear and incomplete information, such as discretionary decisions by police personnel and justices (Pritchett & Woolcock 2004). In the cases of police and informal providers of justice, these decisions lack specificity—and thus are difficult to monitor (Fukuyama 2004). The combination of transaction intensity, discretionary decisionmaking, and low specificity places police and justice among the most difficult areas of public administration. The experience of the Liberian government in underwriting its own justice and security needs when the United Nations withdrew its mission illustrates the problem (box 4-2).

Difficult areas of public administration are the type of challenge that multilateral development banks and bilateral aid agencies normally take up. However, these banks interpret the clauses of their charters that prohibit political interference as keeping them from becoming involved in criminal justice. Bilateral agencies are constrained by having to work within their own government's organization, made difficult when policing and justice are linked to concerns about cross-border crime, migration, and terrorism. Other parts of the international system that could claim a mandate, like the UN, the EU, and other regional organizations, tend to lack capacity and internal coherence. In addition, there is a lack of consensus among international actors about the nature of support. Policing and justice depend on local factors, which may demand different approaches to those adopted in industrialized countries: a greater role for informal mediation than for formal justice, for justice to be restorative rather than retributive, and for policing to be a combination of a national gendarmerie and local forces accountable to communities.[26]

---

26. See Carothers (2003) and Jensen (2008) for analyses on justice in fragile situations.

Box 4-2. *Justice and Security in Liberia*

The Liberian government was struggling in 2014 to find additional income of US$25 million a year, the amount estimated by the UN and the World Bank that Liberia would need to take over the justice and security services provided by the departing UN mission. The government was already the primary provider of security in the country, but it was having difficulty filling this funding gap, even though the amount was just 5 percent of the annual US$500 million that the international community was spending on the UN mission. The international community regarded the savings from the departure of the UN mission as needed elsewhere and was not prepared to provide a small proportion of it to help during the transition phase. Even though Liberia's taxes were high for a low-income country (26 percent of GDP) and had been growing, they were not growing as fast as the rate at which the UN mission was drawing down. Lack of funding meant that the police force would have limited mobility in comparison to the UN mission. Liberia received US$120 in long-term development aid per person living in extreme poverty, less than the global average of US$190. Since its foreign direct investment ratio to GDP in 2013 was over 100 percent, Liberia clearly has substantial capacity to absorb additional external aid (especially if the aid was used to purchase imported vehicles).

The governments of the g7+ complain that foreign aid flows to donors' priorities rather than to theirs. An example of this is the underfunding of the fourth PSG, economic foundations (infrastructure and job-creating private investment). East Asian countries that successfully reduced poverty invested heavily in infrastructure, and the state played a critical role in coordinating private investment.[27] Infrastructure in fragile states is seriously neglected, except by new partners such as China, but they often need to create infrastructure to establish the most basic services and provide the connectivity that makes nation building possible. South Sudan's experience with road building is a case in point (box 4-1).

The financing of reconstruction and basic infrastructure is inadequate in countries emerging from prolonged crisis. These may be one-off costs needed for private markets to operate and for regions of the country to be brought together. This neglect of infrastructure is due to lack of specialization among donors and to the inadequate efforts of the multilateral development banks to catalyze private investment in all low- and mid-income countries. Infrastructure investment falls naturally to these banks and to large, risk-averse bilateral

---

27. On the role of the state in facilitating and coordinating private investment, see Lin and Monga (2010).

donors, which prefer ring-fenced projects. Because of the MDG paradigm, these financiers have incentives to finance programs that reduce poverty directly in order to gain recognition by global and domestic constituencies. There is thus often a mismatch between what a large bilateral donor will finance and what people in poor countries want (Leo 2013).

Regarding the coordination of international assistance, the integration of political, security, justice, humanitarian, and development policy communities in a fragile state remains elusive. This is partly due to lack of capacity and partly to the 1940s international assistance architecture that leads to lack of coherence among international partners. While the administrative capacity of fragile states may be low, it takes only a few well-qualified individuals supported by the head of government (to ensure cross-ministry coordination) and a few international advisers to manage international assistance. Fragile states are usually critically dependent on foreign aid and security assistance and may be willing to accept what their partners propose rather than risk going without their assistance.

OECD partners also struggle to be internally coordinated despite the recent creation of "whole of government" offices at the center of their governments. Internal coordination is even harder to achieve if the cabinet itself is made up of competing interests and if external relations are dominated by a large player, such as the defense or foreign ministries.[28] Coherence is complicated further by interests within the legislature that may be ill informed about conditions in the country or have its own fixed views on appropriate institutional arrangements in fragile states, usually similar to those in the donor country. The multilateral architecture, too, has problems. While the UN has the institutional mandate to operate across all policy communities, its capacity is weak in, for example, expeditionary military capacity and policing, or is underfunded and thus often able to respond to a crisis only after raising additional resources.

Further, the proliferation of UN agencies and departments makes internal coordination within the UN system problematic. It is difficult to see the UN system adopting a more rational organization in return for more core funding without a financing crisis. Despite a broad mandate, the EU has similar issues.[29] The World Bank and regional development banks are well resourced but have been reluctant to become engaged in political and security matters. The current international architecture has difficulty in incorporating new state players,

28. Neustadt and May (1986) describe the presidential system of government as "a government of strangers," since cabinet secretaries may not have known each other before their appointments. The same is probably true in fragile states emerging from prolonged conflict, where government ministers may be revolutionary figures who stayed in the country during the conflict and technocrats who lived outside the country during that time.

29. See Gavas, Davies, and McKechnie (2013) for an assessment of the EU's performance in fragile states.

such as the BRIC countries, which may have their own views on what constitutes international legitimacy and the effectiveness of the current approach to assisting countries emerging from crisis. Voting power within the IMF and the World Bank in particular reflects the economic order of the late 1940s and underrepresents emerging economies of the twenty-first century, such as China. Consequently, the legitimacy of the Bretton Woods institutions is in decline, and emerging powers are establishing their own development banks and aid agencies. Even greater issues arise in bringing civil society and private sector actors into a coherent strategy, despite their importance in innovation, service delivery, and job creation. Finally, the international system has generally failed to address new challenges: the corrosive effect of drug trafficking throughout West Africa, organized crime in Central America, the fragility of middle-income countries in the Middle East, and subnational fragility in otherwise well-performing countries.

Multilateral development banks have a potential role in evening out the distribution of development finance across countries, but the performance-based allocation used by these banks for sizing country programs spreads money too thinly across eligible countries. Aid allocations could be spread further if donors facilitated lower cost of service delivery by supporting nonstate actors (Glennie, McKechnie, and Rabinowitz 2013). In addition, multilateral development banks could free up more resources for fragile states by mobilizing private investment and remittance flows in nonfragile countries. Performance-based allocations do not distinguish particular development opportunities among countries with similar average performance and do not address the aid orphan problem.

The most recent replenishment of the World Bank's IDA window for concessional finance did seek to address this misallocation.[30] It recognized the value of providing additional funding to "turnaround" countries, but the additional financial allocations will be marginal. In most fragile states access to incremental resources is possible only after a country has demonstrated years of successful performance. As a result, high-return projects will go unfunded for years. For example, in Liberia, many years after the conflict, there were many unfunded road projects offering very high rates of return, some in excess of 100 percent. Also in Liberia, no partner had sufficient resources to finance hydropower rehabilitation, delaying by years the shift from high-cost, carbon-emitting, thermal power production, which has been a drag on the recovery of the private sector.

---

30. The African Development Bank's special window for fragile states, the Fragile States Facility (FSF) was also replenished in 2014. The FSF will receive US$1 billion out of the total US$7.3 billion for the 2014–16 programming cycle (www.afdb.org/en/news-and-events/article/participants-reaffirmed-their-commitment-to-africa-at-adf-13th-replenishment-12314/).

Changing Donor Practices

The challenges for donors in fragile states do not concertn just aid finance and allocation but also how donors operate. Five issues stand out in particular: fragility itself, ownership, institution building, speed, and risk taking.

Focusing on the Causes of Fragility

At the core of the New Deal is the recognition that development partners need to focus much more on the key challenge in fragile states, and that is reducing fragility. The revolution required is of the same scale as that of the introduction of the MDGs. In the late 1990s development partners recognized that, for all their efforts, poor people were not benefitting enough. This lay behind the first MDG: reducing the number of people living in extreme poverty. It was also the reason for the introduction of the primary condition for debt relief for heavily indebted poor countries (HIPC) and preparation of a poverty reduction plan. It also led to a major (but still insufficient) effort to monitor poverty reduction and to a major research effort in new approaches to tackle poverty, such as cash transfers.

The same revolution is needed on fragility. The intellectual challenge is even harder, as it is not even clear how to measure fragility.[31] The New Deal offers some general pointers; the peace-building and state-building goals are a ready checklist. But although the New Deal was endorsed back in 2011, it is doubtful that many staff in fragile states could list all five goals. There needs to be a major effort to make everyone aware of the five PSGs, just as there was for the eight MDGs.

In addition, the collective experience of the g7+ states shows that peripheral areas of each country distrust the central government and see few government services. Development agencies reinforce this bias, as their staffs are typically concentrated in the capital city and see only the daily needs of the central government, rarely visiting the peripheral areas to assess their needs. In many countries it might be reasonable to favor developing decentralized services (Bennett and others 2010). But development assistance always seems to focus first on the central ministries. For example, public financial management reform always seems to focus on the center, when arguably it is basic financial management at the subnational level that needs to be changed first—or at least needs to be built in parallel. Similarly, transparency is often seen as a second priority. Yet as Timor-Leste has found, transparency is critical to building

---

31. While measuring fragility is inherently difficult, much effort is being taken to obtain indicators grounded in theory, indicators both objective and acceptable to most governments and practitioners. For an example of a practical approach, see Hesselbein (2011).

confidence and trust at the national level, so that people can see where the money is going. The argument that transparency reforms are too difficult is contradicted by experience. As De Renzio from the International Budget Partnership has noted, "Transparency does not need to wait—some of the countries that have made the most progress in the Open Budget Index in recent years have been fragile states."[32]

The major challenge for development partners prioritizing reducing fragility is that most staff know how to deliver the MDGs or at least the goals that are the focus of their agency.[33] In a time of fiscal austerity, most politicians want to focus on headline issues with clear, measurable results, such as reducing the number of children dying. By contrast, the war that never happened is never a headline, and even the most sophisticated evaluation techniques could not work out which project was the most effective in achieving that result. As the former USAID administrator Andrew Natsios notes, "The counter-bureaucracy ignores a central principle of development theory—that those development programs that are most precisely and easily measured are the least transformational, and those programs that are most transformational are the least measurable" (2010).

Ensuring Country Ownership

Despite their rhetoric, international partners continue to find it difficult to respect country ownership and political processes in fragile countries. Recipient governments may not wish to question aid in case the offer is withdrawn and overall resources decline. International partners often come with ideas and solutions mandated by their governing bodies, ideas and solutions that are inappropriate to the recipient country. Partners may impose their agenda on public expenditure and leave national priorities unfunded. Ownership of development assistance is intertwined with its legitimacy. Such ownership involves the political leadership of the country and its advisers, with broad support among agencies of the state and civil society, which decide the desirability, nature, and timing of change and build this change into policy and administration.[34] Ownership with legitimacy implies deciding *with the country* on courses of action, a process that would include a wide range of viewpoints, accountability, and transparency, particularly about the interests and intentions of the parties (DIE 2010).

32. Cited in Manuel, Gupta, and Ackroyd (2011).
33. See Manuel (2011), for example, on how this might apply to the IMF.
34. This paraphrases the definition of Killick, quoted in Brinkerhoff (2007).

One of the OECD principles for engagement in fragile states is Do No Harm. Yet the implementation record is mixed. An OECD report on country studies shows that international partners' strategic objectives and the combination of their aid and other instruments could negatively affect state building (Putzel 2010). In extreme cases, partner-driven priorities, such as premature elections and economic reforms, could actually contribute to renewed conflict. South Sudan is an example in which IMF-sponsored economic reforms, which were sensible from a technical economic perspective, were blocked by the legislature, probably because they changed the distribution of economic rents underlying the political settlement. This in turn led to a withdrawal of partner support for the compact agreed under the New Deal, and the country returned to conflict a few weeks later. While there is insufficient evidence to draw a causal chain, South Sudan illustrates the risks of pushing otherwise rational reforms onto a fragile country without analyzing potential unintended consequences. Too much aid can reduce incentives for government to collect taxes and develop institutions.[35] Bypassing country systems to achieve fast results along a partner's time scale or to avoid fiduciary risks can retard the development of effective country institutions that underlie the transition from fragility to resilience. International partners of fragile states should be aware of the harm they can cause to peace and to the development of local institutions. Aid levels need to be calibrated so as not to exceed the absorptive capacity of the country or to create excessive rents that maintain power holders who lack domestic legitimacy. Aid should be predictable and recognize that institutional transformation involves steps backward as well as leaps forward. Aid that uses country budget and treasury systems, that reinforces the development of country institutions and accountability, and that supports legitimate authority and permanent service delivery mechanisms is likely to be more effective, in terms of both peacekeeping and development, than aid delivered through parallel systems.

35. Brautigam and Knack (2004) show that high levels of aid in Africa are associated with deteriorating governance, creating soft budget constraints and so making it difficult to solve collective action problems. Earlier work by Knack (2000) suggests that donors should provide more aid as budget support rather than displacing the government in the design and implementation of projects, so that the government can build administrative capacity and negotiate with civil society over service provision and taxes. Arcand and Chauvet (2001) show that aid can create rents that reduce conflict—a finding also of Brautigam and Knack—but that aid unpredictability is associated with conflict. Birdsall (2007) argues that aid unpredictability affects middle-income countries disproportionately and can weaken institutions. Rubin (2002) finds that the start of Afghanistan's civil wars in the 1980s followed a sharp reduction in Western and Soviet aid. Mavrotas (2003) finds that bilateral project aid and food aid appear to displace public investment and government consumption, unlike program aid and technical assistance.

Since country context matters and solutions need to build on local institutions, decisions on the design of country programs and the projects that implement them need to emerge from a process of dialogue and problem solving involving international and local actors. This cannot take place without decentralization of decisionmaking to in-country offices that include staff of appropriate seniority. Establishing country offices in fragile states is expensive due to logistical challenges and the costs of locating staff in areas sometimes plagued by crime and insecurity. Local conditions and uncertain prospects for successes on which career promotions depend can make it difficult to recruit high-caliber staff to field positions. Few bilateral and international agencies have put in place the decentralization, budget, and human resources needed to establish effective offices in fragile states. The quality of dialogue with these countries and the ability to develop country ownership has suffered as a result.

Building Effective Institutions

There is a consensus among academics and practitioners that fragility is associated with weak, ineffective institutions that cannot deliver basic services. Resilient states have institutions that are effective in service delivery, are capable of resolving differences, embody a sense of nationhood, and are considered legitimate by their population and international partners. Moreover, institutional development is a homegrown process: outsiders can facilitate and advise, but each country needs to find its own institutional arrangements that meet its needs. Informal local institutions are persistent, influential, diverse, and matter for development outcomes (DfID 2010).

Attempts to transfer international best practices are often said to fail because of lack of political will, but the problem is usually the failure by partners to understand local power relationships. Institutional development is not about transferring best practices or global solutions. Such approaches lead to isomorphic mimicry—Potemkin states that appear modern but that fail to perform like their models (Acemoglu and Robinson 2012; OECD 2010, 2011; Pritchett, Woolcock, and Andrews 2012; World Bank 2011a). Billions of dollars have been poured into capacity building in fragile states and have achieved only modest results. Building on institutions that already exist rather than making new laws and organizations is a more promising approach to effective service delivery (Tavakoli and others 2013; Manuel and others 2010).

A new approach is needed to help fragile states build their own institutions. There also needs to be realism as to what can be achieved and over what time scale. Institutions in OECD countries have evolved over hundreds of years. Even with today's better information flows, effective institutions take at least twenty years to build (World Bank 2011a). Many of the obstacles to development are collective action problems: the inability of elites to make decisions that would be in their collective interest and in the interest of society as a whole. This requires a different way for international actors to deliver capacity-building support; rather than more studies and technical assistance, emphasis should be placed on facilitation and dispute resolution. Breaking the link between investment finance and advisory services provides the space and time for collective action problems to be resolved (Booth 2012). In a similar vein, shifting assistance for capacity building from grand strategies and master plans, which often have unintended consequences or are too rigid to respond to uncertainty, toward an approach that works with countries to identify and solve particular problems of concern to them seems to have promise for more effective institutional development support (Andrews, Pritchett, and Woolcock 2012).

Support for an effective civil service and for better public financial management is critical to institutional development; international partners would, first, avoid doing harm and, second, see their financial assistance have an impact well beyond expectations. Pay reform is a critical aspect of both, as Richard Manning, the former chair of DAC, notes: "Until governments are able to be competitive employers of their own people, we will never be able to build sustainable institutions" (Manuel and others 2010). Yet support for pay reform is normally considered too expensive and is rarely tackled. Partners continue to invest in training and the provision of very expensive international technical assistance. This also is a classic example of collective action failure. Pay reform is too complex for any one partner, and so each one continues to provide its own small-scale training and technical assistance programs. Since the fiduciary risks of both are easy to control and the inputs and outputs are highly visible, such programs are attractive to partners. As the quality of their outcomes is difficult to measure, hard evidence of the long-term value of training and technical assistance is largely unknown.

At the same time, partners can actually cause harm. After the conflict in Liberia the UN mission was employing 1,500 professional staff at salaries several times what the government could afford. Many of these people would have been strong candidates for the government's own under-resourced Senior Executive Service, which numbered just a hundred people. This was a direct result of the imbalance of partner financing for Liberia, where the resources for the UN mission were two to three times greater than total development aid.

Speeding up Delivery

Under the New Deal, development partners have committed to faster delivery—for example, introducing simplified fast-track procurement. The World Bank already has such procedures and used these to great effect in Afghanistan for over ten years, although use of these procedures in other fragile settings has been patchy. While procurement may be seen as a technical issue, procurement delays can become a political issue. Fragile states complain frequently that partners are too slow. As a fragile state recovers from conflict, there is an urgent humanitarian case for infrastructure rehabilitation; high economic rates of return are another indicator of the value of speed. An even stronger case for moving quickly is political, as rapid improvement in infrastructure can help build confidence in the new government.

Working faster is costly for development agencies. The success in Afghanistan was due to the decision to place experienced World Bank staff in country to implement the streamlined procurement policies. Yet in times of fiscal austerity, multilateral banks are increasingly judged by simple aggregate cost ratios, such as the ratio of administration costs to loan disbursement. A large road project in a stable middle-income country is always going to have a much lower cost ratio. If partners do not recognize the higher costs of working in fragile states, they will not be able to deploy the experienced staff needed to facilitate peace and development. Unless there is flexibility for fragile states—or recognition of the higher rates of return (including the value of avoiding a return to conflict)—internal incentives will continue to disadvantage fragile states.

A longer-term perspective is also needed for activities in fragile states. Even if fragile states work at the fastest rate of reform, it will take decades to deliver the needed change (World Bank 2011a). Activities need to be designed for the duration—that is, set up for ten years, with break points. Arguably the need for a longer-term perspective might suggest that those multilateral development partners less driven by short-term budgets would be better placed to lead support. Most transitions involve the active engagement of at least one bilateral partner or small core group, which can help hold the multilaterals to account.[36]

Countering Risk Aversion

Fragile states are considered by donor country politicians and publics as risky for foreign assistance, but these risks are often exaggerated (figure 4-3). There are always trade-offs among the main categories of risk; fiduciary risk, the risk that a program will not deliver its results, and the risk that the country will fail strategically, even though the particular program is successful and the money is properly accounted for. There is also a trade-off between minimizing risk and value for money. Fiduciary risk perceptions and concerns about the ability of low-capacity countries to deliver quick development results have led donors to bypass government budget systems and to provide aid in the form of projects, rather than programmatically.

36. For example, the United Kingdom in Sierra Leone, the United States in Liberia, and the United States, Norway, and the United Kingdom in South Sudan.

Figure 4-3. *Risk Management: Myth and Reality*

Trying to have it all: risk trade-off myth when bypassing country systems

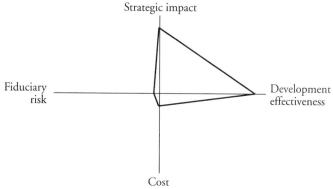

Risk trade-off reality when bypassing country systems: high risks of failure at high cost

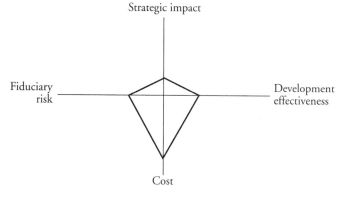

Different risk-reward trade-offs when using country systems and mitigating risks

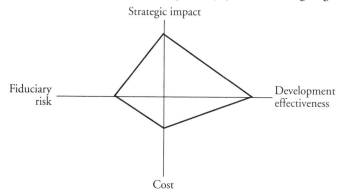

Source: Authors' calculations, based on McKechnie and Davies (2013).

Such aid modalities can undermine state building, as the population sees services provided by foreign agencies rather than their own government. Accountability for service provision shifts away from the government to the international community, and capacity-building opportunities are taken away. Governments are reluctant to budget operations and maintenance for projects they do not "own," which perpetuates aid dependency. Project-driven aid may not reach a scale sufficient to address national-level problems and may be high cost, in contradiction to donor concerns about value for money.[37] The Afghanistan example shows that externally driven project aid has high fiduciary, programmatic, and strategic risks, while government-executed programs can be less risky and better value for the money.

While it is impossible to eliminate fraud, corruption, and collusion in any country, the risks of directing aid through budget systems in fragile states are probably exaggerated. Much corruption in fragile states involves abuse of power, extortion by state agents, informal payments to access services, illegal transfers of state property, and unpaid loans from banks rather than diversion of funds from the treasury or misprocurement, although these can still take place. Excessive aversion to fiduciary risk adds to the cost of development projects, as donors subcontract to international firms that in turn subcontract to other firms. Donor funds may appear safe (although there is often corruption in the chain of subcontractors), but projects are more expensive, lack country ownership, and can fail in operation. Citizens may become disillusioned at the waste and lack of sustainable service delivery and at the impotence of their government contributing to renewed conflict. Oversight agencies in donor countries believe that aid delivered through their own parallel channels has little risk of going astray, is effective, and represents value for money. These are often misperceptions. After fiduciary risks have been mitigated, directing aid through country systems is usually more effective, is cheaper, and has very little additional fiduciary risk (see figure 4-3).[38]

Corruption in fragile states is intertwined with economic rents and with the relationship between government and the private sector. It can have positive as well as negative impacts. It can prevent conflict, or it can undermine support for public institutions. Petty corruption can strengthen the service orientation of officials, or it can lead to abuse of poor citizens and the undermining of the state.[39] While all governments create rents to some extent, rents and corruption tolerated by government are common in the neopatrimonial political systems

37. See Ghani and Lockhart (2008) and Glennie and others (2013) for more on the disadvantages of project-based aid and bypassing country systems.

38. See McKechnie and Davies (2013) for a more exhaustive treatment of risks.

39. Abuse of street vendor Mohamed Bouazizi by corrupt police in Tunisia led to his self-immolation and sparked protests that ignited the Arab Spring; see Fisher (2011).

that characterize many fragile states. As Khan (2003) argues, rents have been a factor in countries that have been successful in economic development, and the association between high economic growth and lack of corruption is not statistically robust. He argues that in a dynamic state undergoing economic and social transformation, growth-enhancing rents that drive technological innovation and learning are favored over growth-reducing rents that permit capture of service delivery systems and open-ended transfers to privileged groups. Negative rents arise from monopolies and the protection of market incumbents that have ceased to innovate or whose productivity has plateaued. Managing the dynamics of rents to strike a balance between building the private sector and avoiding firms without competition becoming dependent on the state and corruption is a challenge for a government and its international partners.

Unless a better balance can be struck between fiduciary risks and the risks of failing to achieve program and strategic goals, there is a risk that support for development assistance in fragile states will evaporate in donor countries. Donor governments will simply shift assistance to military and humanitarian channels, neither of which has a good track record in building the public institutions that enable the transition out of fragility.

Excessive aversion to fiduciary risks by partners could be changed by the following:

—Understanding and mitigating fiduciary risk through options that include strengthening public financial management, applying special procurement and accounting rules, contracting out government fiduciary services while strengthening its capacity, and a dual sign-off on key decisions by government and donor agents. New aid instruments can also mitigate fiduciary risks, such as U.S. FARA grants, which reimburse governments for spending on specific budget items but only after spending on the items has been has been independently verified.

—Differentiated approaches for countries with weak governance. The test for determining whether a government merits a special response is not how it came to office but whether the development assistance it controls will reduce poverty, strengthen peace, and build better institutions. It is unrealistic to expect aid to be effective in countries where government has little public support and is not committed to development. In such cases, all that may be possible is to alleviate the worst manifestations of poverty through humanitarian assistance. In other countries there may be development-focused ministries within an otherwise dysfunctional government, where support for capacity development may generate longer-term benefits and where funds could be well spent. The UK's Department for International Development has financed items in government budgets, such as health supplies, in countries with governments lacking public legitimacy or abusing minorities but with funds not flowing through treasury systems. In situations of pervasive anarchy, where minimally capable government is only slowly emerging, a trusteeship arrangement under UN or regional political auspices is an option, but this would test the limits of the current definitions of national sovereignty and the administrative capacity of the UN or the regional organization.

—Shifting aid to multilateral channels better able to insulate risk management from donor politics. Multilateral organizations are governed by consensus and react to risk events with more consideration than bilateral organizations driven by day-to-day pressures from politicians, the media, and public opinion. Pooling funds through multilateral organizations or pooled funding arrangements such as multidonor trust funds also pools risk. Risk exposure is reduced from 100 percent with a purely bilateral project to the share in the pooled fund. Responsibility for managing risk is delegated to an organization such as a multilateral development bank that has experience operating in risky environments.

—Changing governance arrangements in multilateral organizations to strengthen risk management, effectiveness, and accountability. Shifting risk to multilateral organizations would require them to be efficient, effective, and accountable. Surveys such as those by MOPAN show that the multilaterals usually entrusted to manage pooled funds are effective, particularly mainstream funds from the International Development Association and the African and Asian Development Banks.[40] However, there have been instances in which the management of single-country multidonor trust funds has fallen short. A shift to pooling risks through multilateral channels would require changes to their governance and accountability arrangements. The boards of multilateral development banks may need strengthening and may need to shift their focus from project approvals to oversight of program implementation and results. Since comprehensive UN reforms are not politically feasible, donors to UN-managed funds could use their financial leverage to insist on management reforms at the fund or country level. Finally, a shift in governance of multilateral development banks to a more even balance between contributing and receiving shareholders would enable a better balance between fiduciary risks and the risks to recipients, not least the risks that programs fail to deliver results.[41]

—Better communications with legislatures and publics on risks, rewards, and the nature of corruption in fragile states.

40. MOPAN is the Multilateral Organization Performance Assessment Network, a network of eighteen donor countries (www.mopanonline.org/).

41. The implications of more balanced ownership can be illustrated to the differences in fiduciary policies for budget support between the African Development Bank, which is dominated by recipient shareholders, and the World Bank, which is dominated by a few large industrialized countries. The AfDB requires evidence that fiduciary management is improving in order to permit budget support, while the World Bank usually requires diagnostic work and basic standards to be in place.

A New Compact That Brings in the Private Sector

In the future, the private sector will need to play a much larger role in the development of fragile states. This stems from the private sector's ability to create sustainable jobs, mobilize remittances, and transform natural resources revenues into infrastructure. Private sector development in fragile settings is an enormous challenge, since so many things need to fall in place: security, factor markets, the laws and regulations that rule the business environment, finance, justice, infrastructure, serviced land, skilled labor, management, and organizational capacity, to name a few.

So far, international support for private sector development in fragile states has been disjointed and incoherent and without much impact. There has been an overreliance on business climate reforms, which are likely to meet resistance from vested interests and prove no easier to put in place in a fragile setting than other reforms. Even if such reforms were implemented, investors would be unlikely to materialize due to risks that deter foreign investors and the lack of capacity and resources available to local investors.

A new approach—a new compact for the private sector—is needed to mobilize the private sector in fragile states. This would entail obligations by donor governments, governments of fragile states, and adherence to agreed principles and to laws by the local and foreign business sector.

The international community needs to work with governments in fragile states to implement actions that increase local and foreign private investment. These actions could range from supporting the skills development of local businesses, to supplying critical inputs, to managing borders, to improving infrastructure. International agencies can shape procurement to enable local firms to compete, especially in labor-intensive sectors like construction, giving preference to such firms in bid evaluation, much like affirmative action and small business programs in industrialized countries.

To bridge the infrastructure gap in fragile states, multilateral financial institutions will need to deploy all their financial instruments and better coordinate the parts of their organizations responsible for managing them. This is likely to involve a mix of risk mitigation instruments such as publicly supported guarantees and insurances that cover political risks and extend debt maturities, as well as conventional long-term development finance with and without sovereign guarantees. Infrastructure investments especially will require the blending of public and private financing, particularly in countries where risk exposure constrains both private and development finance that does not have a sovereign guarantee. However, a more coherent array of financing instruments is not sufficient; multilateral institutions need a nuanced approach to country risk, an approach that recognizes low-risk opportunities in otherwise risky environments, possibly seeking to securitize a blend of loans to fragile and nonfragile states. They also can develop the capacity of the local private sector through supporting training, management development, and finance. Furthermore, aligning their staff incentives and skills with their operational procedures would facilitate greater international and local private investment in fragile states.

Governments of fragile states need to resolve policy and investment bottlenecks to private investment and to contract out equitable delivery of public services where this will produce efficiency and better coverage. They should weaken the links between the private sector and political patronage, enable competitive markets to flourish, establish transparent, simple, and predictable taxes for private enterprises, and focus the regulatory system on the promotion of competition and of health and safety. The Extractive Industries Transparency Initiative (EITI) is an example of countries voluntarily adopting a code of practice for the governance of natural resources.[42]

The local private sector should register and pay taxes and comply with local laws, and in return its assets should be protected by the state. Such a compact could involve regularizing assets accumulated during conflict or when public administration was weak, in a process (analogous to the truth and reconciliation process) that transforms ill-gotten funds into legitimate assets. The international private sector also would participate in a compact by complying with international standards on health, safety, and environment and address the interests of project-affected people. The performance standards promoted by the International Financial Corporation would be one basis for this (IFC 2012). The Equator Principles are a commitment from firms, not just from OECD countries, to adopt minimum standards on environmental and social and human rights aspects of their operations.[43] These principles are models for the international private sector. Action in other areas would multiply the positive impacts of private investment and give investors more security in fragile situations. Current initiatives of the G-20 and the OECD include reduction of tax avoidance, corruption, and money laundering.

The existing platform of the g7+, bilateral donors, and multilateral organizations could be broadened to incorporate the private sector. This initiative could lead to core standards for private investment in fragile states. One global platform that already involves private firms, trade associations, international organizations, and government that might facilitate a new compact for the private sector is the World Economic Forum. Other options are the World Bank Group, the OECD, and the United Nations.

42. For more on EITI, see http://eiti.org/.
43. For more on the equator principles, see www.equator-principles.com/.

Conclusions

Experience from the international engagement in fragile states during the past two decades suggests three challenges ahead. First, a major refunding and redirection of aid finance is needed. Too much is spent globally on national defense relative to development aid. In addition, the distribution of development aid across developing countries is regressive and inconsistent with the objective of poverty reduction. Countries that could do more to help themselves get three times as much aid as poorer countries for tackling poverty. The international community lacks the mechanisms for timely financing of peacekeeping and humanitarian missions and for sharing the costs between UN missions and national governments when UN missions finish. Too much aid in conflict-affected countries has been spent on directly reaching Millennium Development Goals at the cost of building the foundations of peace on which poverty reduction could take place. Insufficient resources have gone to achieving peace-building and state-building goals, including justice, jobs, and infrastructure.

Second, the way international partners deliver aid requires major change. Partners have yet to prioritize working on the fundamental causes of fragility. One possible lesson from the tragic events in South Sudan is that partners may have spread their efforts far too widely, diverting both their and the government's attention to tackling decades of marginalization and intercommunity violence. Partners are still struggling to respect country ownership and to build effective institutions. Related to this is the reluctance to channel aid through country systems, unlike the Marshall Plan, which directly financed some very fragile European states in the late 1940s. Instead, aid uses modalities that can be destructive to institutions. Partners' approach to risk is still too simplistic; their internal budgets fail to provide for greater staff presence in fragile states. They also fail to deliver critical short-term results in those fragile situations where a few early quick wins are needed to build public confidence in legitimate institutions. There are approaches that could be adopted to deliver results while building local institutions. But ramshackle aid delivery just perpetuates aid dependency.

Third, the private sector, the international community, and the g7+ all need to undertake a new compact for fragile states that reduces the blockages for foreign and local private firms to sustain peace, development, and well-paid jobs. Too much of the burden of financing peace and development is being taken by aid. The private sector can make an enormous contribution through innovation, organizational capacity, and finance. Better solutions are needed for fragile states to address those critical obstacles to private investment and to contract out equitable and efficient provision of public services and infrastructure. With their international partners, fragile states can share risks that the private sector cannot bear alone and can create more level playing fields for foreign and local firms. International partners will need to provide a more and better integrated package of finance and risk management instruments and technical support to governments and local businesses. The private sector and its financiers need to be more imaginative about the possibilities that exist in fragile states and should commit to internationally agreed codes of conduct that include health, safety, and local taxation.

Without progress on addressing these three challenges, all the resources in the world will fail to solve the problems of fragile countries. Eliminating extreme poverty at the global level will not be possible by the target date of 2030, even though evidence shows that progress is possible. The ultimate question is whether it is possible to reorganize global efforts to achieve this goal. Without the necessary changes fragile states will be a major development challenge for the next fifteen years and more and a source of regional and global instability. It does not have to be that way.

References

Acemoglu, Daron, and James A. Robinson. 2012. *Why Nations Fail: The Origins of Power, Prosperity, and Poverty.* London: Profile.

Albrecht, Peter, and Paul Jackson. 2009. "Security System Transformation in Sierra Leone 1997–2007." Global Facilitation Network for Security Sector Reform (www.ssrnetwork.net).

Andrews, Matt, Lant Pritchett, and Michael Woolcock. 2012. "Escaping Capability Traps through Problem-Driven Interactive Adaptation." Working Paper 299. Washington: Center for Global Development.

Arcand, Jean-Louis, and Lisa Chauvet. 2001. "Foreign Aid, Rent-Seeking Behaviour, and Civil War." Working Paper. Oxford, UK: Centre for the Study of African Economies.

Belasco, Amy. 2011. "The Cost of Iraq, Afghanistan, and Other Global War on Terror Operations since 9/11." Report RL33110. Congressional Research Service (www.fas.org/sgp/crs/natsec/RL33110.pdf).

Bennett, Jon, Sara Pantuliano, Wendy Fenton, Anthony Vaux, Chris Barnett, and Emery Brusset. 2010. "Aiding the Peace: A Multi-Donor Evaluation of Support to Conflict Prevention and Peacebuilding Activities in Southern Sudan 2005–2010." Hove, UK: ITAD Ltd. (www.oecd.org/countries/southsudan/46895095.pdf).

Berman, Eli, Joseph H. Felter, Jacob N. Shapiro, and Michael Callen. 2010. *Do Working Men Rebel? Insurgency and Unemployment in Afghanistan, Iraq and the Philippines.* Working Paper 15547. Cambridge, Mass.: National Bureau of Economic Research.

Berman, Eli, Jacob N. Shapiro, and Joseph H. Felter. 2011. "Can Hearts and Minds Be Bought? The Economics of Counterinsurgency in Iraq." *Journal of Political Economy* 119, no. 4: 766–819.

Birdsall, Nancy. 2007. "Do No Harm: Aid, Weak Institutions and the Missing Middle in Africa." Working Paper 113. Washington: Center for Global Development.

Booth, David. 2012. "Development as a Collective Action Problem." London: Overseas Development Institute (www.institutions-africa.org/filestream/20121024-appp-synthesis-report-development-as-a-collective-action-problem).

Brautigam, Deborah A., and Stephen Knack. 2004. "Foreign Aid, Institutions and Governance in Sub-Saharan Africa." *Economic Development and Cultural Change* 52, no. 2: 255–85.

Brinkerhoff, Derik W. 2007. "Where There's a Will, There's a Way? Untangling Ownership and Political Will in Post-Conflict Stability and Reconstruction Operations." *Whitehead Journal of Diplomacy and International Relations* (Winter/Spring): 112–20.

Carothers, Thomas. 2003. "Promoting the Rule of Law Abroad: The Problem of Knowledge." Working Paper 34. Washington: Carnegie Endowment for International Peace.

Chandy, Laurence. 2011. "Ten Years of Fragile States: What Have We Learned?" Brookings Institution.

Collier, Paul. 2007. *The Bottom Billion: Why the Poorest Countries Are Failing and What Can Be Done about It*. Oxford University Press.

———. 2010. *The Plundered Planet: Why We Must, and How We Can, Manage Nature for Global Prosperity*. Oxford University Press.

Collier, Paul, and Anke Hoeffler. 1998. "On Economic Causes of Civil War." *Oxford Economic Papers* 50, no. 4: 563–73.

———. 2004. "Greed and Grievance in Civil War." *Oxford Economic Papers* 56, no. 4: 563–95.

Cramer, Christopher. 2002. "Homo Economicus Goes to War: Methodological Individualism, Rational Choice, and the Political Economy of War." *World Development* 30, no. 11: 1845–64.

Cowper-Coles, Sherard. 2012. *Cables from Kabul: The Inside Story of the West's Afghanistan Campaign*. London: Harpers.

DfID (UK Department for International Development). 2010. "The Politics of Poverty: Elites, Citizens and States." London.

DIE (German Development Institute). 2010. "Legitimacy of Future Development Cooperation. Conference Report." November (www.die-gdi.de/CMS-Homepage/openwebcms3. nsf/(ynDK_contentByKey)/MSIN-8A8CJ9/$FILE/German-Development-Institute_ Conference%20Report_Legitimacy-of-Future-Development-Cooperation_November-2010.pdf).

Fishbein, Paul, and Andrew Wilder. 2012. "Winning Hearts and Minds? Examining the Relationship between Aid and Security in Afghanistan." Feinstein International Center, Tufts University. January (http://fic.tufts.edu/publication-item/winning-hearts-and-minds-examing-the-relationship-between-aid-and-security-in-afghanistan).

Fisher, Marc. 2011. "In Tunisia, Act of One Fruit Vendor Unleashes Wave of Revolution through Arab World." *Washington Post*, March 26.

Fukuyama, Francis. 2004. *State-Building: Governance and World Order in the 21st Century*. Cornell University Press.

———. 2011. *The Origins of Political Order: From Prehuman Times to the French Revolution*. New York: Farrar, Straus, and Giroux.

Gavas, Mikaela, Fiona Davies, and Alastair McKechnie. 2013. "EU Development Cooperation in Fragile States: Challenges and Opportunities." Report PE 433.724. Brussels: Directorate-General for External Policies, European Parliament.

Ghani, Ashraf, and Clare Lockhart. 2008. *Fixing Failed States: A Framework for Rebuilding a Fractured World*. Oxford University Press.

Glennie, Jonathan, Alastair McKechnie, Gideon Rabinowitz, and Ahmed Ali. 2013. "Localising Aid: Sustaining Change in the Public, Private and Civil Society Sectors" (www.odi. org.uk/publications/7320-localising-aid-public-private-civil-society).

Hesselbein, Gabi. 2011. "Patterns of Resource Mobilisation and the Underlying Elite Bargain: Drivers of State Stability or State Fragility." Working Paper 88. Crisis States Research Centre, London School of Economics (www.lse.ac.uk/internationalDevelopment/research/crisisStates/download/wp/wpSeries2/wp882.pdf).

IFC (International Finance Corporation). 2012. "Performance Standards on Environmental and Social Sustainability." Washington.

International Dialogue on Peacebuilding and Statebuilding. 2014. "New Deal Implementation Progress Overview (October 2014)" (www.pbsbdialogue.org/newsandevents/2013/ND%20implementation%20progress%20overview_Oct%202014.pdf).

Jensen, Erik. 2008. "Justice and the Rule of Law." In *Building States to Build Peace,* edited by Charles Call and Vanessa Wyeth. Boulder: Lynne Rienner.

Khan, M. 2003. "State Failure in Developing Countries and Institutional Reform Strategies." Annual World Bank Conference on Development Economics: Europe.

Knack, Stephen. 2000. "Aid Dependence and the Quality of Governance." Working Paper 2396. Washington: World Bank.

Leo, Ben. 2013. "Is Anyone Listening? Does US Foreign Assistance Target People's Top Priorities?" Working Paper 348. Washington: Center for Global Development (www.cgdev.org/publication/anyone-listening-does-us-foreign-assistance-target-peoples-top-priorities-working-paper).

Lin, Justin Y., and Celestin Monga. 2010. "Growth Identification and Facilitation: The Role of the State in the Dynamics of Structural Change." Working Paper 5313. Washington: World Bank (http://elibrary.worldbank.org/doi/book/10.1596/1813-9450-5313).

Livingston, Ian S., and Michael O'Hanlon. 2012. "Afghanistan Index." Brookings Institution (www.brookings.edu/~/media/Programs/foreign%20policy/afghanistan%20index/index20121213.pdf).

Manuel, Marcus. 2011. "Ten Steps to Improve IMF Performance in Fragile States." London: Overseas Development Institute.

Manuel, Marcus, Sanjeev Gupta, and Paul Ackroyd. 2011. "Accelerating the Transition out of Fragility: The Role of Finance and Public Financial Management Reform." Report of sixth annual CAPE conference. London: Overseas Development Institute.

Manuel, Marcus, and others. 2012. "Innovative Aid Instruments and Flexible Financing: Providing Better Support to Fragile States." London: Overseas Development Institute.

Mavrotas, George. 2003. "Which Types of Aid Have the Most Impact?" Discussion Paper 2003/85. United Nations University, World Institute for Development Economics Research.

McKechnie, Alastair J., and Fiona Davies. 2013. "Localising Aid: Is It Worth the Risk?" London: Overseas Development Institute.

Nagl, John A. 2005. *Learning to Eat Soup with a Knife: Counterinsurgency Lessons from Malaya and Vietnam.* University of Chicago Press.

Natsios, Andrew. 2010. "The Clash of the Counter-Bureaucracy and Development." Washington: Center for Global Development.

Neustadt, Richard E., and Ernest R. May. 1986. *Thinking in Time: The Uses of History for Decision-Makers.* New York: Free Press.

North, Douglass C., John Joseph Wallis, Steven Benjamin Webb, and Barry R. Weingast. 2013. *In the Shadow of Violence: Politics, Economics, and the Problem of Development.* Cambridge University Press.

OECD. 2010a. "The State's Legitimacy in Fragile Situations." Series: Conflict and Fragility. Paris.

———. 2010b. "Resource Flows to Fragile and Conflict-Affected States." Paris.

———. 2011. "Supporting Statebuilding in Situations of Conflict and Fragility." Policy Brief. Paris.

———. 2012. "International Development Statistics, Online Database on Aid and Other Resource Flows."

OECD/DAC. 2013a. "Fragile States 2013: Resource Flows and Trends in a Shifting World." Paris.

———. 2013b. "Statistics on Resource Flows to Developing Countries." Aid statistics (www. oecd.org/dac/stats/statisticsonresourceflowstodevelopingcountries.htm).

Pritchett, Lant, and Michael Woolcock. 2004. "Solutions When the Solution Is the Problem: Arraying the Disarray in Development." *World Development* 32, no. 2: 191–212.

Pritchett, Lant, Michael Woolcock, and Matt Andrews. 2012. "Looking Like a State: Techniques of Persistent Failure in State Capability for Implementation." Working Paper 2012/63. United Nations University, World Institute for Development Economics Research (www.wider.unu.edu/publications/working-papers/2012/en_GB/wp2012-063).

Pushak, Nataliya, and Vivien Foster. 2011. "Sierra Leone's Infrastructure—A Continental Perspective." Policy Research Working Paper 5713. Washington: World Bank.

Putzel, James. 2010. *Do No Harm: International Support for Statebuilding*. Paris: OECD.

Rubin, Barnett R. 2002. *The Fragmentation of Afghanistan*. Yale University Press.

SIPRI. 2014. "SIPRI Military Expenditure Database." Stockholm International Peace Research Institute (www.sipri.org/research/armaments/milex/milex_database).

Srivastava, Vivek, and Marco Larizza. 2012. "Working with the Grain for Reforming the Public Service: A Live Example from Sierra Leone." Policy research working paper. Washington: World Bank.

Tavakoli, Heidi, Rebecca Simson, Hellen Tilley, and David Booth. 2013. "Unblocking Results: Using Aid to Address Governance Constraints in Public Service Delivery." London: Overseas Development Institute.

World Bank. 2011a. *World Development Report 2011: Conflict, Security and Development*. Washington.

———. 2011b. "Operationalizing the 2011 World Development Report: Conflict, Security, and Development." Development Committee Paper DC2011-0003. Washington.

———. 2013a. "World Bank Group Assistance to Low-Income and Conflict-Affected States: An Independent Evaluation." Independent Evaluation Group. Washington.

———. 2013b. "Liberia Public Expenditure Review Note: Meeting the Challenges of the UNMIL Security Transition." Washington.

5

A Thousand Paths to Poverty Reduction

GARY MILANTE

The global goal of poverty eradication by 2030 is an admirable endeavor for any generation, and it has fallen to ours.[1] The goal is incredibly ambitious; it means creating the means, capacity, and opportunity for approximately a billion people to climb out of extreme poverty over the next fifteen years. Ignoring reverses, life cycles, and demographic shifts and setting aside the problems associated with a poverty measurement of $1.25 a day, to achieve this goal, 181,729 people would have to move out of poverty every day for the next fifteen years. That equals 7,572 people moving out of poverty every hour.

For even the most stable developing countries with good growth, low inequality, and low inflation, this rate of poverty reduction would be ambitious. For conflict-affected and fragile countries it will be very difficult. An analysis using an extremely optimistic scenario suggests that we could expect a poverty rate of 15–20 percent in these countries in 2030; more realistic scenarios suggest poverty rates of 20–27 percent. Estimates suggest that many, if not most (38–62 percent),

The author is indebted to Suyoun Jang for tireless research assistance and support, Laurence Chandy and Homi Kharas for thoughtful guidance on the chapter's approach, Alex Thier as discussant, as well as participants at the Brookings workshop and numerous commenters on earlier versions.

1. Poverty eradication has been laid out by the World Bank and the U.S. government as a target for 2030 and will likely be adopted through the UN post-2015 Millennium Development Goals process, but for a visionary look at both the prospects and the imperative for ending poverty, see Sachs (2005).

of the world's extreme poor will live in fragile and conflict-affected states by 2030.[2] These estimates reflect the average effects of attempting poverty reduction in countries affected by conflict and instability, not the effects of such attempts in the midst of civil wars, mass killings, and displacements; interstate conflicts; and climate events (Torres and Anderson 2004). Complicating matters is the increase of income inequality in many developing countries. This is particularly evident in countries with economies noticeably divided between rural and urban and reliant on natural resources or extractives (which may benefit only a small part of the population); countries divided by terrain; and countries divided along other dimensions, like ethnicity and language. Lagging regions of nonfragile countries often exhibit the characteristics of fragile states.[3]

If we apply the figures of past poverty reduction to future poverty eradication, the future does not look bright.[4] Average progress over the past thirty years has been a drop in the poverty rate of 1 percentage point a year. Less than 25 percent of countries over this time period reduced poverty by more than 2 percentage points a year. Even if extreme poverty were to be reduced by 3 percentage points a year starting January 1, 2016, many countries still wouldn't eradicate poverty by 2030. Included among these countries are the Central African Republic, Chad, the Democratic Republic of Congo, Haiti, Liberia, Madagascar, Malawi, Mali, Mozambique, Nigeria, Rwanda, Sierra Leone, Tanzania, and Zambia. (Only 10 percent of all countries have ever achieved a reduction in poverty of 3 percentage points a year—and none has achieved it for fifteen consecutive years.) Progress on poverty eradication in the rest of the world will likely result in "poverty enclaves" in fragile and conflict-affected countries.

The next two sections introduce the rationale behind using a systems approach and what we can learn from the past to inform projections and practice. The section after that introduces the methodology of what I'm calling a thousand paths, an approach for using past experiences to inform current possibility space. The section on country examples walks the reader through three

2. Burt, Hughes, and Milante 2014, tables 1 and 2, summarize estimates and forecasts from Chandy, Ledlie, and Penciakova (2013), Edward and Sumner (2013), Ravallion (2013), World Bank (2014a), and simulations from the International Futures project. Ranges vary depending on estimation assumptions and definitions of fragility and conflict affected. Projections reported here reflect the updating of results in Burt, Hughes, and Milante using rebased purchasing power parity numbers. The International Futures modeling system was developed by Barry B. Hughes. Version 7.04 is based in the Frederick S. Pardee Center for International Futures, Josef Korbel School of International Studies, University of Denver (www.ifs.du.edu).

3. See Clemens and Moss (2005) for an insightful critique of the "unattainability" of the MDGs for many countries.

4. Note that, for the purposes of this analysis, a poverty rate below 3 percent (using the $1.25-a-day cutoff, also referred to as extreme poverty) is considered eradication, following the World Bank's definition.

cases: the Democratic Republic of Congo, Nepal, and Yemen, identifying relevant country comparators and applications from those cases, derived by applying the thousand paths approach. The chapter concludes with the results for certain countries of interest, pointing to practical applications of what we've learned in the past about poverty reduction and what can be done differently to truly eradicate poverty by 2030.

Alternate Paths

Development is a highly complex systems process, involving (at the minimum) the social, political, economic, and security spheres in a society, which are composed of diverse actors representing a variety of interests and constituencies and, often, external actors with their own interests and objectives (Anderson and others 2005). As a result, challenges and development problems, like poverty reduction, must be solved using a systems approach—policymakers must be aware of the consequences, intended and otherwise, of their actions across all of these spheres. It is not possible to approach development challenges apolitically. Sen (1999) objects to treating political and economic issues independently: "Our conceptualization of economic needs depends crucially on open public debates and discussions, the guaranteeing of which requires insistence on basic political liberty and civil rights." Sachs (2005) sums up the systems approach nicely by suggesting that "development economics" should be treated like "clinical economics," drawing a parallel to clinical medicine: "Economies, like individuals, are complex systems," so economists should "learn the art of differential diagnosis."[5]

When undertaken in fragile countries or countries affected by violence and war, development is often more complicated than even a systems problem and can become a "wicked problem." Wicked problems (Rittel and Webber 1973; Conklin 2006) have unique features that make them unsolvable in a traditional sense. Three of the most salient features of wicked problems for our present purposes are as follows:

—There is no right or wrong solution.

—There is no stopping rule for finding solutions.

—Every solution is unique—it is a one-shot solution, and without a counterfactual, we may never know if the selected solution is the best.

---

5. Sachs has five recommendations for treating development economics like clinical economics. In addition to treating economies like complex systems and applying differential diagnosis, Sachs proposes that economists approach their "patients" with a family medicine mind-set, considering the environment, neighbors, and other interests; increase monitoring and evaluation to adapt "treatment" to changing conditions; and adopt principles and ethics expected of medical practitioners, given the possible importance of development interventions.

In this chapter, I use paths to represent the possible outcomes that may result from applying various solutions. In other words, many paths are solutions, but not all solutions are "good paths." With that in mind, the three features of wicked problems suggest that, for these development challenges, there will be a number of paths that policymakers can take, many of which could be deemed as "right" in the sense that they are good solutions given the limited capacity in solution space defined by many pressing needs and limited time.

Acknowledging that we are dealing with a wicked problem is both frustrating and liberating. It is frustrating because policymakers expect experts to assess the situation and propose a single solution set, but problem solving in the realm of wicked problems implies that for every solution proposed there is an alternate solution that may be preferable on other dimensions (cost, impact, effectiveness, beneficiaries, and so on). Months and years can be spent cycling through these alternative solutions, with no clear stopping rule to end this cycling through solution space. This can be extremely frustrating to national and international actors. It is the reason people can go to endless meetings, can feel that they are working hard, yet not make any forward progress. Recognizing wicked problems can be liberating, though, allowing policymakers to acknowledge that there are many possible paths they can take, that they won't be able to identify any one path as the universal best solution, and that they will have to settle for one, using some sort of stopping rule. This rule could be a self-enforced deadline or other commitment built into the planning process.

As development experts, we're often called upon to give guidance to policymakers. Acknowledging that socioeconomic development is a systems process reminds us that the guidance will often not be a single set of directions but rather guidance about the many paths that could be taken. Much like giving directions, once we know there are many possibilities and that many of them are viable, and that we may never know whether the path taken is actually the best, then experts can be most effective by providing guidance on what paths are preferred and what paths should be avoided. This is consistent with the approach outlined in the *World Development Report 2011*, which recommends finding the "best fit" for development in a particular, fragile context: "Don't let perfection be the enemy of progress—embrace pragmatic, best-fit options to address immediate challenges" (World Bank 2011, 248). Unfortunately, economists and their econometrics often give the impression that there is a single best global solution for any development problem. Development practitioners on the ground, however, understand that the world is much more complicated than that. They explore the solution space for paths that are not only feasible but also fiscally and politically possible, given the many constraints of difficult environments.

Context and Knowledge Transfer

The advice of the OECD (2007) is to "take context as the starting point. It is essential for international actors to understand the specific context in each country and develop a shared view of the strategic response that is required." In the context of poverty reduction in the most difficult development environments, we are interested in not only what is possible but also what is probable. Because development is a complex systems process and often in these countries is a wicked problem, many solutions may be viable and may be preferable but may not be considered "best." How can experts guide policymakers toward these paths—the viable and the preferable?

Expertise is developed both in learning and practice, and poverty reduction expertise is no different. Poverty reduction experts are products of their own experiences: they've seen where development projects have worked and where they haven't. They may have biases formed by their own experiences in other countries and bring those biases to their own solution space. Of course, comparative analysis isn't new (see Arif and Farooq 2012 on China and Pakistan); we've been learning by comparing since Aristotle began categorizing the world. This chapter and the approach spelled out below is intended to supplement development expertise by extending the solution space for consideration by policymakers and experts, who might be limited by their own experiences. It uses more than 300 country periods from the last three decades, matches them to current conditions in the countries of interest, and asks: What if these countries followed the paths of their most relevant historical examples?

How can we use historical experiences to inform current estimates and practice? We know from Heraclitus that every situation is different ("One cannot step twice in the same river"). And, indeed, as development practitioners we've enshrined this as the first principle for good international engagement in fragile states and situations (OECD 2007). Yet admonitions from George Santayana and Eleanor Roosevelt remind us not to ignore past experience.[6] We would be foolish to try to reinvent the wheel, and so we have invested in building a cadre of global experts on development and poverty reduction, specialists (both national and international) who have a lifetime of experience working on these challenges. If we are to truly scale up development and eradicate poverty in the next fifteen years, then that expertise should be applied in these contexts, not ignored. How do we navigate the straits between Scylla and Charybdis, where "context matters yet knowledge transfers"?[7]

---

6. "Those who cannot remember the past are condemned to repeat it" (Santayana). "Learn from the mistakes of others. You can't live long enough to make them all yourself" (Roosevelt).

7. I thank Laurence Chandy for letting me use the clever and concise phrase he coined for this section.

Collier (2007), in his insightful *The Bottom Billion*, describes a meeting with his counterparts in the Central African Republic:

> When I settled into discussions with the government, I asked them a question that I always ask when advising a government, because it forces people to get concrete and also serves as a measure of ambition: which country did they wish to be like in twenty years' time? The group of government ministers discussed it among themselves for a while, then turned back to me with the answer: Burkina Faso. Burkina Faso! In fact, it was not a foolish answer by any means. The two countries share some important characteristics, and Burkina Faso has been doing about as well as possible given those conditions.

Development practitioners, advisers, policymakers, and experts often use other country experiences not as models to be replicated but as heuristics for identifying a path forward. Other country examples can be used as touchstones, testing whether a country can benefit from similar programs; as waypoints, demonstrating when a country is on a similar positive path; and as warning signs or cautionary tales, if a country is on a similar but undesirable path. They can offer concrete examples of where progress has been possible and how it was achieved. Other country experiences are also more useful than vague econometric estimates (which are themselves just generalizations based on aggregated country experiences). As Collier notes, comparative analysis can give insights into both the ambition and the pragmatism of the actors.

As Collier learned in the Central African Republic, such comparisons can be concrete, but of course the solution is not simply to adopt the Burkina Faso model or import any other model whole cloth. In addition to recognizing that there are many paths that countries can take for poverty reduction, we've also learned that development practice is not just about mimicking reforms, projects, and institutions that have been successful elsewhere. Andrews, Pritchett, and Woolcock (2012), at the Center for International Development at Harvard, have held a mirror up to development practice and developed the problem-driven, iterative adaptation approach, which reminds us not only to find local solutions to local problems (again, context matters) but to encourage experimentation and adaptation, scaling up successes, and allowing programs and projects to evolve over time. This is important guidance when applying the thousand paths approach: We are identifying a variety of country experiences as possible guideposts, waypoints, or cautionary tales for the country of interest, without suggesting that these paths can be mimicked to fit a certain context. In the next section, the actual methodology is described.

A Thousand Paths to Poverty Reduction

Because poverty reduction is highly context specific, estimates and averages should be starting points, not the conclusion of analysis, if they are to be at all useful to decisionmakers at the national level. Knowing how long it takes to get somewhere is not the same as having directions, yet economists often confuse regression results with policy implications. In other work, I have collaborated with the International Futures program to project what is possible (Burt, Hughes, and Milante 2014), using complex systems models that take into account the interaction of thousands of variables. Such approaches are useful for describing the range of possible worlds we could achieve by 2030, but they give little guidance on the paths that can be taken to achieve any particular outcome. The thousand paths approach uses a different, simpler tactic to increase our understanding of poverty reduction in complex development environments, attempting to operationalize the wisdom of Collier, Sen, and Sachs and other development experts by linking informative historical cases to our countries of interest.[8] Essentially, this approach compares the experiences of other countries with poverty reduction over the last three decades and identifies similar historical experiences that might inform prospective and potential exemplary experiences for current poverty reduction efforts.

The eight steps of the comparative process follow. To be accessible to all readers, technical specifics on the approach are relegated to footnotes.

First, identify the country of interest.

Second, identify a sample of historical country experiences (308 country period observations for which poverty reduction data are available).[9] When this coding process is applied to poverty data, 172 observations are identified for seventy-five countries with data using the $1.25-a-day measure; 136 observations are identified for seventy-five countries with data using national poverty rates. Each observation is defined by a country, a start year, length of period, poverty rate at the beginning of the period, and poverty rate at the end of the period. Below is an example period observation:

---

8. The title of this section is inspired by the "nomadic thought" approach of Deleuze and Guattari (1987). Although schizophrenic rationality may seem incongruous with modern economic theory, it is extremely useful when considering contingencies and various state outcomes associated with systems thinking and wicked problems.

9. Data based on both the $1.25-a-day measure and the national poverty level are used, though these two measures are treated separately in the analysis and the simulation. Simple coding rules are used to break up these data systematically, including the following: periods must be at least three years long, as many periods as possible must be identified, and periods should be as equal in length as possible.

Country	Start year	Initial poverty rate	End year	Ending poverty rate
Cambodia	1994	44.50	2004	37.69

The example shows that Cambodia achieved an average reduction of poverty of 0.7 percentage point per year for this decade. The period is relatively long compared to other sample periods because there were no additional data points between 1994 and 2004.

Third, using a number of criteria (including population, poverty level, income level, urbanization, region, and composition of the economy—agriculture and natural resource dependency), identify the most relevant historical periods for the country of interest.[10] However, because development is a systems process, it isn't always the case that all of these components interact in the same way in all country experiences to result in poverty reduction. Furthermore, the relationship between country experiences may vary by case and relevant socioeconomic conditions. For example, are countries of the same size more similar to each other than countries of the same income level? A valid case could be made for many of these indicators in identifying similarity. For this reason, the weighting for each indicator is allowed to vary across iterations.[11]

Fourth, simulate what poverty reduction might be for the country of interest if it followed paths like three randomly drawn historical experiences over the fifteen years 2015–30. Countries with higher affinity under current weighting rules are more likely to be used as examples than countries with lower affinity. Three historical country experiences are drawn, assigned random lengths

10. These indicators are chosen because of availability and basic relevance to level of poverty and rate of poverty reduction (among many others, see Alkire and Vaz 2014; Deaton 2002; Sachs 2005; and Torres and Anderson 2004). Natural resources include oil, coal, and minerals, as well as forest products and, thus, can overlap with agricultural products. Unless otherwise specified, all data are from the World Bank's World Development Indicators. Where values are missing, most recent values are used to fill gaps. Where no data exist for a series, the value is left blank. For simplicity, for each variable, a band approximately equal to one standard deviation is introduced, and the country observation for that variable is assigned a dummy value of 1 if it falls within the band for the same variable for a given country of interest.

11. Because development is a systems process, we remain agnostic on the weights associated with any particular indicator. We are attempting to explore the solution space associated with possible development paths and avoid limiting our results to cases that would be biased by preassigned individual weights. Indeed, most of the contribution of the thousand paths approach comes from allowing the weights to vary for each iteration, looking for commonalities regardless of weighting assumptions. While the weights are random for each run, they are uniformly distributed over proportional ranges. That is, the ranges for each weight are predefined: poverty rates are weighted higher than other variables. On average, similarity on poverty is weighted 50 percent higher than similarity on five other relevant variables (population, GDP per capita, urbanization, agriculture, and natural resources share of GDP). These five variables are, in turn, weighted (on average) double that of the three other variables (year of observation, statistical capacity in country, and region).

(ranging from three to seven years, all summing to fifteen), creating a country chain of three observations. The annual poverty reduction rate for each of the countries in the chain is calculated and applied to the starting poverty rate in 2015 for the country of interest. This might result in a chain like this one: four years of progress like Tanzania's progress from 2000 to 2007, followed by six years of progress like Rwanda's from 2000 to 2006, followed by five years of progress like Mali's from 1994 to 2001.

Fifth, repeat (a thousand iterations) the fourth step, creating a thousand country experience chains. Tabulate the average outcome for each chain and identify the thirty country chains most similar to the country of interest (using the weighting from the third step to measure similarity).[12]

Sixth, repeat (a thousand iterations) the fifth and sixth steps, tabulating the ten countries with most relevance and that are the most impactful in driving the highest and lowest simulated poverty reduction outcomes from all of the (million) chains. At this point, patterns in performance start to emerge, as some country experiences with high affinity are repeated in a number of chains (see figure 5-1 for an example applied to the Democratic Republic of Congo).

The ten highest affinity results with the best performance (on top) have outcomes in 2030 that range between 47 and 65 percent poverty rates. The ten highest affinity results with the worst performance (on bottom) have outcomes in 2030 that range between 67 and 85 percent poverty rates. The outer bounds are shown by dashed lines, representing the minimum and maximum outcomes for the thirty highest-affinity outcomes. For comparison purposes, the results of a pooled regression are also shown; the best outcomes are similar and crowded around the "average" regression results, while all of the worst outcomes do worse than the regression results. These results demonstrate how difficult poverty eradication in the DRC might be: no combination of similar country historical experiences would result in a poverty level less than 34 percent in 2030, and the median outcome is significantly worse than the average expected outcome of 59 percent in 2030.

The highest affinity chains for each run are captured, and the program tabulates the number of times that a historical country experience is in the top twenty highest affinity chains and also drives either a positive or a negative result (not both). Countries that show up frequently are then identified as either positive (waypoint and guideposts) country experiences or less positive (warning signs and cautionary tales) country experiences.

---

12. The affinity score is the distance measure of a particular chain, using the weights described above and normalized across runs of the model (since weights vary across iterations). Higher affinity scores are used in the next step, to identify the most relevant country chains.

Figure 5-1. *Likely Prospects for Fifteen-Year Poverty Reduction, Democratic Republic of Congo: The Good, the Bad, and the Likely, 2015–30*

Poverty rate (percent)

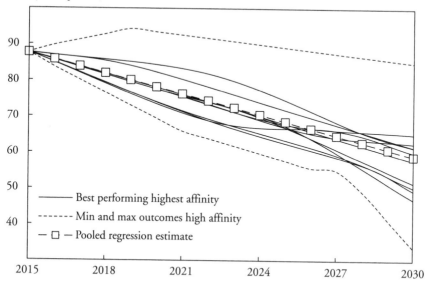

Poverty rate (percent)

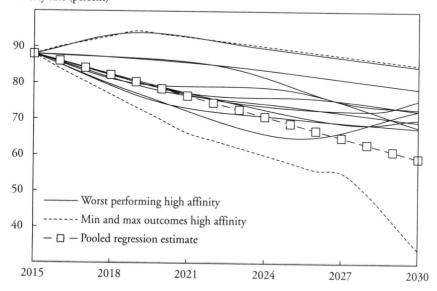

Source: Author's calculations based on thousands path methodology described above.

Seventh, run the above for both $1.25-a-day poverty measures and national poverty measures. This results in twenty country historical experiences that might be relevant touchstones or examples. These historical experiences are the starting point for inquiry into relevant examples. For the DRC, countries like Cambodia in 2004, Thailand in 1988, and Tajikistan in 2003 are relevant (based on the dimensions identified above) experiences that the DRC might want to look to for paths to follow on poverty reduction. Meanwhile, the DRC might want to avoid experiences like Nigeria's in 1986 and 1996 and Tanzania's in 1992 and 2000. Policymakers could then avoid the design and implementation of programs from these periods to avoid replicating those outcomes (that is not to say that the programs or projects might not succeed but that the implementation might be avoided).

Eighth, run the above for each country of interest. (For the results of this exercise, including trajectories and relevant country experiences, see the appendix.) This approach is not a standard regression analysis (though regression results are included in the figure and the appendix for comparison purposes). Instead, it uses modeling and simulation techniques to expand on event analysis as undertaken in Chen, Loayza, and Reynal-Querol (2008). This approach was further expanded to explore relevant experiences for Afghanistan's postconflict transition in Byrd, Milante, and Anye (2013).

In the Afghanistan paper, the post-2001 transition and the prospects for 2014 were compared to twenty-four relevant country comparators lined up against similar precipitating events (ending of conflict, signing of peace treaties, significant political transitions). The comparative analysis presents results for economic, political, governance, and social indicators over a ten-year period for countries; these are broken into three groups based on development performance. The comparative analysis provides a nuanced picture of how Afghanistan's performance since 2001 compares to similar cases and what might be reasonable and possible in a post-2014 context.

The philosophy underlying the approach is also similar to Azevedo and others (2013), who use a decomposition approach to unpack poverty reduction processes. While the methodology is much different and the thousand paths approach is much less econometrically rigorous, both eschew average effects from regressions in favor of identifying interaction effects that reflect context. Also, it should be noted that, in the sense that this chapter develops possible trajectories based on the experience of similar countries, it follows Pritchett and de Weijer (2010), who looked at historical governance reform paths for all countries since 1960 to determine what was possible and what was "fastest ever" in terms of speed of reform. The benefit of the thousand paths approach is that it allows for contextualizing the results, linking countries to experiences relevant to them. Rather than using statistics to generalize, it can be used to search

Box 5-1. *A Note on Poverty Data*

Data on poverty are notoriously difficult to use in econometric analysis. Drawn as they are from household living standards surveys, they can be quite expensive to collect, may be collected only irregularly, and may not be comparable over time. Other observers highlight the challenges associated with these data (Deaton 2002; Chandy and Gertz 2011). Fortunately, for the purposes of comparing historical episodes, rectangular panel data (same first and last year) with full coverage (no missing years) is not necessary. Like difference-in-difference approaches, we are interested in the change over time; therefore, the length of the time periods for the observations need not be the same. As long as the number reported in any year is measuring the same thing as that reported in another year (however many years later), the historical period observation can be used—and even if the levels are biased, it works as long as the bias is consistent across cases.

Data for both the $1.25-a-day and the national poverty levels reveal a great diversity. Some countries have one observation or none, other countries have ten or twenty, dating back to 1978 (India). Honduras, Thailand, Venezuela, and Brazil are the only countries with thirty or more data points for both measures of poverty from 1960 to 2012, which is to say that of more than a hundred possible observations (two data series, fifty-three years each), only four developing countries have greater than 28 percent coverage.

locally over relevant experiences or to identify country experiences that might not be immediately apparent to the policymaker or the international expert.

The exercise allows us to explore the data space around poverty reduction on a number of dimensions, described above. As might be expected from a systems problem, there is no clear universal theory for how poverty is reduced. Poverty reduction functions quite differently in different countries, in different contexts, and over time. Poverty reduction is often associated with economic growth, but it is also highly context specific, particularly if that growth is concentrated in particular sectors or regions and is in a complex development environment (Anderson and others 2005). And, often, what can be called a success depends on how poverty is defined (see box 5-1) and methodology of analysis. To demonstrate this complexity, figure 5-2 shows a Venn diagram displaying the "best" poverty reduction successes identified in three recent papers (Alkire and Vaz 2014; Azevedo, Atamanov, and Rajabov 2013; and Fosu 2010). These papers agree only on Ghana as a clear poverty reduction success.[13] While there is some

---

13. Indeed, the data used in this chapter confirm a consistent 1- to 2-point reduction in poverty in Ghana over the last twenty years.

Figure 5-2. *Poverty Reduction Successes from Three Studies*

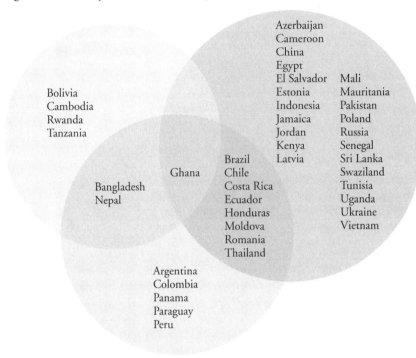

Sources: Alkire and Vaz (2014); Fosu (2010); and Azevedo and Rajabov (2013).

overlap with other analyses, the majority of cases in the Alkire and Vaz paper and the Fosu paper are not listed in Azevedo, Atamanov, and Rajabov paper.

Poverty reduction may function differently at different levels of development and may depend crucially on the sectoral composition of the economy, the type (rural/urban, for example), and the concentration (ethnic, caste, regional). Not only that, the term may mean different things in different contexts (poverty is a multidimensional concept; see Alkire and Vaz 2014). This further supports the present approach, which holds that there is no single path to poverty reduction. This is also evidenced by figure 5-3, which plots level of poverty against level of income for all of the country periods in the sample.

The size of the bubble shows the level of poverty reduction that the country managed to achieve in the period, with dark bubbles showing increases in poverty.[14] Maldives, Swaziland, China, and Uganda all managed impressive poverty reduction during periods of high economic growth, while Namibia, Tajikistan,

---

14. A number of country cases used in the analysis are left out of this figure because of dubious outcomes on poverty reduction. They include Guinea, Gambia, Niger, Mali, and Swaziland.

Figure 5-3. *Poverty Reduction, Progress across All Cases*[a]

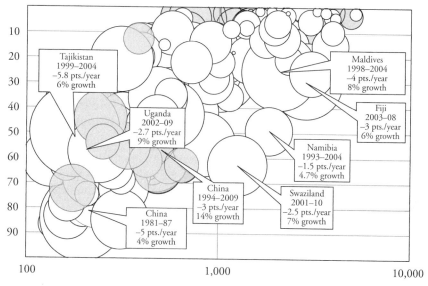

Initial poverty rate[b]

GDP per capita at beginning of period (US$)

Source: Author's calculations based on World Bank data described in note 10.

a. Boxes in chart describe select poverty reduction spells, stating (1) the country; (ii) the time period; (iii) the average annual percentage point reduction is $1.25 poverty; and (iv) the average annual economic growth rate.

b. $1.25 poverty line.

and China achieved poverty reduction with low economic growth. The figure shows that levels of poverty and income do not predetermine progress on poverty reduction, since there are equally large bubbles at the lower left corner and the upper right corner of the figure. Also, it is worth noting that a number of lower-middle-income countries, particularly at lower levels of poverty, have reversions (dark bubbles), so development is not proof against poverty relapse. Despite the consensus in the papers described above, Ghana, with a steady 1–2-point a year poverty reduction from 1992 to the present, is an average-sized bubble in the middle of the chart.

Country Examples of the Thousand Paths Approach

This section shows the results of applying the thousand paths approach to three countries—the DRC, Nepal, and Yemen—to identify experiences that might open up the solution space for policymakers and experts to inform current planning. Recall that the exercise is intended to supplement the expert assessment. The relevant comparators listed below don't reflect many important elements of poverty reduction or eradication that a full-fledged participatory poverty assessment would identify (Donnelly-Roark, Nata, and Zami 2008). For example, such an assessment would include at the minimum a thorough measurement of poverty, inequality, and social welfare, capital accumulation and assets of the poor (Moser 2006), the urban/rural divide and agricultural investments, horizontal inequalities (Narayan and Petesch 2010), natural resources and natural resource management, social safety nets, and such human development areas as health and education (World Bank 2002).

Democratic Republic of Congo

The Democratic Republic of Congo may be facing the world's most difficult poverty eradication challenge, considering its depth, scale, and complexity. Estimates suggest that, if spending for a typical Congolese household were to increase by 3 percent a year, it would take twenty-three years for that household to move out of poverty. To achieve population control, economic growth, security, governance, institutional capacity, resource mobilization, environmental protection, and decentralization, economic growth would have to average 7.2 percent a year, and 900,000 jobs a year would have to be created. To put this ambitious agenda into perspective, consider the poverty reduction strategy paper for the period 2006–11 (IMF 2007a; this was the first strategy document to identify national priorities in poverty reduction). This study identifies job creation, road construction, and education as the three priorities for poverty reduction in the DRC. Even so, delivery on just these three basic priorities was mixed during 2006–11. How then will the DRC deliver on a much wider development agenda? What paths might it take to 2030?

The DRC is a very low-income country, with an average annual GDP per capita of US$262. In a country of more than 65 million people, 87 percent (55 million people) are estimated to live on less than $1.25 a day, and 71 percent (46 million people) survive on incomes lower than the national poverty line. Food consumption accounts for 62 percent of household expenditures, demonstrating how vulnerable the population is to fluctuations in food prices. For example, the 2007–08 food crisis saw economic growth drop by 2.8 percentage points.

The DRC is one of the few countries in the world where poverty has worsened over the last two decades. In 1995 its national poverty rate was 62 percent; national planning at the time aspired to cut poverty to 37 percent by 2015, with sufficient economic growth. Persistent instability and economic contraction in the late 1990s resulted in an increase in the national poverty rate to 73 percent in 2001, but economic growth has been insufficient since 2001 to result in significant poverty reduction. In addition to missing targets on poverty reduction, the DRC has also made little to no progress in the last decade on education, child health, the fight against malaria, and sanitation, all of which speak to the capacity challenges the DRC faces with respect to delivery of large-scale public goods.

Urban poverty is a major challenge for the DRC. Approximately 35 percent of the population lives in urban areas, where six in ten households are poor, according to the national poverty line. Eradicating urban poverty would lift nearly 14 million people out of poverty. Urbanization is expected to continue and even accelerate in the future, with projections that 40 million people will live in cities by 2025, 15 million of these in Kinshasa alone.

Still, most poverty in the DRC is in rural areas (eight in ten rural households are poor, or approximately 31 million people). The rural poor are particularly difficult to reach, and they subsist with little access to markets, infrastructure, and social services. Because of ongoing conflict and instability from a variety of sources, large numbers of internally displaced persons and economic and social migrants live in rural areas. Before these people can begin to climb out of poverty, they will need to settle into a life where they feel secure and will invest their time, assets, and labor in a future. At the same time, ex-combatants number among the displaced and have little or no prospects in the formal economy; given this, they may well revert to criminality or violence if it remains an option.

The government estimates that agricultural productivity dropped by 60 percent from 1960 to 2006. Agricultural products were 40 percent of exports in 1960; now they are just 10 percent. Many of the rural poor rely on subsistence agriculture and have little access to improved methods, including fertilizers and high-yield crops. Even if they had access to these agricultural inputs, they have little or no credit to buy them. Also, without secure property rights, they have little incentive to invest in farming. Other rural poor rely on artisanal, small-scale mining, which remains largely informal, unregulated, and dangerous.

The sectoral differences in economic activity across the provinces demonstrate how poverty eradication will need to be tailored to provincial and local needs. Most of the value-added production of Bandudo, Equateur, and Sud Kivu is from agriculture. Meanwhile, the economy of Bas Congo is primarily composed of mining. As would be expected, services compose most of the economy in Kinshasa, but this is also true of Kasai Orientale and Nord Kivu. Mixed economies are present in Katanga (mining and services) and Province Orientale (agriculture and services). There is very little economic activity in Kasai Occidental and Maniema. This reflects the current composition of the economy: some of the weak sectors in these provinces may be a result of current inefficiencies, but these differences suggest that poverty reduction approaches in Maniema will be very different from those in Kinshasa if they are to be successful.

Socioeconomic conditions further complicate the poverty reduction strategy. According to government surveys, rural households headed by women have lower incidence of poverty than those headed by men; this relationship is reversed in urban households. Young households headed by apprentices or those working in the informal agricultural sector have the highest incidence of poverty. Regardless of location, larger households in the DRC are poorer, as would be expected, but population growth is such that economic growth must be greater than 6 percent (twice that of population growth, which is 3.1 percent a year) to make significant headway against poverty. More than 50 percent of the labor market is young, due to high population growth, further stressing school and health systems and the job market. Unemployment rates have been as high as 28 percent. And these effects compound each other: poor health and nutrition lead to lost productivity. HIV infection is a leading cause of morbidity and mortality in the most productive age group (twenty to forty-nine years old).

Because of sectoral and socioeconomic heterogeneity across the country, government responses are multifaceted. To promote rural development, the government has increased efforts to decentralize and empower local communities. The Ministry of Decentralization has launched local and provincial committees for the fight against poverty, but it is not clear what impact these committees have had. One program, TUUNGANE, has delivered approximately US$3.7 million in grants through community assistance to 280 villages in eastern DRC, with some positive impact. Still, the scale of the initiative is minor compared to the depth of the poverty. TUUNGANE delivered only approximately $1 per capita over two years. Similar initiatives in Sierra Leone delivered $5 per capita and, in Aceh, $20 per capita; the target for the Millennium Villages is $120 per capita (Humphreys, Sanchez de la Sierra, and van der Windt 2012). Financial initiatives proposed by the government to promote local rural development include credit unions, mutual insurance companies, microcredit cooperatives, microfinance institutions, and national and provincial agricultural and rural development funds. In response to labor challenges, the government is increasing investment in highly labor-intensive projects and programs, streamlining regulations of the private sector to facilitate private investment and jobs, promoting employment in public contracts, and empowering the Employment Promotion Unit in Public Investments.

Thus the challenges for poverty eradication in the DRC are many and complex. What paths might the DRC follow to replicate some of the successes we've witnessed in other countries over the past thirty years (table 5-1)? Of course, the DRC would like to reduce poverty as quickly as possible, but the DRC of today is nothing like Chile, Peru, or Romania were when they began their exceptional periods of poverty reduction. Using the criteria set out in the previous section,

Table 5-1. *Democratic Republic of Congo: Results from a Thousand Paths Approach*

	Poverty rate at $1.25 a day	Poverty rate at national poverty line
Most recent or estimated value	87.7	71.3
Scenario based on:		
High progress, similar countries	53.4	40.6
Low progress, similar countries	73.1	57.2
Pooled regression outcome	59.0	35.9

Warning signs and cautionary tales: Nigeria (1986, 1996), Chad (2003), Malawi (2004), Guinea-Bissau (2002)

Mixed success: Rwanda (2000, 2006), Niger (1992, 2005), Tanzania (1992, 2000), Mozambique (2003)

Guideposts and possible examples to follow: Mali (1994), Burkina Faso (1998), Tajikistan (2003), Kyrgyz Republic (2006), Cambodia (2004), Thailand (1988)

the DRC is unlike nearly all of the countries that made exceptional progress on poverty reduction identified in Azevedo and otherts (2013). Relevant cases identified through the thousand paths approach include Cambodia (2004), Thailand (1988 and 1996), Tajikistan (2003), and a cautionary tale from the last decade of development in Tanzania.

DRC Comparisons: Cambodia, Thailand, Tanzania, Tajikistan

The Cambodia of 2004 is similar to the current DRC in terms of urbanization and the importance of agriculture in the economy, so the takeaways from the Cambodian experience may be most relevant for farming provinces like Bandudo, Equateur, Province Orientale, and Sud Kivu. Over the period 2004–08, Cambodia experienced annual economic growth of nearly 12 percent and managed to convert that into poverty reduction through increased rice production and higher revenue from nonfarm businesses. The country benefited from the price shocks of 2008, which brought higher prices for its rice. In addition, the government encouraged higher rural wage rates and more salaried jobs in urban areas. The government has invested in infrastructure improvement, including roads and rural irrigation. The latter increases productivity and reduces exposure to climate vulnerabilities (drought and flooding). Early efforts at decentralization and deconcentration, like the Seila program, gave voice and local ownership to the rural poor (Anderson 2004). Farmers have benefited from a commune system that contributes to social safety nets as well as encourages collective action. Innovations like forestry groups have also helped to reduce poverty in less developed, less agricultural areas (Sunderlin 2006). Current concerns are whether this progress on poverty reduction can continue now that the low-hanging fruit (increased rice production and access to markets) has been plucked, particularly if much of the population is reliant on single-crop production and is vulnerable to climate-change-related natural disasters (FAO 2011; Thomas and others 2013; World Bank 2014b).

The Thailand of 1988 to 1996 enjoyed an average economic growth rate of 13 percent following political reforms and increasing economic openness, despite numerous changes in government. Thailand at the time was most similar to the modern DRC in terms of population size, level of poverty, and level of urbanization. Like the DRC, most of the poverty in Thailand was (and continues to be) concentrated in rural areas, in large households led by persons with low education. Initiatives like the Community Development Master Plan, the Village Fund (discussed below), One Tambon, One Product (OTOP), the Poverty Alleviation Project, the People's Bank, and Health for All have contributed to the success of poverty reduction in Thailand over the past two decades. Current concerns are that poverty reduction will stall as income inequality continues to increase, but the challenges associated with sharing prosperity in modern Thailand do not impact the relevance of Thailand's past experiences, two of which are described in more detail below.

Population growth was quite high in Thailand in 1988, despite the population policy launched in the 1970s. The growth rate began to fall in the late 1980s and early 1990s, thanks to economic growth and innovative outreach like that of the private, nonprofit Population and Community Development Association, which introduced contraceptives and family planning and moved into water access and agricultural lending, including "pig banks" and "rice banks," where loans were made in animals and commodities at the beginning of the season and repaid at the end of the season. Development initiatives (combined with population policy that follows the Buddhist maxim, *Many children make you poor*) have been very effective in reducing poverty (Frazer 1992; Lindelow, Hawkins, and Osornprasop 2012). Indeed, according to Warr (2011), "Since 1988, the largest absolute decline in poverty incidence occurred in the poorest [rural] region of the country, the northeast."

Recent innovations in microfinancing through local credit associations have also contributed to increased income and expenditure, lifting millions out of poverty in Thailand since 2001. The Village Fund was launched, pledging a million baht to every village and urban community in Thailand. Over four years, nearly US$8 billion was loaned to nearly 80,000 villages and urban communities, through average loans of only around $500. This represented 99 percent of all villages; 98 percent of the original funds were distributed in just four years. Most of the borrowers were poor and agricultural. Interestingly, there was little crowding out of borrowing from the national agricultural bank. Participants in the program experienced increases in income (of 1.9 percent), in expenditure (of 3.3 percent) and in ownership of durable goods (of 5 percent). One should be careful drawing implications for the DRC from this experience, however: per capita income in Thailand in the early 2000s was an order of magnitude greater than per capita income in the DRC, so the capacity to roll out such a program may not be present in the DRC. Still, the microfinance experience in Thailand demonstrates that it is possible for a central government to deliver at scale to local village credit associations (Boonperm, Haughton, and Khandker 2009).

The experience in Tanzania, from 2000 to 2007, serves as a possible cautionary tale for the current DRC as it considers paths forward. The Tanzania of 2000 was very similar to the modern DRC in terms of income levels, urbanization, portion of the economic product derived from agriculture, and poverty levels. During this period, Tanzania experienced economic growth, but progress on poverty reduction was small, primarily attributed to drought and global food and oil price shocks (Wedgwood 2007; Treichel 2005; Minot 2008; International Monetary Fund 2011). The poor identify the main obstacles to overcoming poverty as lack of access to land for agriculture, lack of nonfarm business opportunities, lack of salaried employment, lack of opportunities for trading, and lack of agricultural inputs. Poverty escapes are uncommon, but where people have succeeded, life histories reveal that upward mobility is often linked to assets, personal loans, and access to infrastructure (Higgins 2010).

As in the DRC, a large number of Tanzania's poor are engaged in artisanal and small-scale mining. This income can help reduce poverty and diversify income sources and so protect against shocks. However, in Tanzania as in the DRC, people are often unable to obtain a formal mineral claim or use a claim, particularly if government policy is directed toward large-scale mining interests and remains unconnected to local planning, regulation, and enforcement (Fisher and others 2009). Because of the value of small-scale mining as an alternative source of income for the poor, particularly in rural Africa, it has been suggested that artisanal mining and agricultural policy should be integrated, rather than handled independently, to promote local development (Hilson 2013). Despite, or perhaps because of, these challenges to poverty reduction in Tanzania, and given the proximity and the value of regional cooperation on some issues related to artisanal mining and rural development, a DRC-Tanzania knowledge exchange may be fruitful in identifying best practice for both.

The poverty reduction experience of Tajikistan in 2003–07 is a positive example that the DRC could aspire to replicate. Tajikistan in 2003 resembled the modern DRC in terms of poverty, income, and urbanization. While the composition of its economy is quite different from that of the DRC (it relies primarily on cotton and aluminum production), Tajikistan does, like the DRC, have rich mineral deposits that remain largely untapped due to difficult terrain and infrastructure gaps. Tajikistan has enjoyed a decade of solid growth, low inflation, and effective political reforms, despite being landlocked and in a difficult neighborhood. Much of the poverty reduction and recent progress in socioeconomic development has been attributed to catch-up growth following a decade of instability. Tajikistan faces similar constraints to the DRC's in terms of weak infrastructure and difficult terrain that make development in rural areas difficult (IMF 2012b).

There have been multiple drivers of poverty reduction in Tajikistan over the last decade, namely labor earning, infrastructure investments (roads in mountainous regions), and improved access to markets and the regional economy (Azevedo, Atamanov, and Rajabov 2014; Jones, Black, and Skeldon 2007). Tajikistan, like the DRC, has high rates of population growth for the region. While remittances are very high, there is mixed evidence on its poverty reduction (Buckley and Hoffman 2012). One area of undisputed success is in increased labor earnings. At least some of this success can be attributed to vocational education programs that have been launched countrywide. These training centers are intended to replace outmoded production methods, teach new skills, and close skill gaps among the rural population—helping them to, for example, add beekeeping or animal breeding to their productive activities and therefore to diversify their sources of income. These initiatives were coupled with microcredit training and institutions and have resulted in higher incomes and less rural-to-urban migration (Wallenborn 2009).

Nepal

Unlike the DRC, Nepal has managed to escape large-scale civil conflict and has enjoyed relative peace in the last decade.[15] While Nepal is extremely poor (with a GDP per capita of US$690), it has managed to consolidate its recent stability into economic growth (3–5 percent per year since 2000) and poverty reduction (the $1.25-a-day headcount reduced from 68 percent in 1996 to 25 percent in 2010). Many MDGs have been or will be met, including targets on primary

---

15. The poverty profile is based on IMF (2007b) as well as supplementary information from BTI (2014), IFAD (2014a, 2014b), and other sources as noted.

education, education gender parity, and under-five mortality. Still, there is much to be done; state institutions are often ineffective, security remains a concern in many areas, the constitutional reform process remains unresolved, and identity issues and grievances loom large in the national dialogue. With uncertainty about the constitutional process, various agreements and legislation have been stalled (these include decentralization, rural infrastructure, power, economic zones, and investment). Many of the processes of the state function ad hoc, key positions remain unfilled, and political contests are often resolved through political forums and street actions.

As long as the political issues remain unresolved, the hard-won gains on economic growth and poverty reduction risk being overturned. Poor law and order remains a key concern among investors and the population. Over the last few years, food prices have risen rapidly (approximately 15 percent annually), and much of the population (an estimated 3.5 million people) remains food insecure. Increases in food prices contribute to inflation of around 9.5 percent a year. Most poor households are large, with low levels of education and high rates of illiteracy, and with no (or small) land and asset holdings. Agriculture is often too small to meet subsistence requirements: 70 percent of households have holdings of less than one hectare, following a legacy of feudal land ownership. In addition, agricultural productivity is low because of lack of machinery, knowledge of new techniques, inputs, and extension services. The government's twenty-year Agricultural Perspective Plan (introduced in 1995) focused on staple crops (rice, wheat, maize, and potatoes) in the relatively fertile Terai plains and on higher value agricultural products (such as honey and silk) in the hills and mountains.

Alongside economic growth and reduced poverty, inequality has been increasing in Nepal. Much of the poverty is horizontal, determined by caste, ethnicity, and gender; the government is attempting to address these inequalities through a poverty reduction strategy that promotes gender equality and social inclusion along with improved governance and accountability. Women were officially recognized in the Interim Constitution as a social group along with Dalits, Madhesis, Muslims, and Janajatis. And the National Planning Commission has introduced special programs to assist these groups, including reserved seats for political representation and inclusion in the civil service.

While the unemployment rate is low, underemployment (those working less than nineteen hours a week) remains high. Remittances from Nepalis working in India, Malaysia, Saudi Arabia, and the UAE are a vital source of income, totaling over US$5 billion in 2012 (Lokshin, Bontch-Osmolovski, and Glinkaya 2010). According to government estimates, 80 percent of these remittances are used for daily consumption and another 7 percent is used for loan repayments; less than 3 percent is used for investment. Because Nepal is land-locked, the government has placed a priority on connectivity to local and global markets for goods, which would also help to reduce vulnerability to food price shocks and climate-change-related disasters.

Three successful Nepali initiatives are worth noting:

—The Rural Access Improvement and Decentralization Project has rehabilitated and maintained more than 4,000 kilometers of rural roads, constructed more than a hundred trail bridges, and constructed small community infrastructure, resulting in a 20 percent increase in trips and cutting average trip times by 75 percent on project roads.

—Community forestry is an important part of poverty eradication and local governance (Acharya and Acharya 2006). An innovative response to the small landholder problem described above is the Hills Leasehold Forestry and Forage Development Project. From 1989 to 2003, the project established public forest land leases for nearly 7,500 hectares, reaching 1,700 groups and more than 12,000 households. This resulted in increased livestock, due to availability of feed and forage, income increases, reduced time collecting forage and firewood (particularly for women), and increased school attendance, as there was less need for children to herd grazing animals. Because the local communities signed extended leases, biodiversity increased and environmental degradation decreased, as the tenants had a vested interest in maintaining the lands (IFAD 2014b; Brett, Ohler, and Tamrakar 2004).

—A third successful Nepali project is the Poverty Alleviation Fund (PAF). Evaluations of the PAF find that two-thirds of the households have an income increase of at least 15 percent, with an average increase of 82 percent in real terms. The PAF has covered forty of the poorest districts, with more than 500,000 households. More than half of the fund went to Dalit and Janajati households. This program is associated with a 10 percent decrease in food insufficiency and a 6 percent increase in school enrollment (IFAD 2014a).

Nepal is a good example of a formerly conflict-affected state that has made the transition out of violent conflict, has reaped the benefit of bounce-back growth following a long period of instability, and is now attempting to consolidate those gains through reform. Like many countries following a similar path, it is focusing on some of the bottlenecks in the economy that are persistent obstacles to development, particularly for those populations that were most aggrieved or were made the most vulnerable by, and during, the conflict.

Nepal Comparisons: Kyrgyz Republic, Tanzania, Uganda

The poorest of the former Soviet satellites, Kyrgyz Republic weathered a difficult decade of political transition, enjoyed a decade of strong economic growth, and nearly halved poverty in the period 2005–08 (ILO 2008). However, the evidence is mixed whether Kyrgyz Republic represents a positive example or a cautionary tale: following social unrest in 2008 and other economic shocks, recent growth has not translated into poverty reduction. Much poverty is chronic and remains concentrated in rural oblasts, owing to difficult terrain, low skills levels, and lack of employment opportunities (World Bank 2013; IMF 2014). As Kyrgyz Republic is landlocked and highly dependent on fuel (Kyrgyz Republic imports 90 percent of all consumed carbons) and food imports, recent shocks have been particularly painful to the most vulnerable (typically the urban poor) and threaten to reverse recent progress, as in Nepal. Like Nepal, remittances feature heavily in the poor's coping mechanisms—much of the skilled labor in Kyrgyz Republic migrates for construction work to Russia and other central Asian states.

While there are social safety nets in place, many subsidies are regressive, with richer households benefiting disproportionately over poorer households in Kyrgyz Republic. However, the monthly benefit for poor families strongly targets the lower quintile and serves as an example of a well-targeted safety net (World Bank 2013). While much of the poverty is rural, planners face increasing challenges in accommodating informal settlements in urban areas and pressures to deliver public services to the poor. Kyrgyz Republic suffers from small agricultural landholdings, much like Nepal does: 97 percent of the farms are at or below the size necessary for subsistence. Recent analysis suggests that, because of these small landholdings, outdated production methods, and incomplete credit markets, Kyrgyz Republic has a US$400 million deficit in machinery. Initiatives that have encouraged the organization of local credit associations to finance long-term machinery lease and service at low cost have been effective in increasing local agricultural output (Guadagni and Fileccia 2009). Such credit mechanisms may be something for Nepal to consider so as to increase its access to the machinery necessary to scale up agricultural production.

Like the DRC, Tanzania also serves as a cautionary tale for Nepal. Tanzania of 1992 and of 2000 are most relevant to current Nepal in terms of population size, urbanization, and composition of the economy (reliance on agriculture and natural resources). However, levels of income are higher and levels of poverty are lower in present-day Nepal than in historic Tanzania. Fuel and food price shocks have set back poverty reduction in Tanzania as they have in Nepal. Like Nepal, a large proportion of the poor in Tanzania is rural and struggle with the challenges of subsistence-level agriculture on small landholdings (Ellis 2003; Minot 2008). Tanzania has experienced mixed success in promoting agricultural development through foreign land investment for biofuels. Slow reform on land titling and investments has led to numerous disputes between large biofuel companies and small landholders (OECD 2013). Nepal would do well to learn from Tanzania's mistakes regarding land reform rather than repeat them.

Just as Nepal is now addressing the aftershocks of its civil war, Uganda continues to face repercussions from the civil war of the 1980s. These have resulted in persisting insecurity in the north of the country, demonstrating that, after a conflict, it can take decades to consolidate the peace in a fragile state. Of course, Uganda has for the most part entrusted peace consolidation to the executive authority, while Nepal continues to use the constituent assembly process, so care should be taken in importing lessons. Despite that, many of the issues are similar in both countries, including a large, poor population, highly dependent on agriculture and small landholdings and a similar level of urbanization. Uganda has enjoyed an 8 percent economic growth rate for much of the early 2000s, yet agriculture grew at only 1 percent per year over the same period, while the share of the labor force engaged in agriculture increased from 66 percent in 2002 to 75 percent in 2006. The current government development plan is promoting agricultural growth, with a target of 2.8 percent growth a year. This growth is expected to reduce the poverty rate to 26 percent (IMF 2010).

Uganda is often cited as a positive example of programs designed for and targeted on pro-poor growth. Uganda's Poverty Action Fund (PAF—not to be confused with Nepal's Poverty Alleviation Fund) dramatically increased financing, particularly focusing new resources made available through debt relief on rural infrastructure, including roads and water, education and health, all of which increased significantly in the early 2000s. However, recently the PAF's usefulness and future have been called into question, as the government pivots toward a pro-growth strategy (Hickey 2013). As a virtual poverty fund that is run through the government budget, the PAF was intended to use country systems and build capacity for delivery, which it has certainly done, increasing in size from 18 percent of the government budget in 1998 to 35 percent in 2002. As more donors participated through debt relief and a multidonor trust fund, financing increased from US$100 million a year in 1998 to US$400 million a year in 2005. With expansion, more programs were included in the PAF, and pro-poor criteria were introduced. This has resulted in an entrenchment of the PAF as a dual process within government systems, with its own monitoring and evaluation and, possibly, perverse incentives on spending. It is suggested that this has created new fragilities in the rural economy, as the rural poor are now highly reliant on government financing, funded by aid. Analysis suggests that a more flexible design could yield the positive outcomes of PAF yet allow a similar program to adapt over time, avoiding entrenchment and the introduction of perverse incentives (Canagarajah and Williamson 2008).

Recent progress on poverty reduction is also evidenced by direct cash transfer programs in northern Uganda. Relatively small transfers (by aid standards), approximately equal to a year's income, result in large returns for the rural poor—increasing employment hours nearly 20 percent and earnings by nearly

50 percent, especially among women. Many of these returns are due to asset purchases and the taking on of new trades, like metalworking and tailoring, suggesting that it is not the skills that are missing locally but credit and fiscal space. Analysis suggests that the success of these unconditional cash transfers is largely due to lifting credit constraints among the rural poor, particularly youth and women. Those who experience the largest gains are those initially with the least capital and credit. Unfortunately, there is little evidence of a relationship between these transfers and increases in social cohesion or collective action (Blattman, Fiala, and Martinez 2013).

Interestingly, in addition to the country experiences discussed above and those identified in the appendix, Nepal also appears as its own good example based on its poverty alleviation during the period 1996–2011. This is a double-edged finding, as it suggests that little has changed on key economic indicators (composition of the economy, urbanization), but it also attests that Nepal has already managed to achieve a significant drop in its poverty rate. As its own positive pathway, Nepal might consider scaling up successful programs like the leasehold land arrangements and the poverty alleviation fund, while adapting them to current contexts and incorporating lessons learned from other countries, like those above.

Yemen

The last thorough assessment of poverty in Yemen was undertaken by the World Bank in 2007, four years before the Arab Spring would pass through the region. At the time, there was already violence in the Saada province in the north, a breakaway region in the south, attacks by al Qaeda, and political opposition and protests in the capital in the lead-up to the Arab Spring. Yemen was (and remains now) the poorest country in the Arab region and the Middle East, and there was little prospect that it would achieve the goal of halving poverty by 2015. The national poverty rate was 35 percent, representing about 7 million people. These were mostly rural, and indeed significant improvements had been made among the urban poor in the period leading up to the Arab Spring. Disparities between regions and clans were in fact a source of grievance. With the change in government and the concomitant instability and political paralysis, little progress has been made on socioeconomic development in the last decade. A national dialogue is now identifying ways forward, but it is unlikely that the poverty situation has improved since the World Bank assessment. Yemen faces—in addition to poverty and instability— environmental challenges, including diminishing water reserves.

Yemen Comparisons: Ecuador, Egypt, Uganda, Thailand

Ecuador's recent poverty reduction of a percentage point a year may be a good path to consider for modern Yemen. In 2000 Ecuador had a similar level of poverty and per capita GDP to Yemen. In both Ecuador and Yemen, agriculture is only a small percentage of total economic output, yet much of the poverty is in rural areas, particularly among the indigenous people of Ecuador. This situation might find parallels in some of the clans of Yemen. Oil is an important export for both Ecuador and Yemen. Recent growth has been in construction, agriculture, commerce, and manufacturing, suggesting an increasing diversification of the economy, a path the government of Yemen has indicated it would like to replicate. It is most notable that Ecuador responded to the global financial crisis by applying some of its oil wealth to a countercyclical stimulus of nearly 5 percent of GDP, increasing housing loans and microcredit programs. A cash transfer program called Bono de Desarrollo Humano directly targeted young mothers, the elderly, and the disabled and reduced poverty while increasing education and health outcomes (Ray and Kozameh 2012). Much of the poverty reduction is attributed to growth in nonlabor incomes, reflecting the importance of safety nets and transfers (Maurizio 2013).

Egypt since 2000 represents a cautionary tale for modern Yemen. Over the last decade, Egypt was similar to current Yemen in terms of GDP per capita, level of urbanization, and composition of the economy (in both agriculture and natural resources as percent of GDP). Obviously, the scale of the poverty challenge differs—there are almost as many poor in Egypt as there are people in Yemen. Yet the environmental and regional pressures are similar, and both could benefit from introducing or expanding price information systems, credit and insurance markets, and geographic targeting of social safety nets (IFPRI 2014). One area that Yemen could watch closely in Egypt is reform of the government's subsidies programs. In 2013 these programs (for fuel, gas cylinders, bread, and ration cards) cost the government nearly US$16 billion annually. Recent efforts to rein in government spending and balance the budget include reforming these subsidy programs for both scale and efficiency.

While subsidies are an important part of the social safety net for millions of Egyptians, corruption is such that, due to black market wheat sales and leakages in the system, little actually gets to the poor (Coleman 2012). As the government reforms these programs in attempts to reduce costs, prices for basic consumables will likely go up, leading to unrest (IRIN 2013). These reform processes were initiated under President Morsi and his Muslim Brotherhood administration, and so it is unclear how and if they will continue. Still, as Yemen contemplates its own safety nets and subsidy programs, it could learn from the history of implementation and attempts at subsidy reform in Egypt, including addressing sequencing and targeting issues, possibly introducing nutrition programs and transfers as substitutes for or complements to subsidies.

In addressing rural poverty, modern Yemen might also look to recent Uganda, which was similar in 2005 on measurements of poverty, population size, urbanization, and reliance on natural resources. The lessons from Uganda's experiences with the Poverty Action Fund and cash transfers programs described above (with respect to Nepal) might also be applicable to Yemen (Canagarajah and Williamson 2008). Such interventions may be particularly relevant in less developed regions in the Houthi north and targeted at more vulnerable or previously alienated populations. Indeed cash transfers and other redistributive elements might work as substitutes for or complements to reformed subsidies programs (see Fiszbein, Kanbur, and Yemtsov 2014 for a discussion of targeting efficiency and budgetary adequacy in social protection programs).

Perhaps one of the most interesting cases for comparison with modern Yemen is 2004 Thailand. This is not an immediately apparent comparison, but Thailand had the same level of national poverty, same degree of urbanization, and a similar composition of the economy (agricultural and natural resource production) as Yemen, making Thailand of 2004 perhaps more similar than many modern countries in the Middle East. Certainly the 2006 coup and political instability in Thailand that followed affected poverty reduction and economic performance, similar to the current era of transition in Yemen. And of course, the recent coup in Thailand raises doubts about the Thai experience as a path for others to follow (notwithstanding the link between the coup and the political impasse). But despite the political uncertainty, pro-poor initiatives like the Village Fund were adopted early by the relatively marginalized and vulnerable communities of Thai Muslims in the south, providing access to reliable and low-cost credit for the poor, replacing high-cost informal and illegal financing (Boonperm, Haughton, and Khandker 2009, Taneerananon 2014).

Summary of the Thousand Paths Approach

Once the thousand paths approach has been run for all countries, some countries emerge as consistently positive examples and others as consistently negative examples. Of course, a country experience can be both a positive example for one country and a cautionary tale for another, reflecting the reality that countries are both at different points in development and have different ranges of what is possible or realistic. Some results for the frequency with which countries appear most as waypoints (positive examples) or cautionary tales (negative examples) are shown in table 5-2. The numbers in the table indicate the number of times a country appears in the thousand paths analysis for all countries of interest. Some countries in this table emerge as cautionary tales for a number of other countries; for example, Côte d'Ivoire, Mauritania, and Guinea are cautionary tales for a number of countries. Further study could unpack specific country success stories, starting with the countries that are positive examples for a number of other countries; for instance, can whatever Cambodia, Cameroon, Pakistan, Kyrgyz Republic, and Tajikistan have been doing right be replicated elsewhere?

Table 5-2. *Positive Waypoints and Cautionary Tales, Incidence of "Examples" for Fifteen Countries*

	Positive examples	Negative examples
Kyrgyz Republic	28	0
Cambodia	35	2
Tajikistan	22	0
Senegal	18	5
Cameroon	26	11
Pakistan	29	14
Ghana	12	8
Rwanda	12	8
Mozambique	9	13
Mali	10	15
Guinea	19	39
Mauritania	7	23
Honduras	0	24
Philippines	0	25
Côte d'Ivoire	0	51

Additionally, it is important to note that some countries often appear as cautionary tales for themselves. Examples include Côte d'Ivoire, Guinea-Bissau, Mozambique, Nigeria, Zambia, Lesotho, and Malawi. These countries have already experienced periods of ineffective poverty reduction and, because the underlying conditions have not changed, risk repeating these experiences in the future. This reflects possible fragility traps, in which underlying structural constraints do not lead to investment and do not change because of a slow growth, poor governance equilibrium trap, as identified in Andrimihaja, Cinyabuguma, and Devarajan (2011).

Conclusions

The thousand paths approach asks, "What is a country like now and what could it be like in fifteen years?" It is intended to meet the demand of practitioners who don't have time to understand complex econometrics and interactive marginal effects. It moves all of the conditional averages (how initial conditions are related to each other) forward to the country cases themselves, rather than burying them in coefficients and statistical significance. No doubt there are other ways (thousands?) to run similar types of exercises that are illustrative over large data sets and a number of examples, and perhaps this approach will help to spur the development of such approaches.

This approach attempts to reconcile twin dangers: overgeneralizing (particularly dangerous in complex development environments like fragile countries) and ignoring previous knowledge. This is nothing new: skillful development practitioners have been adapting lessons they have learned in other contexts for years. A good example of this is recent knowledge exchanges between Mozambique and the DRC, hosted by the Congolese Poverty and Inequality Observatory (IMF 2013). This approach simply facilitates wider comparisons across a larger sample of successes and failures. This approach is not a menu or a cookbook; the poverty reduction specialist would do well to draw from the suggested country cases with care. Even if other country experiences evoke new solutions, the solution space available to policymakers will still be restricted by the capacity and the willingness to implement these solutions (Anderson and others 2005). The appendix is intended as a useful reference for the practitioner, to quickly leaf through, find a country of interest, and compare the expected outcomes with those of similar countries. The appendix yields six quick estimates of poverty rates in 2030 for each country: good cases, bad cases, and estimates from a regression for both measures of poverty.

It is hoped that this chapter properly conveys the complexity and wickedness of the challenge in poverty eradication in fragile states. Better understanding of this challenge would move us collectively toward more strategic and comprehensive poverty reduction strategies. Too often, current strategies are designed by national actors with international guidance as if they are a shopping list. This shopping list approach—often the result of horse trading by development sectors, line ministries, and other actors—promotes the false belief that if country *A* simply built *X* kilometers of road, connected *Y* households to the Internet, and enrolled *Z* children in primary education, development would be achieved. And development experts are not to blame for this result—they've personally witnessed the positive impact of roads and education in other development experiences. But knowing a path is a good path is not the same as knowing it is the appropriate path. To succeed, we must understand that development at the strategic and generational level over the next fifteen years, is much more complex than just the sum of sectoral wish lists, and indeed, in conflict-affected and fragile countries, it is often a wicked problem, where the first- or second-best solution may not be possible.

Beyond informing practice—say through design of a poverty reduction strategy, a needs assessment, or other national visioning exercise—the findings from this approach could also inform practice on the ground. Perhaps multilateral agencies hiring poverty specialists should consider hiring experts with relevant experiences from other countries that have been successful. Indeed, increasingly, national actors are not waiting around for donors to bring this expertise to bear on their challenges: they are inviting specialists and experts from other relevant countries through poverty labs and other initiatives. Not one of the people who managed to eradicate extreme poverty in the United States or Denmark is alive today, but there are thousands of people who have succeeded in their lifetime in significantly reducing poverty in Cambodia, Kyrgyz Republic, Uganda, and Bhutan. And while the cases are unique, the expertise is transferable.

Looking more broadly than poverty, other inquiries using something like the thousand paths approach could examine other processes we know to be path dependent. These might include transition processes (peace processes and institutional reform processes) as well as paths for development (composition of the economy, access to markets, investment in education, for example). Optimally, this would be presented in a dynamic form, through an online interface, where policymakers could identify the country of interest, identify their variables of interest and their weighting for similarities, and explore policy and outcome space with relevant comparator historical experiences. This would help policymakers and practitioners, both national and international, better introduce scenario building into their planning.

While the results of this analysis are presented around extreme poverty and national poverty levels, the results should not be interpreted as an endorsement of conceptualizing poverty reduction or eradication as threshold or unidimensional measures. Like all indicators, poverty rates are useful mathematical simplifications for measurement and simplify the modeling in this chapter, but such blunt measures cannot reflect the depth of poverty or local conceptualizations of what poverty means. (For a thicker conceptualization of poverty, see among many others, Narayan, Pritchett, and Kapoor 2009; Narayan and Petesch 2010; and Alkire and Vaz 2014.) This understanding extends to the policy implications for donors as well; all too often "successes" will be measured by how poverty reduction has moved people above a threshold, has contributed to economic growth, or has become sustainable, rather than by the depth and degree to which poverty has been alleviated (Barder 2009). As Barder further notes, mundane interventions like immunizations and bed nets remain chronically underprovided, despite their proven cost effectiveness, because they require long-term commitments—demonstrating how we as development actors follow political targets rather than the deeper objectives of poverty alleviation.

Finally, the reader should remember that the estimates from this analysis are based on past performance (like any statistical analysis) and that this is no guarantee of future performance. Learning from successes and adapting them to new contexts and the challenges that lie before us are our best hopes for improving the poverty reduction rates of the last fifty years over the next fifteen years.

While the prospects of poverty eradication by 2030 are not optimistic, we've never had the skill sets, international expertise, resources, ingenuity, and global agenda directed at poverty eradication that we are now assembling. Admittedly, there will be new challenges—including those associated with climate change, geopolitical events, demographic shifts (urbanization and population growth), and the movement of people—that will test the limits of our ability to reduce poverty globally. Because of the depth of poverty, the vulnerability of those near the poverty line to fall back into poverty, and the compounded effects of growth over time, heavy, early investment will be the most effective in making and securing gains against poverty. If we hope to achieve the noble goal of poverty eradication by 2030, and "bend the arc of history," as President Kim of the World Bank has asked us to, we will need to apply every possible trick we've learned about development over the last fifty years to navigate the thousands of paths before us.

Appendix
Possible Outcomes and Country Waypoints for High-Poverty, Low-Progress Countries

Country	Poverty measure	Most recent value	Simulated outcomes from thousand paths approach		Pooled regression outcomes
			High-progress similar countries	Low-progress similar countries	
Benin	$1.25/ day	47.3	18.0	39.2	23.3
	National poverty level	33.3	24.2	43.0	27.1
Burundi	$1.25/ day	81.3	47.4	68.0	50.0
	National poverty level	66.9	36.7	51.1	42.7
Central African Republic	$1.25/ day	62.8	42.7	56.6	40.7
	National poverty level	62.0	32.3	48.8	39.8
Comoros	$1.25/ day	46.1	19.5	36.2	29.5
	National poverty level	44.8	26.5	39.0	34.3
Democratic Republic of Congo	$1.25/ day	87.7	53.4	73.1	59.0
	National poverty level	71.3	40.6	57.2	35.9
Côte d'Ivoire	$1.25/ day	23.8	5.8	19.6	9.1
	National poverty level	42.7	17.3	35.6	29.8
Eritrea	$1.25/ day	20.0	0.6	9.0	6.3
	National poverty level	69.0	34.2	57.1	44.6
Guinea-Bissau	$1.25/ day	43.3	24.2	39.5	27.9
	National poverty level	69.3	43.9	64.8	40.9
Haiti	$1.25/ day	61.7	25.2	47.4	11.9
	National poverty level	78.0	51.8	74.2	36.2

Countries with warning signs and cautionary tales	Countries with mixed success	Waypoints and guideposts: countries offering possible examples
Côte d'Ivoire (1985, 1993), Dominican Republic (2000), Zambia (1998), Timor-Leste (2001), Pakistan (1999)	Guinea (2003), Mauritania (1987, 1993), Mali (2001, 2006)	Senegal (1991, 2001), Indonesia (1993), Albania (2002), India (2005), Georgia (2003), Cameroon (1996)
Burundi (1992), Niger (1992), Guinea-Bissau (2002)	Burkina Faso (1994, 1998), Guinea (1991, 2007), Malawi (1998, 2004), Mozambique (2003), Uganda (1992, 2000), Rwanda (1985, 2000, 2006)	Mali (1994), China (1981), Tajikistan (2003), Cambodia (2004)
Georgia (2003), Zambia (1998), Tanzania (1992), Moldova (2003), Guinea-Bissau (2002)	Mali (2001, 2006), Ghana (1988, 1992), Guinea (2003, 2007)	Kyrgyz Republic (2005, 2006), Pakistan (1997), Senegal (1991), Malaysia (1970), Cambodia (2004)
Sierra Leone (2003), Mauritania (1987, 2000), Guinea-Bissau (1991), Mozambique (2003), Timor-Leste (2001), Côte d'Ivoire (1993, 2002)	Mali (2001, 2006), Ghana (1988, 1992)	Nepal (2003), Guinea (2003), Bhutan (2003), Indonesia (1993), Namibia (2004), Cameroon (1996), India (2005)
Nigeria (1986, 1996), Chad (2003), Malawi (2004), Guinea-Bissau (2002)	Rwanda (2000, 2006), Niger (1992, 2005), Tanzania (1992, 2000), Mozambique (2003)	Mali (1994), Burkina Faso (1998), Tajikistan (2003), Kyrgyz Republic (2006), Cambodia (2004), Thailand (1988)
Morocco (1991), Mauritania (2000), Côte d'Ivoire (1993, 2002), Kenya (1997), Colombia (1991), El Salvador (2005), Egypt, Central Arab (2005)	Cameroon (1996, 2001)	Armenia (2001), Kyrgyz Republic (2005), Bhutan (2003), Bolivia (2000), Romania (2000), Kazakhstan (2001), Belarus (1998), Albania (2002)
Guinea (1994, 2003, 2007), Honduras (2001), Sri Lanka (1991), Côte d'Ivoire (1993), Kenya (1997), Pakistan (1999), Mozambique (2003)		Kyrgyz Republic (2005, 2006), Tajikistan (1999, 2003, 2004), Senegal (1994), Ecuador (2000), Botswana (1986), Cambodia (2004)
Sierra Leone (1990), Lesotho (1987), Guinea-Bissau (1991, 2002), Malawi (2004)	Cambodia (1994, 2004), Ghana (1988, 1991, 1992), Mauritania (1993, 2000), Guinea (1991, 2003, 2007)	Pakistan (1997), Kyrgyz Republic (2006), Mozambique (1996), Mali (2001), Rwanda (2006)
Zambia (1991, 1998, 2004), Dominican Republic (2000, 2002), Honduras (2001, 2005), Côte d'Ivoire (1985)	Senegal (1991, 2005), Tunisia (2000, 2005)	Gambia, The (1998), Rwanda (2006), Mali (2001), Indonesia (1993), Azerbaijan (2001), Peru (2004), Kyrgyz Republic (2006), Ukraine (2002)

Country	Poverty measure	Most recent value	Simulated outcomes from thousand paths approach		Pooled regression outcomes
			High-progress similar countries	Low-progress similar countries	
Kenya	$1.25/ day	43.4	12.2	28.0	22.7
	National poverty level	45.9	23.9	39.6	35.5
Liberia	$1.25/ day	83.8	40.7	77.1	47.5
	National poverty level	63.8	44.4	62.6	36.5
Madagascar	$1.25/ day	81.3	23.7	61.7	40.8
	National poverty level	75.3	47.0	63.4	47.2
Mauritania	$1.25/ day	23.4	4.5	18.2	14.1
	National poverty level	42.0	10.1	26.3	22.8
Mozambique	$1.25/ day	59.6	27.0	48.2	31.3
	National poverty level	54.7	30.9	44.8	37.2
Nigeria	$1.25/ day	68.0	50.1	70.6	41.3
	National poverty level	46.0	22.7	41.1	26.8
Papua New Guinea	$1.25/ day	35.8	7.1	22.2	14.7
	National poverty level	37.5	11.8	26.9	11.4
Zambia	$1.25/ day	74.5	30.2	60.6	36.6
	National poverty level	60.5	20.1	45.6	36.5
Zimbabwe	$1.25/ day	20.0	7.0	22.6	4.2
	National poverty level	72.3	48.2	68.3	44.6

Countries with warning signs and cautionary tales	Countries with mixed success	Waypoints and guideposts: countries offering possible examples
China (1987), Lesotho (1987), Mali (2006), Mauritania (1987, 2000), Malawi (2004), Mozambique (2003), Côte d'Ivoire (1993), Guinea (2003)	India (1994, 2005)	Senegal (1991), Cambodia (2004), Pakistan (2002), Nepal (2003), Kenya (1992), Rwanda (2006), Ukraine (2002)
Zambia (1998, 2004), Mauritania (2000), Armenia (1996), Nigeria (2004), Guinea-Bissau (2002), Malawi (2004)	Guinea (1991, 2003), Mozambique (2003)	Kyrgyz Republic (2005, 2006), Pakistan (1987), Malaysia (1970), Cambodia (2004), Rwanda (2006), Ghana (1992)
Indonesia (1984), Tanzania (1992), Zambia (1991, 2004), Côte d'Ivoire (2002), Honduras (2001), Sri Lanka (1991), Guinea-Bissau (2002)	Guinea (1991, 1994, 2003)	Niger (2005), Senegal (1991), Nepal (2003), Kenya (1992), Kyrgyz Republic (2006), Rwanda (2006), Mozambique (1996), Thailand (1988), Tajikistan (2003)
Paraguay (1990, 2003), South Africa (1993), Georgia (2003), Côte d'Ivoire (1993, 2002), Honduras (1986), Congo (2005)		Bhutan (2003), Armenia (2001), Fiji (2003), Tajikistan (2004), Costa Rica (1981), Azerbaijan (2001), Kazakhstan (2001), Mongolia (2010), Pakistan (2002), Moldova (2007)
Nigeria (2004), Zambia (1998, 2004), Kenya (1997), Malawi (2004), Mozambique (2003), Guinea (2003, 2007), Mauritania (2000)	Mali (2001, 2006)	Nepal (2003), Uganda (2002), China (1994), Niger (2005), Pakistan (1997), Cameroon (1996), Rwanda (2006), Kyrgyz Republic (2006), Cambodia (2004)
Zambia (1998, 2004), Nigeria (1986), Mauritania (2000), Côte d'Ivoire (1993, 2002)	Ecuador (1987, 1994, 2000), Guinea (2003, 2007)	Senegal (1991), Niger (2005), Bhutan (2007), Bangladesh (2000), Kazakhstan (2001), Albania (2002), Pakistan (2002), Cameroon (1996)
Lesotho (1987), Rwanda (1985), Burundi (1992), Ecuador (1994), Tanzania (2000), El Salvador (2005), Ethiopia (1995), Timor-Leste (2001)	Cambodia (1994, 2004), Pakistan (1999, 2002)	Tajikistan (1999), Bhutan (2003), Kenya (1992), Mongolia (2010), Paraguay (2007), West Bank and Gaza (2007), Kazakhstan (2001)
Yemen (1998), Zambia (2004), Swaziland (2001), Senegal (2005), Honduras (2001)	Guinea (1991, 2003, 2007), Cameroon (1996, 2001), Ecuador (1987, 1994, 2000)	Niger (2005), Mozambique (2003), Kazakhstan (2001), Cambodia (2004), Botswana (1986), Tajikistan (2003)
Honduras (1986, 2001, 2005), Bolivia (1991), Côte d'Ivoire (1985, 1993, 2002)	Ecuador (1994, 2000)	Cameroon (1996), Tajikistan (2003, 2004), Armenia (2001), Burkina Faso (2003), Kyrgyz Republic (2006), Botswana (1986)

References

Acharya, Krishna, and Sushanta Acharya. 2006. "Small Wood-Based Enterprises in Community Forestry: Contributing to Poverty Reduction in Nepal." Paper prepared for the International Conference on Managing Forests for Poverty Reduction. Ho Chi Minh City, Viet Nam, October 3–6.

Alkire, Sabina, and Ana Vaz. 2014. "Reducing Multidimensional Poverty and Destitution: Pace and Patterns." Oxford Poverty and Human Development Initiative.

Andersen, Henny. 2004. *Cambodia's Seila Program: A Decentralized Approach to Rural Development and Poverty Reduction.* Washington: World Bank.

Anderson, Michael, Andrew Branchflower, Magui Moreno-Torres, and Marie Besancon. 2005. "Measuring Capacity and Willingness for Poverty Reduction in Fragile States." PRDE Working Paper 6. London: DFID.

Andrews, Matt, Lant Pritchett, and Michael Woolcock. 2012. "Escaping Capability Traps through Problem-Driven Iterative Adaptation." Working Paper 240. Washington: Center for Global Development.

Andrimihaja, Noro Aina, Matthias Cinyabuguma, and Shantayan Devarajan. 2011. "Avoiding the Fragility Trap in Africa." Policy Research Working Paper 5884. Washington: World Bank.

Arif, G. M., and Shujaat Farooq. 2012. "Poverty Reduction in Pakistan: Learning from the Experience of China." Monograph. Islamabad: Pakistan Institute of Development Economics.

Azevedo, Joao Pedro, Aziz Atamanov, and Alisher Rajabov. 2014. "Poverty Reduction and Shared Prosperity in Tajikistan." Policy Research Working Paper 6923. Washington: World Bank.

Azevedo, Joao Pedro, Gabriela Inchauste, Sergio Olivieri, Jaime Saavedra, and Hernan Winkler. 2013. "Is Labor Income Responsible for Poverty Reduction? A Decomposition Approach." Policy Research Working Paper 6414. Washington: World Bank.

Barder, Owen. 2009. "What Is Poverty Reduction?" Working Paper 170. Washington: Center for Global Development.

Blattman, Chris, Nathan Fiala, and Sebastien Martinez. 2013. "Generating Skilled Self-Employment in Developing Countries: Experimental Evidence from Uganda." *Quarterly Journal of Economics* 129, no. 2.

Boonperm, Jirawan, Jonathan Haughton, and Shahidur Khandker. 2009. "Does the Village Fund Matter in Thailand?" Policy Research Working Paper 5011. Washington: World Bank.

Brett, Nigel, Frits Ohler, and Jamuna K. Tamrakar. 2004. "Case Study: Providing the Poor with Secure Access to Land in the Hills of Nepal." Paper prepared for the Shanghai Poverty Conference on Scaling up Poverty Reduction. Shanghai, May 25–27.

BTI (Bertelsmann Stiftung's Transformation Index). 2014. "Nepal Country Report."

Buckley, Cynthia, and Erin Trouth Hofmann. 2012. "Are Remittances an Effective Mechanism for Development? Evidence from Tajikistan, 1999–2007." *Journal of Development Studies* 48, no. 8.

Burt, Alison, Barry Hughes, and Gary Milante. 2014. "Eradicating Poverty in Fragile States: Prospects of Reaching the 'High-Hanging' Fruit by 2030." Policy Research Working Paper 7002. Washington: World Bank.

Byrd, William, Gary Milante, and Kenneth Anye. 2013. "A New Approach to Understanding Afghanistan's Transition." Peaceworks 87. Washington: United States Institute of Peace.

Canagarajah, Sudharshan, and Tim Williamson. 2008. "Uganda's Virtual Poverty Fund: Pro-Poor Spending Reform." Washington: World Bank.

Chandy, Laurence, and Geoffrey Gertz. 2011. "Poverty in Numbers: The Changing State of Global Poverty from 2005 to 2015." Policy Brief 2011-01. Brookings Institution.

Chandy, Laurence, Natasha Ledlie, and Veronika Penciakova. 2013. "The Final Countdown: Prospects for Ending Extreme Poverty by 2030." Policy Brief 2013-04. Brookings Institution.

Chen, Siyan, Norman Loayza, and Marta Reynal-Querol. 2008. "The Aftermath of Civil War." *World Bank Economic Review* 22, no. 1.

Clemens, Michael, and Todd Moss. 2005. "What's Wrong with the Millennium Development Goals?" Washington: Center for Global Development. September.

Coleman, Isabel. 2012. "Reforming Egypt's Untenable Subsidies." Expert brief. New York: Council on Foreign Relations.

Collier, Paul. 2007. *The Bottom Billion: Why the Poorest Countries Are Failing and What Can Be Done about It*. Oxford University Press.

Conklin, Jeffrey. 2006. *Dialogue Mapping: Building Shared Understanding of Wicked Problems*. Chichester: Wiley.

Deaton, Angus. 2002. "Is World Poverty Falling?" *Finance and Development* 39, no. 2.

Deleuze, Gilles, and Felix Guattari. 1987. *A Thousand Plateaus: Capitalism and Schizophrenia*. Translated by Briam Massumi. University of Minnesota Press.

Donnelly-Roark, Paula, Georges Tshionza Nata, and Moise Zami. 2008. "Participatory Poverty Assessments in Conflict-Affected Countries." Washington: World Bank.

Edward, Peter, and Andy Sumner. 2013. "The Geography of Inequality: Where and by How Much Has Income Distribution Changed since 1990?" Working Paper 341. Washington: Center for Global Development.

Ellis, Frank. 2003. "Livelihoods and Rural Poverty Reduction in Tanzania." *World Development* 31, no. 8.

FAO (Food and Agriculture Organization). 2011. "Cambodia and FAO: Achievements and Success Stories." Rome.

Fisher, Eleanor, Rosemarie Mwaipopo, Wilson Mutagwaba, David Nyange, and Gil Yaron. 2009. "The Ladder That Sends Us to Wealth: Artisanal Mining and Poverty Reduction in Tanzania." *Resources Policy* 34, nos. 1, 2.

Fiszbein, Ariel, Ravi Kanbur, and Ruslan Yemtsov. 2014. "Social Protection and Poverty Reduction: Global Patterns and Some Targets." *World Development* 61.

Fosu, Augustin Kwasi. 2010. "Growth, Inequality, and Poverty Reduction in Developing Countries: Recent Global Evidence." Background paper. Paris: OECD.

Frazer, Edorah. 1992. "Thailand: A Family Planning Success Story." *In Context* 31.

Guadagni, Maurizio, and Turi Fileccia. 2009. "The Kyrgyz Republic: Farm Mechanization and Agricultural Productivity." Country highlights paper. Washington: World Bank/FAO.

Hickey, Sam. 2013. "Beyond the Poverty Agenda? Insights from the New Politics of Development in Uganda." *World Development* 43.

Higgins, Kate. 2010. "Escaping Poverty in Tanzania: What Can We Learn from Cases of Success?" Paper prepared for conference on chronic poverty. Chronic Poverty Research Centre. Manchester. September.

Hilson, Gavin. 2013. "Picks and Ploughs: Revitalizing Local Economic Development in Rural Sub-Saharan Africa." Proceedings. Crawford Fund 2013 Annual Conference. Canberra.

Humphreys, Macartan, Raul Sanchez de la Sierra, and Peter van der Windt. 2012. "Social and Economic Impacts of Tuungane." Paris: OECD.

IFAD (International Fund for Agricultural Development). 2014a. "Enabling Poor Rural People to Overcome Poverty in Nepal." Factsheet. Rome.

———. 2014b. "Fighting Poverty and Land Degradation with Leasehold Agreements." Country brief. Nepal.

IFPRI (International Food Policy Research Institute). 2014. "Building Resilience to Conflict through Food Security Policies and Programs: An Overview." Conference Brief 3. Vision 2020. Washington.

ILO (International Labor Organization). 2008. "Kyrgyzstan: Economic Growth, Employment, and Poverty Reduction." New York: United Nations Development Program.

IMF (International Monetary Fund). 2007a. "Democratic Republic of the Congo: Poverty Reduction Strategy Paper." Country Report 07/330. Washington.

———. 2007b. "Nepal: An Assessment of the Implementation of the Tenth Plan/PRSP." Country Report 07/176. Washington.

———. 2010. "Republic of Uganda, National Development Plan." Country Report. Washington.

———. 2011. "Tanzania: Poverty Reduction Strategy Paper. Country Report 12/118. Washington.

———. 2012a. "Republic of Congo: Poverty Reduction Strategy Paper." Country Report 12/242. Washington.

———. 2012b. "Republic of Tajikistan: Poverty Reduction Strategy Paper." Country Report 12/33. Washington.

———. 2013. "Republic of Congo: Growth and Poverty Reduction Strategy Paper, Second Generation." Washington.

———. 2014. "Kyrgyz Republic: Poverty Reduction Strategy Paper." Country Report 14/247.

IRIN (Integrated Regional Information Networks). 2013. "Briefing: Egypt Rethinks Its Subsidy System for the Poor." News Report 98031. Nairobi.

Joliffe, Dean, Peter Lanjouw, Shaohua Chen, Aart Kraay, Christian Meyer, Mario Negre, Espen Prydz, Renos Vakis, and Kyla Wethil. 2014. "A Measured Approach to Ending Poverty and Boosting Shared Prosperity: Concepts, Data, and the Twin Goals." Policy Research Report 91350. Washington: World Bank.

Jones, Larissa, Richard Black, and Ronald Skeldon. 2007. "Migration and Poverty Reduction in Tajikistan." Working Paper C11. Brighton, UK: Development Research Centre on Migration, Globalisation, and Poverty.

Lindelow, Magnus, Loraine Hawkins, and Sutayut Osornprasop. 2012. "Government Spending and Central-Local Relations in Thailand's Health Sector." Health, Nutrition, and Population discussion paper. Washington: World Bank.

Lokshin, Michael, Mikhail Bontch-Osmolovski, and Elena Glinkaya. 2010. "Work-Related Migration and Poverty Reduction in Nepal." *Review of Development Economics* 14, no. 2.

Maurizio, Roxana. 2013. "Current Trends in Poverty Reduction in Latin America: The Role of Labour Market and Social Protection." Poverty Brief 14. Bergen, Norway: CROP.

Minot, Nicholas. 2008. "Are Poor, Remote Areas Left Behind in Agricultural Development: The Case of Tanzania." *Journal of African Economics* 17, no. 2.

Moser, Caroline. 2006. "Asset-Based Approaches to Poverty Reduction in a Globalized Context." Global Economy and Development Working Paper 01. Brookings Institution.

Narayan, Deepa, and Patti Petesch. 2010. *Moving out of Poverty: Rising from the Ashes of Conflict.* Washington: World Bank.

Narayan, Deepa, Lant Pritchett, and Soumya Kapoor. 2009. *Moving out of Poverty: Success from the Bottom Up.* Washington: World Bank.

OECD. 2007. "Principles for Good International Engagement in Fragile States and Situations." Paris.

———. 2013. "Overview of Progress and Policy Challenges in Tanzania." In *OECD Investment Policy Reviews: Tanzania 2013.* Paris.

Pritchett, Lant, and Frauke de Weijer. 2010. "Fragile States: Stuck in a Capability Trap?" Background paper. Washington: World Bank.

Ravallion, Martin. 2013. "How Long Will It Take to Lift One Billion People out of Poverty?" Policy Research Working Paper 6325. Washington: World Bank.

Ray, Rebecca, and Sarah Kozameh. 2012. "Ecuador's Economy since 2002." Washington: Center for Economic Policy and Research.

Rittel, Horst, and Melvin Webber. 1973. "Dilemmas in a General Theory of Planning." *Policy Sciences* 4.

Sachs, Jeffrey. 2005. *The End of Poverty.* New York: Penguin.

Sen, Amartya. 1999. *Development as Freedom.* New York: Anchor.

Sunderlin, William D. 2006. "Poverty Alleviation through Community Forestry in Cambodia, Laos, and Vietnam: An Assessment of the Potential." *Forest Policy and Economics* 8, no. 4.

Taneerananon, Sirirat. 2014. "Ultra-Poor Revisited: A Case of Southern Thailand." *International Journal of Social, Management, Economics, and Business Engineering* 8, no. 4.

Thomas, Timothy S., Tin Ponlok, Ros Bansok, Thanakvaro De Lopez, Cathy Chiang, Nang Phirun, and Chhim Chhun. 2013. "Cambodia Agriculture: Adaptation to Climate Change Impact." Working Paper 1285. Washington: International Food Policy Research Institute.

Torres, Magui Moreno, and Michael Anderson. 2004. "Fragile States: Defining Difficult Environments for Poverty Reduction." PRDE Working Paper 1. London: DfID.

Treichel, Volker. 2005. "Tanzania's Growth Process and Success in Reducing Poverty." Working Paper 05/35. Washington: International Monetary Fund.

Wallenborn, Manfred. 2009. "Skills Development for Poverty Reduction: The Case of Tajikistan." *International Journal of Educational Development* 29, no. 6.

Warr, Peter. 2011. "Thailand's Development Strategy and Growth Performance." UNU-WIDER Working Paper 2011/02. Helsinki.

Wedgwood, Ruth. 2007. "Education and Poverty Reduction in Tanzania." *International Journal of Educational Development* 27, no. 4.

World Bank. 2002. *A Sourcebook for Poverty Reduction Strategies.* 2 vols. Washington.

———. 2007. *Yemen Poverty Assessment.* 4 vols. Washington: World Bank and United Nations Development Program.

———. 2011. *World Development Report 2011: Conflict, Security, and Development.* Washington.

———. 2013. "The Kyrgyz Republic: Poverty Update, 2011." Report 78213-KG. Washington.

———. 2014a. "Global Monitoring Report 2014/5: Ending Poverty and Sharing Prosperity." Washington.

———. 2014b. "Where Have All the Poor Gone? Cambodia Poverty Assessment 2013." Country Study 4545. Washington.

PART II

Creating Jobs

6

Agriculture's Role in Ending Extreme Poverty

JOHN W. McARTHUR

Roughly 80 percent of the world's extremely poor people are estimated to live in rural areas, and around 60 percent work in agriculture (Olinto and others 2013).[1] As of late 2014 it remains difficult to translate these proportions into precise headcount figures, but a reasonable approximation suggests that approximately 800 million extremely poor people live in rural areas, and more than 600 million are engaged in agriculture.[2] Amidst the world's extraordinary recent declines in extreme poverty, the foremost last mile challenge of

I thank Steven Rocker, Brandon Routman, Madelyn Swift, and especially Julie Biau and Christine Zhang for outstanding research assistance. Comments from Gero Carletto, Uma Lele, Marcus Manuel, Steve Radelet, and other Last Mile conference participants were extremely helpful. Laurence Chandy and Homi Kharas provided countless generous suggestions and insights, especially pertaining to global measures of extreme poverty.

1. These researchers estimate that, as of 2010, 77.8 percent of people living on less than US$1.25 a day were living in rural areas and that 62.8 percent of the same group worked in agriculture.

2. In April 2014 the International Comparison Program published new global purchasing power parity (PPP) estimates for the baseline year 2011 (ICP 2014). These estimates represented a major update from the 2005 PPP benchmarks previously used to calculate extreme poverty globally. In October 2014 the World Bank announced that the new PPP data would not be incorporated into global poverty estimates until 2015. In the meantime, the World Bank and IMF's October 2014 *Global Monitoring Report 2014/2015* estimate that 1.01 billion people were living in extreme poverty as of 2011. The figures in this paragraph thus represent best estimates, with acknowledged imperfections, based on available data.

Figure 6-1. *Official Development Assistance to Agriculture, Forestry, and Fishing, 1985–2012*[a]

ODA (US$ billion)

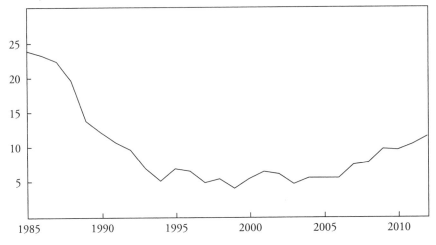

Source: OECD (2014).
a. Data presented in constant 2012 US$.

eliminating extreme poverty by 2030 will be to ensure that these farm families and local economies can reliably boost their incomes for the long term.

Fortunately, agriculture has enjoyed a renaissance of attention and global public resources in recent years. This has included a doubling of official development assistance for the sector since 2006, reversing a trend of long-term decline and stagnation. However, as shown in figure 6-1, the recent aid levels of more than US$11 billion still represent (in real terms) less than half the amount invested in agriculture in the mid-1980s. By historical standards the renaissance remains in its early stages.

Increased attention to agriculture has also reinvigorated debates around the sector's role in economic growth and poverty reduction. At one end of the spectrum, scholars downplay agriculture and instead emphasize the "pull" mechanisms of higher value added sectors like manufacturing and services as the key to economic growth. At the other end of the spectrum, scholars emphasize the central role agricultural productivity plays in feeding societies, keeping real wages competitive, and freeing up labor for other sectors.

In its simplest form, the last mile for agriculture hinges on whether it is easier to boost incomes on the farms where 600 million poor people already live or to create long-lasting, higher-wage, off-farm jobs to support all the same people. One central theme of this chapter is that each economy's agricultural circumstances are unique. But the bulk of the evidence suggests that—absent natural resource discoveries or other windfall opportunities—agriculture will continue to play a pivotal role in eliminating extreme poverty.

The Last Mile's Agricultural Contours

Aggregate assessments of agriculture can be difficult to penetrate because the term *agriculture* itself encompasses such a vast array of crop dynamics, ranging from storable grains like rice and maize, to highly perishable foods like apples and tomatoes, to stimulants like coffee and tea, to industrial inputs like cotton and rubber. Some crops are planted and harvested on a seasonal basis. Others grow on trees that only become productive after multiple years required to reach minimum maturity. And unlike other economic sectors, agricultural technologies are not universally diffusible, since most plants grow under particular conditions. This is the opposite of, say, mobile phone technology, which applies consistently across the planet. Coffee and rubber grow only under certain circumstances. Wheat is broadly diffusible across temperate but not tropical climates. Maize has localized germinating properties that are extremely difficult to transplant across geographies—quite different, for example, from paddy rice's relative adaptability across similar growing environments.

Since agriculture's products, investments, and local system dynamics are highly plant and place specific, the first step in a last mile strategy is to specify the relevant locations. While potentially significant revisions to global poverty estimates remain pending at the time of writing, a reasonable proxy of country-by-country poverty levels can be taken from purchasing power parity (PPP) adjusted "actual individual consumption" (AIC) data that were published in April 2014 (ICP 2014). The indicator assesses the mean value of household-level goods and services consumed in each country, incorporating both those purchased in private markets and those provided through government programs. The AIC measure is thereby a useful approximation of average material well-being in each country, even if it does not provide information on within-country distributions.

Table 6-1 lists the sixty-one countries with reported annual AIC of less than $5,000 in PPP terms. Note that this is not a comprehensive list of countries with extreme poverty, since AIC data are not available for all economies, such as Afghanistan, Papua New Guinea, South Sudan, and Timor-Leste. Nonetheless, for the purposes of this chapter the countries with relevant AIC data are separated into two categories. Group 1 includes the poorest thirty-one economies, with AIC of less than $2,000. These countries have a population of 550 million altogether. Group 2 includes twenty-eight countries with AIC values between $2,000 and $5,000. These countries have an aggregate population of 1.2 billion.

Table 6-1. *Annual Actual Individual Consumption (AIC per Capita),*
Sixty-One Focus Countries, 2011
US$ (PPP)

Group 1: AIC per capita < $2,000			Group 2: $2,000 < AIC per capita < $5,000		
Country	Region	AIC per capita	Country	Region	AIC per capita
Dem. Rep. Congo	SSA	447	Nigeria	SSA	2,075
Liberia	SSA	606	Mauritania	SSA	2,089
Comoros	SSA	621	Bangladesh	SA	2,138
Burundi	SSA	648	Ghana	SSA	2,242
Niger	SSA	719	Myanmar	EAP	2,273
Guinea	SSA	789	Cambodia	EAP	2,277
Central African Rep.	SSA	869	Cameroon	SSA	2,297
Mozambique	SSA	890	Sudan	SSA	2,309
Guinea-Bissau	SSA	928	Lao PDR	EAP	2,341
Burkina Faso	SSA	953	Lesotho	SSA	2,524
Ethiopia	SSA	979	Yemen	MENA	2,762
Malawi	SSA	1,006	Vietnam	EAP	2,991
Tanzania	SSA	1,029	Tajikistan	ECA	3,025
Mali	SSA	1,047	Sao Tome and Principe	SSA	3,340
Togo	SSA	1,193	Kyrgyz Republic	ECA	3,506
Sierra Leone	SSA	1,194	Nicaragua	LAC	3,587
The Gambia	SSA	1,221	Bolivia	LAC	3,661
Rwanda	SSA	1,293	Honduras	LAC	3,748
Madagascar	SSA	1,332	Maldives	SA	3,883
Zimbabwe	SSA	1,349	Pakistan	SA	3,926
Uganda	SSA	1,390	Bhutan	SA	3,998
Benin	SSA	1,473	West Bank and Gaza	MENA	4,070
Chad	SSA	1,476	Morocco	MENA	4,309
Congo	SSA	1,513	Angola	SSA	4,319
Haiti	LAC	1,688	Philippines	EAP	4,490
Djibouti	MENA	1,719	Cape Verde	SSA	4,747
Zambia	SSA	1,778	Indonesia	EAP	4,805
Nepal	SA	1,848	Equatorial Guinea	SSA	4,916
Senegal	SSA	1,923			
Kenya	SSA	1,937	*Uniquely large countries*		
Côte d'Ivoire	SSA	1,979	India	SA	3,023
			China	EAP	4,331

Source: ICP (2014).
    EAP = East Asia Pacific; ECA = East Central Asia; LAC = Latin America/Caribbean; MENA = Middle East North Africa; PPP = purchasing power parity; SA = South Asia; SSA = Sub-Saharan Africa

China and India would fall into group 2 based on their AIC levels, but in light of their uniquely large populations, they are listed separately.

Some geographical trends stand out in table 6-1. Twenty-eight of the thirty-one group 1 countries are located in sub-Saharan Africa, according to World Bank regional designations. The other three are Djibouti, Haiti, and Nepal. Group 2 countries are more geographically dispersed, including six in East Asia Pacific, four in South Asia, three in Latin America and the Caribbean, three in the Middle East and North Africa, two in Central Asia, and ten in sub-Saharan Africa.

Table 6-2 presents a range of population-weighted average economic and demographic indicators for the two groups of countries. Group 1 is estimated to have half of its population living in extreme poverty, compared to slightly less than a quarter of group 2. Although many individual countries' headcount assessments have been questioned under the outgoing 2005 PPP standards, the weighted aggregates should provide a reasonable overall approximation of the extent of poverty in the two groups. One implication is that the total number of people living in extreme poverty is similar across the two categories, at roughly 275 million in group 1 and roughly 320 million in group 2.

Other similarities between the groups are limited. Group 2's average per capita income is four times higher than group 1's. Moreover, group 2's real annual per capita growth rates averaged 4.0 percent between 2000 and 2010, compared to only 2.5 percent for group 1. Over the course of a decade this implies a cumulative 20-percentage-point difference in economic outcomes. The population in the lower AIC group is also significantly more rural, averaging 72 percent, while that portion is 58 percent in group 2.

Group 1's average fertility rates are dramatically higher, at 5.3 children per woman, compared to 3.3 in group 2. This helps drive group 1's much faster overall population growth, at 2.7 percent annually, compared to 1.7 percent for group 2. At first glance a 1-percentage-point variation in population growth might not appear significant, but it represents the difference between a population doubling in only twenty-six years and one doubling in forty-one years. Fast population growth in the poorest countries helps to explain why they also have the fastest urban growth rate, at 4.2 percent a year, much higher than even China's 3.2 percent.

The table 6-2 indicators for China and India reflect rapidly shifting economies. Poverty estimates for these two countries of course have major consequences for global aggregates, especially the 25 percent figure indicated for India, which might be as much as 10 percentage points too high (Chandy and Kharas 2014). Other indicators highlight structural differences between the two countries, in addition to the well-known fact of China's much faster long-term economic growth rates. In particular, India's population remains significantly more rural,

Table 6-2. *Population-Weighted Averages by Country Group: Economic and Demography Indicators*[a]

Group	N	(1) Total population, 2010 (million)	(2) AIC per capita ($ 2011 PPP)	(3) Extreme poverty rate in 2011 (2005 PPP) (%)	(4) GNI per capita, 2010 ($ 2011 PPP)	(5) Growth in GNI per capita, annual rate, 2000-10 (LCU %)	(6) Population in rural areas (%)	(7) Total fertility rate, 2010 (%)	(8) Population growth rate, 2010 (%)	(9) Urban growth rate, 2010 (%)
1	31	551	1,185	50	1,289	2.5	72	5.3	2.7	4.2
2	28	1,180	3,363	24	5,015	4.0	58	3.3	1.7	2.9
India	1	1,210	3,023	25	4,589	6.0	69	2.6	1.3	2.4
China	1	1,340	4,331	6	9,187	9.9	51	1.6	0.5	3.2

Sources: World Bank (2014a, 2014c); ICP (2014).
a. Not all countries have data for all variables.

even with China's policy restrictions on rural-urban labor mobility. India also has a much higher population growth rate. This is linked to a higher total fertility rate, although that has declined to 2.6 children per woman on average. India's urban population is also growing quickly, at 2.4 percent annually, although much slower than urban growth in China and than the averages for groups 1 and 2.

Table 6-3 presents a variety of population-weighted agricultural indicators. The first fundamental distinction across country groups lies in the labor force structures. More than 70 percent of group 1 countries' employment is in agriculture, compared to 42 percent of group 2 countries. Agriculture's overwhelmingly dominant role in group 1 underscores the fact that, if those countries are to eliminate extreme poverty in the near future, they require either a major boost in agriculture incomes or a major boost in off-farm rural income opportunities.

Agricultural value added per worker also differs tremendously between the two groups, averaging $399 for group 1 and $1,592 for group 2, nearly four times higher. This is a product of much slower recent growth rates for group 1, at 1.2 percent, versus 3.7 percent for group 2. It is something of a puzzle why China's value added per worker remains so low relative to its much higher average incomes, but this might be linked to low domestic crop prices and excess rural labor due to migration restrictions.

The poorest economies are expanding agricultural area harvested at the fastest rate. The thirty-one group 1 countries saw farmland increase by an average of 30 percent over only ten years. This compares to 16 percent for group 2, 9 percent for India, and 7 percent for China. The differences are likely driven partly by differences in population growth rates and partly by group 1's persistently low yields per hectare, which are reflected in column 5. Group 1 countries still have average cereal yields of only 1.5 tons a hectare, compared to 3.2 for group 2, 2.7 for India, and 5.5 for China. From 2000 to 2010, yields grew at an average of more than 2 percent annually across both groups, a positive signal of general progress although not enough to close the gap between countries.

The variation in yields is highly correlated with differences in input intensity. Group 1 countries still have average fertilizer use of a minuscule 13 kilograms a hectare, which is functionally close to zero. Meanwhile, group 2 countries are an order of magnitude more intensive in their fertilizer usage, at 134 kilograms a hectare on average. These are both significantly lower than India's use of 179 kilograms a hectare and China's 548. Column 8 provides a potential explanation for low fertilizer use (discussed further below). Group 1's average value of indexed distance to fertilizer plants suggests some of the world's highest transport costs in accessing fertilizer. The distance values can be roughly interpreted as cost-adjusted kilometers across land and sea. The final column shows the limited average presence of cash crops across the full sample, although group 2 has roughly twice the relevant share of area harvested as group 1.

Table 6-3. *Population-Weighted Averages by Country Group: Agricultural Indicators*[a]

Group	N	(1) Employment in agriculture, 2010 (%) FAO	(2) Agricultural value added per worker, 2010 ($ 2011)	(3) Agricultural value added per worker, annual growth, 2000–10 (%)	(4) Growth in area harvested, 2000–10 (%)	(5) Cereal yield, 2010 (t/ha)	(6) Growth in cereal yield, annual rate, 2000–10 (%)	(7) Fertilizer use, 2010 (kg/ha)	(8) Distance to fertilizer (index)	(9) Area harvested to cash crops (%)
1	31	71	399	1.2	30	1.5	2.1	13	9,650	8
2	28	42	1,591	3.7	15	3.2	2.2	134	6,030	15
India	1	54	723	2.0	9	2.7	1.6	179	3,235	10
China	1	36	764	4.3	7	5.5	1.5	548	4,695	6

Sources: FAO (2014); World Bank (2014a); McArthur and McCord (2014); National Bureau of Statistics of China (2013).
a. Not all countries have data for all variables.

Academic Debates

Debates on agriculture's role in economic growth and poverty reduction have a long tradition in the economics literature, dating back at least to the seminal arguments advanced by Johnston and Mellor (1961) and Schultz (1968). Scholars like de Janvry and Sadoulet (2009, 2010) argue that agriculture's role in promoting growth in other sectors was widely forgotten or misunderstood in the latter part of the twentieth century, and causality was too often misinterpreted to take place in the other direction. Analysts have apportioned responsibility for agriculture's neglect across a variety of stakeholders, ranging from developing country governments themselves to the international development agencies that set policy advice and implicit policy standards (for example, Bates 1981; World Bank 2007; Anderson, Rausser, and Swinnen 2013).

A significant body of empirical research has helped inform the conceptual arguments. For example, Bourguignon and Morrisson (1998) present evidence suggesting that increasing agricultural productivity is the most efficient path to decreasing poverty. Gollin, Parente, and Rogerson (2002) estimate that 54 percent of developing country poverty reduction from 1960 to 1990 was directly attributable to agriculture and a further 29 percent was indirectly attributable, as increased agricultural productivity freed up labor to shift to higher productivity sectors. Loayza and Raddatz (2010) suggest similarly strong links between labor-intensive agriculture and poverty reduction. Meanwhile, Christiaensen, Demery, and Kuhl (2011) find that agricultural growth has particularly powerful effects in reducing $1 per day poverty, although its record in reducing $2 per day poverty is not as strong.

Policy barriers have historically impeded many countries' agricultural progress, although Anderson, Rausser, and Swinnen (2013) show that many of the distortions have converged toward zero over recent decades. Bates and Block (2013) suggest that African economies saw improved gains in underlying agricultural productivity when political institutions were reformed to be more responsive to rural voters. However, a number of countries with significant poverty still had negative price-distorting policies as of 2005–10, including Bangladesh, Côte d'Ivoire, Ethiopia, Kenya, Mozambique, Tanzania, Uganda, and Zimbabwe. India and Indonesia also have aggregate negative policy assistance for agriculture, even while the two countries continue to provide significant input subsidies (Anderson, Rausser, and Swinnen 2013).

The world's most prominent case of rapid poverty reduction, China, has its own strong roots in agriculture. Ravallion and Chen (2007) estimate that agricultural growth played the dominant role in the country's unprecedented poverty reduction from 1981 to 2000. Christiaensen, Pan, and Wang (2010) also find that boosting lagging regions' agricultural labor productivity had important poverty-reducing effects during the early 2000s.

At the other end of the spectrum, sub-Saharan Africa remains the region to have seen the least progress in poverty reduction and the least progress in boosting agricultural productivity. Diao and others (2006) cite Africa's lack of progress as a key reason that the region has not yet experienced greater long-term economic growth and poverty reduction. The mainly rain-fed nature of the region's agriculture also presents a special challenge. For example, Barrios, Bertinelli, and Strobl (2006, 2010) show that long-term declines in rainfall have contributed to Africa's uniquely increased rates of rural-urban migration and lower long-term economic growth patterns. This is consistent with de Janvry and Sadoulet's (2010) evidence that Africa's rural sector was key to any poverty reduction over the 1993–2002 period but that migration to urban areas was not.

In simple macroeconomic terms, boosting agricultural productivity can support the end of extreme poverty through at least three channels. One is a direct income effect for households primarily engaged in agriculture. More profitable farms mean higher incomes for farmers. A second channel takes shape if increasing food productivity to meet minimum aggregate food needs frees up labor to engage in higher productivity sectors. A third takes shape if a country is predominantly rural and its food production is primarily consumed domestically as a relatively nontraded good. Then boosting food sector productivity can lower the real price of food and thereby lower the real wage, contributing to a more competitive real exchange rate and supporting export-oriented sectors like manufacturing (for example, McArthur and Sachs 2013). Some researchers emphasize the special importance of staple food sector productivity in affecting long-run economywide outcomes (for example, Gollin, Parente, and Rogerson 2007; Restuccia, Tao Yang, and Zhu 2007).

Diao and others (2012) present a variety of case studies indicating that agriculture is more effective for reducing extreme poverty than is growth originating in other sectors and that agricultural growth also makes significant indirect contributions to aggregate growth. However, they stress that the nature of agricultural productivity gains plays an important role in determining its economywide implications and that the broader consequences for growth and poverty reduction are affected by linkages with other sectors. Meanwhile, McArthur and McCord (2014) present evidence indicating that increased agricultural input intensity is linked to higher yields, higher GDP per capita, higher movement of labor to nonagricultural sectors, and higher rates of nonagricultural value added per worker across developing countries. Even though these results suggest a likely role for public investment in agriculture, the evidence remains highly imperfect regarding the specific causal pathways among public investment, agricultural growth, and poverty reduction (see de Janvry and Sadoulet 2009).

The uncertain pathways and opportunity costs of public investment to promote agriculture have prompted caution from some researchers, who argue that agriculture can play an important role in promoting growth and poverty reduction but that other sectors might be more effective in promoting these goals in many countries (Collier and Dercon 2013; Dercon and Gollin 2014). A relevant typology by Dercon (2009) asserts that landlocked countries without major mineral endowments might be well suited to prioritize agriculture but that coastal economies are better suited to promote trade infrastructure, investment climate, and efficient labor markets as a path to competing in global markets. A recent strand of evidence by McMillan and Rodrik (2011) and Rodrik (2013), finding global unconditional convergence in manufacturing productivity, further prompts some analysts to consider that sector to be the key to long-term economic growth and structural transformation. But even here, there is growing evidence that boosting agricultural productivity, especially in countries with a high degree of nontradability of food, might be a key to decreasing real wages and making labor more globally competitive in manufacturing (Gelb, Meyer, and Ramachandran 2013).

The key difference in views seems to hinge on whether agriculture is a *necessary* component of aggregate growth and poverty reduction versus whether it is *sufficient* to achieve economywide goals. Emphasizing agriculture might be less appropriate, for example, in countries with little arable land and whose extractive industries engage the majority of the labor force. And few argue that agricultural investments are always sufficient for promoting widespread growth and poverty reduction throughout a country, especially if infrastructure is sparse and other sectors do not provide enough labor demand to absorb low-skilled workers from rural areas. However, there does seem to be an argument on the extent to which agricultural investments are a necessary priority for public resources in those low-income countries in which agriculture represents the largest share of the labor force.

Overall, the evidence to date indicates that boosting agricultural productivity plays an important role in reducing extreme poverty in rural areas and, in the presence of adequate labor mobility and economic links to other sectors, in promoting structural transformation toward higher-productivity sectors. This does not imply a one-size-fits-all agricultural policy. Quite the opposite: even strong advocates of agriculture emphasize the importance of country-specific strategies, which account for local crop mix, the nature of linkages with other key sectors, and the degree of connectivity with global markets. The key priority is therefore to identify each country's crop-specific opportunities and constraints and how these link with other sectors.

Historical Context

The term *green revolution* was coined after South Asia's rapid increases in cereal yields in the late 1960s and 1970s. The words are typically used to describe

Figure 6-2. *Fertilizer Use and Cereal Yield, China and India, 1961–2002*

Tons per hectare

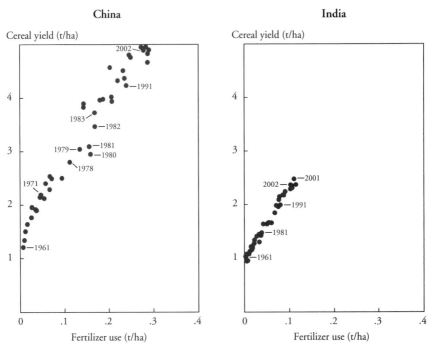

Source: World Bank (2006); McArthur (2013).

the early stage when yields jump from roughly one ton per hectare to two or more tons per hectare. Figure 6-2 shows the history of cereal yields and fertilizer input use in China and India from 1961 to 2002, the full period for which consistent data are available (following McArthur 2013, which draws from World Bank 2006). Cereal yield comparisons are informative because they include the major crops of maize, rice, and wheat, which all have similar yield profiles and responsiveness to fertilizer. Figure 6-2 shows two distinct agricultural productivity histories, which are important for understanding the two countries' respective histories in poverty reduction. Both started the 1960s with cereal yields of roughly one ton per hectare, although China had already developed relatively high-productivity and resource-intensive rice agriculture in its southern regions, well before the 1949 change in political regime.

By the late 1960s, following the staggering human losses during the Great Leap Forward, China was already surpassing two tons per hectare. Then, by the time of Deng Xiaoping's famous market-led agricultural reforms in 1978–79, average yields had reached nearly three tons per hectare, and input use was well over 150 kilograms per hectare. The graph shows a visible vertical jump between data points in the early 1980s, as market reforms took hold. The reforms undoubtedly boosted economic activity, but China was already a relatively highly productive and input-intensive rural economy. In some ways the reforms were tantamount to lifting the lid off an already boiling pot.

Meanwhile, India's green revolution took hold in the years after 1965, first with the advent of high-yield wheat in the temperate zones of Punjab and Haryana and then with the diffusion of high-yield rice throughout the country. India's input intensity and yield metrics have grown steadily in subsequent decades, but as of the early 2000s yields were only roughly 2.5 tons per hectare, less than China had achieved before its late-1970s market-oriented reforms. India has made tremendous long-term advances in agriculture, but when one considers its land productivity graph next to China's, it is not surprising that the latter has experienced more extensive poverty reduction.

Of course, these graphs present a simplified and only partial view of the complexities of agricultural development. Absent are measures of labor intensity per hectare or modern variety seed adoption. Also missing are China's and India's high levels of government-led investments in energy and irrigation, all of which made possible the successful deployment of modern variety, fertilizer-responsive seeds. Large-scale fertilizer use certainly had mixed environmental consequences, including significant problems with runoff into water systems (see Pingali 2012). But examining those variables does not change the fundamental story that China's rural productivity, measured by food production, followed a much more accelerated path than India's for many decades.

Figure 6-3 presents a second important comparison, challenging the long-standing myth that Ghana and Korea started their development trajectories from the same starting point in 1961. Through the period shown in the figure, Ghana had cereal outputs consistently in the range of one ton per hectare, with almost no fertilizer use. Korea's yields, as of 1961, were already more than three tons per hectare, with more than 150 kilograms per hectare of fertilizer use. Note that even the vertical and horizontal axes need to be adjusted from figure 6-2—to eight tons per hectare and 600 kilograms per hectare, respectively—in order to capture the full extent of Korea's agricultural development in subsequent decades.

Korea's starting point of yield and fertilizer use in 1961 was in fact still higher than any mainland sub-Saharan African country had achieved as of 2013, excluding South Africa. The country had already undergone its green revolution in the 1920s and 1930s as part of a policy of research- and infrastructure-driven rice intensification implemented under Japanese colonial occupation. The long-term trends provide important context for Korea's extraordinary postwar

Figure 6-3. *Fertilizer Use and Cereal Yield, Ghana and Korea, 1961–2002*

Tons per hectare

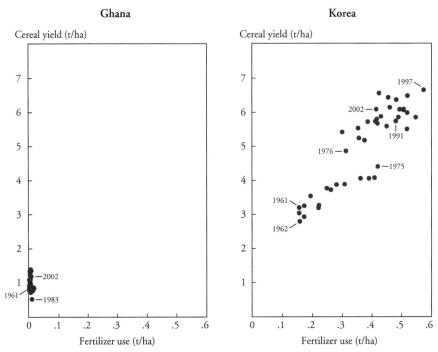

Source: World Bank (2006); McArthur (2013).

accomplishments in economic growth and poverty reduction—and a view of history contrary to the claim that Korea did not invest in agricultural productivity in the period leading up to its industrialization (see, for example, Dercon 2009).

Figure 6-4 compares the same variables for two other coastal African and Asian countries, Kenya and Vietnam. Kenya began the period with yields near one ton per hectare and grew over time to two tons per hectare with modest increases in fertilizer use (approaching roughly twenty-five kilograms per hectare). (Note that the axis scales are again the same as in figure 6-2.) Vietnam began the 1960s at two tons per hectare. Vietnamese farmers were enthusiastic adopters of the famed IR-8 breed developed by the International Rice Research Institute in 1966, although the Vietnam War undoubtedly disrupted productivity gains in many dimensions. Nonetheless, as of the 1980s, the country was on a rapid path of input intensification and yield improvements.

Interestingly, the Vietnam graph shows a horizontal jump around 1994, a critical year of market reforms. Liberalization seemed to lead to increased input

Figure 6-4. *Fertilizer Use and Cereal Yield, Kenya and Vietnam, 1961–2002*
Tons per hectare

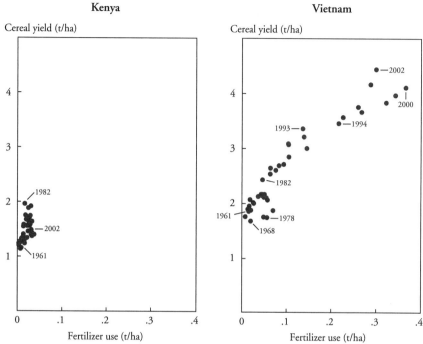

Source: World Bank (2006); McArthur (2013).

use, although not necessarily immediately increased yields, which were already at approximately 3.5 tons per hectare. More broadly, as with China and Korea, the long-term agricultural productivity history provides key insights for understanding Vietnam's remarkable long-term reductions in extreme poverty.

Finally, figure 6-5 presents data for Nepal and Rwanda, two landlocked countries that have historically struggled with agricultural productivity, extreme poverty, and domestic conflict. Nepal has slightly higher yields, but neither country was successful over the period in achieving systematic intensification of inputs or yields. Long-term yield stagnation is particularly notable in Rwanda, which has one of the highest population densities and smallest average farm sizes of any country in the world. If ever there were a test of Boserup's (1965) scarcity-induced land intensification hypothesis, Rwanda would be it. And there the hypothesis fails.

A major challenge for Nepal and Rwanda is that their relative remoteness from the sea means that they face a double-transport cost burden to boosting

Figure 6-5. *Fertilizer Use and Cereal Yield, Nepal and Rwanda, 1961–2002*

Tons per hectare

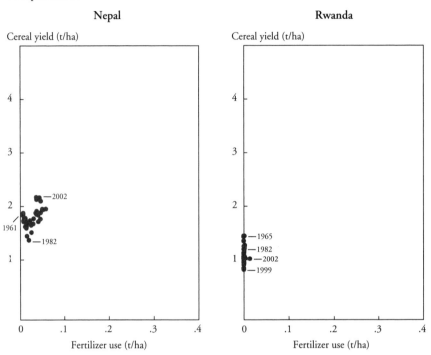

Source: World Bank (2006); McArthur (2013).

agricultural productivity. On one side, fertilizer prices are significantly heightened as a multiplier on overland transport. On the other side, farm gate crop sale prices are suppressed when products must incur heavy costs to reach markets. A landlocked farm therefore faces much lower marginal return to inputs compared to one growing an equivalent crop with low-cost coastal access. This provides important context as to why both Nepal and Rwanda still have such low levels of agricultural productivity and high levels of extreme poverty.

Agricultural Geography

Each country has its own unique agricultural geography, meaning not just its location in global markets but also its domestic mix of current crops and agronomic potential. In practical terms, farms need adequate access to relevant high-potential seeds, water, and plant nutrients, plus low-cost market access for reliably buying inputs and selling outputs. Market access is usually driven by transport costs, which are generally determined by the extent of the road network.

Crop-Level Arithmetic for Three Illustrative Farmers

Much of the last mile agricultural challenge boils down to location-specific options for maximizing value added on a given farm. Each crop has its own physical yield profile, market price per ton, and responsiveness to inputs like fertilizer. To illustrate, consider two farmers in two respective countries, each with 0.5-hectare farms. Farmer A has the opportunity to grow food crop X, with a yield potential of 5 tons per hectare if she uses US$50 of fertilizer and a likely market price of $300 per ton. If she needs 1 ton of output to feed her family, then she can sell 1.5 tons (= $5 \times 0.5 - 1$) for a profit of $400 (= $300 \times 1.5 - 50$). Farmer B has the opportunity to grow food crop Y with a market price of $150 per ton and a yield potential of 3 tons per hectare if she uses $50 worth of fertilizer. If she likewise needs 1 ton of output to feed her family then she can sell 0.5 tons (= $3 \times 0.5 - 1$) for a profit of only $25 (= $150 \times 0.5 - 50$).

However, if Farmer A lives in a coastal economy and Farmer B lives in a landlocked economy (say across a border and far from the coast), the two farmers will probably face different fertilizer prices. The fertilizer cost for Farmer B is likely to be $75 or more, implying zero profit. In this case Farmer B will unlikely bother to use fertilizer, due to climate and broader crop risks. Subsistence farmers facing climate risk do not use fertilizer even when it is expected to be profitable on average, since they cannot afford the losses of a drought year (for example, Dercon and Christiaensen 2011). Farmer B therefore uses no fertilizer and gets a much smaller yield, perhaps 1.5 tons per hectare, which produces only 0.75 tons and is inadequate to feed the family. The household needs to supplement its harvest in order to survive; it therefore pursues some combination of informal side enterprises, or one of its members migrates to a nearby town in a search for employment.

Now imagine Farmer C, who has a 0.5-hectare plot that is entirely dedicated to growing coffee, which yields 0.5 tons per hectare at a predicted global market price of $2,000 per ton. In the absence of severe drought or comparable disasters, the farmer has an anticipated harvest income of $500. The net income might adjust for fertilizer costs. But since the coffee will be sold to reliable wholesale purchasers for the global market, the farmer has both a physical asset (coffee trees) and a tradable, foreign-currency-based income stream with relatively inelastic global demand. Together these provide significant collateral and opportunities for borrowing to invest in farm improvements, including the planting of new coffee trees that will bear fruit after three to five years. The farmer's need to purchase food for the household also provides demand for other food producers, creating spillovers between the local cash crop and food crop farmers.

Although these calculations are only illustrative, they underscore the crop-specific calculus that poor households face across geographies. Farmers A, B, and C each control 0.5-hectare plots, but they face entirely different economic decisions based on expected marginal products per hectare and the nature of their income stream. Their example highlights why strategies to support subsistence farmers across countries need to respect highly localized crop arithmetic. They also help explain why it is so difficult to generalize the lessons from site-specific randomized control trials focused, for example, on fertilizer use, when the marginal products of input use vary so dramatically by crop, time, and geography.

Geography-Linked Profitability of Inputs

The simple calculations above also help illustrate the importance of year-to-year price volatility. Figure 6-6 shows the changing real price of fertilizer since 1990, alongside price variations for natural gas and crude oil, key inputs to fertilizer production and transportation. As of the early 2000s, a conventional wisdom had taken hold presuming the long-term secular decline of fertilizer prices. The graph shows that fertilizer prices had indeed been steady for more than a decade until the early 2000s, but then they shot up over the course of the mid-2000s. Notwithstanding a huge price shock in 2009, real prices now seem to have normalized at levels more than twice as high as a decade ago.

Recent global commodity price volatility has been manifest within the food sector. Figure 6-7 shows variation in real prices for rice, wheat, and maize, the three most prominent global cereals. The first thing to note in this graph is that global food prices have tended to increase significantly since the early 2000s. The second thing to note is the ongoing relative ranking of prices per ton: rice is more expensive than wheat, which is more expensive than maize. This is important because, as mentioned earlier, the three crops have similar physical yield profiles and similar responsiveness to fertilizer. Thus for a given amount of fertilizer and a corresponding amount of crop harvested, rice is more profitable than wheat on global terms, and wheat is in turn more profitable than maize.

The information from figures 6-6 and 6-7 can be merged into a more representative indicator of crop profitability per unit of input. This is presented in figure 6-8, which shows relative crop-to-urea prices for rice, wheat, and maize. Urea is one of the world's most common forms of nitrogen fertilizer. Higher values on the graph suggest greater profitability. Again, the ratios are volatile, and rice tends to be roughly twice as profitable as maize, with wheat somewhere in between, although trending closer to maize. The graph shows that the increases in food prices have not been enough to compensate for the increases

Figure 6-6. *Real Price of Fertilizer, Natural Gas, and Crude Oil, 1990–2013*

Index, 2010 = 100

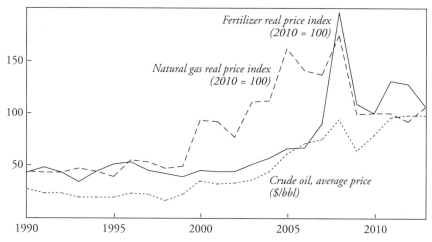

Source: World Bank (2014b).

Figure 6-7. *Real Price of Rice, Wheat, and Maize, 1990–2013*

US$ per metric ton[c]

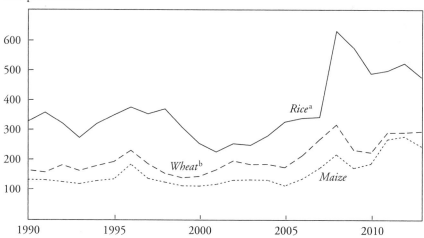

Source: World Bank (2014b).
a. Thailand white rice, 5% broken.
b. U.S. hard red winter wheat, ordinary protein.
c. Data presented in constant 2010 US$.

Figure 6-8. *Ratio of Cereal Crop Prices to Urea Fertilizer Prices, 1990–2013*

Per metric ton

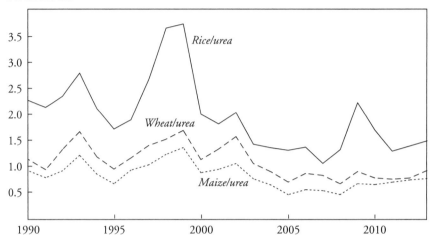

in fertilizer prices. The relevant ratios are for the most part lower in recent years than throughout the 1990s and early 2000s.

These global price ratios provide important context for the last mile, but the localized and relatively nontradable nature of agriculture in many of the poorest countries adds major challenges. In those instances, farmers are likely to earn even less per ton of crop output, due to transport costs and market inefficiencies, and are likely to face even higher costs of accessing fertilizer. In inland areas with high transport costs, fertilizer prices can be multiples higher than in coastal locations. Unfortunately, there is not yet a robust global data set of location-by-location fertilizer costs around the world, so it is not possible to estimate the full variation in relevant prices within and across the poorest countries. However, it is possible to estimate the geographically driven elements of fertilizer prices, based on the approximate distance to the nearest fertilizer production facility.

McArthur and McCord (2014) have constructed such a measure as part of a cross-country econometric study of agricultural productivity and links to economic growth. The variable is calculated by estimating the land- and sea-based distance from each developing country's geographic agricultural center to the nearest urea fertilizer production facility, with land distances weighted more heavily than maritime distances. Fertilizer plants are generally built near liquid natural gas deposits, and most of them are located in developed countries. When

Figure 6-9. *Fertilizer Use and Actual Individual Consumption, Developing Countries, 2010*

Actual individual consumption, 2011, PPP (log scale)

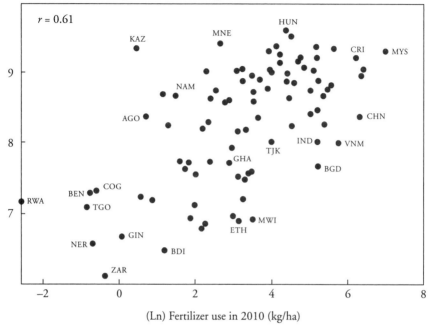

(Ln) Fertilizer use in 2010 (kg/ha)

Source: World Bank (2014a); ICP (2014).

interacted with a global fertilizer price variation in recent decades, this distance index has a statistically robust correlation with historical changes in fertilizer use. It is independently significant as an explanatory variable for yields, alongside adoption of modern variety seeds and annual variations in precipitation.

To illustrate the problem, figure 6-9 shows a scatter plot of fertilizer use per hectare against actual individual consumption across ninety-four developing countries in 2010. The two variables have a strong positive correlation ($r = 0.61$). There is undoubtedly a degree of endogeneity between these two measures, since poor countries can afford less fertilizer and countries that use less fertilizer are less likely to achieve the agricultural productivity gains that help reduce poverty. However, figure 6-10 shows another scatter plot of the indexed distance to a fertilizer plant and average fertilizer use. There is a strong negative correlation between the two variables, with a coefficient of –0.55. It is therefore noteworthy that the correlation coefficient is –0.5 between actual individual consumption and the distance to a fertilizer plant within the same sample.

Figure 6-10. *Indexed Distance to Urea Manufacturer Compared to Fertilizer Use, 2010*

Fertilizer use in 2010 (kg/ha) (log scale)

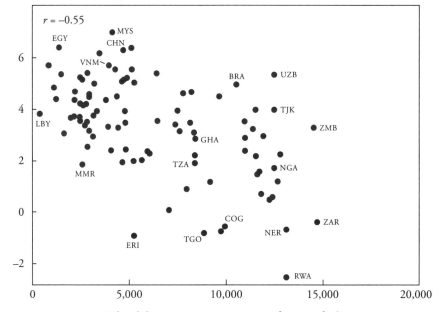

Indexed distance to nearest urea manufacturing facility

Source: McArthur and McCord (2014); World Bank (2014a).

Uneven Challenge of Land

Economists have long grappled with the relationship between farm size and productivity, especially the persistent puzzle of a negative relationship between the two variables (for example, Barrett, Bellemare, and Hou 2010; Eastwood and others 2010). The illustrative farmers A, B, and C above all faced half-hectare, fixed land constraints, but average farm sizes vary tremendously across low-income geographies. Farmers producing staples for own-use consumption in a region averaging 0.2 hectares per worker with no room for land fallow will have an entirely different optimization strategy than farmers in a region growing a mix of cash and staple crops across more than 2.0 hectares per worker and ample opportunities for crop rotation. Several parts of the developing world also still have the potential to expand area under cultivation. Deininger and others (2011) estimate that the developing world has approximately 400 million hectares of nonforestland that is suitable for crops. Roughly half of that total is in sub-Saharan Africa, and approximately 30 percent is in Latin America and the Caribbean. Less than 4 percent is in East and South Asia.

But sub-Saharan Africa's aggregate figures for land availability mask tremendous country-level variation. Countries with high population density like Burundi and Rwanda already have some of the smallest average farm sizes in the world, with minimal opportunities for expansion. Meanwhile, countries like Mozambique and Tanzania still have significant scope for expansion. In aggregate, the sixty-one focus countries are estimated to have expanded their area harvested by 14 percent between 2000 and 2010, from 640 million hectares to 726 million hectares (McArthur forthcoming). This came during a period when most developed countries saw their area harvested shrink by approximately 8 million hectares overall.

The majority of this expansion took place in only a handful of countries. India and China alone accounted for nearly a third of the growth, with 16 million new hectares (9 percent national growth) and 12 million new hectares (7 percent national growth), respectively. Six countries accounted for more than half of the rest of the growth: Indonesia (8.2 million hectares, or a 26 percent increase), Tanzania (6.2 million hectares, an 83 percent increase), Myanmar (5 million hectares, a 38 percent increase), Niger (4.6 million hectares, a 41 percent increase), Ethiopia (3.5 million hectares, a 32 percent increase), and Mozambique (3 million hectares, a 72 percent increase). Seven countries saw a decline in area harvested over the period. This includes Nigeria, which dropped from 41.6 million hectares to 40.5 million hectares.

The opportunity of land expansion must be understood as only applicable in some countries and only offering a temporary solution in those cases, especially when productivity remains low. Moreover, countries with available land are increasingly attractive to foreign investment and need to manage crucial sensitivities around accountability, transparency, and profit sharing, as exemplified by political unrest in Madagascar in recent years. A significant amount of area expansion has been driven by population pressures, and there is a natural limit to how much land is available in any country. The essential nature of biodiversity and ecosystem services only amplifies the need for limits to expansion. The short-term gains from "growing out" through new land harvested need to be complemented with more fundamental investments in "growing up," through higher yields per hectare.

A Snapshot of the Agricultural Last Mile

The crop area composition for each of this chapter's sixty-one focus countries is described in a series of tables presented in the appendix to this chapter. Table 6A-1 shows the share of each country's area harvested by major crop type, including cereals, oil crops, roots and tubers, pulses, fruits and vegetables, and key cash crops. Cereals are prominent across most countries. Weighted averages do not suggest major differences of crop type across groups 1 and 2, although group 1 countries do have a larger share of area harvested to roots and tubers (13 percent versus 6 percent) and a larger share allocated to pulses (11 percent versus 5 percent). These differences are driven somewhat by the dominance of African countries in group 1.

Table 6A-2 considers changes in crop mix between 2000 and 2010 and highlights the general stability in this regard. There is a small but potentially interesting difference between the country categories. Group 1 experienced a 1.1-percentage-point average increase in share of area harvested to cereals over the period and a 1.1-percentage-point decline in area harvest to cash crops. Meanwhile group 2 experienced a 1.9-percentage-point average decline in area harvested to cereals and a 1.9-percentage-point increase in area harvested to cash crops. These changes would be consistent with group 1 countries expanding food production to meet the basic needs of growing populations, while group 2 countries begin to diversify to higher-value-added crops.

The cross-country variation in cereal crop composition is amply demonstrated in table 6A-3. This shows the prevalence of rice in Asia, wheat in temperate countries, and maize in much of Africa and Latin America. A separate calculation of weighted averages indicates that group 2 countries have approximately 29 percent of area harvested to rice, 9 percent to maize, 8 percent to wheat, and 8 percent to other cereals. Meanwhile, group 1 countries have only 7 percent of area harvested to rice, 19 percent to maize, 3 percent to wheat, and 17 percent to other cereals.

Table 6A-4 then shows that only a small number of countries have a significant share of agricultural land (and presumably labor) allocated to cash crops. Only eleven of the sixty-one countries have more than 15 percent of area harvested to cash crops. Côte d'Ivoire has the most, at 44 percent, the majority of which is in cocoa. Liberia is the only other group 1 country with a sizable share of area in cash crops. In South Asia, Pakistan has the greatest share, at 16 percent, composed mostly of cotton and sugar. Indonesia is the highest in East Asia, at 34 percent, made up of coffee, cocoa, oil palm, rubber, sugar, tobacco, and other crops. Honduras has the greatest cash crop concentration in Latin America, at 39 percent, similarly driven largely by coffee, oil palm, and sugar.

Altogether, the crop mapping analysis underscores the fact that only a handful of countries have developed large cash crop sectors, and most of the poorest countries' agricultural sectors remain overwhelmingly focused on staple food production. Moreover, cash crop production forms no guarantee of long-term economic success: the correlation coefficient between focus countries' actual individual consumption and share of area in cash crops is only 0.17. A small amount of cash crop exports can bring significant economywide gains, but they are unlikely to provide the broad-based income or employment growth that is needed to help all rural households rise out of poverty. The last mile will therefore need to focus significantly on boosting staple crop productivity, with attention to each country's unique agricultural geography and the challenges to profitability for its current and potential crops.

Macroeconomic Context

In addition to the issues of crop composition, each country's last mile agricultural challenge needs to be appreciated for its macroeconomic context, demographic dynamics, and geographic situation. Appendix table 6A-5 presents a simple diagnostic framework for assessing each of this chapter's sixty-one focus countries across the relevant dimensions. Among macroeconomic factors, twenty-six of the thirty-one group 1 countries and five of the twenty-eight group 2 countries were still at official low-income status as of early 2014, implying only a limited domestic capacity to make public investments. Only eight of the thirty-one group 1 countries experienced at least 3 percent average per capita economic growth between 2000 and 2010, meaning that twenty-three of them are stuck in low-growth poverty situations. These could be considered the twenty-three highest priority cases for the world, although fast-growing countries like Liberia and Mozambique are still very poor, so their long-run success still requires support.

Seventeen of the group 1 economies are also officially fragile, according to recent World Bank official designations, so the political and institutional issues addressed in chapters 2 through 5 of this book remain crucial to their long-term success. The growing body of evidence (for example, Hsiang, Burke, and Miguel 2013) regarding causality from negative climate shocks to crop declines to conflict also suggests that investments in boosting agricultural productivity can be a fundamental strategy for minimizing the risks of fragility.

Natural resource revenues provide an important and complex source of revenue for many governments, frequently causing political strain and macroeconomic management problems like Dutch disease. For countries with relatively nontradable local food sectors, increasing staple crop productivity can play an important deflationary role to maintain relative price stability and thereby wage competitiveness for other industrial sectors. These issues will only become more common as recently discovered deposits come online for export in the near future. At the moment, natural resources play a major fiscal role in only three group 1 countries (Chad, Congo, and DR Congo), but they play at least some notable role in another three (Guinea, Mali, and Zambia). The International Monetary Fund (IMF 2012) estimates that seven more will soon have major resource revenues (CAR, Madagascar, Mozambique, Sierra Leone, Tanzania,

Togo, and Uganda). Among group 2 countries, nine are already established resource exporters and three are scheduled to begin exporting soon.

In terms of demographics, agriculture is likely to play a proportionately larger role in national strategies for countries where the population and workforce are still predominantly rural. The flip side is that agriculture might play less of a priority role in countries with highly urbanized populations and also in small island economies, where other approaches to boosting marginalized populations' incomes might be more successful in the medium term. However, even in areas with low shares of the population in agriculture, if the relevant households are still stuck in extreme poverty, then a successful last mile strategy might still imply targeted support for boosting productivity among those households.

Population growth and fertility rates indeed remain a pressing concern for most of the focus countries, especially those in group 1. Eighteen of the thirty-one countries with AIC below $2,000 still have total fertility rates of 5 or greater, as do four group 2 countries. Only two group 1 countries, Haiti and Nepal, have fertility rates below 3.5, although nineteen group 2 countries have crossed the same threshold. For countries with persistently high population growth and fast-growing pressures on the agricultural environment, a voluntary reduction in fertility can be pursued through a combination of efforts to promote child survival, girls' secondary education, and access to family planning.

In terms of agricultural geography, eighteen group 1 countries are "far" from a urea fertilizer plant, measured as an indexed distance value of 8000 or greater, and thirteen countries are landlocked. The corresponding numbers for group 2 are ten and six countries, respectively. In terms of crop mix, table 6A-5 lists each country's staple crop with the largest share of area harvested. Lead crops across group 1 countries include cassava, rice, bananas/plantains, millet, maize, sorghum, teff, beans, and yams. A similarly diverse mix of lead crops emerges across group 2 countries.

The range of key staple crops does prompt caution for interpreting cereal yield as a benchmark of overall agricultural land productivity, but the measure offers the best cross-country proxy available and provides useful information. Only three group 1 countries had cereal yields of at least two tons per hectare as of 2010. The vast majority still require major boosts in agricultural productivity. Meanwhile, twelve group 2 countries were still below the two tons per hectare threshold. Fertilizer use still remains below twenty-five kilograms per hectare in eighteen group 1 countries and twelve group 2 countries.

Some General Priorities

One central implication of this chapter is that there is no one-size-fits-all last mile strategy, since there are many components to agricultural systems and their nature differs tremendously across economies. Nonetheless, some general priorities can be identified, especially for the African countries that make up the majority of the poorest countries that constitute group 1. A proper multi-pronged strategy needs to address priorities like rural health systems and universal access to secondary education, which will promote productive labor forces and a smooth demographic transition. The following are some priorities linked directly to agricultural productivity.

Transport Infrastructure

Little will do more to help the economics of smallholder agriculture than a major scale-up of investment in transport infrastructure. This is especially important in Africa, where baseline transport costs are so high that policymakers need to replace standard thinking around percentage improvements with new measures of percentage gaps. Landlocked areas have the most to gain in this regard, since the return on investment will be affected by the lower relative price of inputs and the higher profitability of outputs.

Public Assistance for Inputs, Targeted to the Poorest Households

One of the great global policy advances of the past decade has been a blunt recognition of the previous generation's failure adequately to support access to inputs, especially in Africa (World Bank 2007). The success of Malawi's initially controversial input voucher program played a seminal role in changing the debate. Carter and colleagues (2014) find evidence for persistent gains resulting from vouchers for fertilizer and improved seeds in a randomized experiment in Mozambique. However, some recent studies have raised concerns regarding efficiency (for example, Pauw and Thurlow 2011, and Pan and Christiaensen 2012) suggest that elite capture has been a problem with input voucher programs in Tanzania. In light of many countries' structural disadvantage in accessing the global fertilizer market, ongoing policy refinements will be needed to support profitable local price ratios for inputs.

Public Incentives for Warehousing and Pooling Sales

One of the major challenges in low-income agricultural environmental is the lack of infrastructure to help smallholders protect their product from postharvest losses, pool their sales to enhance market power, and time their sales in pursuit of optimal pricing across the calendar. Small differences in margins can have especially pronounced consequences among extremely poor farmers, so national and local governments need to promote the regulatory frameworks and warehousing facilities that allow farmers to benefit from scale economies.

Climate Insurance

Although subsistence farmers often avoid the cost of rainfall insurance (see, for example, Giné and Yang 2009), precipitation insurance mechanisms have made gains in recent years. For example, researchers at Columbia University's International Research Institute for Climate and Society reviewed historical precipitation data to measure probabilities of extreme weather events and created a real-time satellite-based vegetation measurement index that can be used to trigger a strike price on an options contract. Early field testing showed that the method was initially economically unviable in multiple rural African settings due to cost ratios for staple crop farmers, but it has since been successfully deployed by Oxfam and Swiss Re, working with coffee growers in Ethiopia. This represents an important early step toward broader market-priced risk management instruments for low-income agriculture.

The most obvious other mechanism to mitigate climate risk is groundwater-based irrigation, which can ensure a more reliable source of hydration for plants and support the introduction of multicropping, which is especially valuable in geographies with unimodal rainy seasons. The cost is generally modest, on the order of $3,000 per hectare, and typically has a high net present value for small-scale farmers. However, $3,000 is typically prohibitively expensive for farmers living in extreme poverty, and the high costs of rural loan administration tend to prevent commercial banks from entering the market. There is a "missing rural middle" in credit systems throughout rural Africa in particular.

Multilateral Agricultural Credit Facilities

To bridge the rural finance gaps, farmers require access to market-based credit on risk-adjusted terms. This needs to be structured over extended maturities to allow for season-to-season experimentation as farmers introduce new crops. Farmers also need to tackle scale economies in order to access inputs, credit, and market connections at manageable cost. This likely implies pooled efforts in the form of private cooperatives or farmers' associations. In practical terms, there needs to be a vehicle whereby smallholder farmers can coordinate to access "patient capital" loans of perhaps $25,000 to $100,000 at a time. A relevant financing facility could focus on the risk-adjustment component to incentivize private loans. A rough calculation suggests that sub-Saharan Africa's total international public financing requirements are $5 billion annually, which could allow private credit to reach 25 million farmers over five years (McArthur 2011).

National Investor Roundtables

One of the more promising initiatives in recent years has been the creation of country-by-country investor forums to bridge public and private capital. One of these has taken shape under the label Grow Africa, launched through a partnership of the World Economic Forum and the New Economic Partnership for African Development. Another, dubbed Grow Asia, is getting under way. It is too early to judge results, but to date the Africa roundtables are reported to have mobilized $7 billion in planned investments for ten African countries (Grow Africa 2014). It is crucial for such processes to be anchored in basic standards of public transparency and corporate accountability, including those embodied in the recently adopted Principles for Responsible Agricultural Investments. If these public-private approaches gain widespread citizen support, they can serve as an important contributor to reaching the last mile.

Public Research for Seed Varieties Resistant to Drought, Floods, and Pests

A growing body of scientific research is developing new disaster-resistant seed varieties for staple crops. Pest resistance is a challenge everywhere, especially in areas with soil nutrient depletion. In Asia some of the most exciting advances are in flood-resistant rice breeds, while in Africa a major initiative for drought-resistant maize is now under way. Although a considerable amount of relevant research is now pursued by private companies, the Consultative Group for International Agricultural Research and national agricultural research bodies have historically provided, and continue to provide, many of the frontline technological advances. Public funding and institutional support for these organizations remain essential.

Mobile Technology

Legal and regulatory frameworks need to ensure that advances in digital technology are translated into ever-greater support for farmers. Some of these will directly help farmers to become more productive. For example, in countries with inadequate agricultural extension staffing, entrepreneurs starting "m-farming" businesses (using mobile devices) can deliver wireless services like image-based or video-based technical support. Some advances will help with government program efficiency, such as digital tracking of vouchers or similar subsidies targeted to those with greatest need. Other advances could bypass agricultural technicalities and instead simply ensure minimum income standards for all farmers around the world, through, for example, unconditional cash transfers as pioneered by GiveDirectly. These transfers might be particularly impactful in fragile states, where infrastructure constraints and service delivery can be most challenging.

Conclusion

This chapter focuses on specifying the location-specific components of agriculture most pertinent to the last mile of ending extreme poverty. Anchored in historical context, it emphasizes the common challenges that apply across most of the poorest countries alongside the tremendous country-specific variations. These economies are predominantly still rural in nature, with high fertility rates, fast-growing populations, very small cash crop sectors, and very low and slow-growing staple crop productivity. The upshot is that efforts to boost farmers' staple crop productivity should be considered essential if several hundred million people are going to escape extreme poverty. In addition to the importance of each country's macroeconomic environment, returns on investment will be determined by geography-specific factors such as crop type, crop price, farm size, yield potential, input responsiveness, and forms of available irrigation. Moreover, many of the countries facing the greatest hurdles to boosting crop productivity—like distance-driven constraints to accessing global fertilizer markets—are also the poorest countries, so targeted approaches are required to help farmers surmount relevant market barriers, including physical barriers.

The chapter points to many topics that would benefit from more refined analysis and research. For example, what are the actual prices of fertilizer, seeds, and irrigation across the world's poorest farming areas? What crops are the poorest people within the poorest countries actually farming, and what higher-value-added crops are agriculturally and ecologically suitable to grow? What new public instruments could be designed to help the poorest farmers enjoy more advantageous price ratios between their inputs and their outputs?

A tremendous amount is also already known about what to do, and many policy efforts simply need to be scaled up accordingly. The poorest farmers need support for local agricultural system inputs, including germ plasm, fertilizer, irrigation, credit, insurance, and storage warehouses. As each link in the chain is addressed, and each country and farm community boosts its productivity and income incrementally, the distance to the last mile's goal line will shrink ever smaller. Within a generation, hundreds of millions of people could, and indeed should, literally be able to grow their way out of poverty.

Appendix 6A

Table 6A-1. *Share of Area Harvested, by Major Crop Groups, Sixty-One Focus Countries, 2010*[a]

Percent

Country	Cereals	Oils	Roots and tubers	Pulses	Fruits and vegetables	Cash crops	Other
Sub-Saharan Africa							
Angola	41	8	27	17	6	2	
Benin	37	15	15	5	4	7	17
Burkina Faso	59	15		17	1	7	
Burundi	19	2	18	22	35	4	
Cape Verde	49	3	2	40	4	2	
Cameroon	30	12	10	10	16	22	
Central African Republic	21	29	34	3	8	5	
Chad	66	21	3	5	1	4	
Comoros	20	32	15	13	11	9	
Congo, Rep.	9	16	43	4	16	13	
Congo, Dem. Rep.	32	11	35	7	8	7	
Côte d'Ivoire	11	5	17	1	10	44	12
Equatorial Guinea		4	53		14	28	
Ethiopia	65	6	6	10	3	6	3
Gambia	63	32	1	2	1	1	
Ghana	25	7	24	4	7	32	1
Guinea	56	8	6	2	14	14	
Guinea-Bissau	31	9	4	2	6	3	45
Kenya	49	5	5	25	6	9	1
Lesotho	84		3	9	4		
Liberia	44	3	13	1	10	29	
Madagascar	53	3	20	3	8	12	1
Malawi	48	11	10	18	5	7	
Mali	75	12		5	2	5	
Mauritania	61	1	1	34	3		
Mozambique	38	16	20	17	3	5	2
Niger	62	6		31	1		
Nigeria	38	11	20	7	9	13	1
Rwanda	21	5	26	20	25	3	
Sao Tome and Principe	3	29	10		15	43	
Senegal	50	39	1	5	3	2	1
Sierra Leone	43	8	29	8	6	6	
Sudan (former)	70	22	1	3	3	1	

(*continued*)

Table 6A-1 (*continued*)

Country	Cereals	Oils	Roots and tubers	Pulses	Fruits and vegetables	Cash crops	Other
Sub-Saharan Africa (continued)							
Tanzania	40	18	13	12	9	6	2
Togo	49	9	13	12	2	14	1
Uganda	21	16	14	15	27	7	
Zambia	53	20	12	3	3	9	
Zimbabwe	62	18	2	2	2	13	
South Asia							
Bangladesh	80	3	3	2	6	6	1
Bhutan	61	2	7	4	20	4	2
India	49	20	1	13	7	10	1
Maldives	2	24	11	2	52		10
Nepal	70	9	4	6	8	3	1
Pakistan	56	15	1	7	5	16	
East Asia and Pacific							
Cambodia	81	4	7	2	4	2	
China	51	16	5	2	20	6	
Indonesia	43	11	4	1	4	34	3
Lao PDR	73	4	2	1	13	6	
Myanmar	48	21		21	4	4	1
Philippines	51	26	3	1	14	6	
Vietnam	64	4	5	3	10	11	3
Middle East and North Africa							
Djibouti				53	44		3
Morocco	72	12	1	5	7	1	2
West Bank and Gaza	18	56	1	2	18	1	3
Yemen	71	4	2	4	14	6	
Latin America and Caribbean							
Bolivia	30	42	7	2	7	10	1
Haiti	42	3	20	10	14	10	
Honduras	41		1	11	8	39	
Nicaragua	46	4	2	25	5	19	
Europe and Central Asia							
Kyrgyz Republic	63	9	9	3	11	4	1
Tajikistan	42	18	3	2	17	17	1

a. Figures are rounded to nearest percentage point. Values less than 0.5 percent not included.

Table 6A-2. *Change in Share of Area Harvested, by Major Crop Groups, Sixty-One Focus Countries, 2000–2010*

Percent

Country	Cereals	Oils	Roots and tubers	Pulses	Fruits and vegetables	Cash crops
Sub-Saharan Africa						
Angola	−0.05	0.03	−0.03	0.06	0.01	−0.02
Benin	0.03	−0.05	0.01	0.00	0.00	−0.08
Burkina Faso	−0.06	0.02	0.00	0.04	−0.01	0.01
Burundi	0.01	0.01	−0.01	−0.03	0.03	0.00
Cape Verde	0.05	0.00	0.00	−0.07	0.01	0.01
Cameroon	0.10	−0.03	−0.01	0.02	−0.01	−0.06
Central African Republic	0.02	0.00	0.03	0.00	0.00	−0.04
Chad	0.10	−0.06	0.00	0.00	0.00	−0.05
Comoros	0.03	−0.01	0.01	0.00	−0.01	−0.03
Congo, Rep.	0.03	−0.03	0.02	−0.01	−0.01	0.00
Congo, Dem. Rep.	−0.01	0.00	0.00	0.01	0.00	0.00
Côte d'Ivoire	−0.01	−0.02	0.03	0.00	−0.03	−0.07
Equatorial Guinea	0.00	0.01	0.21	0.00	0.05	−0.27
Ethiopia	−0.03	0.02	0.00	−0.01	0.01	0.01
Gambia	0.15	−0.12	−0.01	−0.02	0.00	0.00
Ghana	−0.01	0.01	0.00	0.01	−0.02	0.00
Guinea	0.10	−0.01	−0.01	−0.01	−0.04	−0.03
Guinea-Bissau	−0.04	0.03	0.01	0.01	0.00	0.00
Kenya	0.04	0.00	0.00	−0.02	0.00	0.00
Lesotho	−0.04	0.00	0.01	0.01	0.01	0.00
Liberia	0.14	−0.01	−0.02	0.00	−0.03	−0.08
Madagascar	0.04	−0.01	0.01	0.00	0.00	−0.04
Malawi	−0.04	0.04	−0.02	0.02	0.00	0.00
Mali	0.14	−0.06	0.00	−0.03	0.00	−0.05
Mauritania	−0.01	−0.01	0.00	0.04	−0.01	0.00
Mozambique	−0.06	−0.02	−0.04	0.12	0.01	0.00
Niger	−0.05	0.03	0.00	0.02	0.01	0.00
Nigeria	−0.04	0.02	0.02	−0.02	0.00	0.01
Rwanda	0.03	0.02	−0.01	−0.01	−0.03	0.00
Sao Tome and Principe	0.01	0.03	0.02	0.00	0.03	−0.09
Senegal	0.01	−0.01	0.00	0.00	0.01	0.00
Sierra Leone	−0.03	0.01	0.19	−0.04	−0.06	−0.07
Sudan (former)	0.08	−0.09	0.00	0.01	0.01	−0.01
Tanzania	0.08	0.01	−0.03	−0.03	−0.02	−0.01

(continued)

Table 6A-2 (*continued*)

Country	Cereals	Oils	Roots and tubers	Pulses	Fruits and vegetables	Cash crops
Sub-Saharan Africa (continued)						
Togo	0.04	−0.05	0.01	0.03	−0.01	−0.01
Uganda	0.00	0.02	−0.01	0.02	−0.01	−0.02
Zambia	0.01	0.03	−0.04	0.00	−0.01	0.01
Zimbabwe	0.07	−0.05	0.00	0.00	0.00	−0.03
South Asia						
Bangladesh	−0.01	−0.01	0.01	−0.02	0.03	0.00
Bhutan	−0.08	−0.04	0.02	0.02	0.07	0.00
India	−0.06	0.01	0.00	0.02	0.02	0.01
Maldives	0.00	−0.39	−0.07	0.01	0.41	0.00
Nepal	−0.03	0.00	0.01	0.00	0.02	0.00
Pakistan	0.02	−0.01	0.00	0.00	0.01	−0.02
East Asia and Pacific						
Cambodia	−0.05	0.01	0.06	0.01	−0.02	−0.01
China	−0.02	−0.01	−0.01	−0.01	0.04	0.01
Indonesia	−0.05	−0.03	−0.01	0.00	0.00	0.10
Lao PDR	−0.03	0.01	0.00	0.00	0.01	0.01
Myanmar	−0.06	0.03	0.00	0.03	0.00	−0.01
Philippines	−0.02	0.00	0.00	0.00	0.02	0.00
Vietnam	−0.05	0.00	0.01	0.00	0.01	0.02
Middle East and North Africa						
Djibouti	0.00	0.00	0.00	−0.08	0.07	0.00
Morocco	−0.03	0.03	0.00	0.00	0.01	0.00
West Bank and Gaza	0.02	0.02	0.00	−0.01	−0.03	0.00
Yemen	0.05	−0.02	0.00	−0.01	−0.01	−0.01
Latin America and Caribbean						
Bolivia	−0.04	0.05	−0.01	0.01	−0.03	0.01
Haiti	0.00	−0.01	0.03	0.00	−0.04	0.02
Honduras	−0.06	0.00	0.00	0.00	0.00	0.06
Nicaragua	−0.02	0.00	0.01	0.00	0.00	0.00
Europe and Central Asia						
Kyrgyz Republic	−0.01	−0.01	0.02	0.02	0.01	−0.03
Tajikistan	0.06	−0.05	0.01	0.01	0.04	−0.06

Table 6A-3. *Share of Area Harvested to Major Cereal Crops, 2010*
(3 year period average)[a]

Percent

Country	Rice	Maize	Wheat	Other	Total
Sub-Saharan Africa					
Angola	1	36	0	5	41
Benin	2	30	0	5	37
Burkina Faso	2	11	0	47	59
Burundi	2	10	1	6	19
Cabo Verde	0	49	0	0	49
Cameroon	2	14	0	14	30
Central African Republic	2	13	0	6	21
Chad	3	6	0	57	66
Comoros	18	2	0	0	20
Congo, Rep.	1	4	0	5	9
Congo, Dem. Rep.	7	24	0	1	32
Côte d'Ivoire	5	4	0	2	11
Equatorial Guinea					
Ethiopia	0	13	11	41	65
Gambia	15	9	0	38	63
Ghana	3	15	0	7	25
Guinea	25	14	0	17	56
Guinea-Bissau	20	3	0	8	31
Kenya	0	39	3	7	49
Lesotho	0	63	9	12	84
Liberia	44	0	0	0	44
Madagascar	45	8	0	0	53
Malawi	2	43	0	3	48
Mali	13	10	0	52	75
Mauritania	6	6	0	49	61
Mozambique	3	24	0	10	38
Niger	0	0	0	62	62
Nigeria	6	11	0	21	38
Rwanda	1	10	2	7	21
Sao Tome and Principe	0	3	0	0	3
Senegal	5	5	0	40	50
Sierra Leone	37	2	0	5	43
Sudan (former)	0	0	2	68	70
Tanzania	8	23	1	9	40

Table 6A-3 (*continued*)

Country	Rice	Maize	Wheat	Other	Total
Sub-Saharan Africa (continued)					
Togo	3	30	0	17	49
Uganda	1	13	0	7	21
Zambia	1	47	1	4	53
Zimbabwe	0	45	0	16	62
South Asia					
Bangladesh	76	1	3	0	80
Bhutan	23	26	2	10	61
India	21	4	14	10	49
Maldives	0	1	0	1	2
Nepal	31	18	15	6	70
Pakistan	11	4	38	3	56
East Asia & Pacific					
Cambodia	75	6	0	0	81
China	17	18	14	2	51
Indonesia	33	10	0	0	43
Lao PDR	59	15	0	0	73
Myanmar	43	2	1	2	48
Philippines	32	19	0	0	51
Vietnam	55	8	0	0	64
Middle East & North Africa					
Djibouti	0	0	0	0	0
Morocco	0	3	40	28	72
West Bank & Gaza	0	0	12	6	18
Yemen	0	4	11	55	71
Latin America & Caribbean					
Bolivia	6	11	6	7	30
Haiti	4	28	0	10	42
Honduras	1	35	0	5	41
Nicaragua	8	34	0	4	46
Europe & Central Asia					
Kyrgyz Republic	1	8	41	13	63
Tajikistan	1	1	33	7	42

a. Figures are rounded to nearest percentage point. Crop values less than 0.5 percent not included.

Table 6A-4. *Share of Area Harvested by Major Cash Crops, 2010*
(3 year period average)[a]

Percent

Country	Cocoa	Coffee	Oil palm	Rubber	Cotton	Sugar	Tea	To-bacco	Other	Total
Sub-Saharan Africa										
Angola	0	1	1	0	0	0	0	0	0	2
Benin	0	0	1	0	6	0	0	0	0	7
Burkina Faso	0	0	0	0	6	0	0	0	0	7
Burundi	0	2	1	0	0	0	1	0	0	4
Cabo Verde	0	0	0	0	0	2	0	0	0	2
Cameroon	11	3	2	1	2	2	0	0	0	22
Central African Republic	0	1	0	0	2	1	0	0	0	5
Chad	0	0	0	0	4	0	0	0	0	4
Comoros	0	1	0	0	0	0	0	0	8	9
Congo, Rep.	1	3	3	1	0	5	0	0	0	13
Congo, Dem. Rep.	0	1	3	1	1	1	0	0	0	7
Côte d'Ivoire	31	6	3	2	2	0	0	0	0	44
Equatorial Guinea	9	13	4	0	0	0	0	0	2	28
Ethiopia	0	3	0	0	1	0	0	0	2	6
Gambia	0	0	1	0	0	0	0	0	0	1
Ghana	25	0	6	0	0	0	0	0	0	32
Guinea	1	2	9	0	1	0	0	0	0	14
Guinea-Bissau	0	0	2	0	1	0	0	0	0	3
Kenya	0	3	0	0	1	1	3	0	1	9
Lesotho	0	0	0	0	0	0	0	0	0	0
Liberia	8	1	3	13	0	5	0	0	0	29
Madagascar	0	4	0	0	0	3	0	0	4	12
Malawi	0	0	0	0	2	1	1	4	0	7
Mali	0	0	0	0	5	0	0	0	0	5
Mauritania	0	0	0	0	0	0	0	0	0	0
Mozambique	0	0	0	0	3	1	0	1	0	5
Niger	0	0	0	0	0	0	0	0	0	0
Nigeria	3	0	8	1	1	0	0	0	0	13
Rwanda	0	2	0	0	0	0	1	0	0	3
Sao Tome and Principe	39	0	4	0	0	0	0	0	0	43
Senegal	0	0	0	0	1	0	0	0	0	2
Sierra Leone	3	1	2	0	0	0	0	0	0	6
Sudan (former)	0	0	0	0	1	1	0	0	0	1
Tanzania	0	1	0	0	3	0	0	1	1	6

(continued)

Table 6A-4 (*continued*)

Country	Cocoa	Coffee	Oil palm	Rubber	Cotton	Sugar	Tea	To-bacco	Other	Total
Sub-Saharan Africa (continued)										
Togo	8	2	1	0	4	0	0	0	0	14
Uganda	1	4	0	0	1	1	0	0	0	7
Zambia	0	0	0	0	5	1	0	3	0	9
Zimbabwe	0	0	0	0	9	1	0	3	0	13
South Asia										
Pakistan	0	0	0	0	12	4	0	0	0	16
India	0	0	0	0	6	2	0	0	1	10
Bangladesh	0	0	0	0	0	1	0	0	4	6
Bhutan	0	0	0	0	0	0	0	0	3	4
Nepal	0	0	0	0	0	1	0	0	1	3
Maldives	0	0	0	0	0	0	0	0	0	0
East Asia & Pacific										
Indonesia	4	3	14	9	0	1	0	1	2	34
Vietnam	0	4	0	3	0	2	1	0	1	11
Lao PDR	0	4	0	0	0	1	0	1	1	6
Philippines	0	1	0	1	0	3	0	0	1	6
China	0	0	0	0	3	1	1	1	0	6
Myanmar	0	0	0	1	2	1	0	0	0	4
Cambodia	0	0	0	1	0	0	0	0	0	2
Middle East & North Africa										
Yemen	0	3	0	0	2	0	0	1	0	6
Morocco	0	0	0	0	0	0	0	0	1	1
West Bank & Gaza	0	0	0	0	0	0	0	0	0	1
Djibouti	0	0	0	0	0	0	0	0	0	0
Latin America & Caribbean										
Honduras	0	22	9	0	0	6	0	0	0	39
Nicaragua	1	11	0	0	0	5	0	0	1	19
Haiti	2	6	0	0	0	1	0	0	1	10
Bolivia	0	1	0	0	4	5	0	0	0	10
Europe & Central Asia										
Tajikistan	0	0	0	0	17	0	0	0	0	17
Kyrgyz Republic	0	0	0	0	3	0	0	0	1	4

a. Figures are rounded to nearest percentage point. Values less than 0.5 percent not included.

Table 6A-5. *Macroeconomic Agricultural Diagnostics, Sixty-One Focus Countries, by Country Group*

	Poverty	Macroeconomic context				Demography			Geography		Agriculture			
	AIC (PPP 2011)	Income group	Growth in GNI pc, 2000–10	Resource revenues	Fragile situation	% Pop. in rural areas	% Labor in agric (FAO)	Total fertility rate, 2010	Land-locked	Dist. to fertilizer plant	Lead staple crop (% of area harvested)	Cash crop role	Cereal yield, 2010	Fertilizer use, 2010
Group one														
Congo, Dem. Rep.	447	LIC		M	F	R	57	V high		Far	Cassava (31)		Low	Low
Liberia	606	LIC	Fast		F	M	62	V high			Rice (41)	Major	Low	
Comoros	621	LIC			F	R	69	High			Rice (18)		Low	
Burundi	648	LIC			F	R	89	V high		Far	Bananas (29)		Low	Low
Niger	719	LIC				R	83	V high	L	Far	Millet (44)		Low	Low
Guinea	789	LIC		L		R	80	V high	L		Rice (25)	Mid	Low	Low
Central African Republic	869	LIC		*	F	R	63	High	L	Far	Cassava (24)	Mid	Low	
Mozambique	890	LIC	Fast	*		R	81	V high		Far	Maize (24)		Low	Low
Guinea-Bissau	928	LIC		*	F	R	79	V high			Rice (20)		Low	
Burkina Faso	953	LIC				R	92	V high	L	Far	Sorghum (27)		Low	Low
Ethiopia	979	LIC	Fast			R	77	High	L		Teff (18)		Low	Low
Malawi	1,006	LIC			F	R	79	V high	L	Far	Maize (43)		Low	
Tanzania	1,029	LIC	Fast	*		R	76	V high		Far	Maize (23)		Low	Low
Mali	1,047	LIC		L	F	R	75	V high	L	Far	Millet (29)		Low	Low
Togo	1,193	LIC		*	F	R	53	High		Far	Maize (30)		Low	Low
Sierra Leone	1,194	LIC	Fast	*	F	R	60	High		Far	Rice (37)	Mid	Low	
Gambia	1,221	LIC				M	76	V high	L		Millet (30)		Low	
Rwanda	1,293	LIC	Fast			R	89	High		Far	Plantains (18)		Low	Low
Madagascar	1,332	LIC			F	R	70	High			Rice (45)	Mid	Low	Low
Zimbabwe	1,349	LIC		*	F	R	56	High	L	Far	Maize (45)	Mid	Low	Low

(continued)

Table 6A-5 (continued)

	Poverty	Macroeconomic context				Demography			Geography		Agriculture			
	AIC (PPP 2011)	Income group	Growth in GNI pc, 2000–10	Resource revenues	Fragile situation	% Pop. in rural areas	% Labor in agric (FAO)	Total fertility rate, 2010	Land-locked	Dist. to fertilizer plant	Lead staple crop (% of area harvested)	Cash crop role	Cereal yield, 2010	Fertilizer use, 2010
Uganda	1,390	LIC	Fast	*		R	75	V high	L	Far	Plantains (22)		Low	Low
Benin	1,473	LIC				M	44	V high		Far	Maize (30)		Low	Low
Chad	1,476	LIC	Fast	H	F	R	66	V high	L	Far	Millet (25)		Low	
Congo, Rep.	1,513	LMIC		H	F		32	V high		Far	Cassava (39)	Mid	Low	Low
Haiti	1,688	LIC			F	M	59				Maize (28)	Mid	Low	
Djibouti	1,719	LMIC					74	High			Beans (53)		Low	
Zambia	1,778	LMIC		L		R	63	V high		Far	Maize (47)			
Nepal	1,848	LIC			F	R	93		L		Rice (31)			Low
Senegal	1,923	LMIC				M	70	V high			Millet (34)		Low	Low
Kenya	1,937	LIC				R	71	High			Maize (39)		Low	
Côte d'Ivoire	1,979	LMIC			F	M	38	High		Far	Yams (11)	Major	Low	
Group Two														
Nigeria	2,075	LMIC	Fast	H		M	25	V high		Far	Sorghum (12)	Mid	Low	Low
Mauritania	2,089	LMIC		L		M	50	High			Sorghum (46)		Low	
Bangladesh	2,138	LIC	Fast			R	45				Rice (77)			
Ghana	2,242	LMIC	Fast	*		M	54	High		Far	Maize (15)	Major	Low	Low
Myanmar	2,273	LIC			F	R	67				Rice (43)			Low
Cambodia	2,277	LIC	Fast			R	66				Rice (75)			Low
Cameroon	2,297	LMIC		M		M	48	V high		Far	Maize (14)	Major	Low	Low
Sudan	2,309	LMIC	Fast	H	F	R	47	High		Far	Sorghum (50)		Low	Low
Laos	2,341	LMIC	Fast	L		R	75		L		Rice (59)			
Lesotho	2,524	LMIC	Fast			R	39		L	Far	Maize (63)		Low	

Country	GNI pc	Income	Growth	Resource	Fragile	Rural		TFR		Distance	Cash crop	Role	Cereal yield	Fertilizer use
Yemen	2,762	LMIC		H	F	R	39	High			Sorghum (41)			Low
Vietnam	2,991	LMIC	Fast			R	63				Rice (55)	Mid	Low	
Tajikistan	3,025	LIC	Fast			R	27	High	L	Far	Wheat (32)	Mid		
Sao Tome and Principe	3,340	LMIC		*			57	High			Bananas (11)	Major		Low
Kyrgyz Republic	3,506	LIC		*		R	21		L	Far	Wheat (41)			Low
Nicaragua	3,587	LMIC				M	15				Maize (34)	Mid		
Bolivia	3,661	LMIC		M			41		L	Far	Maize (11)			Low
Honduras	3,748	LMIC				M	24				Maize (35)	Major		Low
Maldives	3,883	UMIC	Fast			R	15				Vegetables (35)		Low	
Pakistan	3,926	LMIC				R	39				Wheat (38)	Mid		Low
Bhutan	3,998	LMIC	Fast			R	93				Maize (26)			Low
West Bank and Gaza	4,070	LMIC			F		8	High	L		Wheat (12)		Low	
Morocco	4,309	LMIC	Fast			M	25				Wheat (40)		Low	
Angola	4,319	UMIC	Fast	H		M	69	V high			Maize (36)		Low	
Philippines	4,490	LMIC				M	34			Far	Rice (32)		Low	
Cape Verde	4,747	LMIC	Fast				17				Maize (49)			
Indonesia	4,805	LMIC	Fast			M	41				Rice (33)	Major	Low	
Equatorial Guinea	4,916	HIC	Fast	H		R	64	V high		Far	Cassava (25)	Major		
India	3,023	LMIC	Fast			R	54				Rice (21)	Mid		
China	4,331	UMIC	Fast			M	36				Maize (18)			

Sources: FAOSTAT (2014); ICP (2014); IMF (2012); Government of Sudan (2012); UNCTAD (2014); World Bank (2014a).

Growth in GNI pc: "Fast" if >3% in constant LCU 2000–10

Resource revenues: "H" if >50% of fiscal revenues; "M" if 25–50%; "L" if <25% of fiscal revenues or if >20% of exports; "*" if prospective resource exporter; IMF (2012)

Fragile situation: World Bank list for FY2014

Population in rural areas: "R" if >60%; "M" if 40–60%

TFR: "V high" if >5; "High" if 3.5–5%

Distance to fertilizer plant: "Far" if index >8,000

Cash crop role: "Major" if >20% of harvest area; "Mid" if 10–20% of harvest area

Cereal yield: "Low" if <2 tons/ha

Fertilizer use: "Low" if <25 kg/ha

References

Anderson, Kym, Gordon Rausser, and Johan Swinnen. 2013. "Political Economy of Public Policies: Insights from Distortions to Agricultural and Food Markets." *Journal of Economic Literature* 51, no. 2: 423–77.

Barrett, Christopher B., Marc F. Bellemare, and Janet Y. Hou. 2010. "Reconsidering Conventional Explanations of the Inverse Productivity-Size Relationship." *World Development* 38, no. 1: 88–97.

Barrios, Salvador, Luisito Bertinelli, and Eric Strobl. 2006. "Climatic Change and Rural-Urban Migration: The Case of Sub-Saharan Africa." *Journal of Urban Economics* 60: 357–71.

———. 2010. "Trends in Rainfall and Economic Growth in Africa: A Neglected Cause of the African Growth Tragedy." *Review of Economics and Statistics* 92, no. 2: 350–66.

Bates, Robert H. 1981. *Markets and States in Tropical Africa: The Political Basis of Agricultural Policy.* Series on Social Choice and Political Economy. University of California Press.

Bates, Robert H., and Steven A. Block. 2013. "Revisiting African Agriculture: Institutional Change and Productivity Growth." *Journal of Politics* 75, no. 2: 372–84.

Boserup, Esther. 1965. *The Conditions of Agricultural Growth: The Economics of Agrarian Change under Population Pressure.* Chicago: Aldine.

Bourguignon, François, and Christian Morrisson. 1998. "Inequality and Development: The Role of Dualism." *Journal of Development Economics* 57: 233–57.

Carter, Michael R., Rachid Laajaj, and Dean Yang. 2014. "Subsidies and the Persistence of Technology Adoption: Field Experimental Evidence from Mozambique." Working Paper 20465. Cambridge, Mass.: National Bureau of Economic Research.

Chandy, Laurence, and Homi Kharas. 2014. "What Do New Price Data Mean for the Goal of Ending Extreme Poverty?" Brookings Institution blog (www.brookings.edu/blogs/up-front/posts/2014/05/05-data-extreme-poverty-chandy-kharas).

Christiaensen, Luc, Lei Pan, and Sangui Wang. 2010. "Drivers of Poverty Reduction in Lagging Regions: Evidence from Rural Western China." UNU-WIDER Working Paper 2010/35. United Nations University.

Christiaensen, Luc, Lionel Demery, and Jesper Kuhl. 2011. "The (Evolving) Role of Agriculture in Poverty Reduction—An Empirical Perspective." *Journal of Development Economics* 96: 239–54.

Collier, Paul, and Stefan Dercon. 2013. "African Agriculture in 50 Years: Smallholders in a Rapidly Changing World?" *World Development* (http://dx.doi.org/10.1016/j.worlddev.2013.10.001).

Deininger, Klaus, Derek Byerlee, Jonathan Lindsay, Andrew Norton, Harris Selod, and Mercedes Stickler. 2011. *Rising Global Interest in Farmland: Can It Yield Sustainable Benefits?* Washington: World Bank.

de Janvry, Alain, and Elisabeth Sadoulet. 2009. "Agricultural Growth and Poverty Reduction: Additional Evidence." *World Bank Research Observer* 25, no 1: 1–20.

———. 2010. "Agriculture for Development in Africa: Business-as-Usual or New Departures?" *Journal of African Economies* 19, AERC Supplement 2: ii7–ii39.

Dercon, Stefan. 2009. "Rural Poverty: Old Challenges in New Contexts." *World Bank Research Observer* 24, no 1: 1–28.

Dercon, Stefan, and Luc Christiaensen. 2011. "Consumption Risk, Technology Adoption and Poverty Traps: Evidence from Ethiopia." *Journal of Development Economics* 96, no. 2: 159–73.

Dercon, Stefan, and Douglas Gollin. 2014. "Agriculture in African Development: Theories and Strategies." *Annual Review of Resource Economics* 6: 471–92.

Diao, Xinshen, Peter Hazell, Danielle Resnick, and James Thurlow. 2006. "The Role of Agriculture in Development: Implications for Sub-Saharan Africa." DSGD Discussion Paper 29. Washington: International Food Policy Research Institute.

Diao, Xinshen, James Thurlow, Samuel Benin, and Shenggen Fan. 2012. *Strategies and Priorities for African Agriculture: Economywide Perspectives from Country Studies.* Washington: International Food Policy Research Institute.

Eastwood, Robert, Michael Lipton, and Andrew Newell. 2010. "Farm Size." *Handbook of Agricultural Economics: Volume IV.* Burlington: Elsevier.

FAO. 2014. FAOSTAT online database.

Gelb, Alan, Christian Meyer, and Vijaya Ramachandran. 2013. "Does Poor Mean Cheap? A Comparative Look at Africa's Industrial Labor Costs." Working Paper 325. Washington: Center for Global Development.

Giné, Xavier, and Dean Yang. 2009. "Insurance, Credit, and Technology Adoption: Field Experimental Evidence from Malawi." *Journal of Development Economics* 89, no. 1: 1–11.

Gollin, Douglas, Stephen L. Parente, and Richard Rogerson. 2002. "The Role of Agriculture in Development." *AEA Papers and Proceedings* 92, no. 2: 160–64.

———. 2007. "The Food Problem and the Evolution of International Income Levels." *Journal of Monetary Economics* 54: 1230–55.

Grow Africa. 2014. *Agricultural Partnerships Take Root across Africa: 2nd Annual Report on Private-Sector Investment in Support of Country-Led Transformations in African Agriculture.* Report produced by Grow Africa Secretariat. May.

Hsiang, Solomon M., Marshall Burke, and Edward Miguel. 2013. "Quantifying the Influence of Climate on Human Conflict." *Science* 341, no. 6151.

ICP (International Comparison Program). 2014. "Purchasing Power Parities and Real Expenditure of World Economies: Summary of Results and Findings of the 2011 International Comparison Program." Washington: World Bank.

IMF (International Monetary Fund). 2012. "Macroeconomic Policy Frameworks for Resource-Rich Developing Countries." IMF policy paper. August.

Johnston, Bruce, and John W. Mellor. 1961. "The Role of Agriculture in Economic Development." *American Economic Review* 51, no. 4: 566–93.

Loayza, Norman V., and Claudio Raddatz. 2010. "The Composition of Growth Matters for Poverty Alleviation." *Journal of Development Economics* 93: 137–51.

McArthur, John W. 2011. "An International Credit Facility to Support Commercialization of African Smallholder Staple Crop Farmers." Concept Note for World Economic Forum, Global Agenda Council on Poverty and Economic Development. January 9.

———. 2013. "Good Things Grow in Scaled Packages: Africa's Agricultural Challenge in Historical Context." Brookings Institution. Africa Growth Initiative Working Paper 11. May.

———. Forthcoming. "What Does 'Agriculture' Mean Today? Assessing Old Questions with New Evidence." Global Views Policy Paper. Brookings Institution.

McArthur, John W., and Gordon C. McCord. 2014. "Fertilizing Growth: Agricultural Inputs and Their Effects in Economic Development." Global Economy and Development Working Paper 77. Brookings Institution, September.

McArthur, John W., and Jeffrey D. Sachs. 2013. "A General Equilibrium Model for Analyzing African Rural Subsistence Economies and an African Green Revolution." Africa Growth Initiative Working Paper 12. Brookings Institution. June.

McMillan, Margaret S., and Dani Rodrik. 2011. "Globalization, Structural Change, and Productivity Growth." Working Paper 17143. Cambridge, Mass.: National Bureau of Economic Research.

National Bureau of Statistics of China. 2013. *China Statistical Yearbook.*

OECD (Organization for Economic Cooperation and Development). 2014. "International Development Statistics Online Database" (http:// stats.oecd.org/).

Olinto, P., K. Beegle, C. Sobrado, and H. Uematsu. 2013. "The State of the Poor: Where Are the Poor, Where Is Extreme Poverty Harder to End, and What Is the Current Profile of the World's Poor?" Economic Premise Paper 125. Washington: World Bank, October.

Pan, Lei, and Luc Christiaensen. 2012. "Who Is Vouching for the Input Voucher? Decentralized Targeting and Elite Capture in Tanzania." *World Development* 40, no. 8: 1619–33.

Pauw, Karl, and James Thurlow. 2011. "Agricultural Growth, Poverty, and Nutrition in Tanzania." *Food Policy* 36: 795–804.

Pingali, P. L. 2012. "Green Revolution: Impacts, Limits and the Path Ahead." *PNAS* 109, no. 31: 12303–08.

Ravallion, Martin, and Shauhua Chen. 2007. "China's (Uneven) Progress against Poverty." *Journal of Development Economics* 82: 1–42.

Restuccia, Diego, Dennis Tao Yang, and Xiaodong Zhu. 2007. "Agriculture and Aggregate Productivity: A Quantitative Cross-Country Analysis." *Journal of Monetary Economics* 55: 234–50.

Rodrik, Dani. 2013. "Unconditional Convergence in Manufacturing." *Quarterly Journal of Economics* 128: 165–204.

Schultz, Theodore W. 1968. *Economic Growth and Agriculture.* New York: McGraw-Hill.

World Bank. 2006. "World Development Indicators" (CD-ROM). Washington.

———. 2007. *World Bank Agricultural Assistance to Sub-Saharan Africa: An IEG Review.* Washington.

———. 2014a. "World Development Indicators Online."

———. 2014b. Pink Sheet data (http://siteresources.worldbank.org/INTPROSPECTS/ Resources/334934-1304428586133/pink_data_a.xlsx).

———. 2014c. "PovcalNet: The Online Tool for Poverty Measurement Developed by the Development Research Group of the World Bank."

World Bank and IMF (International Monetary Fund). 2014. *Global Monitoring Report 2014/2015: Ending Poverty and Sharing Prosperity.* Washington.

7

Structural Change and Africa's Poverty Puzzle

JOHN PAGE

Sub-Saharan Africa has enjoyed nearly twenty years of sustained economic growth. The region grew at around 4.6 percent a year during the last decade, exceeding the average for the rest of the developing world (excluding China) by about 1 percentage point.[1] Per capita income has been rising steadily, and with six of the world's ten fastest-growing countries, cheerleaders as diverse as *The Economist* and the World Bank have branded Africa the developing world's next "frontier market." At the same time, however, there are growing concerns that rapid economic growth has not produced equally rapid poverty reduction. Poverty has declined, to be sure. An estimated 58 percent of people in sub-Saharan Africa were living on less than $1.25 a day in 2000; by 2010 the poverty rate had fallen to 48.5 percent (World Bank 2013). But while East and South Asia managed to reduce extreme poverty dramatically over the last two decades, sub-Saharan Africa failed to keep pace.

Poverty in Africa presents something of a puzzle. The region has both the lowest responsiveness of poverty to per capita income growth and the lowest responsiveness of poverty to changes in income distribution of any of the world's developing regions. Africa's structural pattern of growth during the last two decades is at least partly responsible. In Asia economies that succeeded

---

1. If South Africa is excluded, the regional average is an even more impressive 5.2 percent (World Bank 2013).

in rapidly reducing poverty experienced significant changes in their economic structure, as workers moved from low-productivity sectors such as agriculture into higher-productivity manufacturing. In Africa structural change has contributed very little to growth and poverty reduction.

Until the turn of the twenty-first century an increasing share of African workers found themselves in low-productivity, low-wage jobs. Since about 2000 there is some evidence that structural change in Africa has been growth enhancing, but even here the news is not entirely good. In contrast with Asia, where a manufacturing revolution drove structural change, recent structural change in Africa has consisted largely of the movement of labor from agriculture to services such as trade and distribution. Manufacturing in Africa has failed to take off. Both cross-country evidence and country-level simulations suggest that Africa's performance in reducing poverty would have been better had the region started its structural transformation earlier and had it experienced more robust growth of manufacturing and other sectors with high value added per worker.

Solving Africa's poverty puzzle will require African governments—and their development partners—to move in new policy directions. First, new initiatives to increase productivity in agriculture are needed. Because Africa is starting from such a low base with respect to high-productivity employment, rapid early progress on poverty requires raising incomes where the poor are already employed. Second, Africa needs an industrialization strategy. Creating dynamism in manufacturing through public actions that emphasize exports and industrial clusters is essential. Africa can also build on its comparative advantage in agroindustry and tradable services. Because these industries without smokestacks share many firm characteristics with manufacturing—including the capacity to create large numbers of good jobs—the types of public action needed to boost manufacturing can be effective here as well.

This chapter unfolds in five sections: the first describes Africa's poverty puzzle; the next presents evidence on the role of structural change in growth in Africa and contrasts it with patterns of structural change in comparator economies when they were at similar levels of development. The following section uses both cross-country evidence and simulations for a number of African economies to show how lack of structural change has impeded poverty reduction in Africa. The next section argues that to eradicate absolute poverty, African governments and their development partners will need to develop a new approach to poverty reduction. A concluding section sums up the chapter.

Africa's Poverty Puzzle

As the global community turns to the ambitious goal of eradicating absolute poverty by 2030, most of the heavy lifting needed will have to come from

Figure 7-1. *Extreme Poverty in the Developing World, by Region, 1980–2010*

Percent of population

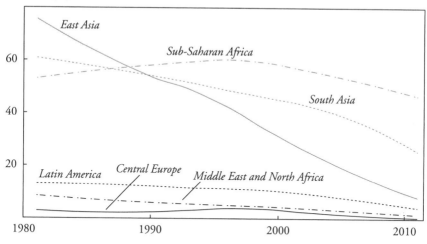

Source: World Bank PovcalNet database.

Africa. China, India, and sub-Saharan Africa account for three-quarters of the world's people living on less than $1.25 a day. For this reason poverty reduction since 1990 has resembled a "relay race in which responsibility for leading the charge on global poverty reduction passes from China to India to sub-Saharan Africa" (Chandy, Ledlie, and Penciakova 2013). This may pose a problem for the last mile.

East and South Asia—regions with the highest poverty rates in the 1980s—managed to reduce extreme poverty dramatically over the last two decades, but sub-Saharan Africa failed to keep pace (figure 7-1). Today more people are estimated to be living on less than $1.25 a day in sub-Saharan Africa—413 million in 2010—than in 1999 (World Bank 2013). In the World Bank's words, "Despite the continent's growth turnaround and progress in the fight against poverty during the last decade, poverty in Africa remains unacceptably high, and the pace of reduction unacceptably slow" (World Bank 2013).

There is a large literature on the relationship between economic growth and poverty reduction (Datt and Ravallion 1991; Chen and Ravallion 2010; Dollar and Kraay 2002). It shows that, across countries and over time, the poverty rate—the proportion of the population falling below a specified poverty threshold—declines as per capita income rises. But differences among countries (and regions) with respect to the rate at which poverty falls with income growth are substantial (Fosu 2011).

Figure 7-2. *Poverty Reduction and Growth in African Countries, 1995–2005*

Change in poverty

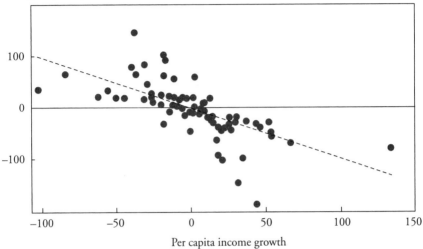

Per capita income growth

Source: Author's estimates using World Bank PovcalNet database.

The usual suspect to account for such differences is income inequality. Cross-country evidence indicates that the growth elasticity of poverty is larger for economies with less initial income inequality (Ravallion 2001; Adams 2004; Fosu 2011). Changes in inequality during growth can also influence the rate of poverty reduction. A number of country studies decompose the contributions of inequality and income growth to poverty reduction. They find that distributional changes during the course of growth have substantial impacts—both positive and negative—on changes in poverty (Datt and Ravallion 1992; Kakwani 1993).

Thus to understand why, despite rapid growth, progress against poverty in Africa has been disappointing it is important to understand how Africa compares to other regions with respect to income growth and inequality.[2] Using comparable household surveys, Page and Shemeles (2014) test the relationship between per capita income growth and poverty reduction for eighteen African countries. The results appear in figure 7-2. While the authors find the expected negative correlation between income growth and poverty

2. One part of Africa's slower pace of poverty reduction is easy to understand: Africa has much higher rates of population growth than Asia; therefore, while GDP growth has been similar between the two regions over the past fifteen years, per capita income growth was much higher in Asia.

incidence—a 1-percent increase in growth results on average in a decline in poverty of about 0.95 percent—the estimated relationship is imprecise and relatively weak, indicating that individual country experiences across Africa vary substantially. The results also confirm an important finding of other cross-country estimates of the relationship between growth and poverty. Africa has the lowest elasticity of poverty with respect to per capita income growth of any of the world's developing regions (Fosu 2011; Christiaensen, Chuhan-Pole, and Sanoh 2013).

The usual suspect matters: Africa has the world's highest level of income inequality (World Bank 2013). This diminishes the impact of growth on the poor, but it is not the full answer. Poverty in Africa also appears to be less responsive to changes in income distribution, controlling for the rate of growth of income, than it is in other parts of the world. Cross-country estimates of the partial elasticity of poverty reduction with respect to income distribution find that they are lowest in Africa, often by wide margins (Fosu 2011). Moreover, there appears to be no systemic relationship between growth and income inequality: countries in Africa that are growing experience increases and decreases in inequality in roughly equal numbers (World Bank 2013).

Thus we are left with a puzzle. Since 1995, growth in per capita income has reduced poverty in Africa but at a slower rate than in other parts of the world. Income inequality has played a role. Africa is the world's most unequal region, but poverty in Africa is less responsive to changes in inequality as well. Neither high inequality nor changes in inequality fully account for the differences between Africa and elsewhere. Why is poverty in Africa less responsive to growth? The answer may lie in the structure of Africa's recent growth.

Structural Change and Growth

Developing economies are characterized by large differences in output per worker across sectors, and those economies that successfully make the transition from low-income status to high-income status typically experience significant changes in their economic structure (Kuznets 1955; Chenery 1986). As factors of production move from lower productivity uses to higher productivity uses, there is a substantial growth payoff (Duarte and Restuccia 2010; McMillan and Rodrik 2011).

There is little evidence, however, that significant structural changes have underpinned Africa's more rapid growth (Arbache and Page 2008). Since 1995, its growth has been driven primarily by strong commodity prices, new natural resource discoveries, and better economic management (Arbache and Page 2009). Africa has the greatest differences across sectors in output per worker (figure 7-3). Research, however, finds that this potential has not been fully

Figure 7-3. *Labor Productivity among Sectors, by Country Group, 2005*

Average ratios of labor productivity in   Average coefficient of variation
highest and lowest sectors, excluding Nigeria   of log of sectoral productivity

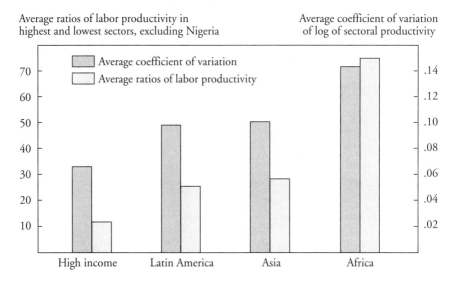

Source: McMillan and Rodrik (2011); author's calculations.

realized (McMillan, Rodrik, and Verduzco-Gallo 2013; de Vries, Timmer, and de Vries 2013).

Changes in output per worker have two components. One is the weighted sum of labor productivity growth within individual sectors, where the weights are the employment shares of each sector in the beginning period. This is defined as the within-sector component of productivity growth. The second component captures the productivity effect of labor reallocations across different sectors. It is the product of productivity levels in the end period with the change in employment shares across sectors. This is defined as the structural change component.

The decomposition is presented for 1990–2005 and for two subperiods, 1990–99 and 2000–05, in table 7-1. Among developing countries, the regional patterns of productivity change are strikingly different, and they change over time. In Asia the movement of workers from lower to higher productivity sectors increased the overall rate of productivity growth in both periods. This was growth-enhancing structural change. In Latin America and Africa over the entire fifteen-year period structural change worked to offset productivity improvements within sectors, reducing overall growth.

Africa's pattern of structural change shifted between the two subperiods. From 1990 through 1999 structural change in Africa looked more like Latin America's than Asia's. While output per worker increased within sectors, the

Table 7-1. *Decomposition of Productivity Growth, Four Country Groups, Various Years*

Percent per year

	Labor productivity growth	Due to within-sector productivity growth	Due to structural change
	1990–2005		
Asia	3.87	3.31	0.57
High income	1.46	1.54	−0.09
LAC	1.35	2.24	−0.88
Africa	0.86	2.13	−1.27
	1990–99		
Asia	3.85	3.25	0.60
High income	1.56	1.54	0.02
LAC	1.75	1.77	−0.02
Africa	−0.20	0.20	−0.40
	2000–05		
Asia	3.87	3.40	0.47
High income	1.21	1.41	−0.20
LAC	1.02	1.90	−0.88
Africa	2.15	1.20	0.95

Source: McMillan and Rodrik (2011); McMillan (2013).

share of workers employed in high-productivity sectors declined. Structural change offset rising within-sector labor productivity and was growth reducing. Structural shifts in employment more than fully offset the positive contribution of within-sector productivity growth to overall productivity growth.

After 2000 labor began to shift from lower productivity to higher productivity employment. This is good news, but it comes with two cautionary warnings. The first is that within-sector productivity growth, despite a significant improvement over 1990–99, remained substantially lower than in Asia and Latin America, with the result that the region's total labor productivity growth rate was about half of Asia's. The second warning lies in the nature of the structural change that was taking place. Historically, industry—and especially manufacturing—has led structural change. It is a high-value-added sector into which labor can flow. Given the very large difference in output per worker between agriculture and industry and its potential to absorb labor, industrialization presents a significant opportunity for growth-enhancing structural change.

Globally, growth in income at early stages of development is associated with very rapid increases of the share of manufacturing in total output (Dinh and others 2013). This pattern of structural change provides a powerful engine of productivity growth. Duarte and Restuccia (2010) find that rising productivity in industry, combined with structural change out of agriculture and into industry, explains 50 percent of the catch-up in aggregate productivity by developing countries between 1950 and 2006. Using a large panel of countries, Rodrik (2013) finds that since 1960 manufacturing industries have exhibited unconditional convergence in labor productivity to advanced economy levels, regardless of country or regional factors.

Africa's pattern of structural change since 2000 is significantly different. The share of manufacturing in GDP has remained the same for more than forty years. In 2010 it was 10 percent, slightly lower than in the 1970s (de Vries, Timmer, and de Vries, 2013). The region's share of manufacturing in GDP is less than half the average for all developing countries, and in contrast with developing countries as a whole, it is declining. Manufacturing output per capita is about one-third of the global developing country average (Page 2012b). Only four African countries—Madagascar, Mozambique, Lesotho, and Côte d'Ivoire—have a share of manufacturing in total output that exceeds the predicted value for their level of income. Many of the region's recent growth success stories—Ethiopia, Ghana, Kenya, Tanzania, and Uganda—have manufacturing value added shares that are well below the predicted values (Dinh and others 2013).

A "Premature" Shift to Services

The structural change that has taken place in Africa since 2000 has been a shift of labor out of agriculture and manufacturing into services. Table 7-2 presents recent estimates of the sectoral distribution of output and employment for eleven African countries over the period 1990–2010. A number of stylized facts emerge from the data. Agriculture's share of the economy has declined in terms of output and employment. Industry—and especially manufacturing—has declined as a share of total output and as a share of total employment. Services have taken up the slack. Between 1990 and 2010 the share of the African workforce employed in market services nearly doubled, from 12.9 percent to 23.5 percent. In 2010 on average 20 percent of the African workforce was employed in distribution services, up from 11 percent in 1990.

This pattern of structural change represents a movement from very low-productivity employment to slightly higher productivity jobs. For the nine African countries in the original McMillan and Rodrik (2011) database, agriculture—at 36 percent of average productivity—is by far the sector with the lowest productivity; manufacturing productivity is six times higher, and that in mining is nearly sixty times higher. These productivity gaps across sectors are enormous.

Table 7-2. *Structure of African Economies, by Sector, 1990 and 2010*[a]

Percent

Sector	Value added share		Labor share		Relative productivity	
	1990	2010	1990	2010	1990	2010
Agriculture	24.9	22.4	61.6	49.4	0.4	0.4
Industry	32.6	27.8	14.3	13.4	3.5	2.6
Mining	11.2	8.9	1.5	0.9	23.9	19.5
Manufacturing	14.0	10.1	8.9	8.3	2.4	1.6
Other	7.3	8.8	3.9	4.2	5.3	2.9
Services	42.6	49.8	24.1	36.8	2.4	1.6
Distribution	28.1	34.0	12.9	23.5	3.0	1.8
Finance and business	5.4	8.6	1.5	3.4	10.4	8.1
Government	11.5	12.2	6.4	8.7	2.5	1.7
Other	2.9	3.5	5.3	5.4	1.0	1.0

Source: Gronnengen Africa sector database, as reported in deVries, Timmer, and deVries (2013).

a. Figures are unweighted averages across eleven African countries. Employment and output data include both formal and informal activity. Other industry includes construction and public utilities. Distribution includes transport services and distributive trade as well as hotels and restaurants. Finance and business services exclude real estate activities. Other services include other community, personal, and household services. Numbers may not sum due to rounding.

The majority of employment in the African sample is in the least productive sectors. Roughly three-quarters of the labor force is in agriculture and wholesale and retail trade.

Africa's shift into services is premature because it has occurred at a much lower level of per capita income than in other countries. In early stages of development, rapidly growing developing countries have typically reallocated most labor into manufacturing. The share of activity in manufacturing follows an inverted U shape: increasing during early stages of development and then decreasing as higher incomes drive demand for services and labor costs make manufacturing more difficult (Chenery 1986; Duarte and Restuccia, 2010; Herrendorf, Rogerson, and Valentinyi 2013).

In Africa workers have been moving into services such as retail trade and distribution (de Vries, Timmer, and de Vries 2013). Today, the share of Africans employed in the distribution sector is about the same level as in the OECD (Jorgenson and Timmer 2011). Moreover, services have been absorbing workers faster than the sector has been increasing output. The relative productivity level of market services fell from 3.0 times the total economy average in 1990 to 1.8 in 2010, suggesting that the marginal productivity of new services workers is low and possibly negative (de Vries, Timmer, and de Vries 2013).

Table 7-3. *Structure of Africa's Economies: Share of Labor Force in Four Sectors*[a]
Percent

Country/benchmark	Agriculture	Manufacturing	Other industry	Services
Least developed country benchmark (US$600–700)	70.0	9.0	3.0	18.0
Ethiopia 2005	83.2	4.1	1.5	11.2
Malawi 2004	77.6	2.9	3.1	16.4
Low-income benchmark (US$900–1,100)	60.9	11.5	2.9	24.7
Mali 2005	66.0	3.1	2.9	28.0
Rwanda 2010	79.0	1.9	2.1	17.0
Tanzania 2005	76.7	2.1	2.7	18.5
Uganda 2005	72.0	3.0	2.0	23.0
Zambia 2005	72.9	3.1	3.4	20.6
Transitioning and lower middle-income benchmark (US$1,200–500)	57.9	13.7	3.0	25.4
Ghana 2005	48.1	11.0	4.1	36.8
Kenya 2010	48.3	12.8	3.6	35.3
Nigeria 2010	59.6	3.9	2.0	34.5
Senegal 2005	52.8	9.0	4.0	34.2
Upper middle-income benchmark (US$10,000)	14.0	25.0	4.0	57.0
Botswana 2005	39.2	5.9	8.4	46.5
Mauritius 2010	7.2	19.1	11.2	62.6
South Africa 2010	15.0	13.2	10.0	61.8

a. Structural characteristics are from the most recent year of available household survey data. The benchmarks used are as follows: least developed, BGD 1994, CAM 1996, CHN 1987, IND 1989, IDN 1982, VNM 1992; low income, BGD 2003, CAM 2002, CHN 1992, IND 1994, IDN 1986, THL 1980, VNM 1996; transitioning, CAM 2005, CHN 1995, IND 2000, IDN 1992, PHL 1982, THL 1985, VNM 2001; middle income, CHL 2003, KOR 1993, MYS 2004.

Benchmarking Africa's Economic Structure

Table 7-3 compares the employment structure of a sample of fourteen African countries with the distribution of employment of four "benchmark" economies, made up of non-African economies—mainly in Asia—that have had sustained success in both growth and poverty reduction. The benchmark countries are Bangladesh, Cambodia, Chile, China, India, Indonesia, Korea, Malaysia,

Philippines, Thailand, and Vietnam. The benchmarks show the structural characteristics of these economies at the time that they were at the same level of per capita income (in international PPP US$) as the contemporary African economies in the sample. The labor share values for the benchmarks in the table are the simple averages of the labor shares of the relevant benchmark countries at the time their per capita incomes (in PPP US$) were equal to the African countries in each subsample. (Some basic descriptive statistics on these countries are presented in appendix table 7A-1.)

The African countries in table 7-3 are broken into four groups: least developed (Ethiopia and Malawi); low income (Mali, Rwanda, Tanzania, Uganda, and Zambia); transitioning (Ghana, Kenya, Nigeria, and Senegal); and middle income (Botswana, Mauritius, and South Africa). Comparisons of the individual country employment structures with the benchmarks confirm the narrative above.

Both Ethiopia and Malawi have larger shares of their labor force in agriculture than the benchmark economy. Both have significantly smaller shares of the labor force engaged in manufacturing. And both have smaller employment shares in services than the benchmark. This suggests that these economies are at very early stages of structural transformation, even in comparison with the benchmark economies at the same stage of development.

The low-income economies are in many ways similar to the least developed countries. With the exception of Mali, a substantially larger share of their labor force is employed in agriculture than the benchmark. The share of the labor force engaged in manufacturing is only about a quarter of the benchmark level, while the services share is somewhat lower. Taken together with the least developed country pattern, these data suggest that, below levels of GNI per capita of about US$1,000 (PPP), most African countries have experienced a delayed structural transformation. Too many workers remain in agriculture and too few have moved to industry relative to other developing countries when they were at similar levels of development.

The transitioning economies display an employment structure that reflects the dominant role of services in structural change in Africa. With the exception of Nigeria, the share of employment in agriculture is below the benchmark value. All of the transitioning economies, with the exception of Kenya, have employment shares in manufacturing that are below the benchmark, some—like Nigeria and Senegal—by wide margins. In contrast, the labor share in services for all countries exceeds that of the benchmark by about 10 percentage points.

The middle-income countries display great diversity. Botswana still has a large share of its labor force engaged in agriculture at very low relative levels of productivity. Mauritius and South Africa have more than 60 percent of their labor force engaged in services. Only Mauritius has a labor share in manufacturing that approximates the benchmark economy.

Structural Change and Poverty Reduction

The very different patterns of structural change and poverty reduction in Asia and Africa suggest that the structural sources of growth may partly determine growth and poverty outcomes. In Asia rising output per worker has been due to two strong, complementary components: within-sector productivity is rising, making it possible for firms to offer increases in wages in line with rising output per worker, and at the same time workers are moving from lower-productivity to higher-productivity employment. The result has been very rapid reductions in poverty. Structural change has played a much smaller role in Africa's growth story, and Africa's progress against poverty has been much less successful.

From 1990 to 1999 structural change in Africa was growth reducing: an increasing share of African workers was forced to find employment in sectors that offered low wages or self-employment incomes. After 2000 structural change in Africa became growth enhancing, but in contrast with Asia, the shift of employment toward higher-productivity sectors was not toward manufacturing. It was toward services, and in particular into retail trade and distribution, which offered only modestly higher output per worker than agriculture.

Moreover, as employment shifted into services between 2000 and 2010 there is evidence that both the average and the marginal product of labor in the sector declined. Unlike manufacturing, which offers the potential for very large increases in employment without sharp declines in marginal productivity—particularly in the early stages of development—Africa's recent services-based pattern of structural change does not appear to offer similar potential for rapid growth of real wages and incomes. Put somewhat differently, Africa's pattern of structural change post-2000 can be interpreted as a symptom of poverty rather than as a source of poverty reduction. Workers in agriculture moved to slightly better urban jobs in the services sector but remained trapped in low-productivity, low-wage employment.

Cross-Country Evidence

Consistent data on productivity growth, structural change, and poverty are sparse, but they permit some simple statistical estimates of the relationship between structural change and poverty reduction. McMillan and Rodrik (2011) present data on employment, output, and productivity for twenty-nine developing countries. Six developing economies—one in Asia, two in Central America, and three in Africa—were added to this sample by drawing on compatible national and international data sources. Poverty data ($1.25 a day) were taken from the World Bank PovcalNet database. Because not all countries in the sample are in the PovcalNet database, thirty-three countries form the final data set on structural change and poverty. (These are listed in appendix table 7A-2.)

Tables 7-4 and 7-5 present the results of some exploratory regressions. In addition to the direct regression on the two variables of interest, two additional

Table 7-4. *Rate of Change of Poverty and Productivity Growth, 1990–2005*[a]

	(1)	(2)	(3)
Constant	0.18	−0.16	−1.48
	(0.11)	(0.09)	(0.68
Productivity growth	−1.13*	−1.16*	−1.16*
	(1.88)	(1.90)	(1.95)
Middle income 1990		1.04	
		(0.44)	
Income relative to U.S. 1990			12.26
			(1.20)
Observations	33	33	33
R^2	0.10	0.11	0.14

t statistics in parentheses; * significant at 10 percent, ** significant at 5 percent, *** significant at 1 percent.

a. Dependent variable is the rate of change of poverty ($1.25 a day). Because poverty at $1.25 vanishes at higher income levels, both the middle-income status of the country in 1990 (as a dummy variable) and income relative to the United States in 1990 were added to test for the stability of the relationship with rising income. Neither variable was significant, and the coefficient estimates of interest were stable.

Table 7-5. *Rate of Change of Poverty and Structural Change, 1990–2005*[a]

	(1)	(2)	(3)
Constant	−2.70**	−3.13**	−4.20**
	(2.54)	(2.25)	(2.47)
Structural change	−1.72***	−1.75***	−1.71***
	(3.12)	(3.11)	(3.11)
Middle income 1990		1.06	
		(0.49)	
Income relative to U.S. 1990			10.63
			(1.13)
Observations	33	33	33
R^2	0.24	0.24	0.27

t statistics are in parentheses; * significant at 10 percent, ** significant at 5 percent, *** significant at 1 percent.

a. Dependent variable is the rate of change of poverty ($1.25 a day).

specifications are used to provide a simple first test of the robustness of the direct relationship. The results show a strong, statistically significant association between the rate of change in poverty and the structural change component of productivity growth. Higher rates of structural change are associated with more rapid declines in poverty, and the reverse. The relationship between

Table 7-6. *Rate of change of Poverty Productivity Growth and Structural Change, 1990–2005*[a]

	(1)	(2)	(3)
Constant	−1.69	−1.85	−2.20
	(0.97)	(0.99)	(1.12)
Productivity growth	−0.46	−0.48	−0.48
	(0.74)	(0.90)	(0.95)
Structural change	−1.52**	−1.55**	−1.53**
	(2.45)	(2.47)	(2.46)
Middle income 1990		1.03	
		(0.49)	
Income relative to U.S. 1990			10.44
			(1.13)
Observations	33	33	33
R^2	0.25	0.25	0.27

t statistics are in parentheses; * significant at 10 percent, ** significant at 5 percent, *** significant at 1 percent.

a. Dependent variable is rate of change of poverty ($1.25 per day).

overall productivity growth and poverty reduction is less clear-cut. The explanatory power of the direct regression is lower and the estimated coefficient, while of the predicted sign, is statistically significant only at the .10 level.

Table 7-6 presents the multiple regression of the rate of change of poverty on the rate of change of output per worker and the structural change component of productivity growth. The results confirm the patterns observed in the direct regressions. The fit of the model to the data is better than for the productivity-poverty relationship alone and similar to that for the relationship between structural change and poverty. The productivity-poverty relationship is of the predicted sign but insignificant. The structural change-poverty relationship is similar in magnitude to that of the direct regression and is significant at the 0.05 level. Neither of the controls for convergence to middle-income status is significant. Figure 7-4 presents the partial scatter plot of the rate of change of poverty and the structural change variable, conditional on change in output per worker.

Although the data are limited and the econometrics subject to the usual uncertainties, they nevertheless suggest a strong conjecture. One of the reasons why Africa's growth since 1990 has produced rates of poverty reduction that many regard as disappointing is that the structural sources of growth have in fact worked against more rapid poverty reduction. Although output per worker was rising within sectors, employment in high productivity sectors was not growing fast enough to absorb a rapidly growing workforce. New workers

Figure 7-4. *Partial Scatterplot of Rate of Change of Poverty and Structural Change, 1990–2005, by Change in Output per Worker*

Rate of change of poverty

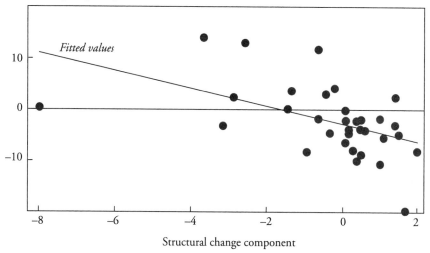

Structural change component

Source: Extended McMillan and Rodrik (2011) database; author's calculations.

were forced into lower productivity, often informal, employment with negative consequences for the overall rate of poverty reduction.

Some Simulations

While the cross-country evidence is indicative of a relationship between structural change and poverty reduction, it is unlikely to convince the skeptics. Another way to assess the extent to which structural change has influenced poverty reduction in Africa is to undertake a set of simulations, using sector-specific poverty data and a counterfactual distribution of employment based on the structural characteristics of the benchmark economies. In effect, this is asking the question, What would the poverty outcome of countries in the Africa sample have been if structural change had been more in line with the observed experience of a benchmark economy at the same level of per capita income?

Sector-specific poverty rates are available from household survey data for twelve of the fourteen countries listed in table 7-3. The poverty data in table 7-7 are reported at the level of three broad sectors—agriculture, industry, and services. Poverty rates are uniformly highest in agriculture. With the exception of Tanzania, they are uniformly lowest in households where the head of household is employed in services. Poverty rates for the industrial sector lie between those

Table 7-7. *Poverty Rates, by Sector of Employment of Head of Household*

Country	Year	Overall	Agriculture	Industry	Services
Botswana	2005	34.36	43.77	30.41	27.63
Ethiopia	2005	41.56	44.31	34.98	25.16
Ghana	2005	22.60	32.58	11.51	8.22
Malawi	2011	65.60	73.78	50.74	32.05
Mali	2005	47.36	53.46	45.03	33.73
Nigeria	2010	66.80	81.64	55.44	52.80
Rwanda	2010	52.80	58.63	44.83	27.76
Senegal	2005	31.09	56.41	19.24	17.54
South Africa	2006	15.91	17.5	5.83	13.03
Tanzania	2007	62.60	70.63	29.2	37.19
Uganda	2005	36.19	43.94	26.3	14.13
Zambia	2003	64.85	70.1	62.49	47.41

Source: AfDB poverty database; author's calculations.

for agriculture and services. This differs from the patterns observed in Asia, where the poverty incidence in industry is generally below that in services, and the poverty incidence in agriculture is more than double that in the other two sectors (World Bank 2012).

The difference lies in the structure of the industrial and services sectors in Africa itself. Manufacturing and services in most African economies are dominated by informal firms. Although informal manufacturing is a source of employment and income, it is not a powerful engine for poverty reduction (Duflo and Banerjee 2004). In Africa, as in other parts of the developing world, formal firms are highly productive and pay higher wages, especially large formal firms; informal firms are small and much less productive (La Porta and Shleifer 2011a, 2011b; Page and Soderbom 2012). The contrast between formal and informal services is equally stark. Clearly, informal firms have an important role to play in providing a livelihood for poor people in Africa, but they do not offer the types of high-wage jobs that draw workers out of poverty. The inability to distinguish between formal and informal segments of manufacturing and services in terms of both their relative size and poverty incidence thus limits the precision of the simulations.

Table 7-8 reports the results of the simulations. While there is considerable variation in the country-by-country results, the main takeaway is clear. Had Africa's economies gone through patterns of structural change that were more like those of the benchmark economies, poverty reduction would have been greater. The median change in the poverty rate for the twelve countries in the sample is

Table 7-8. *Structural Change and Poverty Simulations, Twelve Countries*

Country and year	Observed poverty rate	Simulated poverty rate	Percentage change in poverty
Ethiopia 2005	41.6	39.7	−4.6
Malawi 2011	65.6	63.5	−3.2
Mali 2005	47.4	47.4	0.0
Rwanda 2005	52.8	48.5	−8.1
Tanzania 2007	62.6	55.2	−11.8
Uganda 2005	36.2	34.0	−6.1
Zambia 2003	64.9	63.4	−2.3
Ghana 2005	22.6	22.9	1.3
Nigeria 2010	66.8	66.6	−0.0
Senegal 2005	31.1	40.3	29.6
Botswana 2005	34.4	30.7	−10.8
South Africa 2006	15.9	11.6	−27.0

Source: Author's calculations.

−3.9 percent. The reductions in poverty are largest for the two country groups—high-income economies and low-income economies—that most diverge from their benchmark structural characteristics. Botswana, despite its high per capita income, still has nearly 40 percent of its labor force in agriculture, a sector in which nearly 50 percent of people are poor. South Africa has too few of its workers in manufacturing and too many in services. Poverty would be reduced substantially in Rwanda, Tanzania, Uganda, and Zambia with a further shift of labor out of agriculture into industry and services. In Mali, where the poverty rate in agriculture is relatively low and that in industry is relatively high, a structural change toward the benchmark would leave overall poverty unchanged.

In Ghana and Senegal poverty would have increased if structural change had been in line with the benchmark. Both countries have labor shares in agriculture and industry that are below the benchmark and service sector employment shares that are substantially above it. This means that the reallocation out of services in the simulation shifts the labor share in the direction of the sectors with higher poverty incidence. The effect is particularly striking in Senegal, where the differences in poverty between agriculture and the rest of the economy are very large. Both countries illustrate the limitations of being able to measure structural change only at the level of three broad sectors. Without a finer classification, it is not possible to distinguish between high-productivity and low-productivity subsectors in industry and services.

A New Strategy for the Last Mile

Despite almost two decades of good growth, Africa continues to confront a significant poverty problem. The evidence suggests that one cause of the region's lackluster pace of poverty reduction is its lack of structural change. To succeed in eradicating absolute poverty, African governments and their development partners need to develop a new, two-part strategy for faster poverty reduction. The first objective is to raise agricultural productivity. In the near term, poverty reduction in Africa's low-income economies will need to come mainly from income growth in agriculture. Structural change will take time. Many of the building blocks for higher productivity jobs are long-gestation investments in physical and human capital. An agricultural transformation can both reduce poverty directly and establish the necessary conditions for labor to shift out of agriculture.

The second objective is to pursue public actions that accelerate the movement of workers into higher-productivity, higher-wage jobs. Given the relatively large number of low-skilled workers in most African countries, the structural changes that can have the greatest impact on poverty must be toward sectors that are intensive users of low-skilled labor. While industry—and manufacturing in particular—has been the major driver of structural transformation in Asia, it has not featured prominently in Africa's recent growth story. Africa needs an industrial revolution. And fortunately for Africa, industry no longer needs smokestacks. In addition to manufacturing, tradable services and agro-based value chains offer new opportunities for poverty reduction through structural change.

Back to Basics: Raising Agricultural Productivity

Sixty percent of Africans work in agriculture, and because the region's population growth is so fast and its nonfarm sector is so small, in the near term an increasing number of Africans will have no choice but to earn their living by farming. In the short run, achieving more rapid poverty reduction will depend fundamentally on raising agricultural productivity. While Africa has suffered from underinvestment in new agricultural technologies—especially compared to Asia—there is substantial room for yield increases, even for traditional crops. Thus improving farm productivity offers the potential to directly reduce poverty, as it has done in China, India, and Vietnam, and to strengthen the basis for accelerated movement of labor into higher productivity sectors.

Over the past decade, improved agricultural technologies have played a minor role in output growth in many African countries. Only a small number of smallholders use drought-resistant plant varieties or improved seeds. A similarly small number use productivity-enhancing inputs such as fertilizer (Udry

2010). If the technology available to farmers permits high yields, and farmers choose not to use it, the most likely explanation is that it is not profitable. The price of output is low relative to the prices of inputs.

There is a need to improve rural roads, market access, and irrigation to increase the profitability of new agricultural technologies. Bad roads and poorly developed marketing systems inhibit innovation. Transport costs from the farm gate to primary and secondary markets are high. Poor roads have increasingly negative impacts on adoption of nontraditional inputs. Irrigation can reduce the impact of droughts and also help to enhance productivity through a stable water supply, but the total irrigated area is well below its potential size.

The overall deficit of agriculture and rural development investment in Africa has been put between US$20 billion and $40 billion annually (Kanu, Salami, and Numasawa 2012). Support to the sector by African governments has been far below the 10 percent of fiscal expenditures pledged in the Maputo declaration of 2003. African governments—especially those that have recently experienced significant new natural resources discoveries—need to use some of their increased fiscal space in agriculture. There is also an expanded role for donors. While donor commitments to agriculture have been rising since about 2007, they have not yet reached the share of total official development assistance of the mid-1990s (Page and Shemeles 2014).

Poor rural infrastructure and lack of access to markets are part of the innovation story but not the whole story. We know very little about what else constrains raising agricultural productivity in Africa. Four market failures are commonly thought to be relevant to farmers' decisions to adopt new technologies: credit constraints, lack of insurance, learning externalities, and lack of secure property rights. Any one of these market failures could lead to underinvestment by farmers in the adoption of best practices. Each of these explanations has different implications for appropriate public policy, but there is often insufficient evidence to conclude which constraint is binding (Udry 2010). Most African countries on average spend less than 0.7 percent of agricultural GDP on research (Karugia and others 2009). More money is needed, and more of it needs to be directed toward understanding the behavioral reasons that farmers shun potential yield improvements.

One option to increase agricultural productivity receiving increasing attention by African policymakers—sometimes over the objections of their development partners—is opening the sector to large-scale investors (Collier and Dercon 2009). There are numerous examples of recent investments in out-grower schemes across a wide range of countries that have succeeded in partnering smallholder producers with large foreign firms. Large firms are less susceptible to the types of market failures that affect smallholders, and by partnering with smallholders they can be an important catalyst for productivity growth. For example, formal firms are less likely to face credit constraints or lack of access to adequate insurance. Larger organizations are better able to internalize the benefits of experimentation, allowing faster learning. As a result, a larger organization may be able to diffuse knowledge more effectively (McMillan 2013).

Transforming Manufacturing: The Investment Climate, Exports, and Clusters

Modern manufacturing has the potential to provide good jobs for large numbers of relatively unskilled workers, but rapid growth of manufacturing depends upon the rapid expansion of competitive firms. One set of public actions to support industrial development is largely noncontroversial. It includes mainly policies and investments directed at improving the investment climate—the regulatory, institutional, and physical environment within which firms operate. Indirect costs attributable to the investment climate are higher in Africa than in Asian competitors (Eifert, Gelb, and Ramachandran 2005; Dinh and others 2013). Given the range of investment climate reforms available to African governments and their development partners, however, too much attention has been paid to low-impact but easily measured reforms of business regulations and too little to infrastructure and skills (Page 2012a). Firm-level studies of productivity highlight infrastructure deficiencies as a significant barrier to greater competitiveness. Sub-Saharan Africa lags at least 20 percentage points behind the average for low-income countries on almost all major infrastructure measures. Electric power remains particularly scarce and unreliable (World Bank 2009). There has been little strategic orientation of Africa's infrastructure investments to support industrial development and, until quite recently, little willingness on the part of Africa's development partners to finance infrastructure.

Closing Africa's infrastructure gap will require around US\$93 billion a year, about 15 percent of the region's GDP; 40 percent of total spending needs is for power alone (World Bank 2009). It is clearly unrealistic in the current fiscal environment to count on aid to fill the financing gap. New approaches and products are needed. Guarantee instruments could leverage limited donor financing by reducing the perceived risk of private debt financing for infrastructure. Greater cooperation and coordination between Development Assistance Committee donors and nontraditional donors, like China, can improve the focus and efficiency of resource use. The Infrastructure Consortium for Africa at the African Development Bank, if properly funded and used, could lead the effort.

Africa's skills gap with the rest of the world also constrains its ability to compete. Secondary and tertiary educational access and quality lag other regions significantly. Employer surveys report that African tertiary graduates are weak in problem solving, business understanding, computer use, and communication skills (World Bank 2007a). In manufacturing there is a strong link between export sophistication and the percentage of the labor force that has completed postprimary schooling (World Bank 2007a). There is also evidence that manufacturing enterprises managed by university graduates in Africa have a higher propensity to export and that firms owned by university-educated indigenous entrepreneurs have higher growth rates (Page 2012a). Expanding postprimary education presents at least as daunting a challenge as closing the infrastructure gap. The current funding gap for education across Africa is estimated between US$6 billion and $29 billion (World Bank 2007b). DAC donor commitments to all levels of education in Africa approach only US$4 billion. Confronted with rising unit costs of primary education and limited prospects of external finance, it is time to replace the primary education MDG with a more broad-based measure of human capital.

Investment climate reforms alone, even broadly defined to include greater investment in infrastructure and skills, are unlikely to prove sufficient to meet Africa's industrialization challenge. Africa is a latecomer to the global market in manufactured goods. Rising real wages in China may offer an opportunity to break into global markets in low-wage goods (UNIDO 2009; Dinh and others 2013), but to succeed, African governments—and their development partners—will need to recognize two important realities. First, for the vast majority of African countries the export market represents the only option for rapid growth of manufacturing. Thus an effective strategy for the promotion of nontraditional exports is essential. Second, and closely related, manufacturing and service industries tend to concentrate in clusters, because of the productivity boost that such industrial agglomerations provide.

Africa needs an export push: focused public investment reforms, policy reforms, and institutional reforms that address the critical constraints to exporting. Here is an important role for regulatory reforms. Export procedures—including permits and certificates of origin, quality, and sanitation—can be burdensome. Duty drawback, tariff exemption, and VAT reimbursement schemes are often complex and poorly administered (Farole 2011). Because new entrants to the global trade in manufactures tend to specialize in the final stages of the value chain, improving trade logistics is essential. Value added in final-stage exports is low, amplifying the cost penalties imposed by beyond-the-border constraints to trade. African countries rank at the bottom of the World Bank trade logistics index, and poor trade logistics performance in coastal countries taxes landlocked neighbors (World Bank 2010a). The region ranks especially badly in trade-related infrastructure, but poorly functioning institutions and logistics markets also reduce competitiveness.

International support for an export push should consist of aid to improve trade logistics and policies to increase preferential market access. The Aid for Trade initiative has attracted considerable donor attention. As generously defined by the donors, it makes up about 25 percent of total development assistance. But donors are not fulfilling the promise made at Hong Kong in 2005 to make Aid for Trade additional to existing aid budgets. In fact Aid for Trade's share in total development assistance has fallen steadily since 1996 (OECD 2010). Africa's export push will not succeed unless the international community keeps its promise of additionality. One way to improve trade policy in Africa is to reduce escalating tariffs targeted at higher-stage processing of exports. Here, China must play a leading role. Another step is to develop a simple, time-bound system of preferences for Africa's nontraditional exports to high-income countries. A sensible place to begin would be for the European Union and the United States to harmonize their individual preference schemes for Africa (the Economic Partnership Agreements and the Africa Growth and Opportunities Act).

Africa has few modern industrial clusters, making it both more difficult for existing firms to compete and more difficult to attract new industry. Governments can foster agglomerations by concentrating investment in high-quality institutions, social services, and infrastructure in a special economic zone. This has been one of the keys to the rapid growth of industry in China and Vietnam. In East Asia and Latin America, spatial policies have supported an export push through the creation of export processing zones (Farole 2011; Dinh and others 2013). Africa's experience with spatial industrial policy, however, has been largely unsuccessful. A recent review concludes that most African special economic zones have failed to reach the levels of physical, institutional, and human capital needed to attract global investors (Farole 2011).

Making Africa's special economic zones world class will be a challenge. It will require profound changes in management, including the recruitment of high-quality, business-oriented staff. Surveys of Africa's special economic zones document widespread failure by free-zone authorities to engage constructively in a dialogue with their private sector clients (Farole 2011). Significant upgrading of infrastructure both within and outside the zones is needed. Zone-specific changes in the regulatory regime affecting exports can be introduced to reduce the administrative burdens on exporters. Business support services, training, and skill-upgrading programs focused on the needs of zone-based investors can be introduced. To address the collective action problem, foreign direct investment policy can be designed to encourage a critical mass of investors to locate in a special economic zone within a short period of time.[3] Traditional donors have tended to neglect special economic zones. China, on the other hand—building on its own success with spatial industrial policies—has launched an initiative to

---

3. China has sponsored the development of five "official" special economic zones aimed at supplying the Chinese market. The Chinese government has not involved itself in the design or direct operation of the zones, but it has organized marketing events in China to promote investment in the zones.

promote the construction of export-oriented special economic zones in Africa (Brautigam and Tang 2011). Both governments and donors can learn from the Chinese experience.

Embracing New Options: Industries without Smokestacks

Major technological changes in transport and communications have broadened the range of options for growth-enhancing structural change. Industry no longer needs smokestacks: tradable services and some agricultural value chains increasingly share firm characteristics with manufacturing. With the exception of remote impersonal services, most industries without smokestacks are labor intensive and have mostly low-skilled jobs. And because they share many firm characteristics with manufacturing, the types of public policies needed to promote their rapid growth are similar.

Information and communications technology have made many services tradable that are high-value-added per worker (modern impersonal). The range of business processes that can be traded—processing insurance claims, desktop publishing, the remote management and maintenance of IT networks, compiling audits, completing tax returns, transcribing medical records, and financial research and analysis—is constantly expanding. Like manufacturing, these tradable services benefit from agglomeration, technological change, and productivity growth (Triplett and Bosworth 2004). Global trade in services has grown faster than trade in goods since the 1980s (Ghani and Kharas 2010). From 2000 to 2011 services exports from Africa grew six times faster than goods exports and are now about 20 percent of the total exports of the average non-resource-rich sub-Saharan African country (AfDB 2013).

The transport of fresh produce over long distances became possible with the development of refrigeration and cold-storage chains linking production and consumption points. Keeping products fresh (maintaining the cold-storage chain) and transferring them quickly from farm to shelf adds value. Value is also added through packaging, preparation, and innovation. The global agricultural value chain in horticulture—fresh fruit, vegetables, and flowers—is increasingly dominated by lead firms that coordinate vertical supply chains and have firm characteristics similar to modern manufacturing (Humphrey and Memedovic 2006). Led by Kenya, a number of African producers have succeeded in establishing niche markets in the production of cut flowers and out-of-season crops (Tyler 2005).

Africa has a strong comparative advantage in tourism. Sub-Saharan Africa attracted 33.8 million visitors in 2012, whereas in 1990 there were only 6.7 million. Receipts from tourism in 2012 amounted to over US$36 billion and directly contributed 2.8 percent to the region's GDP (Christie and others 2013). Tourist arrivals to Africa over the next ten years are forecast to grow faster than the world average (World Bank 2010b). Tourism is an employment-intensive industry. There are 5.3 million direct tourism jobs across Africa, but its indirect employment effects are almost three times as large; the World Travel and Tourism Council calculates that the total direct and indirect employment impact of tourism in Africa in 2012 was 12.8 million jobs (WTTC 2012).

Improving infrastructure is as important for industries without smokestacks as it is for manufacturing. Backbone IT infrastructure is central to success in remote impersonal services. Economical and efficient transport and cold-storage chains are essential for horticulture. Half the wholesale cost of African fresh produce in European markets is represented by the cost of transport, storage, and handling. Road infrastructure—crucial to horticultural exports and tourism—has received scant attention. Africa's distance from tourism source markets creates an acute need for higher quality and more competitive air access. Despite having 15 percent of the world's population, the continent is served by only 4 percent of the world's scheduled air service seats (Christie and others 2013). A plethora of small and uneconomical national airlines limits the region's ability to compete in horticulture and tourism (World Bank 2010b).

Trade in services requires high-level cognitive and language skills, and the fastest growing services sectors are the most education intensive (Ghani and Kharas 2010). Policies to build human capital must be tailored to the tradable services that countries want to develop (for example, language skills are essential for call center and tourism markets). Africa has a comparative advantage over Asia in languages, because several important international languages are spoken widely, but relative neglect of postprimary education threatens its ability to compete in many language-based services. Education and training for tourism, both in language skills and in industry specific skills, are deficient (World Bank 2010b). Tourism training institutes often focus on hotel management, though the skills gap is in mid-level skills for hotel and restaurant operations (Christie and others 2013).

Tradable services and agroindustry can benefit as much as manufacturing can from an export push and from spatial industrial policies. Madagascar for example has had success in the development of the fresh vegetable industry through the creation of an export processing zone. The production of vegetables for export has now grown to include almost 10,000 smallholder farmers. Surveys indicate that these farmers on average have higher wages and greater income stability than noncontract growers (Minten, Randrianarison, and Swinnen 2009). In countries with unreliable public infrastructure, services export companies look for customized facilities, such as IT parks (World Bank 2010b). Governments such as Madagascar's and Mozambique's have developed special tourism investment zones (Christie and others 2013).

There are few examples—with the notable exceptions of Rwanda in remote services, Ethiopia in cut flowers, and South Africa in tourism—of African governments developing targeted strategies to promote services and horticultural exports. There are fewer examples still of successful spatial industrial policies to support industries without smokestacks. In part this reflects the general lack of policies in Africa designed to create an export push and support agglomerations, but it also reveals a failure to recognize the potential offered by these new activities.

Conclusions

In the last decade a large number of African countries have experienced moderately high growth in per capita GDP, buoyed by rising commodity prices, better macroeconomic management, and new natural resource discoveries. What is deeply worrying is that, in most cases of this growth, the impact on poverty has been limited. Africa has the lowest elasticity of poverty reduction with respect to per capita income growth and income inequality of any developing area of the world. As a result, completing the last mile in global poverty reduction represents a serious hurdle. In the relay race of poverty reduction, from China to India to Africa, the effort to end extreme poverty may fail on the last leg. Poverty is less responsive to growth and distribution changes in sub-Saharan Africa than in India or China at any poverty rate (Chandy, Ledlie, and Penciakova 2013).

Africa's failure to create enough high-value jobs in the face of a rapidly growing labor force is largely responsible. Lack of structural change has reduced the impact of growth on poverty reduction. There is scope to reverse this trend. To complete the last mile, new ideas and new investments by African governments and by donors will be needed. A two-part strategy for poverty eradication based on intensified agriculture and accelerated industrialization—with and without smokestacks—offers the best hope of Africa successfully finishing the last mile.

Appendix 7A

Table 7A-1. *Some Characteristics of the Benchmark Economies*[a]

Country	GDP per capita, 2012 (current US$)	Rate of GDP growth per capita, 1990–2005	Poverty rate, most recent year	Change in poverty rate, 1990–2005
Bangladesh	752	3.38	43.3	−1.8
Cambodia	944	5.72	18.6	−1.6
Chile	15,452	4.18	1.4	−8.2
China	6,091	9.19	11.8	−10.6
India	1,489	4.13	32.7	−1.7
Indonesia	3,557	2.81	16.2	−5.3
Korea	22,590	4.73	0.0	0.0
Malaysia	10,432	3.86	0.0	−8.8
Philippines	2,587	1.21	18.4	−2.2
Thailand	5,480	3.65	0.4	−19.6
Vietnam	1,755	5.98	16.9	−8.1

a. Change in poverty rate is for the period beginning and ending closest to 1990–2005. Data for Cambodia are for the period 1993–2005.

Table 7A-2. *Countries in the Structural Change and Poverty Reduction Regressions*

Asia	Malaysia	Africa	Nigeria
	Thailand		Senegal
	Indonesia		Kenya
	Philippines		Ghana
	China		Zambia
	India		Ethiopia
	Korea		Mauritius
	Vietnam		Malawi
			South Africa
MENA	Turkey		Tanzania
			Mozambique
Latin America	Brazil		Tunisia
	Argentina		
	Chile		
	Mexico		
	Venezuela		
	Costa Rica		
	Colombia		
	Peru		
	Bolivia		
	Guatemala		
	El Salvador		

References

Adams, R., Jr. 2004. "Economic Growth, Inequality, and Poverty: Estimating the Growth Elasticity of Poverty." *World Development* 32: 1989–2014.

AfDB (African Development Bank). 2013. *African Economic Outlook 2013: Structural Transformation and Natural Resources.* Tunis.

Arbache, J. S., and J. Page. 2008. "Patterns of Long-Term Growth in Sub-Saharan Africa." In *Africa at a Turning Point? Growth, Aid, and External Shocks*, edited by D. Go and J. Page. Washington: World Bank.

———. 2009. "How Fragile Is Africa's Recent Growth?" *Journal of African Economies* 19: 1–24.

Brautigam, D., and Tang Xioyang. 2011. "African Shenzhen: China's Special Economic Zones in Africa." *Journal of Modern African Studies* 49, no. 1: 27–54.

Chandy, Laurence, Natasha Ledlie, and Veronika Penciakova. 2013. "The Final Countdown: Prospects for Ending Extreme Poverty by 2030." Brookings Institution.

Chen, Shaohua, and Martin Ravallion. 2010. "The Developing World Is Poorer than We Thought, but No Less Successful in the Fight against Poverty." *Quarterly Journal of Economics* 125, no. 4: 1577–625.

Chenery, Hollis. 1986. "Growth and Transformation." In *Industrialization and Growth: A Comparative Study*, edited by H. Chenery, S. Robinson, and M. Syrquin. Oxford University Press.

Christiaensen, Luc, Punam Chuhan-Pole, and Aly Sanoh. 2013. *Africa's Growth, Poverty and Inequality Nexus: Fostering Shared Prosperity.* Washington: World Bank.

Christie, Iain, Eneida Fernandes, Hannah Messerli, and Louise Twining-Ward. 2013. *Tourism in Africa: Harnessing Tourism for Growth and Improved Livelihoods.* Washington: World Bank.

Collier, P., and S. Dercon. 2009. "African Agriculture in 50 Years: Smallholders in a Rapidly Changing World?" Expert Paper for the FAO Conference, How to Feed the World in 2050? Rome.

Datt, Gaurav, and Martin Ravallion. 1992. "Growth and Redistribution Components of Changes in Poverty Measures: A Decomposition with Applications to Brazil and India in the 1980s." *Journal of Development Economics* 38, no. 2: 275–95.

deVries, G., M. Timmer, and K. deVries. 2013. "Structural Transformation in Africa: Static Gains, Dynamic Losses." *GGDC Research Memorandum,* no. 136. Groningen Growth and Development Centre, University of Groningen.

Dinh, Hinh T., Vincent Palmade, Vandana Chandra, and Frances Cossar. 2013. *Light Manufacturing in Africa: Targeted Policies to Enhance Private Investment and Create Jobs.* Washington: World Bank.

Dollar, David, and Aart Kraay. 2002. "Growth *Is* Good for the Poor." *Journal of Economic Growth* 7, no. 3: 195–225.

Duarte, M., and D. Restuccia. 2010. "The Role of the Structural Transformation in Aggregate Productivity." *Quarterly Journal of Economics* 125, no. 1: 129–73.

Duflo, E., and A. Banerjee. 2004. "Growth Theory through the Lens of Development Economics." In *Handbook of Development Economics*, vol. 1a. Amsterdam: Elsevier.

Eifert, B., A. Gelb, and V. Ramachandran. 2005. "Business Environment and Comparative Advantage in Africa: Evidence from the Investment Climate Data." Working Paper 56. Washington: Center for Global Development.

Farole, Thomas. 2011. *Special Economic Zones in Africa: Comparing Performance and Learning from Experience.* Washington: World Bank.

Fosu, Augustin. 2011. "Growth, Inequality, and Poverty Reduction in Developing Countries: Recent Global Evidence." Working Paper 2011-07. Oxford: Centre for the Study of African Economies.

Ghani, E., and H. Kharas. 2010. "The Service Revolution in South Asia: An Overview." In *The Service Revolution in South Asia,* edited by E. Ghani. Oxford University Press.

Go, Delfin, and John Page. 2008. *Africa at a Turning Point? Growth, Aid, and External Shocks.* Washington: World Bank.

Herrendorf, B., R. Rogerson, and A. Valentinyi. 2013. "Growth and Structural Transformation." In *Handbook of Economic Growth,* 2nd ed., edited by P. Aghion and S. Durlof. Amsterdam: North Holland.

Humphrey, John, and Olga Memedovic. 2006. "Global Value Chain in the Agri-Food Sector." Vienna: UNIDO.

Jorgenson, D. W., and M. Timmer. 2011. "Structural Change in Advanced Nations: A New Set of Stylised Facts." *Scandinavian Journal of Economics* 113, no. 1: 1–29.

Kakwani, N. 1993. "Poverty and Economic Growth with Application to Côte d'Ivoire." *Review of Income and Wealth* 39, no. 2: 121–39.

Kanu, B., O. A. Salami, and K. Numasawa. 2012. "Inclusive Growth: The Imperative of African Agriculture." Background paper, AfDB Study on Inclusive Growth in Agriculture. Tunis: African Development Bank.

Karugia, J., M. Waithaka, A. Freeman, R. Prabhu, B. Shiferaw, S. Gbegbelegbe, S. Massawe, M. Kyotalimye, J. Wanjiku, and E. Macharia. 2009. 'Responding to Food Price Crisis in Eastern and Southern Africa: Policy Options for National and Regional Action." ReSAKSS Working Paper 27. Nairobi: Regional Strategic Analysis and Knowledge Support System, East and Central Africa.

Kuznets, Simon. 1955. "Economic Growth and Income Inequality." *American Economic Review* 45, no. 1: 1–28.

La Porta, Rafael, and A. Shleifer. 2011a. "The Unofficial Economy and Economic Development." *Brookings Papers on Economic Activity* 39, no. 2: 275–363.

———. 2011b. "The Unofficial Economy in Africa." Working Paper 16821. Cambridge, Mass.: National Bureau of Economic Research.

McMillan, Margaret. 2013. "The Changing Structure of Africa's Economies." Tunis: African Development Bank.

McMillan, Margaret, and Dani Rodrik. 2011. "Globalization, Structural Change, and Productivity Growth." Working Paper 17/143. Cambridge, Mass.: National Bureau of Economic Research.

McMillan, Margaret, Dani Rodrik, and Ignio Verduzco-Gallo. 2014. "Globalization, Structural Change, and Productivity Growth, with an Update on Africa." *World Development* 63, no. 1: 11–32.

Minten, B., L. Randrianarison, and J. Swinnen. 2009. "Global Retail Chains and Poor Farmers: Evidence from Madagascar." *World Development* 37, no. 11: 1728–41.

OECD. 2010. "Aid for Trade: Is It Working?" Paris.

Page, John. 2012a. "Aid, the Private Sector, and Structural Transformation in Africa." Working Paper 2012/21. Helsinki: UNU-WIDER.

———. 2012b. "Can Africa Industrialize?" *Journal of African Economies* 21, special issue 2: ii86–ii124.

Page, John, and Abebe Shemeles. 2014. "Aid, Employment, and Poverty Reduction in Africa." Working Paper 2014/043. Helsinki: UNU-WIDER.

Page, J., and M. Soderbom. 2012. "Is Small Beautiful? Small Enterprise, Aid, and Employment in Africa." Working Paper 2012/94. Helsinki: UNU-WIDER.

Ravallion, Martin. 2001. "Growth, Inequality, and Poverty: Looking beyond the Averages." Washington: World Bank.

Rodrik, D. 2013. "Unconditional Convergence in Manufacturing." *Quarterly Journal of Economics* 128, no. 1: 165–204.

Triplett, J., and B. Bosworth. 2004. *Productivity in the U.S. Services Sector: New Sources of Economic Growth*. Brookings Institution Press.

Tyler, Geoff. 2005. "Critical Success Factors in the African High-Value Horticulture Sector." Background paper for the study "Competitive Commercial Agriculture in Sub-Saharan Africa." Washington: World Bank

Udry, Christopher. 2010. "The Economics of Agriculture in Africa: Notes toward a Research Program." Department of Economics, Yale University.

UNIDO. 2009. *Industrial Development Report, 2009*. Vienna: United Nations Industrial Development Organization.

World Bank. 2007a. "Accelerating Development Outcomes in Africa: Progress and Change in the Africa Action Plan." Washington.

———. 2007b. "Expanding the Possible in Sub-Saharan Africa: How Tertiary Institutions Can Increase Growth and Competitiveness." Washington.

———. 2009. *Transforming Africa's Infrastructure*. Washington.

———. 2010. "Connecting to Compete: Trade Logistics in the Global Economy." Washington.

———. 2010b. *Africa's Trade in Services and Economic Partnership Agreements*. Washington.

———. 2012. "Well Begun, Not Yet Done: Vietnam's Remarkable Progress on Poverty Reduction and the Emerging Issues." Washington.

———. 2013. "Africa's Pulse," vol. 8. Washington.

WTTC (World Travel and Tourism Council). 2012. *Travel and Tourism Economic Impact: Sub-Saharan Africa, 2012*. London.

8

Public Goods for Private Jobs: Lessons from Postconflict Small Island States

SHANE EVANS AND MICHAEL CARNAHAN

Strong, inclusive employment and income growth are more critical to fragile and conflict-affected countries (FCACs) than to other states. Unfortunately, employment and income growth are also difficult to generate. The problem is no less challenging in postconflict small island states. There is often a focus on larger countries because they contribute more to global poverty aggregates. However, going the last mile to end extreme poverty will include addressing the unique challenges facing small island states. Feeny, Iamsiraroj, and McGillivray (2014) describe these challenges as the small size of domestic markets, the great distances some locations are from major markets, and their vulnerability to external shocks.

The particular challenges facing FCACs were documented in the World Bank's 2011 *World Development Report*. Dealing with whole communities of

The authors wish to acknowledge valuable input from Emily Pye and Alice Steele, Nathan Dal Bon, Hien Tran, and Anna Brown. Helpful discussions, comments, and suggestions were provided from DFAT staff operating in Timor-Leste and Solomon Islands, including Vincent Ashcroft, Jonathan Gouy, Colin Johnson, and Sue Connell, and from the academic community, including Hal Hill, Ron Duncan, Brett Inder, Steve Radelet, Johannes Linn, Homi Kharas, Laurence Chandy, and participants in the workshop, The Last Mile in Ending Extreme Poverty, at the Brookings Institution.

The views expressed in this chapter are those of the authors and do not necessarily reflect the views of the Australian Department of Foreign Affairs and Trade, the Minister for Foreign Affairs and Trade, or the Australian Government.

displaced families, high unemployment, the demobilizing of armed groups, restoring the legitimacy of government, and resolving the tensions between combatants emerged as especially difficult problems confronting FCACs and donor governments. These problems reduce the attractiveness of an FCAC to potential investors and, therefore, the prospects for employment and income growth.

The economic conditions that prevail in FCACs are unlike other developing countries. They require a different focus when programing aid for economic growth. The restructuring and stabilization of the economy become critical objectives. Without interventions directed toward achieving and maintaining stability, there is a significant risk of a return to conflict; and without a significant restructuring of the economy, it is unlikely that any initial gains from growth will lead to improvements in the well-being of the population. Without these foundational investments, the likelihood of sustained employment growth and poverty reduction are very limited. Economic growth programs must focus on economic efficiency and growth stimulation through increasing participation and productivity. There must also be a special emphasis on the factors that can reduce the risk of a return to conflict. In FCACs the distribution of the gains from economic growth can be as critical as the rate of economic growth. When the nature of economic growth reinforces or exacerbates conflict drivers, a return to conflict becomes more likely.

Fundamentally, economic growth, and the potential for broad-based economic growth, are driven by increasing the capital stock and the level of productivity-enhancing public goods. The available labor then combines with higher capital stock to produce greater outputs. Certain public goods, taken for granted in nonfragile countries, require deliberate investment in FCACs. Establishing basic security and stability takes more public investment than what is required to maintain them. Resources need to be invested in establishing the legitimacy of the state and in deepening the stock of social capital, a key to a well-oiled, market-based economy.

The challenge for FCACs and the donors that support them is balancing the investments in the different public goods that directly and indirectly support economic growth. The following section sets out a simple framework to highlight these choices. Where aid inflows represent a substantial component of the inflow of revenues to the government in FCACs, these inflows must be coordinated with the other revenue inflows to the government (through taxation). Under the New Deal the total fiscal envelope composed of domestic revenue and aid inflows should be used to frame public expenditure decisions for the economy.[1] So aid and fiscal policy become important interdependent dimensions in influencing a country's growth path.

---

1. The New Deal for Engagement in Fragile States, developed by the International Dialogue on Peacebuilding and Statebuilding (2012), was endorsed by countries and international organizations

The following sections of the chapter apply the framework to two country cases—Solomon Islands and Timor-Leste. In both cases there has been a strong focus in the past ten years on the foundational role of establishing peace, security, and stability. Despite the individual challenges both countries face, these investments have laid a solid foundation for future economic growth. Most important, they have laid a foundation that allows a shift over the next decade into more direct economic productivity-enhancing investments. The World Bank (2011) reports that the average cost of a civil war is thirty years of GDP growth, so measuring these changes in decades does not seem inappropriate.

Conceptual Framework

Economies produce more when they use their resources better (productivity improves) or employ previously unused resources (participation improves). It is increases in productivity (producing more outputs with the same inputs) or participation (more inputs) that lead to more output. When this increase is measured on an annual basis, it is referred to as economic growth. In many cases this economic growth will coincide with reduction in poverty. Any increase in productivity will generally be associated with higher wages for the more productive workers. If this moves these workers or their households above the poverty line, then poverty will decrease. If any increase in participation draws people from below the poverty line into the labor force, poverty will also decrease.

Sustained increases in economic output are always associated with growth in the private sector. Temporary increases in output can be delivered through Keynesian-style stimulus packages, but sustained increases require an expansion of the private sector. Much has been written on laying the foundations for economic growth, but there is a consensus on the importance of peace and stability, investments that increase productivity or participation, policies that support these two elements, and institutions that implement these policies. Investments by governments or aid donors in each of these areas generate the public goods that support the creation of private jobs.

---

in 2011, at the Fourth High Level Forum on Aid Effectiveness in Busan. The three key elements of the New Deal are, one, a focus on peace-building and state-building goals; two, support for country leadership and ownership; and three, a push for international and domestic resources to be better utilized. Several studies, including Barro and Lee (2000) and Dollar and Kraay (2002), have established that the key determinants of growth are education, openness to trade, and financial depth of capital markets. Anand, Mishra, and Peiris (2013) find that macroeconomic stability, and the ability of industries to add value further up the value chain in both export of goods and services, are further proximate factors supporting inclusive growth in developing economies. These studies generally accord with the policies identified by the Spence Commission (2008) as the common characteristics of countries that have successfully achieved sustained growth since 1945. These common characteristics are exploitation of the world economy, macroeconomic stabilization, high rates of saving and investment, market allocation of resources, and committed, credible and capable governments.

Growth in Fragile and Conflict-Affected Countries

Fragile and conflicted-affected countries find themselves with a perfect storm: prone to conflict and instability, low and often atrophied productivity, low participation, weak institutions, and poor policies. As described by Collier and Hoeffler (2004), FCACs have an atypical need of financial flows and advice. The problem for donors is to ensure that the sequencing of these inputs balances the needs across these domains. Investments in creating stability are needed to prevent conflict from breaking out again. Participation needs to be encouraged. Productivity-enhancing investments need to be made—and to be broadly distributed to the conflict-affected segments of the population through public infrastructure, essential services, and human development. Institutions are needed that enable the private sector to flourish by legitimating the state and improving macroeconomic and structural policies.[2] A critical implication of fragility that requires special attention for public expenditures is the establishment and maintenance of peace. An inequitable distribution of wealth or economic opportunity may be responsible for the outbreak of conflict in the first place. Even the perception of inequality can be a conflict driver.

Ncube, Jones, and Bicaba (2013) stress that the likelihood of successfully preventing a return to conflict is increased by reforming the fundamentals of economic growth. However, in the years following the establishment of peace, fragmented and marginalized groups are likely to retain an inequitable distribution of wealth as well. This means that the distribution of the gains from economic growth can either enhance or undermine the sustainability of that growth. This may require an immediate transfer of resources to improve the current welfare of the poor and marginalized.

Stability issues aside, Demekas, McHugh, and Kosma (2002) argue that productive activity is suppressed in FCACs. Conflict typically leaves communities of displaced families in temporary camps. When combatants are unable to return to work, the unemployment numbers are even larger. Getting people back into productive employment is vital for economic growth and for stability. Collier, Hoeffler, and Rohner (2007) demonstrate empirically the link between employment and the risk of return to conflict. They argue that the share of young males in the population is a major risk factor explaining conflict. This supports the need for a strategy to enable productive employment for youth as a priority in fragile states. Ncube, Jones, and Bicaba (2013) quantify the growth

---

2. Cross-country studies generally conclude that, on average, growth is distributional-neutral across countries: the average incomes of the poor tend to rise at the same rate as overall income. Dollar and Kraay (2013) is the most recent empirical study that finds this. However, it is an open question as to whether this relationship still holds at the level of individual FCACs.

cost of fragility in terms of the lower growth trajectory of FCACs leading to missed opportunities for better development outcomes.

Typically, fragile states inherit economic policies that are dysfunctional. Collier (2009) and Demekas, McHugh, and Kosma assert that, during conflict, the weight that governments attach to the future decreases, leading to a change in priorities skewed to the present. Over this period, the government's fiscal position deteriorates as the private sector (and consequently, the tax base) diminishes due to the conflict. Urgent military spending forces governments to resort to inflation financing and costly forms of taxation. In addition, the composition of fiscal expenditures typically gets skewed away from public investment and social spending toward military and patronage expenditures. The low productivity of resources in the private sector is matched by low productivity in the public sector—and therefore weak public institutions. Moreover, Collier and Hoeffler (2004) find that growth is more sensitive to policy in FCACs.

Investments that support peace and stability, productivity and participation, and policies and institutions are highly complementary. Productivity improvements can increase stability by creating employment and increasing incomes, and public investment in infrastructure connecting farmers to markets can create jobs. Reforms in the law and order sector directly influence peace and stability and can indirectly foster productivity through reducing the risk of appropriation of private investment. Collier, Hoeffler, and Soderbom (2008) find evidence that economic recovery substantially contributes to this risk reduction in fragile states. Walton (2010) finds that unemployment is the most likely route through which low growth indirectly affects the risk of a reversion to violence. Moreover, increases in productivity (and therefore income) provide a stronger revenue base, which can fund further productivity-enhancing public goods. The increased funding of public expenditures from domestic revenues drives greater accountability of institutions and the demand for better policies.[3]

Growth Complements and Fiscal Substitutes

Peace and stability, productivity and participation, and policies and institutions complement each other. However, the fiscal constraint on public expenditure means that trade-offs need to be made between spending in these three areas. The choices in how to balance spending both across and within these areas are not straightforward. How the balance across these areas changes across time is also critical.

3. Much of the focus in this area has been on the relationship between the citizen-state relationship and the raising of domestic revenue. The OECD (2009) notes that taxation can also improve governance by creating a shared interest in economic growth between the state and the private sector and that improvements in the state apparatus associated with improved revenue collection may spur improvements elsewhere in the state.

Figure 8-1. *Short-Run/Long-Run Trade-Offs:*
Peace and Productivity as Fiscal Substitutes and Growth Complements

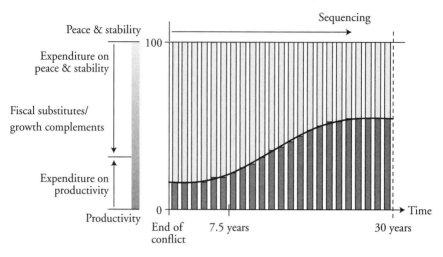

Source: Authors' calculations.

For fiscal decisionmakers and aid programs, there is a stark trade-off between immediate measures to create peace and stabilize the economy versus saving and making specific (direct) productivity-enhancing investments. All things being equal, risk-averse fiscal decisionmakers in fragile countries with a high likelihood of reversion to conflict will need to tilt the balance toward immediate peace-keeping measures. This may slow down the expected pace of the economy's recovery by forgoing direct productivity-enhancing investments. But the slower pace trades off for a more sustained and more sustainable long-term trajectory. Over time, if measures to increase the likelihood of peace and stability are successful, the fiscal trade-off between peace and productivity allows room for the composition of expenditure to shift toward specific public investments. That is, there is a natural sequencing of fiscal expenditures in fragile states. These are the dynamics of the trade-off described in figure 8-1.

Three features of figure 8-1 are noteworthy: the initial division of public expenditures, the time profile of expenditures, and the time horizon over which the expenditures are shown. Underlying the initial division of the budget is the assumption that a large portion of public expenditures devoted to achieving and maintaining peace and stability is a precondition for growth in the initial stages. This is supported by the emphasis recommended by USAID (2007) to provide humanitarian and social assistance and expand physical security in the early stages. The first-order importance of stability to growth is also described succinctly by Dalgaard and Hansen (2001), who show how the risk that producers face of expropriation of investments reduces the marginal product of capital. However, as peace and stability are restored and the basic functions of government are improved, the rate that public expenditures on peace and stability can be substituted for expenditures on productivity under the fiscal constraint to achieve growth increases. Work by Burnside and Dollar (2000) argues that serious policy distortions reduce the marginal productivity of capital and weaken the incentive to invest. To the extent that peace and stability can improve the business-enabling environment, increases in the marginal product of capital can be reinforced by complementary public investments in infrastructure to support growth and also investments in health and education to support longer-term growth.

There are few studies on the timing of the sequencing of expenditures. The timing depicted in figure 8-1 is stylized, but it finds some support in a recent study by Ncube, Jones, and Bicaba (2013). The study estimates that the time for recovery back to the original, preconflict, level in a sample of African nations is between twelve and thirty years. The upper bound is taken as a benchmark against which a postconflict plan might reasonably be considered. Further evidence for such a long horizon is provided in Chand and Coffman (2008), who argue that a donor presence in postconflict countries is required until the government can maintain a monopoly on the use of coercive force and taxation; can provide basic public goods like law and order, health care, and education; and can fund the recurrent budget from internally generated revenues. Finally the World Bank (2011) reports that the average cost of civil war is equivalent to more than thirty years of GDP growth for a medium-size developing country. As for the duration of the devotion of budget expenditures on peace and stability, an indicative time of seven and a half years is chosen, since it is the average time of UN peacekeeping missions to date—a duration that is trending upward (UN 2013). There are two further aspects to consider: how this stylized approach relates to the more standard poverty-growth trade-off and whether the outputs from public expenditure, particularly from the recurrent budget, shift from stability to productivity over time.

Our approach presents a trade-off between investments that enhance peace and stability and productivity-enhancing investments. The traditional trade-off presented in the literature is between investments that drive growth and those that drive poverty reduction. The composition of budget expenditures matters for growth and welfare. Baldacci, Clements, and Gupta (2003) find that fiscal measures for pure redistribution (cash transfers) that raise consumption, and hence welfare, today tend to be associated with lower future growth. However, revenue that is used to pay down debt, invest in public infrastructure, and generally reallocate resources to the most productive sectors in the economy enhances a country's growth potential.

In fragile states the risk of conflict or a return to conflict is a distinguishing factor that adds a layer of complexity and changes the nature of these trade-offs. The nature and distributional impacts of any growth needs to be mapped onto the roots of the conflict to see whether the growth is likely to ameliorate or exacerbate conflict drivers. Spending that disproportionately benefits the poor, the disadvantaged, and the disenfranchised represents an investment in peace and stability.

Through this fiscal lens, helping people in fragile states to reenter the labor force following the onset of peace—that is, increasing the participation rate—needs to be a first-order priority. In the short to medium term, postconflict, the capital endowment is fixed, scarce, and immobile. So the primary objective is to get people back into jobs. Understanding the distributional impact of these investments is critical to understanding their return against peace and stability objectives. Over time the focus needs to shift to ensuring that labor is productively employed—that is, that market failures are corrected through public investments and that policies enable markets to function in order to allocate labor across the sectors of the economy efficiently. Recent work on the links between poverty and growth finds that the poor can be caught in poverty traps. They do not have the basic capability to be participants in and contributors to the economic development that is occurring in their country. So investments that disproportionately benefit the poor may contribute to not only stability and peace but also productivity.

In some cases recurrent expenditure on civil service salaries may be, in and of itself, an investment in peace and stability. Development practice is rife with overcapitalized investment plans—often donor funded—with inadequate operating expenditure. The consequence of this suboptimal capital-operation mix is that a lower level of public goods is produced, with consequentially lower growth. However, in the immediate aftermath of a conflict, recurrent expenditure on civil services can be one of the most effective ways to undertake a rapid Keynesian-style stimulus. Such an approach quickly gets money out into the economy, supporting those service sectors that are labor intensive. Particular care needs to be taken if the civil service has been used as a patronage network, delivering benefits in ways that fuel conflict drivers. In a postconflict economy, a traditional Keynesian stimulus of infrastructure investment may be less effective. It may have a strong longer-term impact, assuming the infrastructure investment is appropriate and there are funds in the recurrent budget for operations and maintenance. However, it will likely have a lower multiplier effect in the short term, because more funds leak out into imported goods. It is also likely to be less rapid, even if emergency procurement and spending rules are applied.

Over time the focus needs to be more and more on the output of the civil service. As the country experiences a period of peace and greater stability, the return on this particular investment in peace and stability decreases, and the marginal impact of continuing to employ civil servants in this way lessens. But this raises the question of when one should start and how rapidly one should undertake major civil service reforms postconflict. The answer may be more art than science, but the answer is likely to be later rather than sooner.

Trade-Offs, Sequencing, and the Role of Donors

Broadly speaking, there is a simple hierarchy of fiscal priorities in fragile countries following the onset of peace. The first priority is measures supporting stability and peace, which includes encouraging participation in the workforce. Other priorities are measures to ignite productivity growth and policies that facilitate efficient use of an economy's resources. From a donor's perspective, sustainable growth strategies that strike the right balance between increasing the income of the poor and enhancing their productive capacity are most effective.[4]

The risk of a return to conflict adds a layer of complexity to the spending choices faced by FCACs. Interactions between donors and the FCAC government and between donor funds and domestic revenue add further layers of complexity. In some cases donor funds will complement domestic revenue and partner government expenditure; in other cases these funds will substitute. In some areas of peace and stability, international partner activity is a clear complement to domestic government activity. In both the case studies discussed in this chapter the domestic government did not initially have the fiscal capacity or the capability to deliver basic law and order functions that were provided by the international community. Domestic forces played a complementary role. In each FCAC there is a question over when and in what way the domestic government reestablishes itself as the deliverer of this most basic public good.

In some key economic areas donors and international partners also have a distinct role to play. Expatriate staff members have occupied major economic roles in FCACs. In some cases this has been because there was not a suitably qualified national to fill the role. In other cases it was because in the immediate period postconflict there was not a candidate for these roles who would have been acceptable to rival groups involved in the conflict. Positions filled by expatriates, including in the two countries in the case studies, have included finance minister, central bank governor, tax commissioner, and CEO of major utilities (water or power). A particular area where donor investments have a

---

4. USAID (2007) describes a number of other trade-offs in programming for growth, including the need for effective versus efficient solutions, urgency of some tasks versus the effect on legitimacy, short- and long-term objectives, and exploiting the window of opportunity versus absorptive capacity.

high complementarity with partner government investments is in strengthening the public financial management system. When international expertise provides capacity building or capacity supplementation, it increases the effectiveness of spending from domestic revenue and can increase the effectiveness of overall donor spending. This supports greater provision of public goods in support of not only peace and stability but also productivity and participation.

A key element of the New Deal is that donors' engagement with fragile states be guided by the principles of country leadership and ownership. Thus by endorsing a fragile state's development plan, donors enter into a compact committing the use of the funds to the terms spelled out in the plan. As such, while the trade-offs and complementarities identified above apply in any postconflict situation, the role of the donor will be sensitive to the domestic resources available to the fragile state and to the level of activity of other donors: the total fiscal envelope. Australia's role in countries where its aid constitutes a large proportion of revenue, such as Solomon Islands, will necessarily be different than in countries where its aid is a fraction of domestic revenues, such as Timor-Leste. This is borne out in the case studies. There are two final points to consider regarding the role of donors: many donors have their own preferences over how their taxpayer funds are spent. Measuring aid effectiveness in FCACs provides additional challenges.

The stylized framework outlined above presents a trade-off within years and over time between investing to support peace and stability and investing to support stronger productivity growth. In practice, investing in stronger productivity growth is often more popular, at least with some donors. In both Solomon Islands and Timor-Leste, Australia has made significant investments in the law and justice area, including prisons and courts. These areas are not popular with some donors for a variety of reasons, including the high risk of failure (World Bank 2011); restrictions on what is included in "official development assistance"; and domestic legislative restrictions on spending.

A particular challenge for donors is in measuring effectiveness. On the cost side, FCACs are by their nature difficult, and therefore expensive, places to do business. They are expensive places for the private sector to set up and to operate in, so it is natural they are expensive places to operate in for those wanting to invest in the provision of public goods. Higher business costs in these countries are due to factors like remoteness, poor infrastructure, weak governments, and lack of peace and stability. Moreover the benefits from any particular investment may be lower in an FCAC compared to other countries. If a country is stable, then investments in its productivity-enhancing public goods have a high rate of return. If a country has a strong economy, then investments in greater security or increased policy stability will generate high returns. This does not mean that aid effectiveness and value for the money should not be pursued.

Figure 8-2. *Non-Oil Real GDP per Capita, Solomon Islands and Timor-Leste, 1990–2013*

Constant 2005 US$

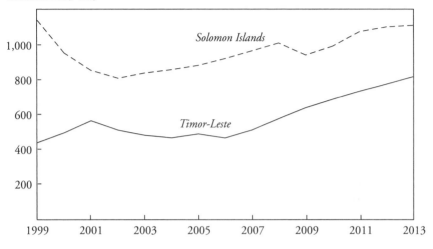

Source: World Bank Indicators.

It simply means that any benchmarking exercise needs to use an appropriate FCAC comparator index, not something more general.

Case Studies: Public Goods for Private Jobs in the Pacific

In the sections that follow we consider the postconflict experience of Solomon Islands and Timor-Leste. Their experiences are examined in the context of the role that donors—and in particular Australia—have played in helping to achieve peace, to invest in the productivity and participation of the workforce, and to form policies and institutions vital for a flourishing private sector.

Both Solomon Islands and Timor-Leste have experienced conflict and then peace over the last decade. And both countries have experienced relatively strong growth in recent years, as can be seen in figure 8-2 (with the exception of Solomon Islands in 2008 to 2009 due to the global economic downturn). However, in both cases the extent of growth across the natural resource and nonresource sectors of the economy needs to be understood. While the two countries share a lot in common, both being resource rich and vulnerable to external shocks, they also have many differences. Most notably, ODA remains a core contributor to public expenditure in Solomon Islands, but Timor-Leste's oil revenues have allowed significant and earlier investment in productivity-enhancing public goods. For Timor-Leste, the challenge may be ensuring the effectiveness of public expenditure without crowding out private investment.

Australian spending data are broken down into three categories: economic, social, and government and stability. This maps closely, but not identically, into the framework presented above, where spending delivers public goods that support peace and stability, investments that increase productivity or participation, policies that support both of these, and institutions that implement these policies. The economic spending category corresponds closely to the second category. The social spending category covers predominantly health, education, water, and sanitation. Provision of these basic public goods can contribute both to peace and stability and, in the longer term, to increases in productivity. The government and stability category includes public goods that contribute to peace and stability and also to the provision of institutional capability supplementation and development. For example, a large portion of the funding from Australia covered the provision of 200 police (directly contributing to peace and stability) and 100 civilian advisers (contributing both to peace and stability and to institutional performance).

A second view is taken from the spending over time that is attributed to the national governments' development and recurrent budgets. Generally speaking, development expenditures are focused on productivity-enhancing investments, such as infrastructure development or investments that deepen the quality of ongoing expenditure in areas like education and health. In contrast, the recurrent budget has a greater focus on peace and stability, as it includes the ongoing costs of administering the country and enforcing the rule of law. Moreover, as discussed above, civil service expenditure in and of itself can have a stabilizing impact.

Solomon Islands

Following the rapid deterioration of Solomon Islands' economy and society before the turn of the twenty-first century, the Australian-led Regional Assistance Mission to Solomon Islands (RAMSI) acted to restore peace and stability to the economy. The United Nations Development Program identifies five interrelated root causes of the conflict (UNDP 2004):

—Mismanagement of land
—A conflict between traditional and nontraditional authority structures
—Access to government services, public resources, and information
—Lack of economic opportunities
—Failure of law and order.

The intention for RAMSI was to lay the foundations for long-term stability, security, and prosperity. Part of this entailed regaining control of the fiscal position of the government and putting in place a sequence of reforms required for the creation of an enabling environment to facilitate Solomon Islands' private sector. Only ten years have elapsed since the onset of peace in Solomon Islands, and the process of reform is slow. While the private sector is yet to fully flourish and take Solomon Islands people forward, there are positive signs of recovery.

Conflict in Solomon Islands

Between 1997 and 2003, ethnic violence brought much of the Solomon Islands economy to a standstill. Rival ethnic gangs from the islands of Guadalcanal and Malaita took advantage of ethnic tensions between Malaitan settlers on Guadalcanal and the island's indigenous residents. The Isatabu Freedom Movement, made up of indigenous residents of the island of Guadalcanal, fought for several years with the Malaita Eagle Force, a militia group consisting mainly of residents and settlers from Malaita. Hameiri (2012) documents how the two groups fought for political power, jobs, and land rights, especially on the island of Guadalcanal; the conflict was foremost about access to land and other resources and was centered upon Honiara. The conflict took place against a backdrop of political economy dynamics driven by a culture of obligation and reciprocity, which had been facilitated for several decades by logging rents.

The conflict brought on a rapid deterioration of the government finances: RAMSI (2013) reports that against a backdrop of a 50 percent collapse in GDP, revenues fell by around 15 percent of GDP due to the eroding tax base. This precipitated a default on all of official Government of Solomon Islands debts, as well as a large backlog of informal debts related to government guarantees of state-owned enterprises and unpaid trade creditors. Solomon Islands' debt position was considered, at that stage, to be unsustainable. The debt crisis also led key multilateral institutions to stop lending to the Solomon Islands government, and local suppliers in the private sector services industry lost confidence in dealing with the government. Moreover, an outflow of skilled staff from Honiara's public service meant that the capacity for managing public finances was stretched. The consequence of this was that provision of public services and public goods by the government rapidly deteriorated.

The private sector was also affected. Less than a third of the population had paid work, the greater part of the population being involved in low-productivity subsistence and small cash-crop agriculture (Solomon Islands Census Office, 1999). Of the small formal private sector, the vast majority of businesses in Solomon Islands are classified as small or medium sized (employing fewer than 200 people), and they are mostly located in, or close to, Honiara and the Western Province (DFAT 2004). The adverse shocks that affected private sector firms were weak local demand, rising transport and travel costs, deteriorating infrastructure, an overall lack of confidence, and security problems from civil unrest. In May 2003 Prime Minister Allan Kemakeza's request for an international military intervention to restore law and order was accepted, paving the way for RAMSI.

The motivation behind the development of RAMSI was to consolidate efforts to help Solomon Islands lay the foundations for long-term stability, security, and prosperity. With its intent of creating a stable environment within which the private sector could recover, RAMSI's framework aligned with and complemented the Solomon Islands government's National Economic Reform, Recovery, and Development Program (NERRDP), which focused on the development of the private sector. The official objective of RAMSI was to facilitate "a peaceful Solomon Islands, where key national institutions and functions of law and justice, public administration, and economic management are effective, affordable and have the capacity to be sustained without RAMSI's further assistance."[5]

Fiscal Choices in Solomon Islands

Australian assistance to Solomon Islands has been heavily weighted toward supporting stability, with a modest shift more recently into some productivity-enhancing investments. This is consistent with the framework: the primary focus for the first decade has been on stabilization. However, it is important to emphasize that a focus on improving government institutions is a long-term issue. Pritchett and de Weijer (2010) argue that institutional development needs to be understood as a generational project. Australia has allocated over 70 percent of its official development assistance to government and stability (figure 8-3). This portion was over 80 percent until 2011 and over 90 percent in some years. Over two-thirds of this expenditure directly contributed to peace and stability through spending on the RAMSI policing component and on the law and justice sector. The remaining funds contributed to peace and stability by supporting the government in its provision of basic public services. More recently there has been an increase in spending in economic areas and a slight increase in spending on social areas. Spending to support increases in productivity has focused on improving transportation and increasing productivity in the agricultural sector. There has also been some spending to support the power and water sectors and the expansion of financial services.

The pattern of recurrent versus development public expenditures in Solomon Islands' total budget expenditure also displays a switch in emphasis from the former to the latter from about 2005 (figure 8-4). To the extent that development expenditures represent productivity-enhancing investments, this change

5. See www.ramsi.org/Media/docs/SIG-RAMSI_PartnershipFramework-f69fa231-cc6a-47bf-99a3-3e88eba95414-0.pdf.

Figure 8-3. *Composition of Australia's ODA to Solomon Islands, 2003–12*[a]

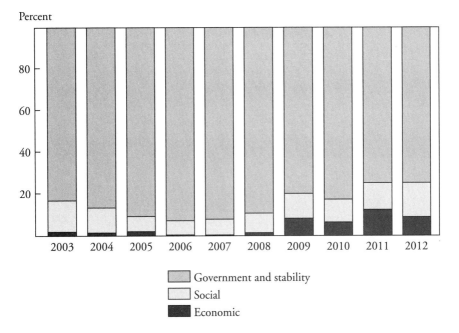

Percent

Government and stability
Social
Economic

Source: OECD (2014).

a. Formally, the shares of spending presented in figures 8-3 and 8-5 to the categories of government and stability, social, and economic categories are calculated by Government and stability = GCS/(SI+EI+PS); Social = (SI–GCS)/(SI+EI+PS); and Economic = (EI+PR)/(SI+EI+PS), where SI, GCS, EI, and PS are taken to be the OECD/DAC purpose codes: 100: I. Social Infrastructure and Services, total; 150: I.5 Government and Civil Society, total; 200: II. Economic Infrastructure and Services, total; and 300: III. Production Sectors, total.

in emphasis is also consistent with the fiscal substitutes/growth complements framework presented above

Job Creation in Solomon Islands

RAMSI moved quickly to support peace and stability, with successful interventions in several areas: restoring law and order, arresting ex-militants, and retrieving most of the guns that had been raided from police armories during the conflict. A rapid economic recovery ensued, following new ownership of the palm oil plantation and, most important, a dramatic increase in logging. Sectoral changes in paid employment from 1999 to 2009 are listed in table 8-1. Employment growth over the period averaged 4 percent a year, outstripping population growth of approximately 2 percent a year. However to evaluate this properly, it is necessary to compute growth in the labor force over the period

Figure 8-4. *Solomon Islands, Recurrent and Development Expenditures, 1998–2012*

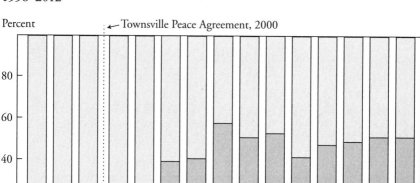

Source: IMF (various years).

and some measure of the subsistence economy. Paid employment increased by 43 percent over the period, a substantial increase, albeit from a low base.

Without going as far as attribution to RAMSI, the two notable changes over this time period are a doubling of paid agricultural employment (accounting for approximately half the increase in paid employment) and large increases in paid employment in forestry and logging, fishing, construction, public administration, and education (although these account for a small proportion of the increase in paid employment). The number of paid manufacturing sector employees, however, declined, reducing that sector's contribution to paid employment. These employment numbers confirm the dominance of agriculture in Solomon Islands' formal economy—and presumably in the private sector. On the other hand, while the rise in employees in public administration and education appears large in absolute terms, even when combined their impact is under half the contribution to the change in total employment as much as the agriculture sector.

Interestingly while logging experienced a boom in value over the period, it did not lead to a commensurate increase in employment. Given the capital-intensive nature of most resource projects, the absolute impact on employment

Table 8-1. *Paid Employment, Solomon Islands, by Sector, 1999 and 2009*[a]

Sector	1999	2009	% change	% share of employment growth
Agriculture	11,859	23,346	96.9	48.3
Forestry and logging	3,375	4,611	36.6	5.2
Fishing	3,367	5,736	70.4	10.0
Mining and quarrying	574	543	–5.4	–0.1
Manufacturing	7,237	5,242	–27.6	–8.4
Electricity and water	530	377	–28.9	–0.6
Construction	2,997	4,979	66.1	8.3
Retail and wholesale trade	8,140	8,996	10.5	3.6
Transport, storage, communications	3,239	4,003	23.6	3.2
Finance	939	856	-8.8	–0.3
Public administration, social security	4,337	6,092	40.5	7.4
Education	4,324	7,449	72.3	13.1
Other services	6,554	9,010	37.5	10.3
Total	57,472	81,240	41.4	100.0

Source: Solomon Islands Census Office (1999, 2009).
a. No strong inference should be drawn from the table, given the informality of the labor market.

will be limited. However, the lack of even a commensurate increase in employment suggests either productivity improvements in the logging sector or the use of foreign workers on logging projects.

Timor-Leste

Despite its high poverty, Timor-Leste's GDP per capita is relatively high compared with Solomon Islands and other fragile states. This is due to the country's oil revenue from its Petroleum Fund. For instance, in 2012 Timor's GDP per capita (which includes oil income) was US$5,643, compared with nonoil GDP per capita of only US$1,175 (IMF 2013). This dominance of the oil sector is also reflected in Timor-Leste's petroleum revenues, which have accounted for around 90 percent of government revenue in recent times (IMF 2013).

While large oil revenue flows take pressure off taxation and aid dependence, Timor-Leste's strong fiscal position has not yet translated into increased employment in the economy overall—nor reallocation into the higher-productivity sectors. Like Solomon Islands, Timor-Leste has made great progress in the decade since achieving independence, but as a postconflict state that is emerging from fragility, it will not achieve long-lasting development results for some time.

Conflict in Timor-Leste

In 1999, after twenty-five years of Indonesian rule, a United Nations–monitored referendum for Timor-Leste's independence precipitated a two-week outburst of violence. The conflict drove hundreds of thousands of Timorese into West Timor, destroyed Timor's infrastructure, and reduced much of its capital, Dili, to rubble. Up to 80 percent of private sector businesses and 50 percent of homes in Dili were lost to the violence ("Conflict Profile: East Timor" 2007). Before independence, Timor's provincial government had relatively little control over its fiscal management, resulting in limited management capacity, an inability to control the structural erosion of its tax base, and little room to maneuver in the face of the Asian financial crisis and increasing social unrest.[6] Moreover, following the Asian financial crisis the Indonesia central government curtailed transfers to its provinces. The effect of this, combined with a decline in revenue, led to a sharp contraction in capital expenditures just before the outbreak of violence.

From this precarious base the public sector in Timor-Leste ground to a halt in the aftermath of the violence. A major factor was the loss of capacity associated with the departure of senior civil staff. This resulted in the inability to operate government structures, systems, and buildings; little capacity for revenue collection (particularly in the absence of a trade regime or controls on international trade); and the loss of almost all public service delivery apart from a few rudimentary services. Hence, while Timor-Leste gained independence, it faced the prospect of starting from a very low base in terms of public administration capacity and public institutions.

The impact of the violence in Dili was sharp and destructive. In addition to a loss of nearly 40 percent of real GDP, the violence drastically disrupted agriculture, destroyed local inventories of manufactured goods, closed the border with West Timor, and restricted access to ports. Moreover, the violence resulted in a wholesale loss of human capital from high-end services and the public sector, as commercial bankers and civil servants fled to Indonesia. In fact, the financial sector up to 1999, although feeling the effects of the Asian financial crisis, had been operating well. Its payments system was clearing an

---

6. A comprehensive discussion of the public and private sector impact of the conflict can be found in Valdivieso and others (2000). The centralization of budget priorities to the Indonesian government meant that Timor's fiscal management capacity was limited. Before independence, as little as 10 percent of total revenues accrued directly to the provincial Timor administration, with the rest finding its way first to the Indonesian government. Whereas Timor might have generated revenues from customs, border taxes, transshipment, and procedures, instead both imports and exports were taxed in other localities in Indonesia. These arrangements underscore Timor's lack of authority over its own fiscal decisionmaking.

increasing number of items with efficiency. But the loss of these services after the initial conflict all but eliminated access to capital and public services underpinning the private sector. Many other business support systems were de facto Indonesian and were operated with Indonesian backing, backing that was withdrawn after independence.[7]

In September 1999 the United Nations–mandated International Forces East Timor (INTERFET) coalition deployed to Timor-Leste in the midst of a rapidly deteriorating security environment. This peacekeeping force remained for the interim, during which the United Nations transitional administration in East Timor oversaw operations until the country became fully independent in 2002. INTERFET's objectives were to restore peace and security, protect and support the United Nations Assistance Mission East Timor in carrying out its tasks, and facilitate humanitarian assistance operations (UN 1999).

Peace and stability were sustained in Timor-Leste following independence until April 2006, when simmering tensions, this time within the military, spilled over into the streets of Dili. The violence that ensued displaced up to 150,000 people, who took shelter in camps throughout Dili and Baucau (UN 2012). In response to this conflict, Australia deployed over 800 Australian federal police to United Nations missions within Timor-Leste. They carried out operational activities to reestablish law and order and then followed on to strengthen the foundations for a local police service, the Policia Nacional de Timor-Leste.

Fiscal Choices in Timor-Leste

Similar to the Solomon Islands case, Australian aid disbursements to Timor-Leste under the government and stability category are predominantly for public sector policy and the law and justice sector (figure 8-5). From 2003 to 2005 the share of spending on government and stability was between 70 and 80 percent. This spiked in 2006 and 2007 to almost 90 percent. This was due to both the renewed conflict in 2006 and support of the election in 2007. Since 2009 the share of spending on government and stability has decreased to between 50 and 60 percent. This is in part the transition from conflict to recovery to investment, which is articulated in the previous section. However it also reflects the fiscal capacity from oil revenues. Government spending to maintain peace and stability allows some room under the total fiscal envelope for Australia to substitute into productivity-enhancing investments. This is seen in Australia's aid disbursements shifting into areas such as education and health and transport, communications, and energy.

This more recent shift resulting from greater fiscal resources is further supported by the recurrent versus capital breakdown of Timor-Leste's budget

---

7. We are grateful to Hal Hill for providing this insight.

Figure 8-5. *Composition of Australia's ODA to Timor-Leste, 2003–12*[a]

Percent

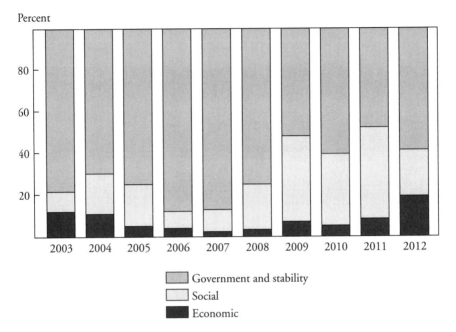

☐ Government and stability
☐ Social
■ Economic

Source: OECD (2014).

a. Formally, the shares of spending presented in figures 8-3 and 8-5 to the categories of government and stability, social, and economic categories are calculated by Government and stability = GCS/(SI+EI+PS); Social = (SI−GCS)/(SI+EI+PS); and Economic = (EI+PR)/(SI+EI+PS), where SI, GCS, EI, and PS are taken to be the OECD DAC purpose codes: 100: I. Social Infrastructure and Services, Total; 150: I.5 Government and Civil Society, Total; 200: II. Economic Infrastructure and Services, Total; and 300: III. Production Sectors, Total.

expenditures (figure 8-6). Until recently there was a lack of essential and complementary public infrastructure required for private investments in the nonservice sector. However, large oil revenues have meant that the situation is improving for some infrastructure but not others. Inder, Brown, and Datt (2014) argue that an optimistic view of the use of these petroleum revenues is that, while they are available, the focus on investment in infrastructure lays the foundation for strong nonoil growth for the economy in future.

Timor-Leste's Strategic Development Plan (2010) puts equal emphasis on infrastructure spending and recurrent spending. This is consistent with the sequencing of investments outlined in previous sections: once peace and stability are attained, the fiscal trade-off between peace and productivity allows room for the composition of expenditure to shift toward specific public investments. However, while the sequencing of these expenditures is consistent with

Figure 8-6. *Timor-Leste, Budget Expenditure, Recurrent and Capital, 2000–11*

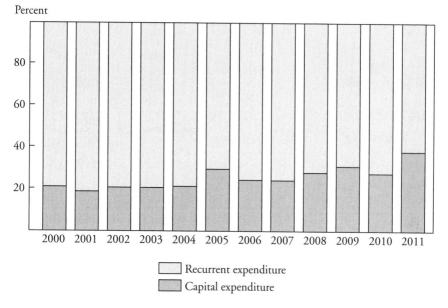

Percent

Source: IMF (2004, 2011).

the pattern in the fiscal substitutes/growth framework, a question is whether the timing of the shift from peace to productivity expenditures is optimal for Timor-Leste. Porter and Rab (2010) argue that, in the period following the near-fatal shooting of President Ramos-Horta and the assassination attempt on Prime Minister Xanana Gusmao, a shift in expenditure priorities and administrative streamlining helped to consolidate peace. More specifically, Porter and Rab note that by investing heavily in public transfers, social protection, and infrastructure the government was able to build confidence among its constituents.

However, there is concern among some policymakers that Timor-Leste's prevailing long-term fiscal strategy locks in social expenditures on recurrent transfers (such as veterans' and widows' payments). The thesis in this chapter is about balancing investments in peace and stability with investments that enhance productivity. The particular challenge in this case is whether long-term entitlement programs limit the gradual rebalancing of public spending toward more productivity-enhancing investments.

Job Creation in Timor-Leste

In addition to the disruption to agriculture, the loss of human capital, and the setback of public sector institutions caused by the conflict, the economy of

Table 8-2. *Industry Aid Employment, Timor-Leste, by Sector, 2010*[a]

Sector	Number of employees	% employment
Agriculture	185,137	66.59
Mining and quarrying	1,107	0.40
Manufacturing	5,191	1.87
Electricity and water	456	0.16
Construction	7,505	2.70
Retail and wholesale trade	15,219	5.47
Transport, storage, communications	7,260	2.61
Finance	457	0.16
Public administration, social security	25,065	9.02
Education	9,359	3.37
Other services	21,276	7.65
Total	278,032	100.00

Source: Timor-Leste (2010).
a. No strong inference should be drawn from the table, given the informality of the labor market.

postindependence Timor-Leste also faces fast population growth. The World Bank (2013b) predicts that the consequent youth bulge will result in nearly half a million individuals ready to enter Timor-Leste's labor force over the next twenty years, representing an enormous fiscal and social challenge for the fragile state.

However, job creation has not fared well to date in Timor-Leste. As table 8-2 shows, a large agricultural sector still accounts for the majority of employment, with the public sector the next most significant employer. Only a thin private sector in services exists, and this has essentially transitioned from serving foreign peacekeepers and development agencies to the new public-sector-driven middle class. And while the government relies on oil for revenue, the oil sector does not generate employment. The low productivity but high employment in agriculture is driven by structural, social, and institutional factors that prevail across all regions of Timor-Leste. Inder, Brown, and Datt (2014) contend that there are a number of structural challenges to overcome in seeking to improve agricultural productivity: production is largely small scale, subsistence agriculture, with minimal inputs and very low yields. This outcome is compounded by the myriad of land titling arrangements that lead to lack of collateral and therefore inefficient capital markets, hampering private sector development. Inder, Brown, and Datt stress that a key area of interest is in the creation of markets in Timor-Leste. They argue that a lot of production is wasted, with one explanation being that there is no market supply chain, so much production cannot be used effectively.

Outside of agriculture, the most prominent employer is the government, with approximately one in ten jobs being in public service (World Bank 2013b). The public administration serves, on the one hand, as a lubricant for the private sector by providing law and order, by building physical infrastructure, and by providing education and other public goods. This creates the environment in which private production can flourish. On the other hand, the public sector competes with the private sector for labor, which lowers private production.

There is also a significant effect on wages and inflation by the large and relatively well-paid public sector, which negatively affects private sector growth. Carnahan, Gilmore, and Rahman (2005) argue that wage inflation in Dili's public sector was caused by the United Nations wage-setting policy. The absence of local markets meant that the United Nations became the de facto price setter for public service, further removing wages from competitive pressure. Consequent high wage expectations resulted in increased business costs, further inhibiting economic growth. Another question is the extent to which the ongoing scaling up of the public sector is continuing to distort the labor market and thus limiting the scope for long-term sustained private sector expansion.

Conclusion

There has been increasing interest in supporting private-sector-led employment growth as a key component of poverty reduction and stabilization. The *World Development Report 2013* stresses the role of strong private-sector-led growth in creating jobs and outlines how jobs that do the most for development can spur a virtuous cycle. Major donors, including Australia, recognize the importance of job creation in ending extreme poverty and are reorienting their program to support stronger private-sector-led employment growth.

The challenge is greater in FCACs. Security and stability are taken for granted in many countries, although the funds needed to maintain these key foundations for growth are neglected. In FCACs there need to be much larger investments in these areas, but the trade-off between investing in peace and stability and other productivity-enhancing investments is stark. The fiscal substitute/growth framework presented in this chapter provides a simple message on the composition and sequencing of public expenditures in FCACs. The first priority is to devote part of the budget to supporting stability and peace. This includes encouraging participation in the workforce. The second priority is to spend funds on measures to ignite productivity growth and adopt policies that facilitate efficient use of an economy's resources.

This perspective held true in the recent experience of both Solomon Islands and Timor-Leste, small island states where prominence has been given to early expenditures on peace and stability. For donors, this took the particular form of peacekeeping and of investments in the law and justice area. For the respective governments, it was argued that civil service salaries and social transfers, like veterans' payments, may be considered investments in stability. Despite their many differences, Solomon Islands and Timor-Leste have had similar job creation experiences. Both are still very reliant on the agricultural sector for the majority of employment, and both have experienced rapid employment growth in the public sector. Whether the peace and stability dividend can be translated into employment growth in higher-productivity sectors remains to be seen. In part this will be affected by the rate at which public expenditures on peace and stability can be substituted for productivity measures.

There are reasons to be cautiously optimistic about both countries. The foundations for stronger and broader economic growth, with associated employment growth, have been laid over the last decade. Recent history tells us that that successfully rebuilding economies after conflicts takes decades of hard work, good public investments, and strong policy decisions. The challenge is to recognize this and for national governments and their donor partners to stay the course on fundamental policy choices.

Ending extreme poverty in Timor-Leste and Solomon Islands will not make a significant contribution to the global poverty aggregates. However, ending extreme poverty means ending it everywhere, including postconflict small island states with unique and difficult challenges.

References

Anand, R., S. Mishra, and S. J. Peiris. 2013. "Inclusive Growth: Measurement and Determinants." Working Paper WP/13/135.1 Washington: International Monetary Fund.

Baldacci, E., B. Clements, and S. Gupta. 2003. "Using Fiscal Policy to Spur Growth." *Finance and Development* 40, no. 4: 28–31.

Barro, R. J., and J-W Lee. 2000. "International Data on Educational Attainment: Updates and Implications." Working Paper 042. Harvard Center for International Development.

Burnside, C., and D. Dollar. 2000. "Aid, Policies, and Growth." *American Economic Review* 90: 847–68.

Carnahan, M., S. Gilmore, and M. Rahman. 2005. "Economic Impact of Peacekeeping." Interim report, phase 1. New York: United Nations Peacekeeping, Best Practices Unit.

Chand, S., and R. Coffman. 2008. "How Soon Can Donors Exit from Post-Conflict States?" Working Paper 141. Washington: Center for Global Development.

Collier, P. 2009. "Post-Conflict Recovery: How Should Strategies Be Distinctive?" *Journal of African Economies* 18, Supplement 1: i99–i131.

Collier, P., and A. Hoeffler. 2004. "Aid, Policy, and Growth in Post-Conflict Societies." *European Economic Review* 48: 1125–45.

Collier, P., A. Hoeffler, and D. Rohner. 2007. "Beyond Greed and Grievance: Feasibility and Civil War." Oxford: Centre for the Study of African Economies.

Collier, P., A. Hoeffler, and M. Soderbom. 2008. "Post-Conflict Risks." *Journal of Peace Research* 45: 461–78.

"Conflict Profile: East Timor." 2007. Amherst: Political Economy Research Institute, University of Massachusetts.

Dalgaard, C-J., and H. Hansen. 2001. "On Aid, Growth, and Good Policies." *Journal of Development Studies* 37: 17–41.

Demekas, D. G., J. McHugh, and T. Kosma. 2002. "The Economics of Post Conflict Aid." Working Paper WP/02/198. Washington: International Monetary Fund.

DFAT (Department of Foreign Affairs and Trade). 2004. "Solomon Islands: Rebuilding an Island Economy." Canberra: Commonwealth of Australia.

Dollar, D., and A. Kraay. 2002. "Growth Is Good for the Poor." *Journal of Economic Growth* 7, no. 3: 195–225.

———. 2013. "Growth Is Still Good for the Poor." Research Paper 6568. Washington: World Bank.

Feeny, S., S. Iamsiraroj, and M. McGillivray. 2014. "Growth and Foreign Direct Investment in Pacific Island States." *Economic Modelling* 37: 332–39.

Hameiri, S. 2012. "Mitigating the Risk to Primitive Accumulation: State-Building and the Logging Boom in Solomon Islands." *Journal of Contemporary Asia* 42: 405–26.

IMF (International Monetary Fund). 2004. 2011. "Timor Leste." Article 4.

———. 2013. "Democratic Republic of Timor-Leste." Country Report 13/338, article 4 consultation. Washington.

———. Various years. "Solomon Islands." Article 4. Washington.

Inder, B., A. Brown, and G. Datt. 2014. "Poverty and Agricultural Households in Timor Leste: Some Patterns and Puzzles." Working Paper. Centre for Development Economics and Sustainability, Monash University.

International Dialogue of Peacebuilding and Statebuilding. 2012. "New Deal for Engagement in Fragile States" (www.newdeal4peace.org).

Ncube, M., B. Jones, and Z. Bicaba. 2013. "Estimating the Economic Cost of Fragility in Africa." Tunis: African Development Bank.

OECD. 2009. "Taxation, State Building and Aid: Factsheet." Paris.

———. 2014. "Gross ODA Disbursements." Paris.

Porter, D., and H. Rab. 2010. "Timor Leste's Recovery from the 2006 Crisis: Some Lessons." *World Development Report 2011*. Background note. Washington: World Bank.

Pritchett, L., and F. de Weijer. 2010. "Fragile States: Stuck in a Capability Trap?" *World Development Report 2011*. Background note. Washington: World Bank.

RAMSI (Regional Assistance Mission to Solomon Islands). 2013. "Rebuilding a Nation: Ten Years of the Solomon Islands–RAMSI Partnership." Honiara: RAMSI Public Affairs Unit.

Solomon Islands Census Office. 1999. "1999 Population and Housing Census, Main Results." Honiara: Solomon Islands Government.

———. 2009. "2009 Population and Housing Census, Main Results." Honiara: Solomon Islands Government.

Spence Commission. 2008. "The Growth Report: Strategies for Sustained Growth and Inclusive Development." Washington: World Bank Commission on Growth and Development.

Timor-Leste. 2010. "Labour Force Survey." General Directorate of Statistics.

UN. 1999. Resolution 1264, Security Council.

———. 2012. "United Nations Integrated Mission in Timor Leste Completes Its Mandate." Fact sheet. New York: United Nations Department of Public Information.

UNDP (United Nations Development Program). 2004. "Emerging Priorities in Preventing Future Violent Conflict." New York.

USAID (United States Agency for International Development). 2007. "A Guide to Economic Growth in Post-Conflict Countries." Washington: Bureau for Economic Growth.

Valdivieso, L. M, T. Edno, L. V. Mendonca, S. Tareq, and A. Lopez-Mejia. 2000. "East Timor: Establishing the Foundations of Sound Macroeconomic Management." Washington: International Monetary Fund.

Walton, O. 2010. "Youth, Armed Violence and Job Creation Programmes." GSDRC research paper. Oslo: Norwegian Peacebuilding Centre.

World Bank. 2011. *World Development Report 2011: Conflict, UN, and Development.* Overview. Washington.

———. 2013a. "Labour Market Issues in Timor Leste: Current State, Prospects, and Challenges": East Asia and Pacific Region. Washington.

———. 2013b. "Timor Leste Social Assistance Public Expenditure and Program Performance Report." Human Development Sector Unit, East Asia and Pacific Region. Washington.

———. 2013c. *World Development Report 2013.* Washington.

9

Transforming Economies for Jobs and Inclusive Growth: Strategies for Sub-Saharan Countries

AKIO HOSONO

Increasing attention is being paid in debates on development to "inclusive growth." The term has no standard definition, but the meaning is clear. Economic growth is more desirable and beneficial to societies if it is accompanied by productive jobs and if its benefits are widely shared. However, some people, some areas, and some sectors may get left behind, even during periods of rapid growth. Jobs can be a useful lens through which to examine inclusive growth. The World Bank's *World Development Report 2013: Jobs* (World Bank 2012) stresses that jobs are a cornerstone of development, bringing benefits that extend far beyond income. The same report, however, also emphasizes that the benefits from jobs depend on a country's level of development, demography, endowments, and institutions. It calls for an inclusive development agenda that differentiates among countries according to the challenges that they face.

This chapter discusses strategies for inclusive growth in countries where extreme poverty is high, with a focus on sub-Saharan Africa. It begins by exploring why the need for inclusive growth is so great on the continent. It includes lessons from Asia and presents case studies of how development cooperation has contributed to inclusive growth. The East Asian experience has often been characterized as focused on labor-intensive manufactured exports; less well appreciated is the role played by agriculture and agro-industrial links in ensuring that Asian growth is truly inclusive. The case study approach distinguishes this chapter from literature that focuses on the general policy and institutional context for inclusive growth. Through case studies, we see more clearly that inclusive growth is not something that happens automatically but something that requires specific, properly designed interventions.

Understanding Inclusive Development

Although "inclusive development" is a relatively new term, the concept has deep roots. Almost four decades ago, Montek Ahluwahlia, Hollis Chenery, and John Duloy made "growth with equity" a principal concern of the World Bank. This tradition continued with many later studies, including the *World Development Report 2006: Equity and Development*. More recently, several pioneering studies on inclusive development have been published, including Ali (2007), World Bank (2009), and AfDB (2012). In these studies, the concept of inclusive development encompasses the provision of full, productive, and decent employment to maximize economic opportunity; equal access to economic opportunity through the development of human capital; and social safety nets to protect the chronically poor and vulnerable.[1] The Asian Development Bank has operationalized this concept through its Framework of Inclusive Growth Indicators (FIGI) (ADB 2013).

In this regard, diversification and transformation—building new firms and industries from scratch and expanding and upgrading existing firms and value chains—is essential because it creates jobs and opportunities that allow people to participate in economic growth. People's capacity to respond to new opportunities is a prerequisite for job creation and promoting inclusive growth. In other words, the first two policy pillars of FIGI—developing productive jobs and economic opportunities and ensuring equal access to economic opportunities by expanding human capital—are intrinsically related.

A similar vision is presented in the report of the High-Level Panel of Eminent Persons on the Post-2015 Development Agenda (2013) (hereafter, the HLP report), which gives priority to "create[ing] opportunities for good and decent jobs and secure livelihoods, so as to make growth inclusive and ensure that it reduces poverty and inequality." It also emphasizes educating, training, and providing people with the skills that they need to respond to the demands of businesses for workers and to succeed in the job market.

---

1. This definition is similar to Ifzal Ali's "three pillars of inclusive growth: (1) full, productive and decent employment to maximize economic opportunities; (2) social protection to ensure minimum economic well-being; and (3) capability enhancement to ensure equal access to economic opportunities" (Ali 2007).

The Imperative of Inclusive Development in Sub-Saharan Africa

Every country has its own challenges to meet in order to achieve inclusive development, but three factors make this goal especially important and challenging in the African context.

Demographic Transition

In sub-Saharan Africa, the number of young people entering the labor force is growing rapidly. The working-age population (ages fifteen to sixty-four) in these countries will reach 616 million by 2030, a 74 percent increase from 353 million in 2010 (JICA Research Institute 2013). That means that roughly 13 million new jobs will be needed every year just to absorb these workers. In addition, the number of youths aged fifteen to twenty-four in Eastern, Middle, and Western Africa will double in the next forty years (2010–50). Providing job opportunities for this growing working-age population and especially for young people is one of the biggest challenges facing sub-Saharan Africa.

Slow Transformation of the Economic Structure

Trends in agricultural and manufacturing growth in sub-Saharan Africa have not been encouraging, despite robust aggregate growth averaging more than 5 percent since 2004. The industrial sector in sub-Saharan Africa employs only 10.6 percent of the overall labor force, and its share of GDP has been declining since the 1980s (Shimada, Homma, and Murakami 2013). Furthermore, sub-Saharan Africa's share of the world's manufactures and exports decreased from 0.4 percent to 0.3 percent and from 0.3 percent to 0.2 percent respectively from 1980 to 2005 (Dinh and others 2012). Rodrik (2013) warns about "premature deindustrialization" in developing countries, including many in sub-Saharan Africa.

Increasing jobs in rural areas is one of the most promising avenues for inclusive development. Yet the amount of cropland per capita in rural Africa decreased by 59 percent between 1960 and 2009 (Makino 2013). What's more, sub-Saharan Africa's yields are lagging behind those in other regions of the world. Yield growth collapsed in the 1980s, and while it began to turn around in the 1990s, the rate of growth remains much slower than in Asia and Latin America (UNDP 2012). The decrease in per capita cultivated cropland, together with stagnant land productivity, resulted in a 13 percent reduction in per capita cereal production between 1961–63 and 2008–10, when per capita production rose by 44 percent in Asia and 48 percent in South America (Makino 2013). Without growth in food production, rural incomes have faltered and few jobs in rural areas have been created.

Wage employment is not the most prevalent form of work in sub-Saharan Africa. Formal employment on average accounts for less than 10 percent of total employment (World Bank 2012). Inclusive growth therefore has to include consideration of how informal jobs are created in both rural and urban areas, where many jobs are now being created in services.

Natural Resource Curse

Despite sub-Saharan Africa's strong growth rate in the last decade, wage-paying jobs have grown only modestly. Part of the explanation for this lies in natural resource exploitation. The natural resource sector has been an important driver of recent growth, but it creates few jobs and has narrow links to other economic sectors that are pivotal to poverty reduction. Indeed, the connection between resource sector growth, jobs, and inclusive development principally hinges on how government rents are managed. History suggests resource-driven growth can easily exacerbate income disparities between the rich and the poor, especially where initial land and property ownership is unequal. This kind of growth may also contribute to social instability and consequently undermine the sustainability of growth itself.

Strategies for Inclusive Growth: The Asian Experience

Generally speaking, growth opportunities can be created by adding to endowments or by developing technology, know-how, and institutions that make those endowments more productive. The most common approach to inclusive growth is to provide policies and infrastructure that support growth across sectors, geographic areas, and households. Building transport networks that encompass remote populations and provide a connection to world markets and making investments in human capital are good examples. Institutional reforms to promote good governance, macroeconomic stability, the rule of law, and efficient administration are also relevant since they promote growth opportunities that do not discriminate. In order to transform economies to enable job creation and inclusive development, the HLP report envisaged triggering a virtuous circle of growth:

> A second priority is to constantly strive to add value and raise productivity, so that growth begets more growth. Some fundamentals will accelerate growth everywhere—infrastructure and other investments, skills development, supportive policies towards micro, small, and medium-sized enterprises, and the capacity to innovate and absorb new technologies and produce higher-quality and a greater range of products (HLP 2013).

In sub-Saharan Africa, one promising proposal to increase jobs and inclusive growth is to construct growth corridors. The New Partnership for Africa's Development (NEPAD) has advocated the creation of regional hubs and development corridors and poles, emphasizing links with mining, agriculture, tourism, and other economic activities (JICA/JBIC 2008). Asia has successful experiences in that regard. The Greater Mekong Subregion (GMS) Development Program, which was launched by the Asian Development Bank (ADB) in 1992 with the participation of six countries in the Mekong region, is especially relevant. The aim of GMS "was to implement poverty reduction and economic growth by creating a belt that would link impoverished inland areas with port cities, which have access to world markets" (JICA/JBIC 2008). Electricity and communications infrastructure was developed in parallel with roads, bridges, and other transport infrastructure to support the agriculture, mining, and tourism sectors. A GMS Business Forum was established to facilitate collaboration between governments and the private sector.

Another potential vehicle for creating a virtuous circle of jobs and inclusive growth is "inclusive finance." The HLP report states: "Financial services are critical to the growth of business, but also raise the income of individuals. When people have the means to save and invest, or get insurance, they can raise their incomes by at least 20 percent" (HLP 2013). Financial institutions played an important role in encouraging inclusive growth in East Asia (Hosono 2013c). East Asian governments created financial institutions to provide long-term loans at low interest rates, facilitating economic growth through industrialization and infrastructure development. At the same time, they encouraged inclusive development by providing credit to agriculture and to small and medium-sized firms. The World Bank's *East Asian Miracle*, a notable study on the region's dynamic growth, highlighted the following three aspects of its growth: governments created a wide range of financial institutions to fill perceived gaps in the types of credit provided by private entities; they addressed the need for long-term credit for industry by creating development banks; and most also created specialized institutions to provide credit to agriculture and small firms (World Bank 1993).

In ASEAN countries, small and medium-sized enterprises and agricultural enterprises have generally been financed by public financial institutions and local commercial banks. These sectors have been crucial for inclusive development in the region. In Indonesia, earnings from oil and mineral resources were recycled through investments in agriculture and rural development, providing a basis for long-term economic growth. Combining supply-side support measures—such as provision of high-quality seeds, chemical fertilizers, irrigation infrastructure, and agricultural finance—with demand-side support measures, including producer price support, to improve agricultural productivity proved crucial for success (JICA/JBIC 2008). In Thailand and Malaysia, small and medium enterprises were developed to support the establishment of a competitive automobile industry (JBIC 2001).

Despite their different backgrounds, African countries could learn from these East Asian experiences. Strategies and lessons regarding specific sectors are discussed below.

Strategies for Inclusive Growth: A Case Study Approach

In this section, I present case studies illustrating three broad strategies for enabling inclusive growth that go beyond the general approaches to nondiscriminatory growth described previously. The first strategy is to increase the level of food production and smallholder productivity. This strategy directly raises rural incomes, thereby providing immediate benefits from growth, and indirectly leads to inclusive growth by helping to decrease food prices and raise real wages or employment levels in nonfood sectors. This strategy is most suitable for countries that have good potential for increasing cropland, irrigation, and application of modern technologies that can improve yields.

The second strategy is to promote agricultural diversification toward higher-value-added crops in a way that creates an agro-industrial value chain. This strategy is useful where natural endowments are not suitable for intensification of agricultural production or where climate change, other environmental changes, or population increases alter the natural endowment. Both of these strategies are relevant for countries that continue to have large population shares in rural areas, as is the case in most low-income countries.

The third strategy is to focus on industrialization for domestic and export markets. I show that sub-Saharan Africa and East Asia have important differences in their labor market structures and so cannot rely on low wages as a determinant of competitiveness. But a structured approach can still deliver competitive industries in selected subsectors.

Strategy 1: Increasing Staple Crop Productivity

Both India and sub-Saharan Africa were trapped in a low-income equilibrium in the 1970s. However, India succeeded in escaping from it, and the two regions diverged significantly in the 1980s (Fujita 2010). The breakthrough that enabled India's achievement was the second wave of the Green Revolution. The first wave, which occurred from the mid-1960s through the 1970s, was limited to increasing wheat yields in the northwest and in small delta regions of peninsular India. It was the second wave, which unleashed a rapid increase in rice production during the 1980s, that was fundamental to the economic development of hitherto poverty-stricken rural areas. India achieved strong agricultural growth that spread across almost all regions and almost all its major crops.

The most important factor supporting rapid agricultural growth during the 1980s was the widespread diffusion of private tube wells for irrigation, especially small-scale, shallow tube wells, which enabled a highly productive system of double cropping of high-yield varieties (HYV) of rice and wheat over broad rural areas and double cropping of HYV rice in areas with plentiful rainfall. Based on a comparative analysis of India and sub-Saharan Africa, Fujita (2010) concludes:

The most important lesson for sub-Saharan Africa from the Indian experience, therefore, is that it should take steps to raise rural incomes and thereby to strengthen rural markets for non-agricultural products and services. Once this has been realized, sub-Saharan Africa will be in a position to proceed to the next stage of economic development: industrialization. To raise rural incomes to a certain level, productivity growth in agriculture should be increased, especially in terms of staple food output, rather than the horizontal expansion of farm land that has been the practice in most of sub-Saharan Africa. This argument is basically in line with that of Eswaran and Kotwal (1994).

At least two aspects of India's transformation since the 1980s deserve special mention. First, the Green Revolution in India did not take place solely because of the introduction of high-yield varieties of crops. It took decades of incremental and sustained agricultural development since the country's independence for the benefits of the Green Revolution to be realized. Second, the remarkable increase in yields was achieved by combining the planting of HYV crops with increased use of fertilizer and irrigation. The availability of affordable fertilizer and the use of private tube wells for irrigation were essential (Yanagisawa 2014). The remarkable nationwide increase in India's agricultural productivity and subsequent changes in rural society have helped enable India to achieve prolonged growth in its domestic and export markets since the 1980s. Those developments prepared India to respond competitively to globalization and the economic liberalization policies introduced after 1992, which led to India's successful integration into the world economy.

The experiences of Bangladesh also are highly relevant for sub-Saharan Africa. The major factors that changed the rural society of Bangladesh include the rapid spread of microfinance, the construction of rural infrastructure, and the modernization of agriculture based on the adoption of new technology, which enabled farmers to shift from low-yield, single-crop, deep-water rice to high-yield, double-crop, short-maturity rice. Increasing land and labor productivity in rice agriculture in the early 2000s had beneficial effects on the agricultural average wage and hence on rural poverty (Hossein, Sen, and Sawada 2012).

The changes in rural society in Bangladesh have been profound. Higher labor productivity in agriculture made it possible for the massive employment of female workers in the garment industry in two big cities, Dhaka and Chittagong. Bangladesh is an example of a country that was able to rapidly urbanize and integrate into the world economy by absorbing unskilled labor into light-manufacturing industries (World Bank 2012). In the case of Bangladesh, several factors interacted in order to bring about that change, including investments in rural roads, irrigation, market facilities and other rural infrastructure, microcredit, and education. This enhanced the mobility and availability of low-opportunity-cost labor in rural Bangladesh.

Hossein, Sen, and Sawada (2012) contend that in any predominantly agricultural economy that has high population growth and density, the critical challenge is to reduce the burden of surplus labor in agriculture—a "challenge [that] can be met through sustained sectoral and social policies and attendant institutional changes *commensurate to each stage of development* to support productivity/growth-enhancing relocation of 'surplus' farm labor to non-farm and non-agricultural jobs" (Hossein, Sen, and Sawada).

In 1981, ten years after Bangladesh achieved independence, raw jute and jute goods constituted 68 percent of the country's total exports. Thirty years later, in 2011, garments accounted for 76 percent of total exports and textiles for another 9 percent. Businesses in these sectors accounted for 50 percent of all manufacturing establishments in the country (UNCTAD 2012). Today, the garment industry encompasses 5,000–6,000 factories with 7–8 million workers using assembly-line production methods. The wages of workers in this industry are around 35 percent higher than the national average. The Bangladesh success story is even more remarkable because, as a recent World Bank study highlighted, "the country was often held out in the development literature as a hopeless case" (World Bank 2012).

These South Asian experiences demonstrate that increasing rural incomes is crucial for structural transformation and that a key factor in achieving transformation is increasing staple food productivity. Although an Asian-type Green Revolution has not been realized in sub-Saharan Africa, several remarkable increases in staple food productivity have been observed. There is significant potential to focus on rice because the gap between production and consumption of rice in sub-Saharan Africa has been growing. Currently, 40 percent of the rice consumed is imported. *The Economist* stated that "in Africa, where a third of the population depends on rice, demand is rising by almost 20 percent a year. At that rate rice will surpass maize as Africa's main source of calories within 20 years" (Economist 2014). Another reason to focus on rice is that rice cultivation is where the technological gaps (or "yield gaps") between sub-Saharan Africa and India and other Asian countries are especially high. The average yield gap for rice is similar to that for wheat and much larger than the modest yield gap for maize. There is no yield gap for sorghum and millet production (Otsuka 2013). Rice could be considered an entry point for increasing productivity in the agricultural sector as a whole, since in most sub-Saharan African rice-producing countries, those working in the rice value chain are involved in other important crops as well (Kubota 2013, 10). General measures—such as strengthening the capacity of institutions and individuals for research and extension—benefit both rice and other crops. It might be thought desirable to pay more attention to maize because it is the principal subsistence crop among poor African farmers. However, as Otsuka (2013) states, "The prerequisite for a maize Green Revolution is the development of truly profitable and productive maize seeds and farming practices for this crop." In other words, maize is not yet at a stage where research has developed seeds appropriate for Africa's ecology. That may come in a second wave of an African Green Revolution.

The public sector must be in the vanguard. Its efforts to invest in the development and dissemination of high-yield varieties are essential for increasing rice production. As explained in World Bank (2012), since farmers can reproduce varieties of rice, private seed companies cannot reap the benefit of introducing new varieties and so tend not to make the effort.[2] Moreover, the costs of other basic necessities for food crop agriculture need to be reduced to make them affordable to small farmers. For example, fertilizer in sub-Saharan Africa costs roughly twice what it does in Asia.[3]

Addressing post-harvest losses (PHL) is another challenge. World Bank (2011) estimates that the value of PHL in sub-Saharan Africa could reach nearly US\$4 billion a year out of an estimated value of US\$27 billion in total annual grain production. This is equal to the annual value of cereal imports of sub-Saharan Africa. The World Bank emphasizes the importance of a value chain approach to identify optimal interventions for reducing PHL losses.

CASE I: AGRICULTURAL SECTOR DEVELOPMENT PROGRAM AND RELATED INITIATIVES IN TANZANIA. The Agricultural Sector Development Program (ASDP), started in 2006, was the Tanzanian government's main agricultural initiative in the first decade of the 2000s, with some 60 percent of the agricultural sector budget going to the program in its first four years (Therkildsen 2011). ASDP's aim is to increase productivity in the agricultural sector, increase agricultural incomes and food security, and alleviate poverty. ASDP has several distinctive features. Its largest component is irrigation, which accounts for some 80 percent of the total budget. The program considers to be crucial both the empowerment and development of the capacities of farmers and the decentralization of implementation by providing local authorities with funds through central government transfers based on their performance. ASDP, in which several donors participate, is one of the first sectorwide approaches in the agricultural sector in Africa.

Since the launch of the program, land under irrigation has increased by 15,000 to 20,000 hectares per year, from a total of 264,000 hectares in 2006 to

2. In contrast, hybrid seeds of maize, sorghum, and millet cannot be reproduced by farmers; hence, the private sector supplies seeds, although public support is necessary to develop biological and chemical technologies (World Bank 2012).

3. This is roughly true for nitrogen, potassium, and phosphate fertilizers (Hirano 2013).

332,000 hectares in 2010. That result is less than planned under ASDP, but it is still a considerable achievement (Therkildsen 2011). From 2011 to 2012, the expansion per year increased to 30,000 hectares. The most recent estimate of land under irrigation was 461,000 hectares in 2013.[4] This increase is the result of enhanced technical capacity (irrigation institutions and individual technical irrigation officers), the priority given to irrigation by government, and other factors, including small-, mid-, and large-scale irrigation development funds.

Within ASDP's capacity development initiatives, emphasis is placed on improving the technical capabilities of central and local governments and farmer groups and increasing the number of technical personnel such as central and local government engineers, technicians, and surveyors.[5] At the same time, rice cultivation technology has been disseminated through a program called Technical Cooperation in Supporting Service Delivery Systems of Irrigated Agriculture (Tanrice). Tanrice is implemented by specialized training institutes.[6] The training on irrigated rice farming for more than 40 irrigation schemes and 13,000 families covers a package of basic farming techniques, such as ridge management (enclosing paddies with low mud walls, or bunds), field leveling, straight-row planting (planting in lines and at specific intervals), use of handmade weeding machines, irrigation scheme management for women, and rice marketing. The training also provides for the dissemination of NERICA (New Rice for Africa) varieties among key rice stakeholders.

Tanrice is based on the technologies, practices, and experiences in farming in the Moshi Rural District in the Kilimanjaro Region, where the resulting rice yield has already reached 6 tons per hectare due to improved farming techniques and irrigation, easily outpacing the national average, which is about 2 tons per hectare. The Kilimanjaro Agricultural Training Center (KATC) has played a key role since the 1990s in helping to expand that success by establishing and implementing various training programs for agricultural extension officers, irrigation technicians, and farmers. Tanrice has been an important factor in the Tanzanian government's National Rice Development Strategy, launched in 2009, which aims to double rice production to 1.96 million tons by 2018 (from

4. "Project for Irrigation Human Resource Development by Strengthening the Capacity of Arusha Technical College" (http://www.jica.go.jp/tanzania/office/activities/project/44.html).

5. More information on the capacity development initiatives and Tanrice 1 and Tanrice 2 projects can be found in the following: "Technical Cooperation in Supporting Service Delivery Systems of Irrigated Agriculture" (Tanrice 1) (www.jica.go.jp/tanzania/english/activities/agriculture_04.html) and "Project for Supporting Rice Industry Development in Tanzania" (Tanrice 2) (www.jica.go.jp/tanzania/english/activities/agriculture_07.html).

6. Tanrice is implemented by specialized training institutes such as KATC (Kilimanjaro Agricultural Training Centre), MATI (Ministry of Agriculture Training Institute)-Ilonga, MATI-Igurusi, MATI-Ukiriguru, and KATI (Kizimbani Agricultural Training Institute) and the Rice Research Program in Tanzania and Zanzibar.

production in 2008) through the intensification of irrigated paddy production. During this period, yield per hectare is intended to increase from 2.1 tons to 3.5 tons in irrigated areas and from 1 ton to 2 tons in rain-fed lowlands. Based on the achievements of Tanrice, the Project for Supporting Rice Industry Development in Tanzania (Tanrice 2) was initiated in November 2012. This project aims to further disseminate rice-farming technologies nationwide in partnership with seven agricultural training institutes. As rain-fed cultivation also needs to be improved to have the maximum impact on poverty reduction, approaches for disseminating the appropriate rain-fed rice cultivation technologies are being explored. This project also aims to promote the value chain of the rice industry.

There has been a significant increase in the proportion of crop-growing households receiving crop extension advice. The percent receiving advice on crops from government extension staff increased from 33 percent during the agricultural year 2002–03 to 60 percent in 2007–08. Meanwhile, the proportion of households receiving extension advice from NGOs or development projects increased from 5.3 percent to 7.9 percent (ASDP Monitoring and Evaluation Working Group 2011). Positive changes have consequently been recorded in agricultural exports; the production or productivity (yield) of maize, rice, meat, milk, and eggs; and the proportion of farmers using improved seeds or chemical fertilizer and adopting mechanization (tractors and power tillers). ASDP is reported to be on track to achieve its objectives. The rice industry in Tanzania has grown rapidly over the last decade and is now largely self-sufficient. Local production meets 92 percent of consumption, despite a 21 percent price premium over imported rice because of the higher quality of local rice, which is fresh, clean, and aromatic (Bill and Melinda Gates Foundation 2012).

ASDP's achievements are encouraging and offer an interesting experience to be shared among sub-Saharan countries. Otsuka (2013) concludes: "It is clear that a combination of improved seeds, improved production practices, and irrigation leads to significantly high yields, resulting in a 'mini' Green Revolution in Tanzania."

CASE 2: THE COALITION FOR AFRICAN RICE DEVELOPMENT INITIATIVE. The Coalition for African Rice Development (CARD) was launched by the Alliance for a Green Revolution in Africa (AGRA) and the Japan International Cooperation Agency (JICA) in 2008 as an international platform for promoting rice development;[7] its goal is to double rice production in Africa in ten years.

---

7. Participants in CARD include international organizations and donors such as the World Bank and International Fund for Agricultural Development (IFAD) and research institutes such as the International Rice Research Institute (IRRI), the Africa Rice Center (AfricaRice), the Japan International Research Center for Agricultural Science (JIRCAS), nongovernmental organizations, and South-South cooperation countries (such as Vietnam).

CARD has twenty-three African member countries: a first group of twelve countries where the importance of rice is relatively high and a second group of eleven countries that are rapidly increasing their consumption of rice. Within the CARD framework, each country has drawn up a National Rice Development Strategy. In addition, a task force has been set up in each country, where stakeholders jointly produce a list of prioritized possible interventions (Kubota 2013). The development partners in CARD agree to jointly support the formulation and implementation of national strategies drawing on their own comparative advantages and to seek out synergies across their interventions. JICA alone was implementing around sixty projects as of August 2012.

In 2008, the first group of twelve rice-producing sub-Saharan African countries and seven development partners jointly endorsed CARD's overall target of doubling rice production in sub-Saharan Africa in ten years from 14 million tons to 28 million tons in 2018. The twelve countries accounted for about 85 percent of total rice production in sub-Saharan Africa as of 2008. According to data on the current status of rice development compiled by the CARD secretariat, land cultivated for rice has already increased by 17 percent, from 7.8 million hectares (the average for 2002–06) to 9.2 million hectares (the average for 2007–11).[8] A positive yield trend from 1.7 tons per hectare in the base period to 2 tons per hectare in the next five-year period was observed, which is the fastest yield improvement in the past few decades in the region, while still falling far short of yield rates in many Asian rice-producing countries.

Especially notable progress has been observed in the partnership among African rice-producing countries and their five Asian partners, Indonesia, Malaysia, the Philippines, Thailand, and Vietnam. CARD has organized a series of dialogues between African and Asian parties that have been instrumental in making development partners' interventions more flexible and wider in scope. For example, most of the rice-related projects formulated and implemented by JICA since the start of CARD in 2008 have a market orientation and components relating to post-harvest losses.

Strategy 2: Diversification of Agriculture to Include Higher-Value Crops and Enhancement of the Agro-Industry Value Chain

The feasibility of commercial crops is high in some areas because of geographic or climatic conditions, or both, and access to consumers and export markets. In most Southeast Asian countries, diversification to high-value crops and development of commercial agriculture have advanced inclusive growth. An example is Thailand, whose "newly agro-industrializing country" (NAIC) strategy—which became part of the country's economic development plan in the

---

8 Estimate based on thirty-nine countries for which data are available.

1980s—aimed to establish the country as a net exporter of food as a basis for promoting industrialization.[9] In addition, it encouraged the development of agro-industry as an export industry based on Thailand's past achievements in exporting primary products.

Thailand traditionally produced rice and natural rubber for export, but in the 1970s, it diversified to include tapioca and maize. With the introduction of modern quality-control and production technologies, the list of export products continued to grow in size and diversity to include broiler, grilled, and skewered chicken; farmed prawns; tinned tuna; and tinned fruit. Specific measures adopted by the government to support this process included provisions for preferential investments for agro-industry and flexible financing by commercial banks for agriculture-related businesses.

CASE 3: SMALLHOLDER HORTICULTURE EMPOWERMENT PROJECT IN KENYA. Like Thailand, Kenya has considerable potential for commercial agricultural diversification thanks to good market access and the capacity of its farmers. In Kenya, horticulture production has achieved an average annual growth rate of 20 percent since 2000. More than 60 percent of production is attributable to small-scale farmers. Although horticulture is more labor intensive than grain production—requiring finer techniques and bigger inputs, including seeds, fertilizer, and pesticides—land productivity is higher under properly managed horticulture.

The Smallholder Horticulture Empowerment Project (SHEP) was launched in 2006. In 2010, encouraged by the effectiveness of the model, the Kenyan Ministry of Agriculture set up the Smallholder Horticulture Empowerment and Promotion Unit (SHEP Unit) (Aikawa 2013). SHEP's main goal was to develop the capacity of smallholder horticulture farmer groups to raise their incomes. According to the project's final monitoring survey carried out in October 2009, average horticulture-related net income among 114 beneficiary farmer groups increased by 67 percent over the baseline while the average net income per farmer increased by 106 percent.[10] While incomes increased for both men and women, the gap between them fell from 31 percent to 15 percent over the project's duration. Key components of SHEP included the introduction of market-oriented agriculture, improvements in farming efficiency, the introduction of

9. The concept of NAIC was first used by H. Mint (JICA/JBIC 2008). In-depth theoretical and empirical analysis of Thailand was conducted by Suehiro and Yasuda (1987). Thailand's agro-industrial development within the framework of the NAIC strategy and its results are discussed in JICA/JBIC (2008).

10. The survey covered a total of 2,177 individual small-scale farmers belonging to 114 of 122 model farmer groups from which data could be obtained in a manner similar to that used in the baseline survey.

appropriate farming techniques, and capacity development of farmers. Aikawa (2013) explains this process as follows:

> Various techniques were introduced in the project. They were simple and applicable, using materials easily available to the farmers. In fact, in Kenya, a country where they have reached a certain level of technological know-how at the research station, the issue was not how to develop new technologies, but how to validate existing technologies from the farmers' perspective and put them to practical use. Based on this understanding, the project focused on the introduction of techniques that were immediately usable the moment they were learned, such as the technique for correct planting using twine. The guidance on these techniques was provided jointly by Kenyan experts with abundant experience in horticulture and by Japanese experts who could provide advice from an outsider's point of view. Even when introducing technologies quite new to the farmers, the project made sure that they would be applicable with the materials and techniques already existing locally. Such technologies included road maintenance using sand bags (*Do-no*), fermented organic manure (*Bokashi*), and easy-to-handle weeding tools.

Aikawa (2013) submits that the skills of farmers improved significantly because they were empowered to conduct market surveys and to freely determine their target crops based on the survey results. This motivated the farmers to learn techniques more thoroughly during in-field training. When the farmers succeeded in marketing their products, their success further reinforced their sense of competence and motivation. This positive interaction between enhanced intrinsic motivation and increased skill levels provides a powerful model for sustained growth.

SHEP and SHEP UP (SHEP Unit Project) started with the premise that horticultural farming is an industry, no matter how small the scale of the market as a whole or the output of individual farmers. On that basis, the projects developed a series of activities to encourage farmers to respond to the needs of the market. Many African countries are encouraging farmers to transform their current subsistence-oriented agriculture into a more commerce-oriented venture. However, small-scale farmers do not necessarily know how to make that transition. The SHEP and SHEP UP programs filled that gap in knowledge (Aikawa 2013).

Since the 1990s, many donors have been providing support for value chain development. Their support has tended to focus on the downstream part of the supply chain, closest to post-harvest processing and sales. In contrast, SHEP and SHEP UP provided support to small-scale farmers throughout the supply chain, from production through sales. Furthermore, the programs always put the farmer at the center as they designed their activities and refined their methods.

CASE 4: DIVERSIFICATION THROUGH AGROFORESTRY AND THE LIVE-STOCK VALUE CHAIN IN ARID AND SEMI-ARID KENYA. About 83 percent of Kenya is covered by arid and semi-arid land (ASAL), which is vulnerable to global warming and climate change. These areas are also characterized by a high incidence of poverty.[11] Increasing staple crop productivity in these environments is difficult if not impossible. Preventing the desertification of ASALs while reducing poverty requires fostering an inclusive green economy as well as enhancing community resilience against drought.

Kenya relies on firewood and charcoal for more than 70 percent of its total energy consumption and for about 90 percent of the energy consumption in homes. The increasing demand for firewood and charcoal (resulting from the doubling of the population in the last twenty years), overgrazing, and disordered cultivation have devastated forest areas. That devastation has not only greatly reduced the supply of firewood and charcoal but also resulted in a decline in the productive capacity of Kenya's land. In order to address these issues, in 1982 the government set targets for the production of 200 million seedlings a year in a strategy established by presidential order to increase rural tree growth. In June 1986, the Kenya Forestry Research Institute (KEFRI) was established as a parastatal institution. In 1994, the Ministry of Environment and Natural Resources of Kenya launched the Kenya Forestry Master Plan 1995–2000, which identified farm forestry as an important model for forestry development in the country.[12]

Through the farm forestry model, with the KEFRI as an implementing agency, local people were entrusted with the management and ownership of forestry resources. Basic tree nursery and tree planting technologies were strengthened. The Farmer Field School (FFS) approach, an existing and proven extension model in the agricultural sector, was adapted to forestry, and techniques for seedling production, fruit tree planting (mango, grevillea, and others), poultry raising, vegetable cultivation, compost use, and woodlot creation were disseminated. FFSs have promoted ownership, strengthened communities, and increased farmers' capacities by sharing knowledge about forestry. Beneficiary farmers and farmer groups have started to sell forestry products such as mangoes, seedlings, lumber, and firewood. FFSs have recently created networks to carry out market surveys, and the Kenya Forestry Service and Equity Bank are facilitating farmers' production and marketing activities through the Support

---

11. For details of the case of agroforestry in semi-arid Kenya, see Hosono (2013a).

12. In Kenya, farm forestry is considered an essential way of increasing forest cover and diversifying subsistence products and income while contributing to soil and water conservation (Forest Act of 2005). The Agriculture Act on Farm Forestry Rules of 2009 stipulates a 10 percent forest cover on farms. See KEFRI's web page on the Farm Forestry Research Program (www.kefri.org/farmf.aspx).

to Community-Based Farm Forestry Enterprises in Semi-Arid Areas of Kenya Project (SCBFFE). In this way, an increasingly self-sufficient agroforestry industry is being developed.

Through these activities, farmers are increasing their awareness of methods to improve their livelihoods. Wider extension activities are expected as graduate farmers from FFSs share advice with farmers in surrounding areas, leveraging and strengthening social capital in the sector. At the same time, technological research for identifying drought-tolerant tree species is being carried out at KEFRI.

The Project for Enhancing Community Resilience against Drought in Northern Kenya (ECoRAD Project) is a recent initiative to address the challenges of climate change adaptation in arid pastoral societies.[13] Among other goals, this project aims to strengthen sustainable natural resource management and improve the livestock value chain. To address water resource management, an innovative rock catchment facility to collect rainwater effectively and cheaply and solar-powered pumping systems for deep wells were introduced together with the improvement of pipeline systems and water pans. The project introduced the innovative "heifer exchange program," through which heifers are provided to pastoralists, giving them an incentive to sell their castrated animals. These sales not only raise the incomes of pastoralists but help them cope with drought, when water and fodder is reserved for fertile animals. The impact of the project has been promising. In the local livestock market, 46 percent of animals were sold through the influence of the heifer exchange program.

These experiences in the arid and semi-arid regions of Kenya demonstrate the possibility of creating opportunities for inclusive and sustainable growth while coping with the impacts of deforestation and climate change.

Strategy 3: An Industrial Strategy with Links to Agriculture Development

In most Asian countries agricultural development has taken place alongside industrialization, including the apparel industry in Bangladesh and the agro-industry in Thailand described earlier. Vietnam, one of the latecomers to industrialization among ASEAN countries, has achieved impressive progress. Its government has adopted a strategic approach since 2000, emphasizing the importance of domestic and foreign capital mobilization and rural and agricultural development along with industrialization and fostering the growth of small, medium, and microenterprises as well as heavy industry.[14]

Sluggish development of agriculture in sub-Saharan Africa has constrained industrialization in multiple ways—among others, by increasing the prices of

13. This project was started in February 2013. For details, see Ministry of Devolution and Planning, Directorate of ASAL Development (Kenya) 2012.
14. Clearly stipulated by the government's policies, such as its Five-Year Plan for Socio-Economic Development 2001–05 (JICA/JBIC 2008, p. 59).

agricultural inputs and limiting the expansion of the consumer market in rural areas. The transition from an agrarian economy to an early industrializing economy or an urbanizing economy involves important interactions between rural and urban growth. World Bank (2013) states that rural growth in Asia helped to lower food prices and real wages for urban areas and created demand for urban goods. It can also contribute substantially to export competitiveness and manufacturing growth.[15] Higher food prices help to explain the high wages for formal labor in sub-Saharan Africa compared to those in several East and South Asian countries. For example, in 2006–07, annual wages among manufacturing industry workers in Kenya ($3,012) were higher than in Thailand ($2,223) and those in Tanzania ($1,709) were higher than in Indonesia ($1,667) (Hirano 2013). This is despite the fact that in Kenya and Tanzania GDP per capita is significantly lower than in Thailand and Indonesia.

A more robust comparison requires an assessment of comparative skill levels across countries. This has been attempted by Dinh and others (2012). The authors found that skilled and unskilled workers' monthly wages in Ethiopia were significantly lower than wages in Vietnam, while wages in Tanzania and Zambia were generally higher or the same as those for the equivalent labor in Vietnam but lower than in China. Hirano (2013) concludes that while the level of wages in sub-Saharan Africa is not overwhelmingly lower than in some East and South Asian countries, there is great potential for the continent to become competitive in terms of wages in some light-manufacturing sectors.

Several measures to increase labor productivity could be carried out to overcome the disadvantage related to wages: human resource development to improve education and skill levels; infrastructure development to reduce energy and transportation costs; regional integration to get better access to neighboring countries' markets; formation of business clusters and deepening of value chains to obtain economies of agglomeration, scale, and scope; improvements in management skills; and the introduction of *kaizen,* the Japanese practice of continuous improvement of quality and productivity at the plant level. Related to those measures are lowering the cost of production and increasing the quality of agricultural inputs for agro-industry and light manufacturing, which are essential for the formation of agro-industrial value chains. Dinh and others (2012) emphasize that with inputs accounting for more than 70 percent of the total cost of light-manufacturing products, small variations in the prices paid for inputs can wipe out any labor cost advantage that a country may have. Under such circumstances, if manufacturing industries are to become competitive in

15. For example, in Bangladesh the purchasing power of agricultural wages increased dramatically due to the increased productivity of rice, from the monetary equivalent of less than 2.5 kilograms of rice a day in 1983 to more than 6.0 kilograms today (World Bank 2012).

export and domestic markets, a coordinated industrial strategy that takes into account the relationships between agriculture and manufacturing appears to be useful. Simultaneous efforts may be necessary to improve efficiency and competitiveness, to develop human resources, to achieve agglomeration effects, and to improve productivity and quality.

CASE 5: AGRICULTURAL DEVELOPMENT–LED INDUSTRIALIZATION IN ETHIOPIA. The industrial strategy of the Ethiopian government has been in place for more than two decades. Its most recent iteration, the Growth and Transformation Plan, was approved by the Ethiopian parliament in November 2010. The plan incorporates the ideas of agricultural development–led industrialization and democratic developmentalism as well as positive and negative lessons from past development plans (Ohno 2013). Democratic developmentalism envisions positioning the government as the primary driver of development and soliciting foreign investors, bilateral donors, and international organizations to enhance the effort through technology transfer and financial assistance.

The vision of the Growth and Transformation Plan for the economic sector involves "building an economy which has a modern and productive agricultural sector with enhanced technology and an industrial sector that plays a leading role in the economy, sustaining economic development and social justice" (Ohno 2013). Industry is expected to become the major source of employment and foreign exchange by broadening the economy to include import-substitution industries as well as export-oriented industries. In addition, new measures are being introduced to promote micro- and small enterprises, while eight selected medium- and large-scale industries are being actively promoted (textiles and garments, leather and leather products, sugar, cement, metals and engineering, chemicals, pharmaceuticals, and agro-processing). Additional policy instruments, such as the institutionalization of *kaizen*, enhancement of the technical and vocational education and training system, and creation of industrial zones are also being employed. Throughout this process, the Ethiopian government has incorporated the diverse experiences of East Asian economies.

CASE 6: EXPORT PROMOTION IN KENYA. Kenya's exports have traditionally been concentrated in tea, coffee, petroleum products, and cement, although the country has recently begun expanding into nontraditional export industries such as commercial vessels and assembled automobiles and motorcycles. The promotion and diversification of exports have been among the main pillars of the Kenyan government's development strategy. In the past, the government had implemented various measures for export promotion, including the establishment of export processing zones, a partial reduction in sales taxes for the manufacturing industry, and the liberalization of exports and foreign exchange.

However, those efforts failed to address the binding constraints to exports, such as inadequate infrastructure and insecurity (JICA/JBIC 2008).

Against that backdrop, an export promotion master plan was formulated that led to the establishment of the Export Promotion Council in 1992. In 1997, the Kenyan government published a document titled "Industrial Transformation to the Year 2020," envisaging Kenya among a select group of Newly Industrializing Economies (NIES) by 2020. To achieve this target, an Economic Recovery Strategy Paper was published in 2003 proposing wide-ranging policy measures. Under that framework, the Private Sector Development Strategy (PSDS), the Master Plan Study of Kenyan Industrial Development, and other initiatives have been carried out. PSDS started officially in 2007 with five strategic goals: to improve the business environment; promote administrative reforms; develop the capacity of the trade sector through industrial development and trade promotion; increase productivity; and promote micro-, small-, and medium enterprises. This strategy was implemented with the support of 17 donors, coordinating 150 projects.

In view of the increased need for strengthening human resource capacity amid enhanced calls for export promotion, a program to build the capacity of small-scale exporters was implemented in 2007. It was designed to strengthen the trade-related business skills required of Kenyan exporters and the staff of the Export Promotion Council. This program is expected to contribute to the long-term goal of establishing Kenya as an economic hub for surrounding countries and creating a strong export-oriented economic structure (JICA/JBIC 2008).

CASE 7: INTRODUCING KAIZEN IN SUB-SAHARAN AFRICA. In 2009 a pilot project aimed at increasing productivity and improving quality (*kaizen*) at small manufacturing plants started in Ethiopia with the support of the Japan International Cooperation Agency (Shimada, Homma, and Murakami 2013). The results of this project were promising: over six months, the thirty firms that introduced *kaizen* obtained an average benefit equivalent to US$30,000, while the highest benefit achieved by a single company was around US$200,000. With an average of 402 employees per participating company, the pilot project generated benefits of US$74 per employee, which almost equaled the gross monthly wage, US$75, that prevailed at the time. The pilot project ended in June 2011. Encouraged by that achievement, in October 2011 the Ethiopian government established the Ethiopian Kaizen Institute (EKI) under the Ministry of Industry, with sixty-five technical staff. The Ethiopian government and JICA began a Phase 2 Kaizen Project in November 2011 in order to build the capacity of EKI and related organizations to disseminate *kaizen* throughout the country.

JICA's assistance in promoting *kaizen* dates back to 1983, when it started a project in Singapore (Hosono 2013b). Over twenty-nine years (1981–2008), different types of cooperative efforts to introduce *kaizen* were carried out in forty-six countries. Those efforts have demonstrated that *kaizen* can be put into practice in a variety of cultural and socioeconomic settings (Ueda 2009). Ueda concludes that "Kaizen is distinct from many other management tools. It is participatory; frontline workers are expected to contribute and benefit by using their brain power as well as their hands."

Concluding Remarks

This essay has argued that three strategies are relevant to support inclusive growth in the agrarian economies of sub-Saharan Africa: increasing the productivity of staple food crops; diversifying agriculture to higher-value crops while building stronger agro-industry value chains; and promoting light-manufacturing industrialization in conjunction with agricultural development. The total process constitutes a structural transformation that could be triggered, sustained, and accelerated by investments in infrastructure, human capital, technology, and inclusive finance. These strategies for promoting jobs and an inclusive growth agenda are mutually reinforcing but must be explicitly articulated. It is clear from past experiences in sub-Saharan Africa that the growth of GDP alone is not necessarily accompanied by jobs and inclusivity.

The case studies described show, first of all, that many successful experiences have confirmed the feasibility of rapid, inclusive growth in sub-Saharan Africa. Second, they show that human capacity development, especially of farmers, workers, and SME entrepreneurs, is essential. There is a strong interrelationship between the creation of job opportunities on one hand and the capacity of people to respond to those opportunities on the other. Capacity development is needed for people as well as institutions. Third, in the seven cases studied, different measures were taken to scale up the impact of programs. Pilot projects have been scaled up to cover geographically wider areas, to diversify activities, and to disseminate proven technologies and practices from the local to the regional and national levels. In some cases they have been shared with other countries through South-South cooperation. In many of the cases, the roles of government, public institutions, and public-private partnerships have been important.

The cases studied here should not be taken as "best practices" that can be readily transplanted to other countries. Most interventions require careful adaptation to local conditions. Nor are they all of the same importance or priority. For example, of the various strategies, improving the productivity of small farms is the highest priority, while strategies to develop jobs, build human capacity, and create inclusive growth opportunities must take into account local socioeconomic and natural conditions, especially in agriculture, due to the characteristics of natural capital on which they depend. As the HLP report noted, "there is no single recipe" for developing a jobs and inclusive growth strategy.

References

African Development Bank (AfDB). 2012. "Briefing Notes for AfDB's Long-Term Strategy: Briefing Note 6: Inclusive Growth Agenda" (http://www.afdb.org/fileadmin/uploads/afdb/Documents/Policy-Documents/FINAL%20Briefing%20Note%206%20Inclusive%20Growth.pdf).

Aikawa, Jiro. 2013. "Initiatives of SHEP and SHEP UP: Capacity Development of Small-Scale Farmers for Increased Responsiveness to Market Needs." In *For Inclusive and Dynamic Development in Sub-Saharan Africa*. Tokyo: JICA Research Institute (http://jica-ri.jica.go.jp/publication/booksandreports/for_inclusive_and_dynamic_development_in_sub-saharan_africa.html).

Ali, Ifzal. 2007. "Inequality and the Imperative for Inclusive Growth in Asia." *Asian Development Review* 24, no. 2. Manila: Asian Development Bank.

ASDP Monitoring and Evaluation Working Group. 2011. *ASDP Performance Report 2009–10*. Dar es Salaam, Tanzania.

Asian Development Bank (ADB). 2013. *Framework of Inclusive Growth Indicators 2013*. Manila.

Bill and Melinda Gates Foundation. 2012. *Developing the Rice Industry in Africa: Tanzania Assessment*. Dar es Salaam, Tanzania.

Dinh, Hinh T., and others. 2012. *Light Manufacturing in Africa: Targeted Policies to Enhance Private Investment and Create Jobs*. Washington: World Bank.

Economist. 2014. "The New Green Revolution: A Bigger Rice Bowl," May 10.

Fujita, Kouichi. 2010. "The Green Revolution and Its Significance for Economic Development: The Indian Experience and Its Implications for Sub-Saharan Africa." Working Paper. Tokyo: JICA Research Institute.

High-Level Panel of Eminent Persons on the Post-2015 Development Agenda. 2013. *A New Global Partnership: Eradicate Poverty and Transform Economies through Sustainable Development*. New York: United Nations.

Hirano, Katsumi. 2013. *Keizai Tairiku Afrika: Shigen, Shokuryou Mondai Kara Kaihatsu Seisaku Made* [Africa, an Economic Continent: From Resources and Food Problems to Development Policies]. Tokyo: Chuokoron Sha.

Hosono, Akio. 2013a. "Catalyzing an Inclusive Green Economy through South-South and Triangular Cooperation: Lessons Learned from Three Relevant Cases." In *Tackling Global Challenges through Triangular Cooperation: Achieving Sustainable Development and Eradicating Poverty through the Green Economy*, edited by Hiroshi Kato and Shunichiro Honda. Tokyo: JICA Research Institute (http://jica-ri.jica.go.jp/publication/other/tackling_global_challenges_through_triangular_cooperationachieving_sustainable_development_and_eradi.html).

————. 2013b. "Industrial Strategy and Economic Transformation: Lessons of Five Outstanding Cases." Initiative for Policy Dialogue. Working Papers: Africa Task Force Meeting. Tokyo and Washington: JICA and Columbia University.

————. 2013c. "Development Finance for Structural Transformation and Inclusive Growth: Asian Experience." In *Sustainable Growth and Structural Transformation in Africa: How Can a Stable and Efficient Financial Sector Help?* London: Overseas Development Institute.

————. 2015. "Catalyzing Transformation for Inclusive Growth." In *Japan and the Developing World: Sixty Years of Japan's Foreign Aid and the Post-2015 Agenda*, edited by Hiroshi Kato, John Page, and Yasutami Shimomura. London and New York: Palgrave Macmillan.

Hossein, Mahabub, Binayak Sen, and Yasuyuki Sawada. 2012. *Jobs, Growth, and Development: Making of the "Other" Bangladesh.* *World Development Report* companion volume. Washington: World Bank.

Japan Bank of International Cooperation (JBIC). 2001. "Challenges of Sustainable Development of East Asia: Support for Small and Medium Enterprises in Thailand and Malaysia." JBIC Research Paper 8. Tokyo.

JICA/JBIC. 2008. *Report of the Stocktaking Work on the Economic Development in Africa and the Asian Growth Experience.* Tokyo.

JICA Research Institute. 2013. *Development Challenges in Africa towards 2050.* Tokyo.

Kubota, Hiroyuki. 2013. "Five Years of the CARD Initiative: History, Achievements, and Further Challenges." In *The Coalition for African Rice Development (CARD): Progress in 2008–2013.* Tokyo: JICA Research Institute (https://jica-ri.jica.go.jp/publication/booksandreports/the_coalition_for_african_rice_development_progress_in_2008-2013.html).

Makino, Koji. 2013. "Boosting Sustainable Agricultural Growth in Sub-Saharan Africa." In *For Inclusive and Dynamic Development in Sub-Saharan Africa.* Tokyo: JICA Research Institute (http://jica-ri.jica.go.jp/publication/booksandreports/for_inclusive_and_dynamic_development_in_sub-saharan_africa.html).

Ministry of Devolution and Planning, Directorate of ASAL Development (Kenya). 2012. *Newsletter of JICA ECoRAD Project.* Nairobi, Kenya.

Ohno, Kenichi. 2013. *Learning to Industrialize: From Given Growth to Policy-Aided Value Creation.* London and New York: Routledge.

Otsuka, Keijiro. 2013. "How Promising Is the Rice Green Revolution in Sub-Saharan Africa? Evidence from Case Studies in Mozambique, Tanzania, Uganda, and Ghana." In *The Coalition for African Rice Development (CARD): Progress in 2008–2013.* Tokyo: JICA Research Institute (http://jica-ri.jica.go.jp/publication/booksandreports/for_inclusive_and_dynamic_development_in_sub-saharan_africa.html).

Rodrik, Dani. 2013. "The Perils of Premature Deindustrialization." Project Syndicate.

Shimada, Go, Toru Homma, and Hiromichi Murakami. 2013. "Industrial Development in Africa: JICA's Commitment at TICAD IV and Its Follow-Up." In *For Inclusive and Dynamic Development in Sub-Saharan Africa.* Tokyo: JICA Research Institute (http://jica-ri.jica.go.jp/publication/booksandreports/for_inclusive_and_dynamic_development_in_sub-saharan_africa.html).

Suehiro, Hiroshi, and Osamu Yasuda, eds. 1987. *Tai no Kogyouka: NAIC eno Chosen* [Challenge to NAIC: Industrialization of Thailand]. Makuhari, Japan: Institute of Developing Economies.

Therkildsen, Ole. 2011. "Policy Making and Implementation in Agriculture: Tanzania's Push for Irrigated Rice." Working Paper. Copenhagen: Danish Institute of International Studies.

Ueda, Takafumi. 2009. "Productivity and Quality Improvement: JICA's Assistance in Kaizen." Development Forum: Introducing KAIZEN in Africa. Tokyo: National Graduate Institute for Policy Studies.

UNCTAD. 2012. "Bangladesh Sector-Specific Investment Strategy and Action Plan: G-20 Indicators for Measuring and Maximizing Economic Value Added and Job Creation from Private Investment in Specific Value Chain." Pilot Study Results (http://unctad.org/Sections/diae_dir/docs/diae_G20_Bangladesh_en.pdf).

UNDP. 2012. *Africa Human Development Report 2012: Towards a Food Secure Future.* New York.

World Bank. 1993. *The East Asian Miracle: Economic Growth and Public Policy.* Oxford University Press

———. 2009. *What Is Inclusive Growth?* Washington.

————. 2011. *Missing Food: The Case of Postharvest Grain Losses in Sub-Saharan Africa.* Washington.

————. 2012. *World Development Report 2013: Jobs.* Washington.

————. 2013. *Global Monitoring Report 2013: Rural Urban Dynamics and the Millennium Development Goals.* Washington.

Yanagisawa. 2014. *Gendai Indo Keizai* [The Contemporary Indian Economy]. Nagoya University Press.

PART **III**

Building Resilience

10

Social Policy and the Elimination of Extreme Poverty

RAJ M. DESAI

I n 1990 approximately half of the population in the developing world lived on less than US$1.25 a day. By 2010 some 700 million people had been lifted out of poverty, dropping that rate to 22 percent, and fulfilling the first Millennium Development Goal of cutting extreme poverty in half (UN 2014). Still, a billion people continue to live below the $1.25-a-day line, and achieving the "last mile" in eradicating poverty will require a different set of instruments, institutions, and policy regimes than has been commonly used.

This chapter argues that, although much progress against extreme poverty in low- and middle-income countries has been accomplished through so-called inclusive growth, the elimination of consumption-based poverty will require greater attention to the political economy of social protection in developing nations. Since the 1990s, increases in labor-based income have been responsible for most of the achievement in poverty reduction. But for the large middle-income countries (where most of the world's extreme poor currently live), evidence suggests that the effect of labor income on consumption will hereafter diminish considerably, with the poorest individuals remaining vulnerable to a variety of shocks, thus requiring a more effective social floor below which they cannot fall. In middle-income countries, it may be that growth has lifted

The author is indebted to Christine X. Zhang for invaluable research assistance.

all the poor out of extreme poverty who can be lifted; for the rest, social policy will be needed.

What kind of social policy mix is needed? While it is technically possible to devise precise, leakage-free, redistributive mechanisms that can raise consumption among the extreme poor and protect those on the edge of poverty, the political reality is that critical support among the nonpoor for these types of schemes is the lowest where it is needed most, namely, in countries with large populations of extreme poor. Consequently, if these countries continue their typical policy mix of "inclusive" growth strategies combined with targeted transfer programs, movement along the last mile will be slow. Instead, the last mile in poverty reduction is more likely to be sustainable through comprehensive, even universal, social policies in which the nonpoor are included.

By 2030, however, most of the world's extreme poor will live in fragile states, many of which are low-income countries. In these countries, of course, there remains much mileage to be gained from growth. However, reforms to social policies in these countries also have their place. Here the challenge is to weave together the various strands of highly fragmentary antipoverty programs into more uniform, effective systems of social protection that preserve cohesion.

Much of this chapter draws upon the history of poverty reduction and social policy reform in advanced, industrialized economies. Of course, countries in the developing world have followed different trajectories—with respect to the timing of industrialization, reliance on service sectors, and the role of the state in the economy in the context of postcolonial development. This chapter argues, however, that the mechanisms by which extreme poverty was reduced in richer countries when those countries were much poorer—through "welfare states" financed through a tax system in which all citizens held a stake, but that also reduced the multiple vulnerabilities faced by the poor—apply with equal force in developing countries today. From Brazil to India to sub-Saharan Africa one already sees hints of these historic forces at work: a long-undermined commitment to the tax system; middle-class resentments against corruption and poor service delivery; and a political awakening that has upended long-lived alliances between ruling elites and particular constituencies in which the middle classes are sidelined. Indeed, the process of welfare-state building—much like state building itself—has not been a peaceful one. In Western Europe and in the United States in the nineteenth and early twentieth centuries, it was characterized by social unrest, political extremism, and economic turmoil. Whether countries where the extreme poor live can develop durable institutions of social protection will depend on a number of factors, including the broader macroeconomic environment, the effect of globalization on the types of risks countries face, the establishment of domestic political alliances between the poor and the nonpoor, and the ability of aid recipients to temper the strong preference for targeting among the donor community.

Inclusive Growth and Its Discontents

The idea of inclusive growth has taken a central role in debates on developmental trajectories and poverty reduction, despite a lack of a consensus on the meaning of inclusive growth and its relative, pro-poor growth (Ranieri and Ramos 2013). The general idea is that a growth strategy should aim at some combination of income growth and progressive redistribution that raises the living standards of lower-income groups along with the mean. The OECD's Development Assistance Committee (DAC) issued its own statement, stating that pro-poor growth focuses attention on the extent to which poor people are "able to participate in, contribute to, and benefit from growth" (OECD 2006). The idea that both the speed and distribution of income growth are critical for achieving economic development as well as poverty reduction is consistent with the findings of the Commission on Growth and Development (World Bank 2008), which notes that inclusiveness—encompassing equity, equality of opportunity, and social protection—is an essential ingredient of any successful growth strategy.

It is important to note that unambiguously inclusive growth has been a rare phenomenon in the past few decades. An IMF study of the developmental trajectories of 101 low- and medium-income countries, for example, finds that 78 of them experienced per-capita income growth of more than 1 percent per year over a twenty-year period (Anand, Mishra, and Peiris 2013). Of these growing countries, fewer than half increased income equity over the same period.

There are several reasons why this has been the case. Many of the major sources of growth—globalization, financial deepening, investment—can each lead to greater inequality even as they raise incomes. Trade openness, for example, can expand wage gaps between skilled and unskilled workers. Similarly, both inward and domestic investment can raise the premiums for workers with higher education. Financial depth, if imperfect markets for credit and insurance are a result, can widen the difference in opportunity costs of capital between the poor and the nonpoor. In particular, price instability during financial liberalization can increase the vulnerability of the poor, who typically do not have access to inflation-hedging instruments. Additionally, as is well known, macroeconomic stability—considered to be one of the proximate factors leading to inclusive growth—can be difficult to achieve in commodity-dependent economies. Growth can also create poverty where economic shifts bring technological advancements, changes in property rights, and labor market dislocations that can dispossess, exclude, or impoverish large numbers (Saad-Filho 2010). Poorer, less-educated workers may be unable to find alternative employment with equivalent pay, or may be unable to obtain the training needed to seek better prospects in other economic sectors. In the Arab world, for example, younger job market entrants have for two generations consistently found fewer employment opportunities than their older counterparts. The policy response to these conditions—the promotion of self-employment—has also foundered due to insufficient access to credit and markets (Assaad and Levinson 2013).

Concerns have been raised about the feasibility of achieving inclusive growth by redistribution alone (Ianchovichina and Lundström 2009). Transfer schemes can impose fiscal burdens, and where average incomes are very low, redistribution with growth may be difficult to achieve. Instead, analyses of the sources of poverty reduction show that labor income growth contributes more to poverty reduction than transfer schemes, with labor income explaining between 40 percent and 50 percent of the reduction in poverty. However, transfers and nonlabor income have a much stronger effect on reducing extreme poverty (Azevedo and others 2013). This is related to studies that have attempted to measure the inclusiveness of growth as a combination of growth in income and growth in equity. These studies find that inclusive growth is most associated with reductions in poverty when the initial extreme poverty rate is high; for those countries with lower extreme-poverty headcounts, inclusive growth has a smaller impact on reducing poverty (Anand, Mishra, and Peiris 2013). These findings, together, suggest that, while labor income has been the key factor behind reducing extreme poverty from very high initial levels, job creation may have diminishing impacts on the last mile of poverty reduction.

Pushing the Limits of Inclusive Growth: The Case of Brazil

Brazil's experience, in this regard, is illustrative. Brazil's industrialization began in earnest in the 1930s under the Estado Novo, which transferred power away from coffee barons, and which led to the expansion of important sectors of the economy including the automobile industry, petrochemicals, and steel, as well as to the initiation and completion of large infrastructure projects (see, for example, Baer 2008). After a brief period of stagnation in the early 1960s, a series of market reforms created the basis for the export-led "miracle" years, primarily by moving the poor out of subsistence agriculture. The impressive growth in income during these decades—among the highest in the world—is shown in table 10-1. Labor income growth was certainly responsible for much of the progress against poverty achieved by Brazil between the 1950s and 1970s. In the 1960s, for example, for three-quarters of Brazil's economically active population, wages were the only source of income, and the income received by wage

Table 10-1. *Growth and Poverty in Brazil, 1951–2008*

Percent[a]

Period	Output growth	Output per capita growth	Output per worker growth	Total factor productivity growth	Extreme poverty rate	Reduction in extreme poverty
1951–66	6.36	3.24	3.27	0.96	40.5	1.40
1967–79	8.90	6.22	5.67	3.08	21.7	1.41
1980–2008	2.47	0.77	–0.38	–1.13	11.4	0.27

Source: Cardoso and Teles (2010); World Bank, Povcalnet Database.

a. Figures are in annual percentages, averaged over the relevant time period.

earners was 71 percent of the total (Fields 1977). By the 1970s, however, the problem of extreme poverty—particularly in rural areas—proved to be resistant to economywide income growth (Heimer 1975). More important, the specter of rural unrest—particularly in the northeast—prompted the military government to act (Schwarzer and Querino 2002; Haggard and Kaufman 2008).

The incorporation of rural workers into an institutionalized relationship with the state, along with the regulation of rural labor relations, became central components of the military's agrarian policies (Houtzager and Kurtz 2000). Social security had been extended to the countryside by law in 1963 but had not been implemented. In 1971, however, the military government in Brazil launched one of its watershed social initiatives, namely, the extension of noncontributory pensions to peasants and the rural poor through the Rural Worker Assistance Fund (FUNRURAL). By the end of the decade, some 90 percent of the population had been given entitlements to a wide range of social assistance programs. With the 1988 constitution, social assistance became a "social right" in Brazil, granting special protection to families, mothers, children, youth, elderly, and persons with disabilities (Robles and Mirosevic 2013).

These noncontributory programs helped Brazil cut the rate of extreme poverty by more than half, from almost 30 percent in 1970 to less than 14 percent in the 1980s (figure 10-1). In subsequent years, these programs were followed by the unconditional Benefício de Prestação Continuada (continuous cash benefit) and the conditional Programa Bolsa Família (cash-transfer programs)—both considered instrumental in poverty alleviation. As indicated in table 10-1, since the 1950s, Brazil has halved its poverty rate approximately every twenty years. For the first forty years, that poverty reduction can be attributed to growth in wages. But the effect of social protection on progress in the last mile in Brazil cannot be understated: after the 1980s, when Brazil (like other Latin American nations) saw poverty rise, the extension of social protection to previously

Figure 10-1. *Rates of Extreme Poverty in Brazil, 1945–2010*

Percent living in poverty ($1.25 a day poverty line)[a]

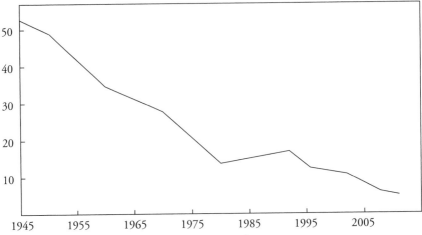

Source: Bourguignon and Morrisson (2002); Maddison (2007); World Bank (various years: *World Development Indicators*).

a. Poverty ratios are calculated from parameterized Lorenz curves derived from historical data.

excluded groups drove poverty down from 12 percent to 6 percent. Transfers from Bolsa Família alone are responsible for lifting over 20 million Brazilians out of extreme poverty since the program was launched. In one of the most income-unequal countries in the world, the incomes of the poorest Brazilians rose seven times as much as those of the richest (Rosenberg 2011). In 2011, the Brasil Sem Miséria (Brazil without misery) program expanded the Bolsa Família, as well as health and education programs. In addition, it directed more money to Brazil's poorest regions, with the goal of lifting the 16 million "most destitute" out of poverty. Early in 2013, Brazil's President Rouseff announced that the last mile would soon be completed.

Social Protection: Building the Welfare State

Significant evidence suggests three main mechanisms by which social protection reduces poverty. First, social protection promotes better access to public services and increases investment in human capital, particularly via health and education, helping raise productivity and labor participation rates among the poor. Second, social protection enables poor people to protect themselves and their assets against shocks and reduces the likelihood that households, during hard times, will engage in behavior that is destructive over the long term, such as withdrawing children from school or selling productive assets. Third, social protection, by enlarging the assets and capabilities of poor people, better enables them to coordinate in factor and product markets, mobilize resources, and gain access and representation in the design and implementation of policies that affect their lives. Critical to the effectiveness of social protection, however, are the public institutions that support social assistance and social insurance—the nature of the "welfare" regime—that facilitates access to the labor force as well as insurance against risk.

An important intellectual innovation in the eighteenth century was that poverty should no longer be thought of as a necessary condition for development, that the afflictions of extreme poverty—hunger, disease—encourage industry and work or that the prospects for upward mobility among the poorest were restricted: "The key contribution . . . was in establishing the moral case for the idea of public effort toward eliminating poverty" (Ravallion 2013). For the better part of a century, that "public effort" largely took the form of mutual aid societies, the workhouse, and compulsory education laws. It did not include any form of protection against shocks or any social "floor."

But after social upheaval among the growing urban, industrial workforce in the late nineteenth century, the political movements—parties, revolutionary communes, labor radicalization—that it spawned were responsible for much of the policy responses to come (figure 10-2). In the 1880s, Bismarck's government enacted the Law Concerning Health Insurance for Workers (1883), the Accident Insurance Act (1884), and the Law on Invalidity and Old Age Insurance for Workers, Journeymen and Apprentices (1889). In this way the modern welfare state was born. The political circumstances behind the expansion of social protection not just in Brazil but all across Latin America partly mirror the nineteenth-century German experience: states seeking to dampen unrest through the extension of benefits to key segments of the population. In Bismarck's own words, "My idea was to bribe the working classes, or shall I say, to win them over, to regard the state as a social institution existing for their sake and interested in their welfare" (Dawson 1894). After the 1890s, France established free medical assistance and assistance programs for the elderly. Facing similar trade union mobilization and electoral threats from the newly formed Labour Party, Britain soon followed suit, with the governing Liberal Party after the 1906 elections enacting a series of welfare reforms that dealt with worker pensions, unemployment, and health insurance. The Great Depression precipitated the Social Security Act and Fair Labor Act in the United States. Beginning in the 1920s, finally, the Japanese government enacted a series of welfare programs, although comprehensive social security was not established until after World War II.

Figure 10-2. *A Century of Social Spending, Five Industrialized Nations,*
1880–1980[a]

Percent of GDP (log scale)

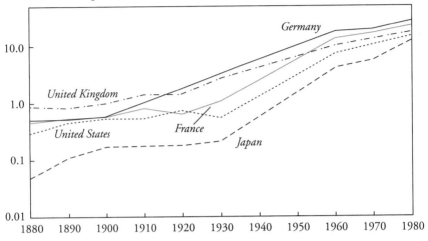

Source: Lindert (1994); OECD.
a. Social spending comprises public expenditures on pensions, health, welfare, and housing.

These rudimentary welfare regimes did not involve large public expenditures in relative terms. As figure 10-2 shows, in all cases all public spending on welfare, pensions, health, and housing remained below 1 percent of GDP in five industrialized economies, at least until the 1930s. Extreme poverty in these states, however, fell during that same period (figure 10-3), with much of that reduction driven by increases in wage incomes. In Lindert's (1994) classic formulation, much of the expansion in social spending began with the organization of labor and the spread of the democratic franchise in these countries in the late nineteenth century. By the post-World War II years, however, these countries had approached their own last mile, with between 3 percent and 5 percent of the populations of the United States, the United Kingdom, Germany, and France living below $1.25 a day in 2005 PPP-adjusted U.S. dollars (Japan's rate was higher, at approximately 15 percent).

The prospect of rising unemployment following the war prompted the British government to investigate the constraints facing social insurance schemes and to reform existing workers' compensation programs. The Beveridge Report (Beveridge 1942) recommended extending the scope of social insurance to cover excluded individuals (for example, children and pensioners), to expand the range of risks against which insurance could be provided, and to raise the rates of benefit. Under the postwar Labour government, the National Health Service

Figure 10-3. *Poverty Rates, Five Industrialized Nations, 1810–1970*[a]

Percent living in poverty ($1.25 a day poverty line)

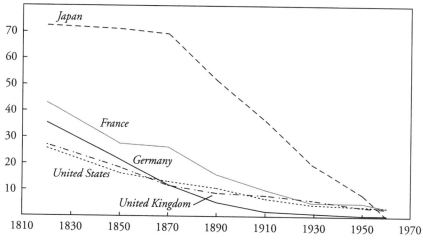

Source: Bourguignon and Morrisson (2002); Maddison (2007); World Bank (various years: *World Development Indicators*).

a. Poverty ratios are calculated from parameterized Lorenz curves derived from historical data.

and a national social security system formed the core components of the current British welfare state. These reforms were to emphasize contributory benefits. Or, as Beveridge put it: "Benefit in return for contributions, rather than free allowances from the State, is what the people of Britain desire" (Beveridge 1942). Thereafter in postwar in Western Europe, similar mixed-economy bargains fueled much of the expansion in social spending and contributed a greater portion to the elimination of extreme poverty in these countries (Shonfield 1965). In the United States, the Johnson administration's War on Poverty similarly aimed at extending social protection to excluded persons and expanding the types of risks covered through such initiatives as Medicare, Medicaid, food stamps, and Head Start. Evidence suggests that the percentage of Americans living above the national poverty line fell from 26 percent to less than 15 percent by the early 1970s, with much of the effect of poverty reduction concentrated among the elderly (Wimer and others 2013).

Divergences among Developing Countries

In the nineteenth century the German economist Adolph Wagner developed the income-effect explanation for social spending for which he is famous: that industrialization would create political pressures for greater social spending. While there is weak support for Wagner's "law" in high-income OECD countries (Lindert 1996), economic development appears to be unrelated to the size or expenditure of government among developing countries (Adsera and Boix 2002; Mares and Carnes 2009). Indeed, explaining variation in social spending among middle- and low-income states has remained something of a puzzle for political economists.

Despite well-known structural differences in welfare states, the postwar systems of social protection that evolved in advanced industrialized economies were principally contributory in nature, with benefits for workers being paid for by their employers through a tax proportional to their wages. Subsequently, social protection regimes expanded to noncontributory programs financed by general tax revenues. While contributory social insurance links the level of contributions to the wages of individuals (ensuring that the rich contribute more than the poor), noncontributory policies finance benefits from general tax revenues. The context in which social protection developed in OECD countries, however, differs from that of middle- and low-income countries along three dimensions: one, the weaker relative bargaining strength of the labor movements; two, a larger informal economy, with consequences for coverage in social programs; and three, greater reliance on targeting in delivering social protection.

Globalization and Organized Labor

Social protection in low- and middle-income countries evolved in an environment in which labor movements have found themselves in a weaker bargaining position relative to the holders of capital. One of the enduring puzzles in the development of social protection around the world is the divergence between high-income OECD countries and developing countries in this regard (Rudra 2002, 2009). While the former were able to prosper and expand social protection programs in an era of capital mobility and international competition, in the latter austerity and neoliberal reforms limited public expenditures on social protection and poverty alleviation (Rodrik 1997, 2008). The divergence is commonly explained by the familiar race to the bottom, whereby economic openness discourages social and welfare spending. As holders of capital push for lower taxation (and expenditures) along with less debt and, at the same time, oppose policies that can lead to rises in unit labor costs, the bargaining ability of workers to resist these pressures shrinks (Garrett 2001). Consequently, for developing nations with large surpluses of low-skilled labor, globalization may have placed labor in a weakened position.

A similar argument makes a distinction between groups within sectors facing shocks (manufacturing sectors exposed to international competition, for example) relative to those less vulnerable. In this view it is distributional conflict between the high- and low-risk sectors, rather than between classes, that shapes social protection. Workers and firms facing high demand volatility, consequently, will favor institutions of social insurance that compensate them for losses of income and that reallocate these costs across sectors; workers and firms in low-risk sectors will oppose these programs that turn them into subsidizers of high-risk sectors (Mares 2005). The outcome of this battle turns both on the relative bargaining strengths of these groups and on the government's ability to manage conflicts and enforce existing policies, which can dampen the effect of external shocks on the erosion of social protection.

Fragmentation and Coverage

While an industrial base of formal sector workers drove the expansion of contributory social protection in OECD countries, informality in many developing countries has fragmented the nature of the social protection regime. The vast majority of the population in low-income countries is not covered by any form of statutory social protection, either insurance based or noninsurance based, with the result that the majority of the workforce is excluded from social insurance. Moreover, the poor find that the social protection services offered by statutory coverage, such as pensions and unemployment benefits, do not match priorities like consumption smoothing, childcare, and basic education (Norton, Conway, and Foster 2001). One explanation stresses the long-term effects of structural changes in the economy linked to "deindustrialization" in the developing world, whereby the growing ranks of self-employed workers in the service sector have very different individual preferences over social policy alternatives (Carnes and Mares 2010). This also potentially explains divergences between East Asia and Latin America.

In Latin America, formal sector workers are forced to consume a bundled set of goods and services largely paid by payroll taxes (and a smaller portion by government subsidies), while in the informal sector workers can choose which goods and services (of the offered menu of social protection) to consume, and their cost is financed out of general government revenues. As a result, employment in the formal sector is taxed (because workers do not value the benefits in full), while employment in the informal sector is subsidized (Levy 2008). In combination, these labor market differences also increase the size of a potential political coalition favoring noncontributory social policies, perpetuating the fragmentation of social policy, and creating an environment in which the temptation to use antipoverty programs for political benefit is strong. Latin America is replete with examples. In Peru, before elections, Fujimori's government often poured money into the FONCODES public works and antipoverty programs (Schady 2000). In Mexico, between 1989 and 1994, the national poverty-alleviation program, Programa Nacional de Solidaridad (PRONASOL) spent 1.2 percent of GDP annually on transfers heavily skewed toward municipalities dominated by the governing Institutional Revolutionary Party (PRI) (Diaz-Cayeros and Magaloni 2003). Whatever their effects on poverty, Mexico's

PROGRESA-Oportunidades and Brazil's Bolsa Família have also yielded electoral rewards for incumbent politicians (De La O 2010).

By contrast, a lower degree of relative informality in East Asia has important implications for its social policy preferences. The expected utility derived from contributory insurance should be higher. Moreover, rising insecurity among this group—due to greater reliance on low-skill, service sector employment, exogenous economic shocks, and demands for labor market flexibility—would also increase support by these workers for policies with a stronger pro-poor bias (Mares and Carnes 2009). Although there is evidence of the relatively larger size of intrafamily transfers in East Asian states (Kwon 2005; Kim 2005), a significant portion of the welfare mix is provided through employer-provided benefits (Kim 2010). Moreover, several East Asian countries are characterized not only by higher levels of coverage but also by high levels of redistribution across income groups when compared to Latin America (Mares and Carnes 2009).

Targeting

Finally, social policy in low- and middle-income countries reveals a strong preference for targeted benefits. In the 1980s and 1990s many developing countries shifted away from broad social policies that emphasized universal benefits toward an approach that targeted public resources to vulnerable segments of the population. Targeted interventions had been designed with a number of specific goals: reducing hunger, increasing income and employment, enhancing the skills of the poor, providing assistance to migrants, launching labor-intensive public works, transforming low-yielding self-subsistence farming into modern agriculture, closing the gap in living standards among ethnic groups, improving education, increasing the share of women in wage employment, combating gender violence, and involving youth in safety enhancement and community awareness projects (see for example, Ocampo 2008).

It is important to distinguish between inefficiently targeted transfers and the inefficient transfers themselves. While the former may be needed to ensure that social programs are politically sustainable, the latter impose distortions on the economy. Pro-poor redistribution sometimes takes a highly distortionary form due to the lack of transparency in budgetary rules or due to high levels of discretion in spending. Some of these extremely inefficient transfers to the poor are well known, like the urban bias in some countries, whereby price subsidies for urban residents are implemented at the expense of poor farmers, and the use of off-budget funds that may have antipoverty components but that constitute a contingent fiscal liability for governments. These distortionary transfers sometimes occur as a way of masking the true cost of the transfer (Acemoglu and Robinson 2001). Thus politicians rely on price subsidies rather than lump-sum transfers, or on off-budget funds rather than budgetary expenditures, in order to avoid revealing the true cost of the transfer and the political relationship between the politician and the beneficiary group. Above all, politicians want to avoid appearing to care about the poor to the exclusion of others.

Although OECD welfare includes minimum wage laws and allowances to those below the poverty line, they have gone much further in the universal provision of education, health insurance, and child allowances. While targeting mechanisms aim to minimize the cost of programs by focusing social protection on the poorest households, over one-quarter of social programs in developing countries were found to have regressive outcomes, indicating that a universal approach would have distributed a greater proportion of benefits to the poor (Coady, Grosh, and Hoddinott 2004). Moreover, the total redistributive effect may be higher in universal systems than in those countries that apply targeting (Korpi and Palme 1998; Ocampo 2008).

Social Protection as a Developmental Process

Before 2000 few middle- or low-income countries provided what might be termed a social safety net with wide coverage. According to the ILO's definition, 80 percent of the world's population has no access to "comprehensive social protection" (Bonilla Garcia and Gruat 2003). The content of social protection programs was either generally highly targeted to certain groups (extreme poor, disabled, elderly, rural residents) or was provided through full-employment policies relying on the public sector (as in the case of several middle-income countries in the Middle East and North Africa). Since then, there have been the spread of cash transfer programs in Latin America and the introduction of universal social policies in Korea, a social protection floor in China, and a countrywide public works program in India.

Moreover, despite the spread in social protection, coverage remains uneven. Figure 10-4 compares coverage ratios across regions of four types of social programs: social assistance (cash and in-kind transfers), social insurance (pensions and social security), labor market programs, and private transfers (remittances). Coverage for the whole population and for the poorest quintile is compared across the upper and lower portions of the figure. The graph highlights three facts about comparative social policy. First, most social programs are not very pro-poor. With the possible exception of social assistance programs in some regions, the coverage shares of the general population and the poorest do not differ remarkably. Second, richer regions appear to rely on social insurance more than social assistance. As one would expect, social insurance coverage ratios are generally skewed to the nonpoor, reflecting their greater participation in contributory social programs. Finally, there is considerable regional variation, both in terms of program coverage, as well as progressivity.

Figure 10-4. *Social Protection Coverage by Program Type and Region*^a

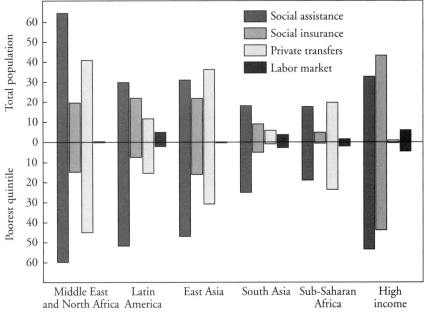

Source: World Bank (various years: *Atlas of Social Protection*).
a. Programs are categorized as social assistance (cash transfers, family allowances, subsidies, and food/cash-for-work programs), social insurance (contributory pensions and social security), labor market programs (unemployment benefits, severance, disability, vocational training), and private transfers (remittances, both domestic and cross border). Data are 2004–11 averages.

The constraints affecting the construction of social protection systems in developing countries can be further seen in table 10-2, which shows that total average budgetary allocations from the general government to social security, health, education, and welfare did not move by much more than 1–3 percent of GDP for low- and middle-income countries, respectively, between the 1970s and 2000s. High-income OECD countries, by contrast, expanded their combined social spending by more than 10 percent of GDP during the same period.

Using historical estimates, one can also compare developing countries to high-income countries in terms of their progress against poverty based on income levels. Figure 10-5 does this for three industrialized and three developing countries over the course of almost two centuries: Germany, United Kingdom, United States, China, India, and Indonesia, between 1820 and 2010. The right side of the curve illustrates the last mile that the richer countries completed several decades ago. But the graph also shows that today's developing

Table 10-2. *Social Spending by Category and Income Group, 1970s–2000s*[a]
Percent of GDP

Income group and category	1970s	1980s	1990s	2000s
Low- and lower-middle-income countries				
Social security and welfare	1.47	1.58	2.07	3.19
Education	3.29	3.37	3.50	4.37
Health	1.32	1.46	1.62	1.58
Total	6.08	6.41	7.19	9.14
Upper-middle-income countries				
Social security and welfare	3.86	4.27	5.40	4.55
Education	3.75	3.80	4.02	4.57
Health	1.59	1.81	2.00	3.04
Total	9.20	9.88	11.42	12.16
High-income OECD countries				
Social security and welfare	14.88	16.71	17.83	22.64
Education	6.18	6.96	6.49	5.35
Health	4.84	6.42	6.75	7.36
Total	25.90	30.09	31.07	35.35

Source: Rudra (2008); World Bank various years (*Atlas of Social Protection; World Development Indicators*).

a. All figures are annual averages expressed as percentages of GDP. Figures for the 2000s are for 2004–11.

nations have higher poverty rates than the industrialized nations did when they were at comparable levels of per-capita income.

More important, these Asian states are also lagging behind in their development of social protection when compared to richer nations at equivalent periods historically. In per-capita income terms (in 2005 purchasing power parity adjusted for international dollars), India today is richer than Germany was in the late 1880s, when Bismarck created contributory social insurance programs for all workers. Indonesia is as rich as the United States was in 1935, when it passed the Social Security Act. And China is richer than Britain was in 1948, when it inaugurated the National Health Service.

Protection of the Poor and Middle-Class Exit

What explains the comparative lag in welfare state development between developing countries and industrialized countries at historically comparable levels of per-capita income? Classic explanations of the expansion of social protection

Figure 10-5. *Progress against Poverty, Six Countries, 1820–2010*[a]

Percent living in poverty ($1.25 a day poverty line)

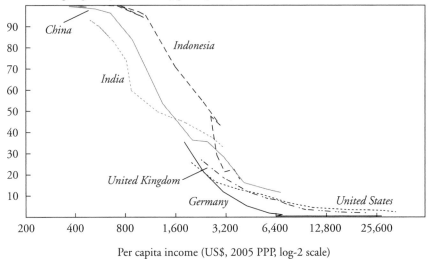

Per capita income (US$, 2005 PPP, log-2 scale)

Source: Bourguignon and Morrisson (2002); Maddison (2007); World Bank, *World Development Indicators;* Luxembourg Surveys.

a. Each line shows poverty headcount ratios for each country against per capita income, starting in 1820 and ending in 2010. Poverty ratios are calculated from parameterized Lorenz curves derived from historical data.

in Western Europe and North America feature the critical role of the emerging industrial (and later white-collar) middle class. From this perspective, the political position of this new middle class was instrumental in consolidating the welfare state (Esping-Anderson 1990). Where the middle class allied with the urban working poor or farmers, for example, governments managed to institutionalize middle-class loyalty to broader systems of social protection. Welfare states in industrialized nations, as described above, were not built for the poor but for workers (to prevent social unrest). But they accommodated needs of the middle class by providing services for which they would be willing to pay taxes (Deacon 2010). In the advanced economies, as the middle class acquired a greater stake in a contributory system, they also demanded accountability, legal protection, and better public services; the poor benefited from all these things (Birdsall 2010). Moreover, the universal education, health, and social insurance programs that served the middle class also greatly supported the poor.

By contrast, the pro-poor focus that has shaped social protection systems in developing economies may have also undermined middle-class support for poverty reduction. A reliance on targeted benefits that exclude the nonpoor— while perhaps making sense in terms of fiscal or technical efficiency—do little to make these programs sustainable. Besley and Kanbur (1990) and Gelbach and Pritchett (2001), among others, argue that targeting to reduce fiscal costs and to reach the truly poor can be counterproductive if the programs as a result lose the political support of the middle class. Some advocate explicitly allowing "leakage" to the nonpoor as means of shoring up broader political support (Pritchett 2005). By contrast, in the richer nations, the universal education, health, and social insurance programs that served the middle class and that have been financed through taxation also served the poor.

Among the nonpoor there is often a widespread belief that poor households will misuse income transfers and that welfare creates dependency. Whether or not these are unfounded perceptions, they are very real in terms of influencing program design and survival (Harvey 2007; Holmes and Jackson 2007). Public opinion regarding antipoverty transfers can dramatically affect the durability of these programs. Evidence from Latin America, for example, shows that those countries whose citizens hold the poor responsible for their own poverty are less likely to support large antipoverty efforts (Graham 2002). Consequently, social policies that tie eligibility for receipt of transfers or investments in human capital are often designed to maintain legitimacy in the eyes of the public (Lindert, Skoufias, and Shapiro 2006).

Conditional cash-transfer (CCT) programs are a prime example. One argument in favor of conditionality—whatever the economic evidence—is that it may facilitate political support for transfers. Policymakers view CCTs as more politically acceptable to voters and taxpayers, since recipients are required, in complying with program rules, to engage in "good" behavior before they can receive cash. Conditionality also dilutes the negative (and often misguided) perceptions of welfare dependence, since association of social assistance with more broadly accepted investments in health and education enhances its attractiveness to voters (Samson, Mac Quene, and van Niekerk 2006).

But sometimes no amount of conditionality can overcome voters' dislike of pro-poor programs. For example, Nicaragua's CCT, Red de Protección Social (social protection network, or RPS) was financed with a loan from the Inter-American Development Bank (IDB), and several evaluations identified positive effects on poverty and inequality (Maluccio and Flores 2005; Fiszbein, Schady, and Ferreira 2009; Moore 2009). However, opposition politicians began to complain about RPS's administrative costs as well as the narrowness of its targeting. The incumbent government was defeated at the polls in 2007, around the same time that the RPS was not renewed (it was replaced by a number of other poverty reduction initiatives). The RPS lasted only for the life of the IDB loan through which it was financed.

Yet program designers in the developing world, appear to have moved even farther in the direction of pro-poor biases for social protection. And the consequence has been middle-class alienation from the idea of social protection.

With the expansion of noncontributory benefits that took place in Mexico in the last decade, the subsidy from formal sector workers to informal employment has increased. Levy estimates that, on average, taxes on low-skilled formal workers amount to 25 percent of their wage, and subsidies to informal workers are equivalent to 8 percent of their remuneration. Meanwhile, poorer workers tend to opt out of the formal sector because their valuation of formal social security benefits is lower—given, for example, the lower quantity and quality of services where poor workers live—while at the same time in the informal (and less productive) sector they can get similar benefits essentially free. The result is not merely an oversized informal, less productive, sector, in which poor workers are overrepresented, but a middle class that has grown increasingly frustrated with poor quality services.

In many low- and middle-income countries, the growing middle class has little stake in the de facto or de jure system of social protection. In the 2005-09 wave of the global World Values Survey, respondents around the world were asked, "Which of these problems do you consider the most serious in your own country?" Table 10-3 shows percentages, averaged by income quintile, of those who responded, "People living in poverty and in need." The table shows two stylized facts. First, poverty is a greater concern in poorer than in richer countries, but the gap varies. Only in Japan and Sweden, for example, do respondents uniformly pick another issue more pressing than domestic poverty (compared to over half of Germans and Australians surveyed). Second, the table shows that the gap in opinion between the first (poorest) quintile and other income groups is generally wider in low- and middle-income countries than in high-income OECD countries. There are exceptions: in Brazil and India, for example, poor and nonpoor alike appear to have similar views on the importance of domestic poverty (in fact, slightly larger percentages of the rich think that poverty is the most pressing problem compared to the poor). However, in other countries the gap between the richest and poorest quintile is large: in Ethiopia (15 percent), Zambia (25 percent), China (30 percent), and Rwanda (38 percent) poverty is a much greater concern among the poor than among the nonpoor.

Even India and China—where social protection is on the rise—have continued a highly targeted, fragmentary approach to social policy. In India various programs—and special measures within programs—have been put in place to reach different sets of the marginalized populations. The National Rural Employment Guarantee Act (NREGA) is, of course, a prime example: it guarantees a hundred days of public employment at a stipulated wage rate. The national Sarva Shikhsa Abhiyan (SSA) focuses on primary education for children of poor, rural families. The Rashtriya Swasthya Bima Yojana (RSBY) provides health insurance for individuals below the poverty line. And so on (see De Haan 2013). In each case, there is a specialized targeting mechanism built

Table 10-3. *Support for Poverty Reduction, by Income Quintile, Selected Countries*[a]

Percent

Country	First	Second	Third	Fourth	Fifth
Brazil	0.60	0.65	0.63	0.65	0.68
China	0.63	0.48	0.52	0.52	0.32
India	0.62	0.52	0.56	0.60	0.72
Ethiopia	0.67	0.40	0.40	0.37	0.51
Rwanda	0.78	0.71	0.72	0.46	0.40
South Africa	0.60	0.56	0.54	0.50	0.52
Zambia	0.78	0.75	0.65	0.52	0.53
Germany	0.50	0.51	0.46	0.42	0.41
Japan	0.06	0.12	0.10	0.07	0.10
Australia	0.54	0.52	0.51	0.48	0.51
Sweden	0.24	0.24	0.25	0.20	0.20

Source: World Values Survey (2008).

a. Figures are average percent of respondents choosing "People living in poverty and in need" as the "most serious problem" facing the country, grouped by within-country income quintiles, with first being the poorest, fifth being the richest.

into the distribution of benefits. Meanwhile, the Indian middle class, which perceives few benefits from these state programs (for example, labor-intensity requirements make it impossible to use NREGA funds to improve transport networks, electrification, food distribution, water or sanitation or other services from which the nonpoor could benefit), has withdrawn into its own privately funded world of utilities, health, and education (Subramanian 2013).

Chinese welfare shares many similarities with India. There are missing components, notably the dimension of family policy; but also missing is income security during illness and health care coverage for dependents, along with shortfalls in the implementation of even obligatory provisions. Meanwhile coordination between central and local authorities is limited (Ringen and Ngok 2013). Still, China has done somewhat better in engaging the middle class in its moves to expand social protection. Indeed, there is a clear government direction toward the expansion of public policies, as China moves to high-income status (De Haan and Shi 2012). China expects to build an integrated social security system, and expansion of the health system is under way. At the same time, government spending will likely remain tightly controlled, and there is a strong aversion to the welfare-dependency trap that is thought to afflict countries with larger welfare states (Lu and Feng 2008).

Special Considerations in Fragile States

Over the next two decades the share of the world's extreme poor who live in stable middle-income countries is expected to fall from 60 percent to approximately 30 percent (figure 10-6). By contrast, the percentage of the extreme poor who live in fragile states will increase from 35 percent to 55 percent (the remaining 15 percent will inhabit stable low-income countries). Consequently, much of the progress in achieving the last mile will have to occur in fragile states, most of these also being low-income countries.

Fragile states face an unattainable triad with respect to the principal goals of social protection, namely, the eradication of extreme poverty, the avoidance of social tension, and cost effectiveness. Given that most fragile states suffer from significant ethnic, religious, or linguistic fractionalization and tension, highly targeted programs (assuming they are cost effective) may be vulnerable to elite capture or resource diversion. Moreover, where the poor are predominantly of a particular minority group, targeted programs can breed wider resentment among the majority. Consequently, social program designers are cautioned to rely, to the extent possible, on more universalistic programs in order to manage social conflicts. But this would raise concerns about cost effectiveness among donors. Were program designers to focus on cost effectiveness and social cohesion, it is possible that targeting would yield programs with significant undercoverage of the poorest groups. In other words, program designers can achieve two, but not all three, of the goals of social protection in fragile states.

The conventional approach by donors in low-income countries, then, is a combination of eradication of extreme poverty and cost effectiveness—that is, antipoverty programs targeted at the extreme poor. The objectives of these social programs are typically designed with concerns about sustainability in the face of severe resource and budgetary constraints and have very little to do with the imperatives of solidarity, citizenship, and nation building. In fragile states, however, these latter concerns should be paramount.

Social protection in weak states raises a host of complexities for governments and donors alike. Given weaknesses in rule-based delivery mechanisms in states rent by factionalism and conflict, the opportunities for program administrators to allocate resources on the basis of loyalty or other factors unrelated to need can abound. Depending on the peculiar lineages of community power relations, local governments may be more prone to capture (and consequently, less accountable) than the central government. Under these conditions, weaknesses in state institutions may simply shelter local elites, who use their position to overprovide essential services to themselves or their families—or to otherwise expropriate wealth (Bardhan and Mookherjee 2006).

Local elites use a number of mechanisms to divert resources from the poor—even predatory behavior. Community-based projects can create an

Figure 10-6. *Poverty and Fragility, Two Types of Countries, 1990–2030*

Share of world poverty ($1.25 a day poverty line)

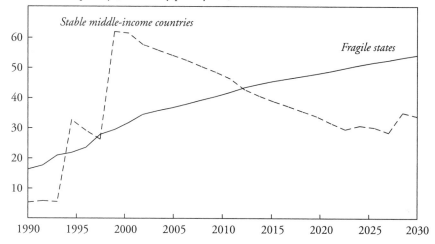

Source: Author's calculations based on Chandy, Ledlie, and Penciakova (2013).

adverse-selection effect wherein individuals likely to obtain leadership roles are precisely those who are able to extract rents (Gugerty and Kremer 2000), to convince donors that their motivations are based on the collective good of their community (Harrison 2002), and to create the façade of community participation (Conning and Kevane 2002). Thus social policies in weaker states often constitute "nothing other than new 'structures' with which [elites] can seek to establish an instrumentally profitable position within the existing structure of neo-patrimonialism" (Chabal and Daloz 1999). There is also evidence of discriminatory practices against minority groups among the poorest, raising the possibility that cleavages among the poor can be induced by social policy. Sri Lanka's Sumurdhi cash-transfer program, for example, once accounted for nearly 1.5 percent of GDP. Survey data indicate that the program discriminated against minorities as well as those in newer settlements (Gunatilaka 2000). In other words, in the hands of highly corrupt officials in states without adequate monitoring mechanisms, social protection can be a tool of oppression.

Moreover, evidence of the cost effectiveness of targeting in weak states is decidedly mixed. Given the extent to which effective targeting relies on information, targeted programs are more likely to suffer from inclusion error as well as higher relative administrative costs in states with fragile institutions. If government capacity is limited, then targeting may overburden the government's administrative resources, while at the same time be more prone to backlash.

Finally, technological innovations have the potential to minimize the cost of more universal programs. India's Unique IDentification Authority of India (UIDAI), which in 2010 launched the Aadhaar program to collect biometric identifying data of all 1.2 billion citizens, was designed in part to enable lower-cost (as well as fairer) access to social benefits and services and, ultimately, to provide entitlements directly to citizens (Daugman 2014). Adopting these innovations in fragile states could overcome resource constraints.

Can the scaling up of social protection in fragile states make similar progress in the last mile of ending extreme poverty? Social protection, when viewed restrictively, is sometimes considered distinct from programs aimed at alleviating extreme poverty. In developing countries, social protection was often traditionally associated with a set of institutions, policies, and programs aimed at providing benefits to individuals and households to enable them to cope with short-term risks. But there is now a greater consensus that social protection can provide an appropriate framework for addressing transient and chronic poverty in ways that should not be limited to addressing short-term vulnerabilities but that can also create conditions for the poor to escape from poverty (Barrientos, Hulme, and Shepherd 2005).

Conclusion

This chapter attempts to make three separate but related points regarding the role of social protection in eliminating extreme poverty. First, inclusive growth—that is, a favorable combination of income growth and inequality reduction—has diminishing effects on the elimination of extreme poverty past a certain threshold. Historical and contemporary evidence suggests that increases in labor incomes in several fast-growing countries have been responsible for the reduction in extreme poverty to approximately 15 percent of the population. Beyond this, reducing extreme poverty requires greater attention to social protection.

Second, the development of institutions of social protection has followed different trajectories in countries that industrialized before, or in the early years of, the twentieth century and in low- and middle-income countries. The latter countries lag in welfare-state development at levels of income comparable to the first group. The conditions under which systems of social protection were scaled up also differ between today's richer and poorer countries: conditions of increased global competition for capital, larger shares of workers in the informal economies, and due to tighter budget constraints, a more prominent focus on the need for targeted benefits. The result in low- and middle-income countries has been to fashion a fragmented set of ad hoc programs from which the non-poor are generally excluded.

Third, this exclusion may have consequences for the political sustainability of social protection efforts. In particular, a group that has historically proven to be pivotal in the scaling up and consolidation of social protection—the middle class—has been denied access to and representation in welfare state benefits and policies. This exclusion appears, here and there across the developing world, in the form of middle-class discontent with social policy and public services as well as in withdrawal into a world of private social insurance, health, and education.

The central obstacle, from this perspective, is not program designers' lack of knowledge, managerial skill, or fiscal resources to create social programs able to eliminate extreme poverty but rather that the domestic politics of developing countries will restrict the scale and duration of redistributive programs. The poor may face high collective action costs, limiting their agenda-setting power. The median voter may not support programs that transfer wealth to the poor. Politicians face strong incentives to use redistributive programs for partisan purposes, limiting the likelihood that these programs will survive political transitions or changes of government. And politicians and public officials may also be prone to create institutional mechanisms that enable them to target different programs to specific groups, potentially limiting their ability to expand in coverage and scale. These interactions between the poor, nonpoor, and public officials—as well as the deliberate political calculations involved in the supply and demand of antipoverty policies—can either limit the scaling up of antipoverty programs or render them unsustainable.

Last, it is also likely that systems of social protection capable of moving countries along the last mile will have to, as one author puts it, rebuild "cross-class solidarities" between the poor and the nonpoor (Deacon 2010). This may seem counterintuitive; after all, if the goal is to reduce the headcount of the extreme poor, why not refine and sharpen targeting mechanisms? This has been the approach of the donor community. But it ignores the need for well-functioning states in managing social protection, at the core of which are durable and accountable programs supported by all social groups. Such an approach would aim at moving from the common, disparate set of safety nets in place in developing countries toward a more comprehensive system that manages the risks and vulnerabilities faced by citizens.

References

Acemoglu, Daron, and James A Robinson. 2001. "A Theory of Political Transitions." *American Economic Review*: 938–63.

Adsera, Alicia, and Carles Boix. 2002. "Trade, Democracy, and the Size of the Public Sector: The Political Underpinnings of Openness." *International Organization* 56, no. 2: 229–62.

Anand, Rahul, Saurabh Mishra, and Shanaka J. Peiris. 2013. "Inclusive Growth: Measurement and Determinants." Working Paper 13-135. Washington: International Monetary Fund.

Assaad, Ragui, and Deborah Levinson. 2013. "Employment for Youth: A Growing Challenge for the Global Community." Background Research Paper Submitted to the High Level Panel on the Post-2015 Development Agenda.

Azevedo, Joao Pedro, Maria Eugenia Davalos, Carolina Diaz-Bonilla, Bernardo Atuesta, and Raul Andres Castaneda. 2013. "Fifteen Years of Inequality in Latin America: How Have Labor Markets Helped?" Policy Research Working Paper 6384. Washington: World Bank.

Baer, Werner. 2008. *The Brazilian Economy: Growth and Development*. 6th ed. Boulder, Colo.: Lynne Rienner.

Bardhan, Pranab, and Dilip Mookherjee. 2006. "Pro-Poor Targeting and Accountability of Local Governments in West Bengal." *Journal of Development Economics* 79, no. 2: 303–27.

Barrientos, Armando, David Hulme, and Andrew Shepherd. 2005. "Can Social Protection Tackle Chronic Poverty?" *European Journal of Development Research* 17, no. 1: 8–23.

Besley, Timothy, and Ravi Kanbur. 1990. "The Principles of Targeting." Policy Research and External Affairs Working Paper 385. Washington: World Bank.

Beveridge, William. 1942. *Social Insurance and Allied Services*. Presented to Parliament, HMSO CMND 6404, London.

Birdsall, Nancy. 2010. "The (Indispensable) Middle Class in Developing Countries." *Equity and Growth in a Globalizing World*: 157.

Bonilla García, A., and Jean-Victor Gruat. 2003. *Social Protection: A Life Cycle Continuum Investment for Social Justice, Poverty Reduction and Sustainable Development*. Geneva: International Labor Organization.

Bourguignon, François, and Christian Morrisson. 2002. "Inequality among World Citizens: 1820-1992." *American Economic Review* 92, 4: 727-744.

Cardoso, Eliana, and Vladimir Teles. 2010. "A Brief History of Brazil's Growth." In *Growth and Sustainability in Brazil, China, India, Indonesia and South Africa*. Paris: OECD.

Carnes, Matthew, and Isabela Mares. 2010. "Deindustrialization and the Rise of Non-Contributory Social Programs in Latin America." Paper prepared for conference, Redistribution, Public Goods Political Market Failures. Yale University.

Chabal, Patrick, and Jean-Pascal Daloz. 1999. "Africa Works: Disorder as Political Instrument." Indiana University Press.

Chandy, Laurence, Natasha Ledlie, and Veronika Penciakova. 2013. "The Final Countdown: Prospects for Ending Extreme Poverty by 2030." Global Views Policy Paper 2013-04, Brookings Institution.

Coady, David, Margaret E. Grosh, and John Hoddinott. 2004. *Targeting of Transfers in Developing Countries: Review of Lessons and Experience*, vol. 1. Washington: World Bank.

Conning, Jonathan, and Michael Kevane. 2002. "Community-Based Targeting Mechanisms for Social Safety Nets: A Critical Review." *World Development* 30, no. 3: 375–94.

Daugman, John. 2014. "Large Data Analysis: Automatic Visual Personal Identification in Demography of 1.2 Billion Persons." *SPIE Proceedings* 9118. Bellingham, Wash.

Dawson, William H. 1894. *Germany and the Germans*, vol. 11. New York: D. Appleton and Company.

Deacon, Bob. 2010. "From the Global Politics of Poverty Alleviation to the Global Politics of Welfare State Rebuilding," Poverty Brief (June). Comparative Research Program on Poverty, International Social Science Council, and the University of Bergen.

De Haan, Arjan. 2013. "The Social Policies of Emerging Economies: Growth and Welfare in China and India." International Policy Centre for Inclusive Growth. Brasília: UNDP.

De Haan, Arjan, and Li Shi. 2012. "Social Protection in China: An Emerging Universal System?" Global Research Network on Social Protection in East Asia. Graduate School of Public Administration, Seoul National University.

De La O, Ana L. 2010. "Do Conditional Cash Transfers Affect Electoral Behavior? Evidence from a Randomized Experiment in Mexico." *American Journal of Political Science* 57, no. 1: 1–14.

Diaz-Cayeros, Alberto, and Beatriz Magaloni. 2004. "The Politics of Public Spending. Part I–The Logic of Vote Buying." Background Paper for *World Development Report 2004*. Washington: World Bank.

Esping-Andersen, Gøsta. 1990. *The Three Worlds of Welfare Capitalism.* Princeton University Press.

Fields, Gary S. 1977. "Who Benefits from Economic Development? A Reexamination of Brazilian Growth in the 1960's." *American Economic Review* 67, no. 4: 570–82.

Fiszbein, Ariel, Norbert Rüdiger Schady, and Francisco H. G. Ferreira. 2009. *Conditional Cash Transfers: Reducing Present and Future Poverty.* Washington: World Bank.

Garrett, Geoffrey. 2001. "Globalization and Government Spending around the World." *Studies in Comparative International Development* 35, no. 4: 3–29.

Gelbach, Jonah B., and Lant H. Pritchett. 2001. "Indicator Targeting in a Political Economy: Leakier Can Be Better." *Journal of Policy Reform* 4, no. 2: 113–45.

Graham, Carol. 2002. "Public Attitudes Matter: A Conceptual Frame for Accounting for Political Economy in Safety Nets and Social Assistance Policies." Social Protection Discussion Paper 0233. Washington: World Bank

Gugerty, Mary Kay, and Michael Kremer. 2000. "Outside Funding of Community Organizations: Benefiting or Displacing the Poor?" Cambridge, Mass.: National Bureau of Economic Research.

Gunatilaka, Ramani. 2000. *The Change Agents' Programme: Reducing Rural Poverty by Catalyzing Economic Change?* Colombo: Centre for Poverty Analysis.

Haggard, Stephan, and Robert R. Kaufman. 2008. *Development, Democracy, and Welfare States: Latin America, East Asia, and Eastern Europe.* Princeton University Press.

Harrison, Elizabeth. 2002. "The Problem with Locals: Partnership and Participation in Ethiopia." *Development and Change* 33, no. 4: 587–610.

Harvey, Paul. 2007. "Cash-Based Responses in Emergencies." Briefing Paper 25, Humanitarian Policy Group. London: Overseas Development Institute.

Heimer, Franz-Wilhelm. 1975. "Education and Politics in Brazil." *Comparative Education Review* 19, no. 1: 51–67.

Holmes, Rebecca, and Adam Jackson. 2007. "Cash Transfers in Sierra Leone: Appropriate, Affordable and Feasible." Freetown, Sierra Leone, and London, UK: Ministry of Finance, EPRU, and ODI.

Houtzager, Peter P., and Marcus J. Kurtz. 2000. "The Institutional Roots of Popular Mobilization: State Transformation and Rural Politics in Brazil and Chile, 1960–1995." *Comparative Studies in Society and History* 42, no. 2: 394-424.

Ianchovichina, Elena, and Susanna Lundström. 2009. "Inclusive Growth Analytics: Framework and Application." Policy Research Working Paper 4851. Washington: World Bank.

Kim, J. 2005. "The Mixed Composition of Welfare State Provision System in Korea." Proceedings of the Fall Joint Meeting of the Korean Academy of Social Welfare, pp. 35–56. Catholic University of Daegu, Korea.

Kim, Pil Ho. 2010. "The East Asian Welfare State Debate and Surrogate Social Policy: An Exploratory Study on Japan and South Korea." *Socio-Economic Review* 8: 411–35.

Korpi, Walter, and Joakim Palme. 1998. "The Paradox of Redistribution and Strategies of Equality: Welfare State Institutions, Inequality, and Poverty in the Western Countries." *American Sociological Review*: 661–87.

Kwon, H. 2005. "An Overview of the Study: The Developmental Welfare State and Policy Reforms in East Asia." In Kwon, H.-J., ed., *Transforming the Developmental Welfare State in East Asia*. London: Palgrave.

Levy, Santiago. 2008. *Good Intentions, Bad Outcomes: Social Policy, Informality and Economic Growth in Mexico*. Brookings Institution Press.

Lindert, Kathy, Emmanuel Skoufias, and Joseph Shapiro. 2006. "Redistributing Income to the Poor and the Rich: Public Transfers in Latin America and the Caribbean." Social Safety Nets Primer Series. Washington: World Bank.

Lindert, Peter H. 1994. "The Rise of Social Spending, 1880–1930." *Explorations in Economic History* 31, no. 1: 1–37.

———. 1996. "What Limits Social Spending?" *Explorations in Economic History* 33, no. 1:1–34.

Lu, Mai, and Mingliang Feng. 2008. "Reforming the Welfare System in the People's Republic of China." *Asian Development Review* 25, no. 1, 2: 58–80.

Maddison, Angus. 2007. *The World Economy*, vol. 2, *Historical Statistics*. Paris: OECD Development Studies Centre.

Maluccio, John, and Rafael Flores. 2005. "Impact Evaluation of a Conditional Cash Transfer Program: The Nicaraguan Red de Protección Social." Washington: International Food Policy Research Institute.

Mares, Isabela. 2005. "Social Protection around the World: External Insecurity, State Capacity, and Domestic Political Cleavages." *Comparative Political Studies* 38, no. 6: 623–51.

Mares, Isabela, and Matthew E. Carnes. 2009. "Social Policy in Developing Countries." *Annual Review of Political Science* 12: 93–113.

Moore, Charity. 2009. "Nicaragua's Red de Protección Social: An Exemplary but Short-Lived Conditional Cash Transfer Programme." Country Study. Brasília: International Policy Centre for Inclusive Growth.

Norton, Andrew, Tim Conway, and Mick Foster. 2001. "Social Protection Concepts and Approaches: Implications for Policy and Practice in International Development." Working Paper 143. London: Overseas Development Institute.

Ocampo, José Antonio. 2008. "Las Concepciones de la Política Social: Universalismo versus Focalización" [Conceptions of social policy: Universalism vs. focalization]. *Nueva Sociedad* 215: 36-61. Caracas.

Organization for Economic Cooperation and Development. 2006. "DAC Guidelines and Reference Series Promoting Pro-Poor Growth Policy Guidance for Donors: Policy Guidance for Donors."

Pritchett, Lant. 2005. "Lecture on the Political Economy of Targeted Safety Nets." Social Protection Discussion Paper 0501. Washington: World Bank.

Ranieri, Rafael, and Raquel Almeida Ramos. 2013. "Inclusive Growth: Building up a Concept." Working Paper. Brasília: International Policy Centre for Inclusive Growth.

Ravallion, Martin. 2013. *The Idea of Antipoverty Policy*. Cambridge, Mass.: National Bureau of Economic Research.

Ringen, Stein, and Kinglun Ngok. 2013. "What Kind of Welfare State Is Emerging in China?" Social Security in China Project, Asian Studies Centre, St. Antony's College, University of Oxford.

Robles, Claudia, Vlado Mirosevic, and United Nations, Economic Commission for Latin America (ECLAC). 2013. *Social Protection Systems in Latin America and the Caribbean*. Santiago: United Nations.

Rodrik, Dani. 1997. *Trade, Social Insurance, and the Limits to Globalization*. Cambridge, Mass.: National Bureau of Economic Research.

———. 2008. *One Economics, Many Recipes: Globalization, Institutions, and Economic Growth*. Princeton University Press.

Rosenberg, Tina. 2011. "To Beat Back Poverty, Pay the Poor." *New York Times*, January 3.

Rudra, Nita. 2002. "Globalization and the Decline of the Welfare State in Less-Developed Countries." *International Organization* 56, no. 2: 411–45.

———. 2008. *Globalization and the Race to the Bottom in Developing Countries: Who Really Gets Hurt?* Cambridge University Press.

Saad-Filho, Alfredo. 2010. "Growth, Poverty, and Inequality: From Washington Consensus to Inclusive Growth." Working Paper ST/ESA/2010/DWP/100. New York: Department of Economic and Social Affairs, United Nations.

Samson, Michael, Kenneth Mac Quene, and Ingrid van Niekerk. 2006. "Designing and Implementing Social Transfers Programmes." Cape Town: Economic Policy Research Institute.

Schady, Norbert R. 2000. "The Political Economy of Expenditures by the Peruvian Social Fund (FONCODES), 1991–95." *American Political Science Review* 94, no. 2: 289–304.

Schonfield, Andrew. 1965. *Modern Capitalism: The Changing Balance of Public and Private Power*. Oxford University Press.

Schwarzer, Helmut, and Ana Carolina Querino. 2002. *Non-Contributory Pensions in Brazil: The Impact on Poverty Reduction*. Geneva: International Labor Office.

Subramanian, Arvind. 2013. "The Economic Consequences of Professor Amartya Sen: Redistributive Policies via Rights and Entitlements Are Ultimately Self-Defeating." *Business Standard*, July 9.

United Nations. 2014. *Millennium Goals Report*. New York.

Wimer, Christopher, Liana E. Fox, Irwin Garfinkel, Neeraj Kaushal, Jane Waldfogel. 2013. *Trends in Poverty with an Anchored Supplemental Poverty Measure*. Institute for Research on Poverty, University of Wisconsin-Madison.

World Bank. 2008. *The Growth Report: Strategies for Sustained Growth and Inclusive Development*. Commission on Growth and Development. Washington.

———. 2012. *China 2030: Building a Modern, Harmonious, and Creative Society*. Washington.

World Values Survey. 2008. *Wave 5 2005-2008 Official Aggregate v. 20140429*. Madrid: World Values Survey Association/Asep/JDS.

11

The Two Fragilities: Vulnerability to Conflict, Environmental Stress, and Their Interactions as Challenges to Ending Poverty

STEPHEN C. SMITH

This chapter examines two types of fragility, environmental and governmental, and their interactions. Increasing environmental fragility, resulting from both external climate change impacts and domestic activities, is a worsening problem in many developing countries. Climate adaptations include large-scale migration and accelerated exploitation of natural resources, leading to heightened risks of conflict. Examples from experiences in such countries as Bangladesh, Kenya, Nigeria, Sudan, and Uganda illustrate the conflict risks of maladaptation by individuals and communities. In addition, maladaptation by governments, such as shortsighted or interest-group-dominated environmental resource mismanagement, can also increase conflict risk and undermine development prospects. Violent conflict can also lead to significant environmental degradation,

I would like to thank Paul Carrillo, Tony Castleman, Elizabeth Chacko, Laurence Chandy, Homi Kharas, Marie Price, and Jonathan Rothbaum for helpful discussions and comments, and particularly acknowledge Arun Malik, with whom I have carried out previous research, some of which has been adapted here. I also gratefully acknowledge comments of participants at the Last Mile in Ending Extreme Poverty workshop at Brookings, January 30–31, 2014, particularly the discussants Manish Bapna and Nigel Purvis. I began writing this essay while I was a visiting fellow in the Brookings Institution Global Economy and Development Program, whose hospitality and support is gratefully acknowledged. I would like also to thank Sixin Li, Britta Schletter, and Grace Mausser for research assistance, Madelyn Swift for editorial assistance, and the Institute for International Economic Policy at George Washington University for research support. Any errors are my own.

as experienced in, for example, Afghanistan, Nepal, Congo, and Sierra Leone. Accordingly, complementarities between the two fragilities—governmental and environmental—are becoming increasingly salient.

The issues raised in this chapter may seem abstract, if not a concern only for the distant future, even where the need to begin contingency planning is acknowledged. But the chapter offers thirty-five examples of how aspects of these problems—and also some promising solutions—have already emerged in recent years. It explores policy options to facilitate peaceful adaptation to environmental change, halt particularly problematic domestic environmental deterioration, and secure the livelihoods of affected populations. Anticipating that environmental stress will worsen in coming decades, the chapter concludes that there are likely to be benefits for both governments and development partners if they adopt an integrated approach to policies—and aid—in addressing conflict and environmental resilience in development and poverty policymaking and program design.

Introduction

The attention of the development community has focused at last on the poorest people in the least developed countries facing the greatest challenges, as exemplified by the 2013 High Level Panel report, the 2013 World Bank commitment to focus on ending extreme poverty and boosting shared prosperity, and the Obama administration's stated development focus on ending extreme poverty. Doing so has brought attention to fragile and conflict-affected countries (FCACs), home to a large and growing fraction of those who are chronically poor and, among the poor, survive on the lowest average incomes. Reports from the IPCC, NOAA (2010), and other groups project that many of the same countries will be among those most negatively impacted by climate change in the coming fifteen-year development goal cycle and for decades to come. In addition, many of these countries face growing domestic-origin environmental stress. Yet the two issues—governmental and environmental fragility—are almost always treated separately. To be successful, these two problems will need to be addressed together, in a way that recognizes their growing interrelationships.

This chapter examines environmental stress and state fragility as two key constraints for ending poverty, with a focus on their interactions. It describes some likely feedbacks between problems of deteriorating environment and climate change and vulnerability to conflict. It considers initial policy implications and options to improve economic development and poverty reduction performance under conditions in which both problems are present; it also looks at the agenda for what we still need to learn. Attention to the quality of interaction between planned (or policy) adaptation by governments and autonomous adaptation by communities to climate change is a priority concern, which requires careful balancing. Generally, in FCACs, greater reliance on well-formulated planned adaptation is called for in the mix of autonomous and planned adaptation, as adaptive responses can worsen social tensions. Yet planned adaptation, and other government policies, need to avoid risking further conflict by thwarting or reducing opportunities for autonomous adaptation. Moreover, policy goals will be better achieved when it is recognized that autonomous adaptation also has the potential to generate positive externalities, including social learning across neighboring communities. To be successful, domestic policy and development partner assistance will also require more integrated attention between climate change and domestic environmental problems. Overall, for FCACs it is essential to maintain a balance in governance reform between strengthening state capacity and improving citizen protections.

The development community recognizes that effectively addressing both conflict and environmental problems is essential to ending poverty and starting development in the least developed countries. For example, in the past two International Development Association (IDA) replenishments (IDA16 and IDA17), special themes include not only attention to FCACs but also attention to the need for low-income countries more generally to prepare for, and respond to, climate change. But relationships between these problems were all but ignored. Policy needs to be designed in an anticipatory way to build climate resilience, even if it is not known whether, for example, future stress will be based on too little or too much water. In the meantime, governments and citizens are beginning to respond to the specific climate change impacts that have already arrived, whether through adaptation or maladaptation.[1]

The World Bank actually produced back-to-back *World Development Reports* on climate change in 2010 and conflict in 2011. Yet surprisingly few explicit connections are made between conflict and environment in these and other major documents.[2] When references are found they typically are general, simulation based, or address one of the issues only indirectly. In-depth studies generally cover only a single country, but they are often insightful concerning more general problems and are described and interpreted in our broader framework throughout this chapter.

---

1. As explained below, some good examples are found in the UN-sponsored NAPA plans and in the plans of member countries of the Pilot Program for Climate Resilience (PPCR). In 2014 the U.S. government announced that climate change had arrived definitively in the United States and more urgent adaptation measures were needed ("U.S. Climate Report" 2014).

2. Indeed, in virtually its only mention, the 2010 *World Development Report* expressed skepticism that there was any convincing evidence at all of a climate-conflict link. It is possible that this is because the report did not systematically examine the indirect effects of maladaptation.

A Preliminary Identification of Countries Potentially at Risk

There is a high degree of overlap between countries affected by the two fragilities. Table 11-1 shows how twenty-two countries rate in separate, well-known reports as vulnerable to or having poor policies regarding governance and conflict, on the one hand, and to climate change and other environmental impacts, on the other hand.[3] A provisional list of countries of high concern for potential interactions emerges from this simple exercise; these countries are concentrated in sub-Saharan Africa, but six from other regions are included. This working list of countries of high concern for the two fragilities (and their interactions) based on standard indexes include Afghanistan, Bangladesh, Burundi, Central African Republic, Chad, Côte d'Ivoire, Democratic Republic of Congo, Ethiopia, Guinea, Guinea-Bissau, Haiti, Liberia, Nepal, Niger, Nigeria, Pakistan, Sierra Leone, Somalia, South Sudan, Sudan, Yemen, and Zimbabwe. As introduced below through illustrations, subregions of many other countries are also at risk of a combination of environmental and conflict stresses.

The purpose in presenting table 11-1 is to assemble some independent assessments of poverty indicators, and either environmental or governmental fragilities, to supplement case studies with a more systematic comparative framework, and to encourage systematic and specific research.[4] Note that there is no implied reason to prefer the set of indicators in table 11-1 as more reliable than others (all rankings are subject to some valid criticisms); there are no explicit rankings of combined risks, nor is this preliminary list of twenty-two countries intended as a claim that some other countries may not be at least as vulnerable (if not more vulnerable) to the two fragilities. In particular, plausible substitutions for a few countries on this list could be made; those substitutions include Eritrea, Kenya, Mali, Myanmar, Syria, and Timor-Leste. Some small island states threatened with storms and sea level rise and experiencing governance challenges, such as Comoros, Kiribati, and Solomon Islands, are also candidates.

---

3. The indicators are not formally weighted. Indeed, availability of rankings for "marginal" countries such as Somalia varies across lists.

4. New indicators could help make further research progress in this area; these will need to address some subtleties. To illustrate, some lists of country vulnerability to climate change are based on the size of expected monetary losses such as reduced crop productivity and cyclone damage; yet other things equal, the magnitude of such losses will be much larger in richer countries with initially high agricultural and building values. Rich countries are also better able to adapt to such losses. Thus indicators based on the absolute size of monetary losses could be misleading for fragility research and policy analysis. If the focus is on ending poverty, indicators are needed to account for the impact on special vulnerabilities of people living in poverty and on the prospects for economic growth of low-income economies. Further, domestic environmental stress needs to be considered in conjunction with exogenous climate risk, among other considerations.

Table 11-1. *Selected Countries of Concern with Comparative Metrics on Poverty, Environmental Fragility, and Governmental Fragility*[a]

Country	Poverty indicators		Environmental fragility indicators			Governmental fragility indicators			
	% below $1.25[b]	MPI score	ND-GAIN rank[c]	EPI rank	On vulnerability list	FSI rank	On WBFS list	WBDBR rank	UNP
Afghanistan	n.a	0.293	170	174	n.a.	7	yes	183	yes
Bangladesh	43.3 (2010)	0.237	139	169	n.a.	29	no	173	no
Burundi	81.3 (2006)	0.442	176	167	no	21	yes	152	no
Central Africa Republic	62.8 (2008)	0.424	174	119	no	3	yes	187	yes
Chad	36.5 (2011)	n.a	178	156	yes	6	yes	185	no
Congo, Democratic Republic	87.7 (2005)	0.399	174	170	yes	4	yes	184	yes
Côte d'Ivoire	35.0 (2008)	0.307	154	129	no	14	yes	147	yes
Ethiopia	39.8 (2010)	0.537	148	131	yes	19	no	132	no
Guinea	40.9 (2012)	0.548	163	162	yes	12	no	169	no
Guinea-Bissau	48.9 (2002)	0.495	169	144	no	16	yes	179	no
Haiti	61.7 (2001)	0.242	170	176	n.a.	9	yes	180	yes
Liberia	83.8 (2007)	0.459	168	172	no	24	yes	174	yes
Nepal	23.7 (2010)	0.197	126	139	n.a.	31	yes	108	no
Niger	40.81 (2011)	0.584	170	142	yes	19	no	168	no
Nigeria	62.0 (2009)	0.239	140	134	yes[d]	17	no	170	no
Pakistan	12.7 (2010)	0.237	122	148	n.a.	10	no	128	yes[e]
Sierra Leone	56.6 (2011)	0.405	160	173	yes	35	yes	140	no
Somalia	n.a.	0.500	n.a.	178	yes	2	yes	n.a.	no
South Sudan	n.a.	n.a.	n.a.	n.a.	yes	1	yes	186	yes
Sudan	19.8 (2009)	n.a.	173	171	yes	5	yes	160	yes[f]
Yemen	9.8 (2005)	0.191	165	157	n.a.	8	yes	137	no
Zimbabwe	n.a.	0.181	146	94	yes[d]	11	yes	171	no

a. MPI (Multidimensional Poverty Index, UNDP); ND-GAIN (Notre Dame Global Adaptation Index, 2013); EPI (Environment Performance Index, 2014); Vulnerability list (Busby and others, Vulnerability list, Africa only); FSI (Failed States Index); WBFS (World Bank Fragile Situations); WBDBR (World Bank Doing Business Ranking, 2014); UNP (UN Peacekeeping presence).

b. World Bank (http://iresearch.worldbank.org/PovcalNet/index.htm?2).

c. ND-GAIN rank 1 (best) to 178 (worst—Chad).

d. 21st century only.

e. Specialized India-Pakistan mission.

f. Mission in Dafur.

Major links in the arguments are illustrated with at least one example with the type of evidence noted; these examples are intended for illustrative purposes motivating the types of research needed and do not constitute systematic case studies. A majority highlights the risks; but a few illustrate policy successes. About half the local cases are situated in countries listed in the table, including Afghanistan, Bangladesh, Côte d'Ivoire, Democratic Republic of Congo, Ethiopia, Nepal, Niger, Nigeria, Sierra Leone, Somalia, and Sudan. Research convincing (to this author) and relevant for present purposes is scarce for many countries on the list. When a key part of the argument can be illustrated more robustly with a relevant study from a developing country not on the list, it is used. For most of these other countries—particularly Guatemala, Kenya, Mexico, Sri Lanka, Syria, and Uganda—both governmental and environmental fragilities are a significant concern. The remaining examples are Bolivia, India, Indonesia, Maldives, Mozambique, Nicaragua, Tanzania, and Zambia, each of which faces at least one of these fragilities to some degree. Figure 11-1 highlights the relationships between the two forms of fragility. Each is affected by, and affects, growth and poverty reduction.

In FCACs, economic growth tends to be erratic or slow; sometimes this is a direct result of conflict, often particularly impacting the poor. Weak governance may also be a factor in violent conflict, again with particular harm to people living in poverty.[5] Moreover, environmental degradation can cause poverty and may cause slower overall growth, as described below.

Environmental degradation can also lead to conflict. The main effects of climate change on conflict will almost certainly operate primarily through the response to observed climate change (adaptation) as well as through actions taken in anticipation of climate change. The direct effects of climate change itself will not be the primary driver. In particular, adaptation (and anticipatory investments in climate resilience) on the parts of government, the private sector, and citizens/civil society is an essential response to the consequences of climate change. Successful adaptation may make individuals and societies less vulnerable to violent conflict (and perhaps even less prone to conflict). But unless managed well, the process of adaptation to climate change by groups in society may precipitate conflict. That is, the primary challenge is not so much that climate change causes conflict, but rather it is the way that people and states respond to the impacts of climate change and other environmental deterioration that can cause conflict.

There will likely also be some direct effects of climate on conflict. For example, studies suggest that higher temperatures can cause more aggressive

---

5. The poverty elasticity of growth is likely lower on average in FCACs; this is known to be the case for economies focused on natural resource exports, which also tend to be countries prone to conflict; but further investigation is needed.

Figure 11-1. *Relationships between the Two Fragilities*

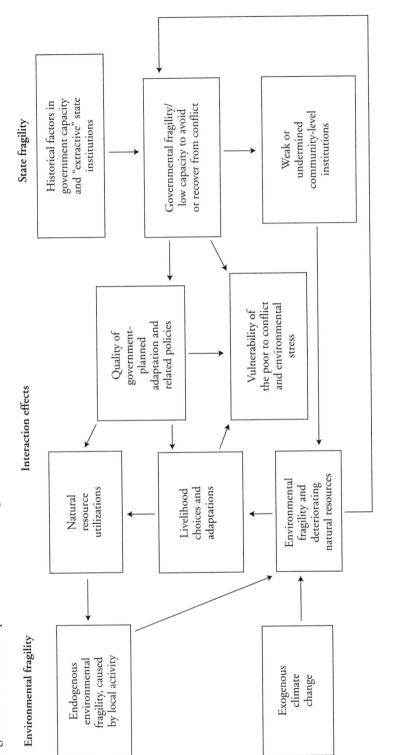

Source: Author.

behavior (Burke and others 2009). But the social response will be crucial, whether through the impacts of adaptation behavior after change occurs or through the impacts of anticipatory actions based on expectations of future change, such as more general resilience policies. There are many ways that humans can adapt to climate changes such as higher average temperatures that do not involve conflict and violence.[6] In such cases the quality of interactions between planned (or policy) adaptation and autonomous local adaptation is of central importance.

Other feedbacks are present, underlining the difficulty of an effective response and again raising the possibility of a trap. One often-overlooked example is that poverty itself can lead to lower growth. The poor's lack of credit constrains their opportunities to escape poverty—this is a rationale for the policy focus on microfinance—but a wider consequence is lower growth due to shutting out some talented entrepreneurs. Similarly, lack of credit robs parents of their chance to educate their children, thus transmitting family poverty to the next generation and also reducing national growth prospects. Moreover, higher population growth leads to lower economic growth; while the lack of financial services also drives the "old-age security fertility motivation" (that is, giving birth to more children to increase the chance that parents will be cared for in old age). Further, chronic health and nutrition deficiencies not only make it difficult to escape poverty but also keep average productivity low.[7]

Finally, poverty and environmental degradation can be mutually reinforcing. For example, when the poor must grow more food they often resort to overusing their farmland, planting aggressively and not resting their soil. Generally, smallholder farmers are aware that the consequences are likely to be worsened soil fertility and lower productivity in subsequent growing seasons. But making this trade-off is less irrational than it may appear, because worse nutrition this year likely means undernourishment for the family, with possibly lifelong damage to their children's cognitive and physical development.[8] And while purchasing fertilizers (and undertaking other land improvements) may be a good investment by conventional calculations, this fact is of no help if the poor have no access to credit. The scope of these difficulties becomes even clearer under the lens of

---

6. For examples, see Das and Smith (2012) and references therein.

7. For a summary of these arguments and references, see Todaro and Smith (2014).

8. For suggestive models of environmental traps, see Sylwester (2004); and Larson and Bromley (1990). There is evidence of poverty trap problems among farmers in Ethiopia, particularly in the impoverished enset growing region (Kwak and Smith 2013). Another example is erosion, as found in Burundi after farming extended to very marginal lands, worsening poverty. Needing closer examination is its possible relationship to conflict, as observers have noted that access to land was restricted due to coffee growing, which was controlled by the elite. See also Bundervoet, Verwimp, and Akresh (2009).

behavioral economics (see for example Duflo, Kremer, and Robinson 2010). Clearly, all of these problems can be greatly magnified under conflict conditions.

In discussions of state fragility, the emphasis is most often on outright conflict, or potential for conflict, against the government and on its implications, such as reduction of government's capacity to enforce favorable national economic institutions. Several significant examples of climate- or adaptation-induced conflict refer to conflict between groups, which are not necessarily threats to (or by) the government per se. Yet such conflicts can also be important contributors to state fragility, which then may be used opportunistically by government opponents.[9] The effects of regional conflict can substantially worsen poverty as well as decrease effective enforcement of environmental protection. There are in addition more direct links between the environment and revolt and civil war. These conflicts, even if localized (indeed even if they have the potential for such conflict) can also lead to state fragility (for a survey, see Miguel, Hsiang, and Burke 2013).

Relatedly, fragility is often regional rather than national and may not lead to governmental fragility at the national level. But even in these cases, fragility is no less important for its location, when our focus is the impact on people living in extreme poverty in these regions.

While major international development and climate partners fail to make these potentially central connections explicit, the issues have not escaped the attention of a much larger player: the military. For example, the U.S. Department of Defense, *Quadrennial Defense Review* (U.S. Department of Defense 2010) notes explicitly that climate change may be "an accelerant of instability or conflict, placing a burden to respond on civilian institutions and militaries around the world." The CNA's "National Security and the Threat of Climate Change" (CNA Military Advisory Board 2014) characterizes climate change as a "threat multiplier" for instability. And the May 2010 White House "National Security Strategy" states that "the change wrought by a warming planet will lead to new conflicts over refugees and resources" (White House 2010).[10] Even so, the nature of any follow-up by the defense sector remains unclear.

Environmental Challenges to Ending Poverty

As a foundation for examining the linkages between the two types of fragility, and their implications for ending poverty, this section first outlines, and

9. The resulting loss of local governmental authority can worsen the prospects of implementing poverty programs as well as of reducing and regulating environmental deterioration (whether for governments inclined to pursue these policies or for civil society or other actors who might otherwise step in).

10. Other security-oriented studies include Gautam (2012).

provides examples of, the effects of the environment on poverty and the effects of conflict on poverty. While the literature offers significantly less regarding how the linkages work in practice, summaries of some currently available examples are presented. Even though still relatively small in number, these examples help to identify gaps in data, research, and policy analysis on environment-conflict linkages.

Confronting Locally and Globally Inflicted Environmental Degradation

Most developing countries are experiencing alarming environmental degradation. Thus far, much of this degradation results from poor national and local environmental policies and practices. In sub-Saharan Africa, more than one-fifth of the population already lives on degraded land, while surface water, including Lake Victoria, suffers from pollution, sedimentation, and over-fishing.[11] In South and West Asia, water quality and water tables are falling alarmingly. The global effects of climate change are inflicting further damage, and there is potential for these exogenous shocks to interact dangerously with domestically caused environmental damage. Agricultural productivity and other environmental resources are almost uniformly harmed by climate change in sub-Saharan Africa and South Asia (IPCC 2007, 2014; World Bank 2011b, 2013).

Broad-brush themes regarding impacts of global climate change are that sub-Saharan African countries will be disproportionately drought afflicted and suffer the worst impacts on agricultural productivity; South Asia will be disproportionately flood affected; countries with high exposure to the Pacific and Indian Oceans within the cyclone belt will be disproportionately storm afflicted; and Southeast Asia and small island developing states will be impacted by sea level rises (World Bank 2013). All countries are predicted to face higher temperatures and increased weather variances. The reports of the IPCC—warnings of prolonged droughts, expanded desertification, increased severity of storms, higher temperatures and more severe heat waves, deteriorated water resources, and reduced crop yields—have been a wake-up call.

Without concerted action, the world faces an approximate 4-degree C increase in average global temperatures this century, again with serious harm to low-income countries.[12] Studies underline that the projected 2-degree C rise within thirty years will lead to growing food shortages in Africa and accentuated water crises in South Asia. The impact of even higher temperature gains and

---

11. For an example of an in-depth study, see Hecky and others (2010). For general coverage see, for example, World Resources Institute and others (2005a).

12. World Bank (2012). As the temperature increase tops 2 degrees C and approaches 4 degrees C, extreme heat waves, rising sea levels, storms, droughts, floods, and losses of grasslands, farmlands, and marine ecosystems will result.

environmental degeneration is far more serious, with potentially calamitous rises in extreme poverty. The worst-case scenarios on poverty impact could turn the last mile into the midpoint of a double marathon.[13] Lest these problems seem far in the future, a World Bank (2013) follow-up study meticulously documents impacts already experienced, including spread of pests, changed growing seasons, extreme weather events, and sea-level rise resulting from the 0.8-degree C average temperature increase thus far.

Regarding domestically generated problems, South Asia suffers from rapidly falling water tables (as well as salinization) due primarily to bad irrigation policies (such as inefficient subsidies) and practice as well as urban pollution. Sub-Saharan Africa suffers from desertification. East and Southeast Asia suffer from industrial pollution, other air pollution problems, and water shortages.[14]

Addressing the New Challenges to Natural Resource–Based Livelihoods

Despite rapid urbanization, a majority of people living in poverty in developing countries still depends on natural-resource-based livelihoods, including agriculture, animal husbandry, and various forms of foraging. Consequently, raising the productivity levels of these activities is an important "path out of poverty" (World Resources Institute 2005).

But such productivity gains are threatened by climate change (IPCC 2014) and domestic environmental deterioration. Environmental stresses on the poor are greatly compounded when they hold weak property rights and have low and often falling control over the resources on which they have traditionally depended. This vulnerability holds both individually and in collectively operated lands. Concerns continue that foreign "land grabs" will threaten domestic food security (von Braun and Meinzen-Dick 2009). Even individually held smallholder farms, as in East Africa, may be locally expropriated; and common property resource areas may be appropriated (whether legally or otherwise) by elites. "Investors" with mysterious government support may suddenly appear from distant cities, with obscure but confusing claims to land. Indeed, risks of

13. The most severe poverty projections naturally result from what are now considered unlikely outcomes, but there is option value in taking action to ensure against such outcomes; for an options approach, see Linquiti and Vonortas (2012). The UNDP compared its baseline forecasts to outcomes under environmental disaster and concluded, "Some 2.7 billion more people would live in extreme income poverty under the environmental disaster scenario than under the base case scenario." Their modeling projected "an increase of 1.9 billion people in extreme income poverty due to environmental degradation." In addition, "environmental calamities would keep some 800 million poor people from rising out of extreme income poverty, as they would otherwise have done under the base case scenario." See UNDP (2012, 95).

14. To be clear, this is only a very broad summary and is not intended to downplay other threats to poverty reduction, such as contamination and deforestation in areas where people depend on natural resources—areas that include parts of Southeast Asia.

appropriation incentivize farmers to treat soils and other natural resources as short-run assets (Jacoby, Li, and Rozelle 2002). Expanding cash crops can grow the economy and help raise incomes of the poor—but usually not when the poor lose control of their only assets (land) in the process. The poor who lose their land may have little or no legal recourse. In the meantime, up to 97 percent of agriculture in sub-Saharan Africa is still rain fed (World Bank 2013). Failure to empower the poor in these circumstances can worsen poverty. Rather than raising long-run productivity, the seeds of conflict are sown.

It may be tempting to consider some of these projected impacts as unimportant to the extent that mass movement of people out of agricultural activities to cities is expected, with potential large-scale agriculture better able to cope with a changing climate. However, agriculture is likely to employ a much higher fraction of people in sub-Saharan Africa in comparison with other developing areas, particularly East Asia. The number of children reaching working age, in comparison to the very low base of manufacturing employment and the low productivity of most urban economic activities, very likely means that smallholder agriculture is here to stay in Africa for decades (Fox and others 2014). Moreover, with the slowdown of growth in India, this also may be the case in South Asia, albeit to a much lesser extent (*Financial Times*, January 16, 2014).

The Long-Lasting Impacts of Natural Disasters

An important predicted consequence of climate change brought about by global warming that is likely to have negative impacts on many countries is more frequent and more severe natural disasters. Baez, de la Fuente, and Santos (2010) document that, rather than transient events, there is considerable evidence that shocks of different kinds (of which disasters are an important example) can have long-lasting negative impacts. Higher-income individuals, just as higher-income economies at a macroeconomic level, recover almost fully from most disasters after a moderate period of time. But despite impressive resilience in many cases, individuals living in poverty (and at a macroeconomic level, low-income economies) often do not recover, at least not fully as measured by income, schooling, and health. Another consequence can be conflict itself.

INCOME. Shocks to wealth and to flows of income can last for a decade or longer. Disasters have severe impacts, as measured by loss of life, decrease in GDP, and poverty in low-income areas (Rentschler 2013). Cross-national evidence that low-income countries face long-term negative consequences is presented in Toya and Skidmore (2007) and Loayza and others (2012), who also provide a brief literature review. As noted earlier, disasters may also raise the likelihood of conflict, magnifying the original effects. Specific country examples focusing on income and wealth impacts on people living in poverty are presented for Côte d'Ivoire, Ethiopia, Nicaragua, Tanzania, and Bangladesh.

—*Example 1*: *Famine in Ethiopia.* The effects of famine in Ethiopia endured for ten years after its initial impact. See Carter and others (2006) and Dercon (2004), using the Ethiopia Rural Household Survey; see also Kwak and Smith (2013).

—*Example 2*: *Drought in Tanzania.* A decade after the 1991–95 drought in Tanzania, the poorest households still had 17–40 percent lower consumption levels (Beegle, Dehejia, and Gatti 2006).

—*Example 3*: *Agricultural shocks in Côte d'Ivoire.* In regions of Côte d'Ivoire that experienced negative agricultural shocks in 1986–87, there were 20 percent lower enrollments compared with unaffected regions (Jensen 2000).

—*Example 4: Floods in Bangladesh.* In Bangladesh floods have destroyed houses, harmed crops, damaged physical capital, and reduced job opportunities. They have led to higher food prices (Islam 2013), with long-term impacts on the very poor (such as effects of malnutrition).

SCHOOLING. Negative shocks to families including but not limited to disasters have been demonstrated to have long-lasting impacts on schooling for families living in poverty.

—*Example 5: Negative income shocks in Mexico.* De Janvry and others (2006) show for the case of Mexico that children taken out of school due to a temporary shock are 30 percent less likely to return to school than similar children who were not taken out of school.

—*Example 6: Hurricane impact on children in Nicaragua.* In Nicaragua in the aftermath of Hurricane Mitch in 1998, child labor increased by over 50 percent (Baez and Santos 2007).

HEALTH. Negative shocks have been demonstrated to have long-lasting harmful impacts on health and nutrition for families living in poverty. Poor nutrition in childhood can have impacts over decades (Baez, de la Fuente, and Santos 2010). Children from nonpoor households can largely catch up to where they would have been in the absence of the disaster, but children from poor families generally cannot, transmitting poverty across generations. Insights can be gained also from positive shocks.

—*Example 7: Nutrition assistance in Guatemala.* Maluccio and others (2006) show that a rural nutrition program for children one to three years old that operated from 1969 to 1977 still showed large impacts on earnings three decades later, including wages that were some 46 percent higher than corresponding untreated stunted children.[15]

15. Background details presented at seminar by John Hoddinott at GWU in 2008.

—*Example 8: Rainfall in Indonesia.* Maccini and Yang (2009) find that women born in a year in which there was 20 percent higher rainfall had a corresponding 0.15 more years of schooling and 5.2 percent higher household incomes twenty-six to forty-seven years after birth.

CONFLICT. Recent evidence suggests that in some circumstances disasters can raise the chance of conflict itself, which in turn increases the likelihood of further negative consequences for people living in poverty, beyond the effect of the disasters themselves (see Miguel, Satyanath, and Sergenti 2004); we return to this topic below.

Environmental Degradation and Conflict: Traps along the Last Mile

Conflict in low-income countries is tragically common; in recent decades more than two-thirds of African countries endured at least one conflict that lasted a year or more (Blattman and Miguel 2010). A number of potential poverty traps relate to environment or conflict or both. The conflict trap "shows how certain economic conditions make a country prone to civil war, and how, once conflict has started, the cycle of violence becomes a trap from which it is difficult to escape" (Collier 2007). Collier concludes that countries are at higher risk of civil war under combined conditions of low income, slow growth, and dependence on primary commodity exports (Collier 2003).

The fragility trap is a related concept describing a low-level equilibrium in which weak institutions, low investment, and slow growth lead to violent conflict, and which in turn keeps institutions weak, investment low, and growth slow (Andrimihaja, Cinyabuguma, and Devarajan 2011). Most countries classified as FCACs remain so for extended periods of time. Many—perhaps hundreds—of descriptive political economy case studies have explored the environment-conflict nexus, though with widely different standards of evidence and viewpoints about root causes.[16]

Environmental degradation alone can thwart efforts to escape from poverty. Overexploitation of resources such as lakes, pastures, and forests for which property rights are not well defined or that lack effective community management (Ostrom 2005) can worsen poverty, whether through the tragedy of the commons or outside theft and encroachment. There have been surprisingly little anticipatory development investments to prevent such breakdowns. With profitable opportunities for resource exports, the incentives to circumvent traditional property rights have also grown. Assisting development for, and

---

16. For a systematic project, see "Inventory of Conflict and the Environment," based at American University, see www1.american.edu/ted/ice/iceall.htm and www1.american.edu/ted/ice/elements.htm.

facilitating the renewal of, local common property institutions in a manner sensitive to local conditions are priorities in addressing the conflict-environment nexus. Indeed, responsible use of shared resources is difficult but not impossible to restore.

—*Example 9: Cooperative common property management in Tanzania.* In the Suledo Forest community in central Tanzania, cooperative common property management was restored after both external and internal stresses led to a serious breakdown. Progress was made with support from SIDA; the Suledo Forest communities won a UNEP/UNDP Equator Prize for their successful combination of economic development and environmental sustainability (Smith 2005; UNDP 2013). However, the community faces continued threats from land grabs, and financial sustainability has become a serious challenge following SIDA's phasing out its support. Once again, it may be dangerously unrealistic to expect financial sustainability for commons management programs, as for poverty programs in the poorest countries more generally (Kremer and Miguel 2007).

Consequences of Conflict and Their Challenges for Ending Poverty

Collier (2007) estimates that "the risk that a country in the bottom billion falls into civil war in any five-year period is nearly one in six." He memorably calls the consequences of conflict "development in reverse." Horrific conditions of refugees receive wide media coverage, while the long-run development impact of conflict gets less attention. Indeed, the evidence shows that most of the economic progress we associate with development—income gains, poverty reduction, and health and education standards—goes into decline during violent conflict (for reviews, see Lindgren 2005; Gupta and others 2002; Plumper and Neumayer 2006; and Stewart, Huang, and Wang 2001). Income growth turns significantly negative. Not surprisingly, conflict can have large fiscal consequences (Gupta and others 2002).

The Damage of Conflict to Economic Development

Lost schooling and other impacts can reduce well-being for a lifetime, and inequality becomes greater as victimized ethnic groups suffer much more human capital loss.[17] Capital is lost through a combination of physical destruction and capital flight (Collier 2003). Government's ability to cushion these blows becomes more limited, with substantial spending cuts for health and

---

17. See, for example, Blattman and Miguel (2010); Blattman and Annan (2010); Bundervoet, Verwimp, and Akresh (2009); Li and Wen (2005); Messer, Cohen, and Marchione (2001); Messer and Cohen (2006); Cassar and others (2013); Chamarbagwala and Morán (2011); and Gupta and others (2002); for an overview see Todaro and Smith (2014, sec 14.5).

education. Social ties are lost when most needed for survival; lost social capital is also destructive to future development opportunities more generally (Blattman and Miguel 2010; Cassar and others 2013).

Akresh and others (2012) find that four decades after the 1967–70 Nigerian civil war those exposed between birth and adolescence have lower adult stature, which is related to lowered life expectancy and life earnings. Bundervoet, Verwimp, and Akresh (2009) find a negative impact on height from civil conflict in Burundi.

—*Example 10: GDP cost of conflict in Sri Lanka.* Ganegodage and Rambaldi (2014) calculate that the civil conflict in Sri Lanka cost that country an annual average of 9 percent of its GDP; this is near the average impact estimated in previous studies on that conflict.[18]

—*Example 11: Human capital cost of civil war in Guatemala.* Chamarbagwala and Morán (2011) show that, in the 1985–96 period of the Guatemala civil conflict, rural Mayan males in district departments where more human rights violations were committed completed 1.09 (23 percent) less years of schooling, while rural Mayan females completed 1.17 (30 percent) less years of schooling. Gender and ethnic disparities in education also apparently increased as a result. The authors found smaller but still significant schooling impacts in two earlier periods of conflict.

Environmental Consequences of Conflict

Conflict can also seriously damage the environment (Biggs 2004). In turn, the environmental impacts cause further harm to the poor. The direct environmental consequences of conflict are quite varied, though most of the impacts are strongly negative. Where governance breaks down in conflict-affected areas, local environmental conservation agreements and arrangements can collapse, while poverty increases; these conditions can accelerate natural resource exploitation (Mitchell 2013).

Encroachments onto protected areas can become more common, including opportunistic poaching. Conflict-related activities can result in chemical pollution of streams and rivers. In addition, a breakdown of state regulation and oversight can lead to unregulated mining, causing severe damage to water quality. There are also cases of deliberate despoilment as a weapon of war. Paradoxically, not all impacts are negative: evacuations of areas in response to conflict can suspend environmental degradation and allow for some ecological renewal. In addition to direct effects, there are also many indirect effects of maladaptation, to which we return in subsequent discussions.

---

18. Such estimates vary widely; Lindgren (2005) found a range of estimated impacts for Sri Lanka of 2.2 to 15.8 percent a year. The Ganegodage-Rambaldi results are in the middle of this pack.

—*Example 12: Impacts of conflict in Afghanistan.* UNEP (2003, 2008) concludes that the legacy of over three decades of conflict in Afghanistan is overuse and depletion of forest, biodiversity, water, and other vital resources, which in turn worsened economic conditions and further undermined safety. Degradation was caused in part by a complete collapse of local and national governance.

—*Example 13: Impacts of conflict in Nepal.* The conflict in Nepal led to destruction of infrastructure for protected areas. Murphy, Oli, and Gorzula (2005, 1) conclude that "a combination of factors, including Maoist attacks on guard posts, reallocation of troops to battle the insurgency, and the loss of political will for environmental conservation may have created conditions conducive for opportunistic resource exploitation" such as poaching. But conflict led to other regions of the county gaining forest regeneration and decreased poaching due to out-migration from the "middle hill region" of the country.

—*Example 14: Impacts of conflict in Sierra Leone.* The conflict in Sierra Leone led to large direct impacts with damaged water systems, agriculture, and forests; pollution from illegal and unregulated mining; and toxins released due to damage to warehouses. As in many countries, indirect effects include several forms of maladaptation (UNEP 2010).

—*Example 15: Impacts of conflict in the Democratic Republic of Congo.* The conflict in the Democratic Republic of Congo has caused environmental damage through battles in protected areas and forests, sabotage of water treatment centers and environmental monitoring equipment, poaching, increases in damaging charcoal production, and other encroachment onto protected areas (UNEP 2008).

Environmental degradation—including damage caused by conflict—harms prospects for ending poverty. At the same time, degradation, whether from local mismanagement or external climate change, can lead to new conflict or amplify existing conflict, deepening the impediments to poverty reduction. To examine this, we take a closer look at responses to environmental stressors and then consider the implications for conflict risks.

Responses to Climate Change and Environmental Degradation

Analysts sometimes draw distinctions between two types of adaptation: autonomous and planned. While planned (or policy) adaptation receives most of the attention, it is inevitable that autonomous adaptation (that is undertaken by individuals, families, and communities below the level of formal government) will predominate over the planned (or policy) adaptation carried out by governments (Mendelsohn 2000; Malik and Smith 2012). Typically, the literature views both planned and autonomous adaptation as cushioning climate change's otherwise harmful effects on people and communities. Among other things, this is thought to reduce the risk that climate change exacerbates tensions—or at least the degree to which it does so (Barnett and Adger 2007; Stark, Mataya, and Lubovich 2009). But under some conditions, either type of adaptation can create or worsen social tensions, thereby increasing the risks of conflict. In low-income countries, the range of risks is likely to be greater from autonomous adaptation because it is more predominant and geographically widespread.

Autonomous Adaptation

There is a wide range of potential autonomous adaptation behaviors (Malik and Smith 2012); and again, they almost certainly add up to a much larger total response than can be expected from planned adaptation (Mendelsohn 2000). Autonomous adaptation takes such forms as farmers responding to drought or worsened crop diseases and pests by altering crop or livestock varieties, altering pesticide use, using more groundwater, and increasing exploitation of common property resources. All these activities benefit those who undertake them, at least in the short run, although they can have negative effects on others. Affected rural residents may further alter their livelihood activities, such as adding day labor to their work mix or attempting an off-farm microenterprise. As conditions worsen further, rural dwellers frequently migrate—whether temporarily or permanently—either to different parts of the country or across national boundaries (Mendelsohn 2000; McLeman and Smit 2006). Autonomous adaptation in cities will also become increasingly important. Urban residents may change location to areas less threatened by storm damage (including flooding and mud slides), alter livelihood activities, and join new informal insurance arrangements.

Again, while these responses are helpful for those who move and change resource use, they can also lead to conflict that must be managed, as illustrated by the experience in Bangladesh.

—*Example 16: Water conflicts in Bangladesh.* In coastal Bangladesh, after tube well water became contaminated with salt water, affected residents began to fetch water from nearby unaffected wells, leading to tensions, including some violent conflict, with residents who depended upon the unaffected wells. Fears, however unwarranted, of reduced water availability or contamination, and perhaps a localized xenophobia, may have played a role (Bangladesh Institute 2009, 15). Conflict between shrimp and rice farmers has been reported (see the Bangladesh Climate Change Strategy and Action Plan).

Planned Adaptation, Government Policies, and Conflict

Active and effective planned (or policy) adaptation is also necessary, as there are many essential activities that autonomous adaptation cannot accomplish, such as provision of large-scale public goods to assist adaptation. These public goods range from climate proofing of infrastructure to improved institutions for managing natural resources.[19] Planned adaptation will be more effective if it recognizes autonomous adaptation and, where possible, works with it rather than ignores or thwarts it. Planned adaptation can also play a crucial role in complementing autonomous adaptation, helping it to be more effective. In this regard, one of its most important roles will be to moderate the risk of conflict.

Investments in climate resilience and planned adaptation encompass both "hard" and "soft" investments, including physical infrastructure, government capacity building at the national and local levels, and institutional activities, such as promulgating regulations and guidelines (to, for example, limit forms of development in low-lying or otherwise vulnerable areas). Governments in developing countries often treat soft investments as of secondary importance to investments in physical infrastructure, but when well planned and implemented, investments in capacity building may leverage the effectiveness of physical investments.

Planned adaptation can facilitate smooth autonomous adaptation by farmers and pastoralists and urban dwellers, reducing the risk of conflict. Examples are drought-resistant seed varieties, crops that can be harvested earlier in the season (when rains end earlier than their historical average), and crops that can better withstand inundation. Smooth autonomous adaptation by urban dwellers can be facilitated with infrastructure for defense against floods and landslides and access to clean water. While building resilience, these responses can decrease poverty and reduce the vulnerability of the poor to conflict. Of course, poorly planned and executed policy-based adaptation can constrain constructive autonomous adaptation or make them more costly. Accordingly, planned adaptation (and government policies more generally) can increase conflict risk when it undermines or restricts autonomous adaptation (Malik and Smith 2012).

Relationships between Planned and Autonomous Adaptation

The relationships between planned and autonomous adaptation to climate change are highlighted in figure 11-2 (which is a subset of relationships shown in figure 11-1 expanded with this special emphasis). The figure indicates that autonomous adaptation can produce negative externalities that can lead to conflict. Planned adaption can either harm or facilitate and assist autonomous adaptation. As experience accumulates, there is growing appreciation of

---

19. The poor generally rely on carefully tuned informal institutions to regulate common property usage (Ostrom 2005), but the delicate balances can be affected by the influx of population, particularly from different ethnic groups—an outcome that is likely to become increasingly common with climate change.

Figure 11-2. *Autonomous Adaptation: Interaction with Policy and Security Implications*

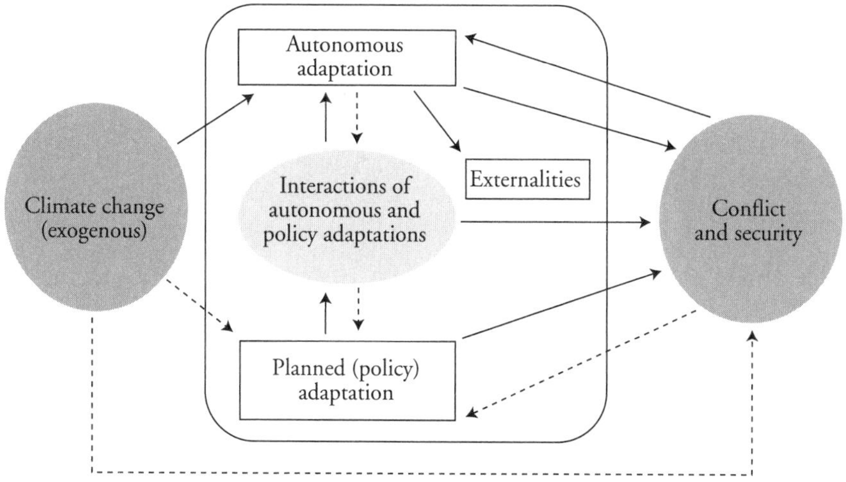

Source: Author.

the importance of ensuring that adaptation is conflict sensitive (Sayne, 2011; Tanzler, Maas, and Carius 2010).

—*Policy example 1: Land use policies.* Consider the example of institutions for land use regulation. Policies of population transfer out of low-lying areas vulnerable to flooding and storm surges—even if well intended—could fuel antistate violence. And when the population moves into nearby regions, social and environmental pressures increase, along with risks of conflict between communities. Even benign and well-meaning policies can have unintended consequences for the two fragilities. For example, constructing barriers to protect vulnerable lands might reduce conflict risks in the immediate area but could also worsen conditions if the barriers adversely affect the environment in nearby areas or otherwise lead to infringement on existing livelihoods.

—*Policy example 2: Migration policies.* Consider the impacts of migration policies. Desired migration on the part of the rural poor is projected to increase in areas most severely affected by climate change, as rural productivity and incomes fall in comparison to incomes elsewhere (whether in urban or relatively unaffected rural areas). Thus on the one hand out-migration can reduce local social and economic pressures; indeed, as climate change accelerates beyond the range of experience and of ready local adaptations, migration may turn out to be the single largest form of an autonomous adaptation response. Under these conditions, curtailing migration can worsen local conflict and accelerate environmental degradation. But on the other hand, to the extent that migration leads to increased social and economic tensions in destination areas, policies to restrict migration either within the country or across national borders might mitigate conflict risks. The way this challenge is handled is of great consequence for the two fragilities, but the scope of the problem is very difficult to predict globally. Warner and others (2009) project that between 50 million and 700 million people will be displaced by climate change by the middle of this century. The wide range reflects the enormous uncertainties about the eventual impacts of climate change. But numbers in the higher part of this range would eclipse the current combined population of international migrants, internally displaced persons, and refugees. Moreover, it is not simply the numbers but the motivations for moving: rather than being attracted by rising incomes and job opportunities elsewhere, climate refugees will be fleeing worsening conditions in their home communities, placing them into more direct competition for resources and employment, thereby heightening the potential for conflict and instability in comparison with more conventional migration patterns.

Relationships between Government and Local Communities

Types and magnitude of planned adaptation may be influenced—positively or negatively—by autonomous adaptations. Planned adaptation can be designed to leverage (and avoid negatively affecting) beneficial autonomous adaptation and to help mitigate the impacts of maladaptation in and among communities. Thus alternatives need to be carefully weighed.

Risks from the two fragilities are strongly influenced by the quality of relationships among government and local communities and identity groups. Even benign neglect can negate community efforts at autonomous adaptation, as their effectiveness may depend on complementary planned adaptation investments and policies. For example, restrictions on migration out of environmentally degraded or climate-affected areas into less affected areas may keep local tensions high and fuel antigovernment sentiment if the destination areas are perceived as being privileged by the state. If at the same time government is actively assisting other communities perceived as specially favored, resentment toward government may build. Other environmental policies may be perceived as even less benign; conflict may result from grievances such as diversion of water from one region to another. Indeed almost any policies that hinder autonomous adaptation could worsen both fragilities, and in mutually reinforcing ways.

A delicate balance is needed, and it will depend upon local conditions. Externalities of autonomous adaptation could push a region that is already vulnerable to conflict into outright conflict. Provided that the central government is competent and responsive, it would be desirable to place greater reliance on well-designed policy adaptation in such regions and less on purely autonomous adaptation than would otherwise be the case. For example, well-designed and implemented policies and regulations can help to moderate resource-related spillovers. Negative externalities are caused by autonomous adaptations that adversely affect neighboring groups through reduced resource availability, including lowered water tables, salinization, deforestation, crop damage, and reduced foraging opportunities.[20] A clear understanding of the local context of such externalities can guide the formation and implementation of policies and programs to contain these spillovers.

The indirect effects of climate change on conflict are likely to prove the most salient in the longer term. But the literature also reports direct effects of weather on violence, including "witch killing" in Tanzania (Miguel 2005), property crimes in rural India (Blakeslee and Fishman 2013), and direct impacts of warming on civil war in Africa (Burke and others 2009). Burke, Hsiang, and Miguel (forthcoming) estimate that a one standard deviation temperature increase is associated with an 11 percent increase in the onset of intergroup conflict; it is unclear how to extrapolate from this.[21] But average temperatures are predicted to rise by at least 1 degree C by midcentury.

Special Challenges of Adaptation for Economic Development

As noted earlier, severe harm to traditional rural livelihoods is projected as a result of climate change (Hatton and Williamson 2003; McLeman and Smit 2006; Naudé 2010; Warner and others 2009). A historically unprecedented level of migration may ensue. Twentieth-century evidence supports these projections. Marchiori, Maystadt, and Schumacher (2012) estimate that "temperature and rainfall anomalies caused a total net displacement of 5 million people during the period 1960–2000." Researchers in security studies note much potential for conflict. In contrast, some analysts take the view that migration will not lead to much conflict (for example, Raleigh, Jordan, and Salehyan 2011). Hopefully, this view will prove correct; however, it is based on past patterns and gives little weight to some recent experience. Climate change is

20. Deforestation can also have broader weather effects over a wider area, notably reduced average rainfall; it can also facilitate larger floods affecting wider geographic areas; the case of deforestation in mountainous Meghalaya (north of Bangladesh) is a case in point.

21. Perhaps a majority of such effects operate through economic channels such as crop losses. But otherwise, it is plausible that these average temperature effects could be mitigated by physiological adaptation, as people become used to greater heat throughout the year. Climate change may also produce greater temperature variation, with more frequent heat waves, featuring larger jumps above the new normal range of temperatures; still, improved knowledge of how to respond to heat waves (Das and Smith 2012) could also have the effect of mitigating violent responses.

leading to weather patterns not experienced previously in many areas. Migration on such a scale could be qualitatively different, resulting in competition for resources and employment. Migration is often rural to rural, not only rural to urban (UNEP 2011; Werz and Conley 2012). The result can be maladaptation, with possibly the largest impacts being farmer-pastoralist conflicts, sometimes called farmer-rancher wars.

A Closer Look at Migration as an Adaptation

Altered patterns of seasonal migration have their own impact:

—*Example 17: Conflict in Sudan among pastoralists and farmers.* A recent example of the potential for problems is reported from Sudan, where changes in water availability and crop cover led pastoralists to alter their seasonal migration patterns, which in turn led to worsened tensions both among pastoralists and between pastoralists and settled farmers (Bronkhorst 2011; UNEP 2007).

—*Example 18: Conflict in Nigeria among pastoralists and farmers.* In Nigeria, shortages of water and livestock feed, caused in part by short-term drought and perhaps longer-term desertification, led pastoralists to alter their traditional grazing routes. At the same time, settled farmers responded to drought and other changes by cultivating larger expanses of land. A result was that pastoralists were squeezed for land, which led to violent farmer-pastoralist clashes, resulting in several hundred deaths (Sayne 2011).

—*Example 19: Pastoralist conflict in Kenya.* In Kenya, severe drought persuaded traditional pastoralists to settle near fixed—but limited—water sources that area farmers already depended upon (Conservation Development Center 2009), again leading to conflict.

—*Example 20: Famine in Somalia.* When famine hit Somalia in 2010, it was already afflicted by conflict and close to being a failed state. Governmental fragility was a multiplier to environmental fragility; migration was a predictable adaptation response, yet millions embarked on a dangerous, all too often fatal, trek to dangerously overcrowded and unsanitary refugee camps (USAID 2012; Todaro and Smith 2014).

Other forms of migration-related conflict are emerging, notably conflict regarding employment opportunities (Reuveny 2007), where migration is intentionally permanent.

—*Example 21: Employment conflict in Bangladesh between locals and climate migrants.* In Bangladesh, tensions—including outright violence—between so-called climate migrants and their new neighbors have been fueled in part by the decline in informal sector wages, as the labor supply of unskilled workers correspondingly rose. There has also been competition for land, causing "high levels of physical insecurity and conflict" (Bangladesh Institute of International and Strategic Studies 2009).

—*Example 22: Employment conflict in Uganda between locals and climate migrants.* In Uganda, migration caused by climate or weather shocks has led to lower employment or wages for both new migrants and the existing residents (Strobi and Valfort 2013), resulting in tensions.

To determine the extent to which climate change can cause outright civil war or similar nationwide upheavals will require more evidence. But once again, generally it is not so much the direct effect of weather and climate as the manner in which government and civil society respond. There is suggestive comparative-historical evidence that large climate shifts in the past have led to violent upheavals and even civilization collapse.[22] Probably the most actively discussed contemporary candidate is the civil war in Syria.[23]

—*Example 23: Extreme drought as a contributory factor in the Syrian civil war.* The harsh impacts of the Syrian civil war include approximately 9 million internal and external refugees, many of whom, living in refugee camps, have fallen into poverty. It cannot be said simply that Syria's severe drought "caused" the civil war, because the government presided over a middle-income economy and had the resources to respond to the hardships due to the drought; and because other factors were clearly present, notably the demonstration effect from other Arab Spring countries. However, it is reasonable to conclude that the failure of government to respond to the economic and social impacts of the drought— such as unemployment among young climate migrants—compounded by the government's prior water resource mismanagement, was likely a significant contributory factor in instigating the civil war.[24]

—*Example 24: Climate change as a cause of the Darfur crisis.* The severe and long-lasting strife in Darfur was also on a nearly national scale, not just encompassing one large region but involving other regions and extensively involving the national government in Khartoum. Analyses by the United Nations Environment Program and analysts such as Andrew Guzman provide evidence that drought and resource degradation was a "spark" for the large-scale genocidal campaign in Darfur.[25]

---

22. For an interesting though somewhat controversial explication of this view with historical examples, see Diamond (2005). Bai and Kung (2011) examine "climate shocks and sino-nomadic conflict," using data on nomadic incursions into settled Han Chinese regions spanning two thousand years. The authors utilize drought and flood data as proxies for precipitation changes and show that nomadic incursions are positively correlated with less rainfall.

23. Another widely discussed candidate is the 2012 upheaval in Mali, which may have been spurred by drought.

24. For examples of studies making these arguments, see Gleick (2014) and de Châtel (2014). The topic has been widely discussed in the media, including by Friedman (2013) and Greenwood (2014).

25. For an overview of the case that the Darfur crisis was triggered by climate change, see Guzman (2013, chap. 5). For UNEP's analysis, see http://postconflict.unep.ch/sudanreport/sudan_website/ and in particular its assessment report, UNEP (2007).

Special Urban Challenges of Governmental and Environmental Fragility

One of the largest adaptations to rural climate change will inevitably be accelerated rural-to-urban migration. Indeed, there is already evidence that some of the high urban migration rates in Africa are driven by environmental stress, such as water availability, that is caused in part by climate change (Marchiori, Maystadt, and Schumacher 2012). The likely movement of affected communities into urban areas could lead to growing numbers of people in informal settlements being exposed to flooding, diseases, and heat waves (the latter would be amplified by the urban heat island effect).

Adaptation in urban areas receives much less attention than that in rural areas, but it will also be important. Even though poverty remains an overwhelmingly rural phenomenon, with over three-quarters of those living on $1.25 or less being rural, urban poverty is increasingly important, as more than half of the population of developing countries will live in cities by 2020 (United Nations Population Division 2013). For example, in China, although urban incomes are rising overall, the average income shortfall of the urban poor in China has worsened due to the influx of people from poor rural areas.[26] Conditions are precarious for some migrants, and there are signs of growing tensions.

Globally, an estimated billion people live in slum conditions, often in high-risk neighborhoods, with low-quality housing and little if any access to public services. Climate change and poor domestic environmental practices, such as unregulated dumping, may worsen water quality and availability in urban areas. Meanwhile, deteriorating rural conditions will bring new climate migrants; new informal settlements can lead to additional obstacles in waterways and untreated waste, worsening the damage to structures as well as to public health. Climate change may also worsen the intensity and frequency of extreme weather in urban areas, particularly heat waves, storms, flooding, and landslides; and sea level rises are a growing threat. A few of the cities most threatened are located in countries, such as Bangladesh, with at least moderate if not high risk for conflict (World Bank 2013; Brecht and others 2012).

Urban neighborhoods lacking infrastructure and basic public services are vulnerable to both environmental and governmental fragilities: to both extreme weather and urban violence.[27] Indeed, in the face of climate change, deteriorating urban slum conditions may aggravate underlying risks of urban violence. Urban dwellers may respond to climate change by building less vulnerable

26. Data from PovcalNet. I would like to thank Tony Castleman for pointing out the China example. Note also that the migrants may arrive from environmentally stressed areas, such as those with growing water shortages.

27. An example is the chronic violence in the *favelas* of Brazilian cities.

housing and participating in informal insurance arrangements. Those who can afford to do so will typically move to higher ground that is less vulnerable to flooding (in areas that are also safer from mud slides), which will bid up the price of land and housing in safer areas. Perhaps paradoxically, low-income families may be more likely to move into environmentally degraded land and areas more vulnerable to storms in response to the increased costs of land and housing in safer areas. Unconstructive government responses (whether interest group motivated or just poorly thought out) can magnify these effects.[28]

Even if socially marginalized climate migrants are unable to organize themselves, they might still be induced to serve as the "troops" for opportunistic government opponents (or otherwise destabilizing criminal organizations). Given such unpredictability, a focus on the problems of urban extreme poverty, including the plight of recent migrants, may be the most effective way to deal with urban conflict.

Investment in urban resilience can mitigate environmental risks and may also reduce conflict risks. Governments may also respond—both to climate threats and to autonomous adaptations by citizens—with regulations on urban growth, land use, zoning, density, and building. Such regulations can be beneficial, correcting negative externalities; but they also can reduce availability of residential land, pushing up land and housing prices (Malik and Smith 2012). In turn, higher land and housing prices, along with stricter regulations, may further limit the ability of lower-income families to enter the formal housing market, potentially resulting in increased homelessness and poverty levels (Buckley and Kalarickal 2005, 2006). Unstable urban conditions will make it more difficult for recent poor rural migrants to adjust to the requirements of urban life. An additional likely result is heightened social tensions, if not violent conflict. Thus once again the quality of interactions between planned and autonomous adaptation is at center stage; in this case, it is likely to be a significant determinant of the risks of conflict in cities and of the rate of urban poverty reduction.

With these examples in mind, it becomes clear that an incremental, piecemeal, or overly compartmentalized approach by government to developing the various forms of urban infrastructure holds dangers of maladaptation. Urban infrastructure has long-term lock-in effects. It is understood that this is a problem for carbon mitigation. For example, if development takes the form of urban sprawl rather than well-planned, dense, city cores, a nation is likely to be locked into high transportation and other energy costs for possibly decades to come; it is in general far more difficult to retrofit buildings for energy efficiency than it is

---

28. For example, Irazabal (2009) notes that "more than one-third of the houses in La Paz, Bolivia, are not connected to the city water line because these low-income houses are located on the steep slopes of the bowl-shaped city, where landslides and floods are common."

to incorporate energy efficiency into the original construction. Redevelopment is costly and often politically infeasible.

But in addition to problems for future climate change mitigation, there are likely to be specific adaptation and general resilience costs of urban maladaptation without systematic and anticipatory infrastructure planning. There is a tendency in the cities of many developing countries to allow settlement to happen and then attempt to address the lack of infrastructure. This is costly, and indeed it is sometimes impossible to build infrastructure later, for political as well as economic reasons.[29] The areas where the poor live are often the most vulnerable. Sound urban resilience planning has a benefit in reducing social tensions and conflict as well as protecting lives and public health. Note that in general adequate planning takes into account the existing urban ecosystem as a whole, not merely addressing shocks or planning for specific shocks. This includes how a city anticipates and addresses current or future water shortages. But the more immediate problem may be the growing incidence of floods.

—*Example 25: Vulnerability to flooding in Mumbai.* In Mumbai, poor slum dwellers live along riverbanks that are at high risk of flooding; after the 2005 flood the poorest residents lost the equivalent of their total savings (Hallegatte and others 2010; see also World Bank 2013).

—*Example 26: Vulnerability to floods and mud slides in Guatemala City.* In 1998 Hurricane Mitch killed at least 5,500 people and caused thousands more to migrate; flooding and mud slides had a severe impact on the poor (McLeman and Smit 2006).

—*Example 27: Vulnerability to sea level rise and storm surges in Lagos.* Lagos, the largest city in Africa (with over 20 million people) is at risk for sea level rise, storm surges, and associated saltwater contamination of its water resources. Such conditions also can have serious public health implications, worsening urban poverty. Sea level rise could cause considerable population displacement both in the city and in the whole low-lying coastal region. Loss of land and water, along with a likely increase in natural disasters, present serious risks for a country that already has a history of serious violent conflicts.[30]

Attending to Containment of International Flashpoints

Climate change impacts take place in ecological zones, not political zones; maps of different climate change effects overlap each other; and they cut through and across countries.[31] Thus attending to containment of international flashpoints will inevitably be part of the way the two fragilities are addressed.

29. I would like to thank Anthony Yezer for helpful discussions on this topic.

30. See the IPCC Nigeria report at www.ipcc.ch/ipccreports/sres/regional/index.php?idp=31. See also Guzman (2013, chap. 5) and Fashae and Onafeso (2011).

31. I would like to thank participants in the Brookings Last Mile workshop, January 2014, for helpful discussion on this topic.

There are growing risks of conflict between developing countries over water, such as the tension between China and India over Himalayan water and between Ethiopia and Egypt over water from the Nile. Facilitation of binational and regional water treaties by development partners may become a priority (De Stefano and others 2010). It cannot be assumed that the climate-conflict nexus in the developing world will be contained within national boundaries. Some international issues are analogous to disputes over natural resources across communities.[32] Analysis of interstate hostility is beyond the scope of this chapter, but it is worth pointing out the tendency of such hostilities to worsen poverty. Moreover, climate-driven migration across national borders is also likely to pose problems. The U.S. military has run simulations of floods in Bangladesh, of the resulting refugee movements into India, and of the predicted religious conflicts, spread of contagious disease, and damage to infrastructure.[33]

Aid: Regional Cooperation and International Development Assistance

The United Nations Development Program (UNDP) played an important role in starting the policy adaptation assistance process, with its National Adaptation Programs of Action (NAPAs). These in turn grew out of global climate meetings.[34] The next step was financing, taken up variously by multilateral development banks and special financing initiatives (such as the Green Climate Fund, headquartered in South Korea). The International Development Association (IDA) and the Pilot Program for Climate Resilience (PPCR) are good cases in point.

General IDA Programing

Attention to climate adaptation and resilience has been slowly building in the IDA in recent years. IDA15 features analytic and advisory activities related to adaptation (IDA 2007). There is a special theme related to climate in IDA16 (along with themes on mainstreaming gender and FCACs), launching this area

32. Despite limited treaties, oceans largely function as international common property, driving the collapse of fish populations (among other problems). Where countries make specific territorial claims, these may overlap (as in the South China Sea) with competing claims for natural resources. Lack of established institutions also drive the intensity of these conflicts.

33. Werz and Conley (2012) cite a 2008 National Defense University exercise that explored the impact of a flood that sent hundreds of thousands of refugees from Bangladesh into neighboring India. See www.boell.org/downloads/climate_migration.pdf.

34. The National Adaptation Programs of Action (NAPA) is a formal UNFCCC process for the least developed countries "to identify priority activities that respond to their urgent and immediate needs to adapt to climate change—those for which further delay would increase vulnerability and/ or costs at a later stage." See UNFCCC (2008).

as a thematic undertaking.[35] In "Special Themes for IDA17" (IDA 2013), climate resilience is featured as one of four themes. There appears to be a new emphasis on staking out an IDA comparative advantage in the area of climate resilience and in the related area of disaster risk management.

The special themes for IDA17, in common with IDA16, also include FCACs. The term *resilience* is used in a social governance context. But written evidence is hard to find, at least evidence that IDA is looking ahead systematically to the complementarities between its two themes, as environmental degradation worsens over time.

PPCR and the Green Climate Fund

One development assistance initiative focused on climate adaptation is the Pilot Program for Climate Resilience (PPCR), one of four targeted programs under the multidonor climate investment funds.[36] The PPCR is designed to demonstrate ways to integrate climate risk and resilience into developing countries' core development planning. It provides incentives for scaled-up action and transformational change and offers additional financial resources in the form of grants and concessional loans (with near-zero interest), to help fund public and private investments for climate-resilient development. One objective of the PPCR is to contribute to knowledge and best practices relating to integrated approaches for climate resilience; another is to reap lessons relating to adaptation financing. All eighteen PPCR countries, plus the Caribbean and Pacific regional programs, have endorsed investment plans, or strategic programs for climate resilience. These programs identify sixty-seven projects to be financed by the PPCR. There is generally little if any explicit connection made to conflict risks.[37]

35. The IDA16 Replenishment document (IDA 2010) states, "IDA will support climate resilience activities through financing as well as enhancing the effectiveness of investments by other development partners."

36. The pilot program for climate resilience is supported by the Strategic Climate Fund, which also supports the Forest Investment Program and the Scaling Up Renewable Energy Program. The Strategic Climate Fund is intended to provide experience and lessons through learning by doing, to channel financing for climate mitigation and adaptation/resilience, to provide incentives for "scaled-up and transformational action," and to provide incentives to restore and enhance natural ecosystems that can maintain or absorb carbon. These efforts fall under the rubric of sustainable development. In contrast, the Clean Technology Fund provides developing countries with incentives to implement technologies with potential savings from controlling greenhouse gas emissions. In climate investment fund documents, the term *contributor* is used, rather than *donor*. Much of the following section draws directly on program websites; see www.climateinvestmentfunds.org/cif/node/4.

37. However, an exception is the project appraisal document for the World Bank (2011a) which sponsored part of the Niger PPCR funding, which notes that one of the risks faced by "Nigerian individual households and communities" is "conflicts over access to and use of shrinking natural resources."

The launch of the Green Climate Fund, attached to the UNFCCC (2013) and based in Seoul, is opening up a new chapter, with a storyline that is still unfolding.[38]

Financing to Jointly Address the Two Fragilities

Policy analysis, development assistance, and practical governance will clearly benefit from moving away from evaluating resilience in a compartmentalized manner, rather than in an integrated way. Both conflict and environmental stressors affect the same social and economic system, and the negative effects of managing one risk inadequately can result in other risks being magnified and tipping over into crisis. Thus effective domestic policy and development planning will be more effective if it can be formulated in a scaled-up and "non-siloed" manner to address not only resilience from climate change and resilience from conflict but perhaps other forms of needed societal and economic resilience (such as financial sector resilience).

More systematic consideration of co-benefits of investments across resilience types would be beneficial. For example, community-driven development (CDD) is often considered helpful with poverty reduction through building conflict resilience.[39] But in addressing specific climate stressors (as has been done in local ecological zones), CDD may also be well suited as a programmatic approach for climate resilience. A CDD project designed and implemented to explicitly address both climate and conflict problems and risks, and to build general resilience, may yield better results, at least as a possibility to be evaluated rigorously.

—*Example 28: CDD in the Niger delta: Rivers State, Nigeria.* In the Niger delta region of Nigeria, fishing and farming livelihoods in delta communities were severely damaged by repeated oil spills. One consequence was antigovernment violence. CDD projects in Rivers State are reported to have had positive impacts on participants' perceptions about these livelihoods and may have led to environmental improvement (via community volunteering) and, potentially, to decreased conflict (Kimenyi and others 2014a, 2014b).

Key Investments: Climate Proofing and Climate Resilience

Enhancing the climate resilience of investments in low-income countries is broadly estimated to increase overall costs by at least 25 percent, with the

38. For details, see http://unfccc.int/cooperation_and_support/financial_mechanism/green_climate_fund/items/5869.php.

39. There is mixed evidence; see for example, Mansuri and Rao (2004). Niger has a major community-driven component in its strategic program for climate resilience and in some of its pilot programs. The same is found, although to a lesser extent, in Zambia.

largest proportional increases experienced in sub-Saharan Africa and small island developing states.

As a general matter, climate proofing investments has recently become a theme of aid. The term has a project-specific connotation, centering on physical investments, including raising dam height and building roads to withstand greater storms and flooding. The term is used in contrast with building climate resilience; the latter is a more systemic concept and addresses wider-scale investments, including capacity building, to respond to shocks, the details or even direction of which may not be predicted in advance.

More explicit prioritizing of investments in adaptation and resilience using criteria that account for co-benefits is needed. Co-benefits of approaches may include investments that provide general risk reduction while simultaneously increasing productivity and resilience and curtailing maladaptation, including conflict risks. Thus project appraisals of climate change investments can at least weigh potential conflict implications explicitly, thereby encouraging active attention to the issues and extending the do-no-harm foundations of development assistance. Similarly, aid for projects in postconflict areas can more carefully appraise and monitor potential environmental impact, since simply checking off the environment boxes in project appraisals does not suffice.

Hydromet: Reducing Both Types of Risks while Improving Productivity

The establishment, expansion, and improvement of hydrometeorological services exemplify an investment that reduces environmental vulnerability (and thus potentially reduces conflict risks). Hydromet includes standard weather services and early warning systems to anticipate environmental emergencies and prevent disasters (which preserves funds for other development efforts).

—*Example 29: Bangladesh preparedness and warning systems.* In Bangladesh, the cost of reinforcing and raising the height of embankments and coastal dykes appears modest in relation to the projected damage. Of equal importance, the impact of cyclones and other extreme weather can be reduced with better early warning systems and government emergency preparedness (Brouwer and others 2007). This may in turn reduce risks of maladaptation.

—*Example 30: Nepal's hydromet development program.* Nepal's program for building resilience to climate-related hazards has been supported financially by PPCR, IFC, and other programs. Its general focus is on hydrometeorological systems, particularly in their relationship to agriculture. It includes both durable assets in modern hydromet systems and "soft" capacity building. The program includes the diverse components needed for short-term and long-term weather forecasting and alerts. In a country still recovering from a long civil conflict and with continued political tensions, hydromet services may reduce conflict risks.

Hydropower, Irrigation, and Flood Control

Hydropower is an example of investments with potential for not only mitigation but also for adaptation and resilience. But poorly planned and located dams also have a history of negative environmental impacts. Dam placement has also led to tensions, especially with involuntary relocations or loss of resources, such as experienced in India. Investments in this area are important and growing. However, attention is needed to preventing conflict both internal and across national borders. Given climate change predictions, another priority is to build storm shelters, flood barriers, and protected roads, bridges, and canals serving areas where the poor live.

—*Example 31: Bolivia's water management programs.* In the face of melting glaciers, Bolivia is planning new and expanded dams to reduce flooding, capture water, and regulate water runoff (UN Habitat 2009).

—*Example 32: Mozambique's hydropower programs.* Mozambique is examining how to adapt its hydropower capacity to likely reduced flows resulting from climate change (Chambal 2010).

—*Example 33: Zambia's rehabilitation of traditional canals.* Zambia's program for "strengthening climate resilience in Zambia and the Barotse sub-basin" in its strategic program for climate resilience includes strengthened adaptive capacity of vulnerable rural communities, specifically rehabilitation, and strengthened management of traditional navigation and irrigation canals.

Awareness Campaigns

Explaining risks to people in vulnerable areas (and helping them to take actions that reduce their risks) can have concrete benefits for reducing poverty and vulnerability.

—*Example 34: Disaster risk management in Odisha State, India.* An awareness campaign addressing improved responses to heat wave conditions (as part of a disaster risk management program) is estimated to have reduced mortality and likely also resulted in other health benefits (Das and Smith 2012).

—*Example 35: Maldives preparedness.* The Maldives has developed an awareness campaign centering on tsunamis; the UNEP finds that the risks are now understood. The approach could be applicable to specifically weather/climate disaster risk management.

Concluding Observations: From Two Fragilities to Combined Resilience

This chapter highlights the need to identify and further investigate the links between two types of fragility, environmental and governmental, and their impacts on poverty—and to orient policy and investments accordingly. Going forward, it will be important for governments and international development partners to take account of the complementarities between the two fragilities.

Some general if preliminary conclusions emerge from the framework, the broad patterns, and the case examples.[40] Among the most important is the interaction between planned policy adaptation and autonomous adaptation. Each of the following six implications readily generates hypotheses for further study.

First, *in FCACs, greater reliance on well-formulated planned adaptation is called for in the mix of autonomous and planned adaptation,* at least as a rule of thumb. But in these situations, implementing sound and transparent approaches to managing interactions between government policy and autonomous adaptation is all the more crucial, with a voice and redress for those affected; reasonable flexibility is required in its application to differing circumstances.

Second, *adaptive responses can worsen social tensions* and thus need early attention. While adaptation often reduces conflict risks by moderating the impacts of climate change, conflict risks can increase when adaptation leads to resource-related externalities in neighboring areas, such as lowered water tables, deforestation, crop damage, worsened sanitation, and reduced opportunities for foraging. A better understanding of how these externalities operate in practice will help in designing policies to contain these spillovers—and thus the conflict and environmental risks they give rise to.

Third, it is essential that *planned adaptation, and other government policies, should not risk further conflict by thwarting or reducing opportunities for efforts at autonomous adaptation.* Many developing countries have promulgated adaptation plans, such as NAPAs; and more plans are being formulated and modified, in addition to conventional government policy formulation that increasingly spans climate adaptation policy. While these are excellent and essential steps, attention is needed to ensure that policies and administrative actions do not unduly restrict migration, undermine viable informal agreements on resource allocation, or divert resources away from affected areas. A crucial step is to help government gain better information about what citizens are already doing in their attempts to adapt autonomously. Governments in many countries solicit input from those who may be especially affected by regulatory and administrative changes.[41] Again, in this case successful policy will provide a voice to autonomously adapting citizens concerning any initiatives that will affect their efforts.

Fourth, *autonomous adaptation has the potential to generate positive externalities that can be encouraged.* The most important example may be social learning

40. I would like to thank Arun Malik for helpful discussions.

41. A recent U.S. example are the 2014 state-level rules promulgated by the United States Environmental Protection Agency to implement reductions in carbon emissions.

across neighboring communities. Encouraging and augmenting this learning process has potential to be a productive part of planned adaptation. Governments can engage in a continuous process of learning what individuals and communities are doing to adapt, their effectiveness and external impacts, and implications for policy adaptation, while facilitating the sharing of lessons. For another example, when communities can (be helped to) solve collective action problems to accomplish locally beneficial reforestation and erosion control, these improvements also provide positive benefits downstream.

Fifth, *domestic policy and development partner assistance will require more integrated attention between climate change and domestic environmental problems.* There is an even narrower tendency—to focus on climate impacts independently from endogenous domestic environmental deterioration. Some of the priority responses need to differ somewhat when environmental problems are considered jointly. It is understandable that development partners have focused on climate change impacts, probably in large part out of a sense of special responsibility. But environmentally sustainable development—which is increasingly foundational to successful economic development—requires a balanced and integrated approach to environmental problems and their potential interactions. This should also help extend benefits to conflict prevention and poverty alleviation and their overlapping challenges.

Sixth, *for FCACs it is challenging but essential to maintain a balance in governance reform between achieving stronger state capacity and improving citizen protections.* Military and other state capabilities must be strong enough to bring violence to a halt and to deter future violence; yet effective institutions must be in place to provide checks and balances to ensure that state power is not abused at the expense of citizens, in particular, people living in poverty. More broadly, the state must be sufficiently resilient and effective to establish and maintain institutions conducive to economic development and to carry out other key functions—and at the same time to govern in a responsive and transparent manner.

Is improved governance sufficient to solve such complex and interrelated problems? Undoubtedly basic reforms would be beneficial, notably attacking corruption, enhancing transparency, strengthening checks and balances, and providing multiple channels for citizen voice. In addition, needed reforms for addressing conflict and environmental distress extend to addressing social exclusion and codifying and enforcing protection of minorities. Another basic component is appropriate and enforced environmental regulation. In countries with diverse identity groups, good regional governance is also needed; but reforms cannot be mandated easily by the central government; nor does central government easily let go of some of its crucial elements, such as regional taxation authority. Attention to informal and localized norms and institutions is also needed—again, very difficult to orchestrate from above. The problems are complex and will require careful policy analysis in the local context to address. While these are all governance-related concerns, this scope stretches the definition and understandings of the meaning of improved governance beyond that of most conventional uses.

Moreover, environmental problems that fuel political conflict (even if usually not violent) are themselves impediments to progress on local governance. This is one reason that attempting governance reform in isolation is unlikely to succeed. In coming years, as climate change impacts and other environmental stressors are magnified, likely with resulting competition over basic resources, governance reforms may become increasingly constrained. More generally, of course, local political conditions make achieving the full gamut of needed institutional reform complex and difficult. In many countries in question, international aid will be needed even with substantive improvements in governance. Aid must be well monitored and well managed, with ongoing attention to governance deficiencies in this broader sense. At the same time, directly strengthening the poor and their communities also helps generate pressure for progress on governance deficiencies. And much aid can directly address localized conflict and environmental problems without requiring a complete overhaul of governance.

The need to account for complementarities between vulnerability to conflict and vulnerability to environmental stress—the two fragilities—becomes very clear when one considers that these are after all stresses on the same system: the failure to manage conflict risks will magnify environment risks, and vice versa. Thus rather than treating resilience in "silo" terms, it makes more sense to plan responses to the full set of risks, taken in combination.

References

Akresh, Richard, Sonia Bhalotra, Marinella Leone, and Una Okonkwo Osili. 2012. "War and Stature: Growing up during the Nigerian Civil War." *American Economic Review* 102, no. 3: 273–77.

Andrimihaja, Noro Aina, Matthias Cinyabuguma, and Shantayanan Devarajan. 2011. "Avoiding the Fragility Trap in Africa." Working Paper 5884. Washington: World Bank.

Baez, J. E., A. de la Fuente, and I. Santos. 2010. "Do Natural Disasters Affect Human Capital? An Assessment Based on Existing Empirical Evidence." IZA Discussion Paper 5164. Bonn: Institute for the Study of Labor.

Baez, J., and I. Santos. 2007. "Children's Vulnerability to Weather Shocks: A Natural Disaster as a Natural Experiment." Working Paper. Pennsylvania State University.

Bai, Ying, and James Kung. 2011. "Climate Shocks and Sino-Nomadic Conflict." *Review of Economics and Statistics* 93, no. 3: 970–81.

Bangladesh Institute of International and Strategic Studies and Saferworld. 2009. *Climate Change and Security in Bangladesh: A Case Study.* Dhaka.

Barnett, Jon, and W. Neil Adger. 2007. "Climate Change, Human Security, and Violent Conflict." *Political Geography* 26: 639–55.

Beegle, K., R. H. Dehejia, and R. Gatti. 2006. "Child Labor and Agricultural Shocks." *Journal of Development Economic* 81, no. 1: 80–96.

Biggs, R., and others. 2004. "Nature Supporting People: Southern African Millennium Ecosystem Assessment." Council for Scientific and Industrial Research. Pretoria (www.unep.org/maweb/documents_sga/SAfMA_Integrated_Report.pdf).

Blakeslee, David, and Ram Fishman. 2013. "Rainfall Shocks and Property Crimes in Agrarian Societies: Evidence from India." Working Paper. George Washington University.

Blattman, Christopher, and Jeannie Annan. 2010. "The Consequences of Child Soldiering." *Review of Economics and Statistics* 92: 882–98.

Blattman, Christopher, and Edward Miguel. 2010. "Civil War." *Journal of Economic Literature* 48, no. 1: 3–57.

Brecht, Henrike, Susmita Dasgupta, Benoit Laplante, Siobhan Murray, and David Wheele. 2012. "Sea-Level Rise and Storm Surges: High Stakes for a Small Number of Developing Countries. *Journal of Environment and Development* 21, no. 1: 120–38

Bronkhorst, Salome. 2011. "Climate Change and Conflict: Lessons for Conflict Resolution from the Southern Sahel of Sudan." Mount Edgecombe, South Africa: African Centre for the Constructive Resolution of Disputes (ACCORD).

Brouwer, Roy, and others. 2007. "Socioeconomic Vulnerability and Adaptation to Environmental Risk: A Case Study of Climate Change and Flooding in Bangladesh." *Risk Analysis* 27, no. 2.

Buckley, R., and J. Kalarickal. 2005. "Housing Policy in Developing Countries: Conjectures and Refutations." *World Bank Research Observer* 20, no. 2: 233–58.

———, eds. 2006. *Thirty Years of World Bank Shelter Lending: What Have We Learned?* Washington: World Bank.

Bundervoet, Thomas, Philip Verwimp, and Richard Akresh. 2009. "Health and Civil War in Rural Burundi." *Journal of Human Resources* 44, no. 2.

Burke, M., S. M. Hsiang, and E. Miguel. Forthcoming. "Climate and Conflict." *Annual Review of Economics.*

Burke, Marshall B., Edward Miguel, Shanker Satyanath, John A. Dykema, and David B. Lobell. 2009. "Warming Increases the Risk of Civil War in Africa." *Proceedings of the National Academy of Sciences* 106, no. 49: 20670–74.

Busby, Joshua W., Kerry H. Cook, Edward K. Vizy, Todd G. Smith, and Mesfin Bekalo. 2014. "Identifying Hot Spots of Security Vulnerability Associated with Climate Change in Africa." *Climatic Change* 124: 717–31.

Carter, Michael, and others. 2006. "Poverty Traps and Natural Disasters in Ethiopia and Honduras." *World Development* 35, no. 5: 835–56.

Cassar, Alessandra, and others. 2013. "Legacies of Violence: Trust and Market Capital." *Journal of Economic Growth* 18: 285–318.

Chamarbagwala, Rubiana, and Hilcías E. Morán. 2011. "The Human Capital Consequences of Civil War: Evidence from Guatemala." *Journal of Development Economics* 94: 41–61.

Chambal, Helder. 2010. "Energy Security in Mozambique, 2010." Policy Report 3. Winnipeg: International Institute for Sustainable Development.

CNA Military Advisory Board. 2014. "National Security and the Threat of Climate Change." (Original 2007). Arlington, Va.

Collier, Paul. 2003. "Breaking the Conflict Trap: Civil War and Development Policy" (www-wds.worldbank.org/external/default/WDSContentServer/IW3P/IB/2003/06/30/000094946_0306190405396/Rendered/PDF/multi0page.pdf).

———. 2007. *The Bottom Billion: Why the Poorest Countries Are Failing and What Can Be Done about It.* Oxford University Press.

Conservation Development Center and Saferworld. 2009. "Climate Change and Conflict: Lessons from Community Conservancies in Northern Kenya." Geneva: International Institute for Sustainable Development.

Das, Saudamini, and Stephen C. Smith. 2012. "Awareness as an Adaptation Strategy for Reducing Mortality from Heat Waves: Evidence from a Disaster Risk Management Program in India." *Climate Change Economics* 3, no. 2.

de Châtel, Francesca. 2014. "The Role of Drought and Climate Change in the Syrian Uprising: Untangling the Triggers of the Revolution." *Middle Eastern Studies* 2014, no. 1.

De Janvry, Alain, Frederico Finan, Elisabeth Sadoulet, and Renos Vakis. 2006. "Can Conditional Cash Transfer Programs Serve as Safety Nets in Keeping Children at School and from Working When Exposed to Shocks?" *Journal of Development Economics* 79, no. 2: 349–73.

Dercon, Stefan. 2004. "Growth and Shocks: Evidence from Rural Ethiopia." *Journal of Development Economics* 74, no. 2: 309–29.

De Stefano, Lucia, James Duncan, Shlomi Dinar, Kerstin Stahl, Kenneth Strzepek, and Aaron T. Wolf. 2010. "Mapping the Resilience of International River Basins to Future Climate Change: Induced Water Variability." Discussion Paper 15. Washington: World Bank, Water Sector Board.

Diamond, Jared M. 2005. *Collapse: How Societies Choose to Fail or Succeed*. New York: Viking.

Duflo, Esther, Michael Kremer, and Jonathan Robinson. 2010. "Nudging Farmers to Use Fertilizer: Theory and Experimental Evidence from Kenya." Working Paper. Massachusetts Institute of Technology.

EPI (Environment Performance Index). Various years. Yale University (http://epi.yale.edu/).

ESI (Environmental Sustainability Index). Various years. Columbia University (http://sedac.ciesin.columbia.edu/data/collection/esi/).

FAO (UN Food and Agriculture Organization). 2010. "Global Forest Resources Assessment 2010" (www.fao.org/forestry/fra/fra2010/).

Fashae, Olutoyin Adeola, and Olumide David Onafeso. 2011. "Impact of Climate Change on Sea Level Rise in Lagos, Nigeria." *International Journal of Remote Sensing* 12, no. 32: 9811–19.

Friedman, Thomas. 2013. "Without Water, Revolution," *New York Times,* May 18.

Ganegodage, Renuka, and Alicia N. Rambaldi. 2014. "Economic Consequences of War: Evidence from Sri Lanka." *Journal of Asian Economics* 30: 42–53.

Gautam, P. K. 2012. "Climate Change and Conflict in South Asia." *Strategic Analysis* 36, no. 1: 32–40.

Gleick, Peter H. 2014. "Water, Drought, Climate Change, and Conflict in Syria." *Weather, Climate and Society* 6: 331–40.

Greenwood, Scott. 2014. "A Hotter, Drier Middle East Climate Could Threaten Stability." *Washington Post*, July 3.

Gupta, Sanjeev, Benedict Clements, Rina Bhattacharya, and Shamit Chakravarti. 2002. "Fiscal Consequences of Armed Conflict and Terrorism in Low- and Middle-Income Countries." Working Paper 02/142. Washington: International Monetary Fund.

Guzman, Andrew T. 2013. *Overheated: The Human Cost of Climate Change*. Oxford University Press.

Hallegatte, S., F. Henriet, A. Patwardhan, K. Narayanan, S. Ghosh, S. Karmakar, and others. 2010. "Flood Risks, Climate Change, Impacts and Adaptation Benefits in Mumbai." Environment Working Paper 27. Paris: OECD.

Hatton, Timothy J., and Jeffrey G. Williamson. 2003. "Demographic and Economic Pressure on Emigration out of Africa." *Scandinavian Journal of Economics* 105: 465–86.

Hecky, R. E., R. Mugidde, P. S. Ramlal, M. R. Talbot, and G. W. Kling. 2010. "Multiple Stressors Cause Rapid Ecosystem Change in Lake Victoria." *Freshwater Biology* 55, supplement 1: 19–42.

IDA (International Development Association). 2007. "IDA and Climate Change: Making Climate Action Work for Development." Resource Mobilization Department. Washington.

———. 2010. " IDA16 Themes and Issues." Resource Mobilization Department. Washington.

———. 2013. "Special Themes for IDA17." Document 78555. Resource Mobilization Department. Washington.

IPCC (Intergovernmental Panel on Climate Change). 2007. Fourth assessment report. *Climate Change 2007: Synthesis Report: Summary for Policymakers.* Cambridge University Press.

———. 2014. Fifth assessment report. *Climate Change 2014: Impacts, Adaptation, and Vulnerability* (www.ipcc.ch/report/ar5/wg2/).

Irazabal, Clara. 2009. "Revisiting Urban Planning in Latin America and the Caribbean." UN-Habitat (www.unhabitat.org/grhs/2009).

Islam, N. 2013. "Urban and Nonagricultural Impacts of Flooding and Their Assessments: The Case of Bangladesh." In *The Economic Impacts of Natural Disasters,* edited by A. Borde, D. Guha-Sapir, and I. Santos. Oxford University Press.

Jacoby, Hanan G., Guo Li, and Scott Rozelle. 2002. "Hazards of Expropriation: Tenure Insecurity and Investment in Rural China." *American Economic Review* 92: 1420–47.

Jensen, R. 2000. "Agricultural Volatility and Investments in Children." *American Economic Review* 90, no. 2: 399–404.

Kimenyi, Mwangi S., Temesgen T. Deressa, Jessica E. Pugliese, Andrew Onwuemele, and Micah Mendie. 2014a. *Analysis of Community-Driven Development in Nigeria's Niger Delta Region.* Brookings Institution.

———. 2014b. *Participant Perception of the Effectiveness of the Rivers Songhai Initiative in the Niger Delta.* Brookings Institution.

Kremer, Michael, and Edward Miguel. 2007. "The Illusion of Sustainability." *Quarterly Journal of Economics* 122, no. 3: 1007–65.

Kwak, Sungil, and Stephen C. Smith. 2013. "Regional Agricultural Endowments and Shifts of Poverty Trap Equilibria: Evidence from Ethiopian Panel Data." *Journal of Development Studies* 49, no. 7: 955–75.

Larson, Bruce, and David Bromley. 1990. "Property Rights, Externalities, and Resource Degradation: Locating the Tragedy." *Journal of Development Economics* 33: 235–62.

Li, Quan, and Ming Wen. 2005. "Immediate and Lingering Effects of Armed Conflict on Adult Mortality: A Time Series Cross-National Analysis." *Journal of Peace Research* 42: 471–92.

Lindgren, Goran. 2005. "The Economic Costs of Civil Wars." Uppsala University (http://carecon.org.uk/Conferences/Conf2005/Papers/Lindgren.pdf).

Linquiti, Peter, and Nicholas Vonortas. 2012. "The Value of Flexibility in Adapting to Climate Change: A Real Options Analysis of Investments in Coastal Defense." *Climate Change Economics* 3, no. 02.

Loayza, N., E. Olaberría, J. Rigolini, and L. Christiaensen. 2012. "Natural Disasters and Growth: Going beyond the Averages." *World Development* 40, no. 7: 1317–36.

Maccini, Sharon, and Dean Yang. 2009. "Under the Weather: Health, Schooling, and Economic Consequences of Early-Life Rainfall." *American Economic Review* 99, no. 3: 1006–26.

Malik, Arun S., and Stephen C. Smith. 2012. "Adaptation to Climate Change in Low-Income Countries: Lessons from Current Research and Needs from Future Research." *Climate Change Economics* 3, no. 2.

Maluccio, John A., John Hoddinott, Jere R. Behrman, Reynaldo Martorell, Agnes R. Quisumbing, and Aryeh D. Stein. 2006. "The Impact of an Experimental Nutritional Intervention in Childhood on Education among Guatemalan Adults." Discussion Paper 207. Washington: International Food Policy Research Institute.

Mansuri, Ghazala, and Vijayendra Rao. 2004. "Community-Based and -Driven Development: A Critical Review." Policy Research Working Paper 3209. Washington: World Bank.

Marchiori, Luca, Jean-François Maystadt, and Ingmar Schumacher. 2012. "The Impact of Weather Anomalies on Migration in Sub-Saharan Africa." *Journal of Environmental Economics and Management* 63: 355–74.

McLeman, R., and B. Smit. 2006. "Migration as an Adaptation to Climate Change." *Climate Change* 76: 31–53.

Mendelsohn, R. 2000. "Efficient Adaptation to Climate Change." *Climatic Change* 45: 75–102.

Messer, Ellen, and Marc J. Cohen. 2006. "Conflict, Food Insecurity, and Globalization." FCND Discussion Paper 206. Washington: International Food Policy Research Institute.

Messer, Ellen, Marc J. Cohen, and Thomas Marchione. 2001. "Conflict: A Cause and Effect of Hunger." *ECSP Report*, issue 7 (ECSP7-featurearticles-1.pdf, available at www.fao.org).

Miguel, Edward. 2005. "Poverty and Witch Killing." *Review of Economic Studies* 72, no. 4: 1153–72.

Miguel, Edward, Solomon Hsiang, and Marshall Burke. 2013. "Quantifying the Influence of Climate on Human Conflict." Paper prepared for the Center for the Study of African Economies Conference, Oxford University.

Miguel, Edward, Shanker Satyanath, and Ernest Sergenti. 2004. "Economic Shocks and Civil Conflict: An Instrumental Variable Approach." *Journal of Political Economy* 112: 725–54.

Mitchell, S. A. 2013. "The Status of Wetlands Threats and the Predicted Effect of Global Climate Change: The Situation in Sub-Saharan Africa." *Aquatic Science* 75: 95–112.

Murphy, Mark L., Krishna Prasad Oli, and Steve Gorzula. 2005. "Conservation in Conflict: The Impact of the Maoist Government Conflict on Conservation and Biodiversity in Nepal." Ottawa: International Institute for Sustainable Development (www.iisd.org/pdf/2005/security_conservation_nepal.pdf).

Naudé, W. 2010. "The Determinants of Migration from Sub-Saharan African Countries." *Journal of African Economies* 19: 330–56.

ND-GAIN (Notre Dame Global Adaptation Index). Various years (http://index.gain.org/).

NOAA (National Oceanic and Atmospheric Administration). 2010. "State of the Climate" (www.noaanews.noaa.gov/stories2010/20100728_stateoftheclimate.html).

Ostrom, Elinor. 2005. *Understanding Institutional Diversity.* Princeton University Press.

Plumper, Thomas, and Eric Neumayer. 2006. "The Unequal Burden of War: The Effect of Armed Conflict on the Gender Gap in Life Expectancy." *International Organization* 60: 731.

Raleigh, Clionadh, Lisa Jordan, and Idean Salehyan. 2011. *Assessing the Impact of Climate Change on Migration and Conflict.* Washington: World Bank.

Rentschler, Jun E. 2013. "Why Resilience Matters: The Poverty Impacts of Disasters." WPS6699. Washington: World Bank.

Reuveny, Rafael. 2007. "Climate Change–Induced Migration and Violent Conflict." *Political Geography* 26: 656–73.

Sayne, Aaron. 2011. "Climate Change Adaptation and Conflict in Nigeria." Special Report 274. Washington: United States Institute of Peace.

Smith, Stephen C. 2005. *Ending Global Poverty: A Guide to What Works.* New York: Palgrave Macmillan.

Stark, Jeffrey, Christine Mataya, and Kelley Lubovich. 2009. "Climate Change, Adaptation, and Conflict: A Preliminary Review of the Issues." CMM Discussion Paper 1. Foundation for Environmental Security and Sustainability.

Stewart, Francis, C. Huang, and M. Wang. 2001. "Internal Wars in Developing Countries: An Empirical Overview of Economic and Social Consequences." In *War and Underdevelopment*, edited by F. Stewart and others. Oxford University Press.

Strobi, Eric, and Marie-Anne Valfort. 2013. "The Effect of Weather-Induced Internal Migration on Local Labor Markets: Evidence from Uganda." IZA Discussion Paper 6923 (www.iza.org/en/webcontent/publications/papers/viewAbstract?dp_id=6923).

Sylwester, Kevin. 2004. "Simple Model of Resource Degradation and Agricultural Productivity in a Subsistence Economy." *Review of Development Economics* 8, no. 1: 128-40.

Tanzler, D., A. Maas, and A. Carius. 2010. "Climate Change Adaptation and Peace." *Climate Change* 1, no. 5: 741–50.

Todaro, Michael, and Stephen C. Smith. 2014. *Economic Development,* 12th ed. Reading, Mass.: Addison-Wesley.

Toya, Hideki, and Mark Skidmore. 2007. "Economic Development and the Impacts of Natural Disasters." *Economics Letters* 94, no. 1: 20–25.

UNDP (United Nations Development Program). .2012. *Human Development Report, 2011.*

———. 2013a. "Case Study: Suledo Forest Community" (www.scribd.comdoc/176680253/Case-Studies-UNDP-SULEDO-FOREST-COMMUNITY-Tanzania).

———. 2013b. *Human Development Report, 2013,*

———. 2014. See http://hdr.undp.org/en/content/table-6-multidimensional-poverty-index-mpi.

UNEP (United Nations Environment Program). 2003. "Afghanistan Post-Conflict Environmental Assessment." Nairobi.

———. 2007. "Sudan: Post-Conflict Environmental Assessment Report." Nairobi (www.unep.org/disastersandconflicts/CountryOperations/Sudan/tabid/54236/Default.aspx).

———. 2008. "Afghanistan's Environment 2008." Nairobi.

———. 2010. "Sierra Leone Post-Conflict Environmental Assessment." Nairobi.

———. 2011. "Livelihood Security: Climate Change, Migration, and Conflict in the Sahel." Nairobi.

UNFCCC (United Nations Framework Convention on Climate Change). 2008. "National Adaptation Programmes of Action" (https://unfccc.int/national_reports/napa/items/2719.php).

UN Habitat. 2009. "Regional Latin America and the Caribbean Report" (www.unhabitat.org/downloads/docs/grhs2009regionallatinamericaandthecaribbean.pdf).

UNP. 2014. "United Nations Peacekeeping Presence" (www.un.org/en/peacekeeping/).

United Nations Population Division. 2013. *World Population Prospects.*

"U.S. Climate Report Says Global Warming Impact Already Severe." 2014. *Washington Post.* May 7.

U.S. Department of Defense. 2010. *Quadrennial Defense Review.*

USAID. 2012. "Horn of Africa: Drought." Fact Sheet 29 (file:///Users/User/Documents/4%20Envir:Adapt%20Rsrch%20/ConflictUSAID&Minerva/hoa_dr_fs29_09-30-2012.pdf).

von Braun, Joachim, and Ruth Suseela Meinzen-Dick. 2009. "'Land Grabbing' by Foreign Investors in Developing Countries: Risks and Opportunities." Policy Brief 12. Washington: International Food Policy Research Institute.

Warner, Koko, Charles Ehrhart, Alex de Sherbinin, Susana Adamo, and Tricia Chai-Onn. 2009. "In Search of Shelter: Mapping the Effects of Climate Change on Human Migration and Displacement" (www.careclimatechange.org).

Werz, Michael, and Laura Conley. 2012. "Climate Change, Migration, and Conflict: Addressing Complex Crisis Scenarios in the 21st Century." Center for American Progress.

White House. 2010. "National Security Strategy" (www.whitehouse.gov/sites/default/files/rss_viewer/national_security_strategy.pdf).

World Bank. 2003. *World Development Report 2003*. Washington.

———. 2011a. "PAD for Niger PPCR Project" [project appraisal document].

———. 2011b. *World Development Report 2011: Conflict, Security, and Development* (http://wdr2011.worldbank.org/).

———. 2012. "Turn Down the Heat Report." Pt. 1 (http://documents.worldbank.org/curated/en/2012/11/17097815/turn-down-heat-4%C2%B0c-warmer-world-must-avoided).

———. 2013a. "Doing Business Ranking" (WBDBR). Washington.

———. 2013b. "State of the Poor: Where Are the Poor and Where Are They Poorest?" (www.worldbank.org/content/dam/Worldbank/document/State_of_the_poor_paper_April17.pdf).

———. 2013c. *Turn Down the Heat II: Climate Extremes, Regional Impacts, and the Case for Resilience*. Washington.

———. 2014a. *World Development Indicators 2014*. Washington.

———. 2014b. "World Bank Harmonized List of Fragile Situations List FY2015." Washington (http://siteresources.worldbank.org/EXTLICUS/Resources/511777-1269623894864/HarmonizedlistoffragilestatesFY14.pdf).

———. 2014c. *Youth Unemployment in Africa*. Washington.

World Resources Institute and others. 2005a. "The 2005 Millennium Ecosystem Assessment" (www.millenniumassessment.org/en/Synthesis.aspx).

———. 2005b. (In collaboration with United Nations Development Program, United Nations Environment Program, and World Bank.) *The Wealth of the Poor—Managing Ecosystems to Fight Poverty*. Washington.

12

Toward Community Resilience: The Role of Social Capital after Disasters

GO SHIMADA

Typhoon Haiyan, one of the strongest storms ever recorded, swept across the central Philippines with gusts of up to 200 miles an hour (320 kilometers an hour) on November 8, 2013. It has been estimated that the cost of reconstruction would reach almost US$6 billion. As figure 12-1 shows, in the last two decades there has been an upward trend in the number of such disasters globally.

As the frequency of disasters increases rapidly, the need to build social resilience becomes more and more important. This is particularly important in developing countries, as many countries that have the hardest task in ending poverty are vulnerable to natural disasters. As figure 12-2 shows, there is a clear correlation between poverty and risk. The world risk index shows that the risk of becoming a victim of an extreme natural disaster is high for 173 countries. The exposure to risk is higher if GDP per capita is low. Further, in any one country, the most vulnerable members of the population, such as the poor, children, the elderly, women, and minorities (linguistic, ethnic, religious, migrant, among others), are usually hit hardest by disasters (Steinberg 2000; Cutter and Emrich 2006; Cutter and Finch 2008). These structural vulnerabilities are rooted in horizontal, or group, inequalities.

Where natural disasters occur frequently, it is difficult for developing countries to eradicate poverty and achieve sustainable development (JICA 2008a,

369

Figure 12-1. *Distribution of Natural Disasters, Five Regions, 1945–2013*[a]

Number of disasters

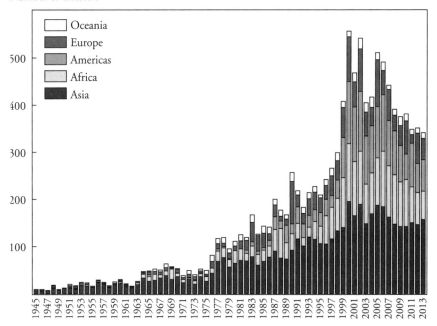

Source: Author's calculations, based on data by the EM-DAT/CREDS.

a. The EM-DAT database is constructed and maintained by the Center for Research on the Epidemiology of Disasters (CRED). The database is global and contains natural disaster data (such as geophysical, meteorological, and climatological natural disasters) from 1900 to the present.

2008b). For instance, Rasmussen (2004) studied several Caribbean islands and found that developing countries tend to be affected the most by natural disasters (a median reduction of the growth rate by 2.2 percentage points in the year of the disaster). International donors have been helping societies cope with disaster in the phases of prevention (mitigation and preparedness), response, and recovery and reconstruction. As the frequency of disasters increases rapidly, however, it is an urgent task for the international community to help developing countries in another task: building resilience. Resilience will reduce risk and thus help eradicate poverty.

This chapter focuses on how countries or societies can be resilient to external shocks, such as natural disasters. Resilience is the capacity to cope with external shocks and restore the previous state. It is known that certain neighborhoods in disaster-hit regions recover more quickly than others (Edgington 2010). What factors render a certain country or society resilient? This chapter considers that

Figure 12-2. *World Risk Index and GDP per Capita*[a]

World risk index 2013

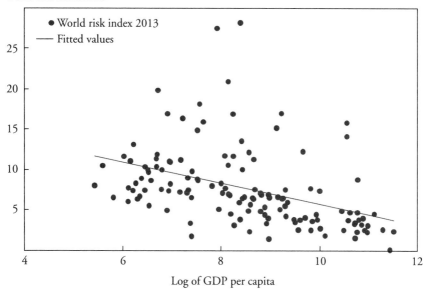

Log of GDP per capita

Source: Author.

a. The vertical axis is the World Risk Index 2013 by United Nations University, Institute for Environment and Human Security (UNU-EHS).

social capital makes a critical difference both in developed countries and in developing countries. How, then, does social capital work?

This chapter first reviews the concept of resilience to determine the ideal conditions for resilient societies. The following discussion looks at how social capital, the essential glue of society, can help build a resilient society.

What Is Resilience?

In 2005 the World Conference on Disaster Reduction adopted the Hyogo Action Framework for Action (UNISDR 2005). It focused on how to build nations and communities resilient to disasters. There is growing interest in resilience in the context of post-2015 studies of Millennium Development Goals (such as World Bank 2013) as well as studies in such fields as psychology, economics, environmental science, and civil engineering (Norman 1971; Anthony 1987; Okada 2005; Norris and others 2008; Longstaff and others 2010; Guillaumont 2009).

The term *resilience* has been used in different contexts and with different meanings. In civil engineering, resilience refers to how fast physical structures such as buildings and expressways can be returned to their predisaster condition. In disaster relief operations, it refers to restoring civilian life. In psychology, it refers to an individual's ability to overcome trauma. In business, it refers to a business continuity plan. Some definitions emphasize the role of community (Aldrich 2012; Tatsuki 2007), and some emphasize physical toughening (Dacy and Kunreuther 1969). The word *resilience* derives from the Latin *resilire*, which means to recoil or leap back.[1] The *Oxford English Dictionary* (*OED*) defines resilience as, first, the ability of a substance or object to spring back into shape, elasticity; and second, the capacity to recover quickly from difficulties; toughness. Hence, there are two important components in the definition of resilience. One is capacity and the other is outcome. Almost every definition of resilience includes the factor of capacity. For instance, Norris, Wyche, and Pfefferbaum (2008) define resilience as the "capacity for successful adaptation in the face of disturbance, stress, or adversity." The main difference among the several definitions lies in the idea of outcome. In the case of the *OED*, outcome is a return to the original shape.

Resilience Frameworks

The resilience framework of the U.S. Multidisciplinary Center for Earthquake Engineering Research (MCEER) is very similar to that of the OED definition in terms of outcome. MCEER defines *resilience* as the capacity to cope with external shocks and bounce back to the previous state. In the MCEER framework, resilience is a measure of how vulnerability can be minimized.[2]

By contrast, the United Nations definition of *resilience* focuses mainly on the ability (or capability) to restore basic functions but not necessarily to restore the predisaster state: "The ability of a system, community or society exposed to hazards to resist, absorb, accommodate to and recover from the effects of the hazard in a timely and efficient manner, including through the preservation and

---

1. The genesis of research on resilience differs depending on the academic discipline. In psychology, it dates back to risk study in the 1970s. Norman (1971) studied children with schizophrenic mothers and children with mothers with mental problems (but not schizophrenia). He found that even facing this risk, some children were highly adaptive and healthy. This high adaptability was the genesis of a resilience study in psychology. Later, Anthony (1987) used the term *invulnerability* to capture this high adaptability. Psychological resilience has three aspects: the competence to endure even under stress, the ability to recover from traumatic shock, and the ability to overcome inequality.

2. To achieve this, the following four Rs are crucial: robustness (inherent strength), redundancy (system properties that allow alternative options), resourcefulness (the capacity to mobilize needed resources), and rapidity (the speed with which disruption can be overcome). Based on MCEER's (2006) resilience framework, Hayashi (2012) proposed three steps to strengthen resilience. These are evaluating the risk in the specific context, preparing for a huge risk, and preparing to recover.

Figure 12-3. *Resilience Framework*

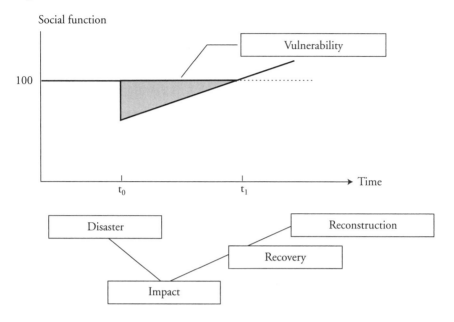

Source: Author, based on Hayashi (2012).

restoration of its essential basic structures and functions" (UNISDR 2012). In this definition, the focus is more on the capacity side rather than the outcome. Here, *resilience* is defined as the ability of social units (government, local administrations, organizations, communities) to mitigate disasters and implement recovery activities while minimizing social cost and preventing future disasters.

Proposed Resilience Framework

The definition by MCEER is very clear about the ideal state to be restored; however, this is difficult to achieve. Although damaged infrastructure can be rebuilt, it is impossible to bring societies or communities back to their original states. Deaths caused by disasters are an absolute loss: the loss is unrecoverable and cannot be compensated afterward through any means. Even if the population or economy recovers, the community is no longer the same. For disaster-hit areas, therefore, in principle all activities afterward go toward creating new societies, rather than returning to the predisaster state.

In this regard, this chapter develops a resilience framework (figure 12-3). The vertical axis is not quality of infrastructure but rather functioning of society. Furthermore, this chapter divides the postdisaster period into two stages: the recovery phase and the reconstruction phase. As discussed above, the capacity of the community is central to the dynamism required to recreate a community in a disaster-hit area. In addition to this engine, capacity is required to take the community in a new direction. This constitutes recovery and reconstruction. This chapter includes the reconstruction phase, which represents a departure from orthodox approaches to disaster. The recovery phase is the short-term period directly after a disaster. This period could last from several months to several years, depending on the magnitude of the disaster. Recovery essentially restores the basic functions of society in the best possible way under the circumstances (McCreight 2010). Those who had left the disaster area come back to live in the area again. One of the important indicators of recovery is population growth.

However, the reconstruction phase is not simply about recovering basic functions but also about recreating a new and vibrant society. The reconstruction phase is crucial to sustaining recovery and putting economic activities back on track. The reconstruction phase is a mid- to long-term process. However, reconstruction itself is a very difficult task, and some areas languish in this phase long after the disasters hit.

Why Are Some Communities More Resilient than Others?

Views are divided regarding the factors affecting resilience (Aldrich 2012). Possible factors suggested are the magnitude of damage to infrastructure (Dacy and Kunreuther 1969; Kates and Pijawka 1977), the quality of governance (Horwich 2000), the quantity of money, or aid, flowing in (Vale and Campanella 2005), and socioeconomic and demographic conditions such as inequality (Katz 2006).

With regard to infrastructural damage, Dacy and Kunreuther (1969) argue that "the speed [of recovery] is determined mainly by the scale of the physical damage," which suggests the benefit of a rapid inflow of capital for reconstruction into a community recovering from a disaster. Kates and Pijawka (1977) argue along the same lines. Is infrastructure, then, the key factor for recovery and reconstruction after disasters?

To examine the logic of this theory, let us look at a case from a developed economy: the population pattern of Kobe, Japan, before and after the great Hanshin Awaji earthquake of 1995. Population recovery is an essential part of disaster recovery (Aldrich 2012; Weil 2010; Davis and Weinstein 2002; Edgington 2010). Vale and Campanella (2005) state that "the numerical resilience of the population may be a reasonable proxy for recovery. For cities that have lost huge percentages of their populations, the restoration of the city as a place of habitation itself is a significant achievement." Figure 12-4 shows the population of Kobe before and after the earthquake. There was a sharp population decline after the earthquake hit in 1995. The earthquake killed

Figure 12-4. *Population of Kobe, 1990–2013, before and after the 1995 Great Hanshin Awaji Earthquake*

Millions

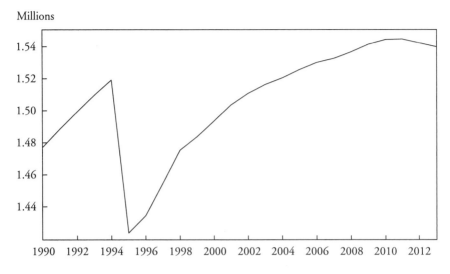

Source: Author.

6,343 people, and around 85,000 people left Kobe that year. It took almost ten years for the population to return to its 1994 level. This curve looks very similar to the resilience framework of figure 12-3. Then can we conclude that Kobe was resilient and recovered well? A review of ward-by-ward data paints a different picture.

Figure 12-5 shows the population of the nine wards of Kobe before and after the earthquake. As the figure shows, population patterns are not unique among these wards. There are four population patterns. One, population declined after the earthquake but bounced back well (Higashi-nada, Nada, Chuo). Two, population declined after the earthquake and continued to decline (Nagata). Three, population decline was small (in other words, damage was minor) at the time of the earthquake but population continued to decline (Suma, Tarumi). And four, there was almost no impact (Kita, Nishi). What, then, are the factors that contributed to this difference among the wards of Kobe? Was infrastructure the most important factor for recovery?

Let us look closely at the case of Nagata. Despite huge infrastructural investment in Nagata ward after the earthquake, the population continued to decline. Nagata is an area that used to be an inner city (a relatively backward area in the city), which housed a cluster of shoe-producing industries and was then redeveloped. During redevelopment many victims were evacuated to temporary

Figure 12-5. *Population of Nine Wards of Kobe, 1990–2013, before and after the 1995 Great Hanshin Awaji Earthquake*

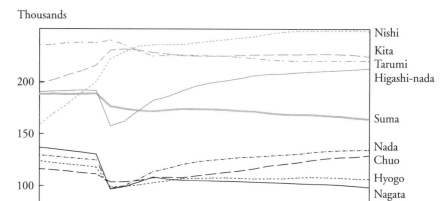

Source: Author.

housing. Most of the residents of the newly developed site are from outside of the community, and most of the predisaster residents have not come back. Therefore, the nature of the community has changed. As Ostrom (2000) states, social capital (or common understanding) is easily destroyed when large numbers of people are rapidly displaced. The redevelopment project in Nagata destroyed the social capital that existed before the disasters. The volume of pedestrian traffic in shopping streets in Nagata ward is also in decline (figure 12-6). In the worst case, the decline was more than 60 percent in 2008 (thirteen years after the earthquake) in the First Avenue shopping street of Shin-Nagata, compared with the preearthquake level.

The same kind of examples can be found anywhere. Although infrastructure is important, infrastructure alone does not contribute to recovery. What other factors, then, can be considered? As mentioned earlier, this chapter considers that it is social capital that makes the difference. This is because infrastructure (physical capital) itself does not create social and economic activities. It is just a means. These activities are created through use. To be used, infrastructure should align with the demands of the area. If infrastructure is connected with the social capital of the area, it will increase the social return on the investment as well as economic return and will become the key driver of societal resilience.

Figure 12-6. *Pedestrian Traffic, Nagata Ward, 2006 and 1992*

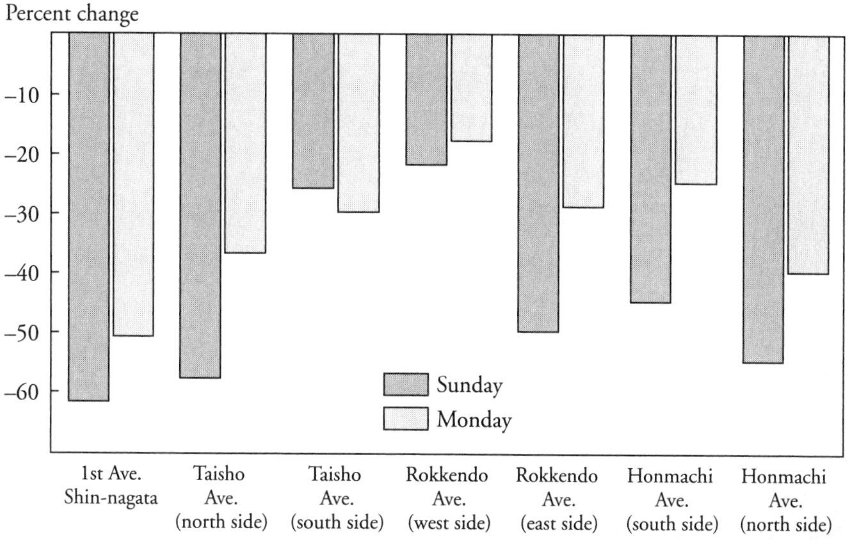

Percent change

Source: Author, based on analysis by Shibanai (2007) and Tatsuki (2005, 2007).

This chapter assumes that if social capital is high in a society, the network will provide the social safety net necessary after devastating external shocks, helping other community/network members to make society resilient. This is particularly true in developing countries, because governments do not function as effectively as those in developed countries. So in many cases in developing countries, social capital is the only available social safety net for the poor, especially in a crisis situation.

How Social Capital Works

This section discusses what social capital is and how the mechanism works to make a society resilient.

What Social Capital Is

Social capital has been studied intensively following the early work of Loury (1977, 1981); Putnam, Leonardi, and Nanetti (1993); Putnam (1995, 2000); Coleman (1988, 1990); Granovetter (1973); and Bourdieu (1986). The idea's genealogy goes back to Tocqueville (1835) and Hanifan (1916). Tocqueville enthused that American citizens worked collectively to realize democracy in their new continent. Recent debate began with Loury. He rejects neoclassical arguments because for him the theory of mainstream economics focuses too much on human capital. Its image of the market is that individuals simply compete with each other on a level playing field, but this image does not explain racial income differences. Loury points out the inadequacies of the individualistic argument but did not develop a concept like social capital. He paved the way for Putnam and Coleman.[3]

The debate became active after the publication of *Making Democracy Work: Civic Traditions in Modern Italy* by Putnam and others (1993). These authors compare the differences between northern and southern Italy in terms of the quality of governance and find that the stock of social capital (measured in terms of groups and clubs) in northern Italy is behind the success of democracy and economic development. Putnam later published another important work, *Bowling Alone: The Collapse and Revival of American Community* (2000), which is celebrated not just by academics but also by the wider public. In this book, Putnam discusses the declining trend of social capital in the United States, pointing out that more people were bowling alone rather than in leagues.

Social capital is broadly understood as community/network relations that affect individual behavior. There are many variations in its definition (Putnam 2000; Fukuyama 1999; Bourdieu and Wacquant 1992; Bourdieu 1986; Granovetter 1973; Coleman 1988; Durlauf and Fafchamps 2004; Aoki 2010).[4]

---

3. Some authors equate social capital with trust and trustworthiness in the community, whereas others regard social capital as a product of class and as belonging to individuals rather than communities. The former view is represented by Coleman and Putnam. The latter view is by Bourdieu. Coleman (1988) argues that social capital is embedded in relationships between people. In other words, his focus is on networks rather than individuals. He points out that the social capital of Catholic communities has positive impacts on the education levels of young people in the United States. He also illustrates how close community ties aided the business transactions of diamond dealers in the orthodox Jewish area in Brooklyn. Coleman started to focus on social capital in his quest to find out the factors that influence an individual's human capital. The causal relationship, in his view, was that social capital has great impacts on the accumulation of human capital. On the other hand, for Putnam the causal relation is in the opposite direction. For him, human capital accumulation is the best way to foster social capital. For instance, in his view, education is the best way to encourage people to participate in volunteer activities.

4. The notion that the social relations referred to by the term *social capital* are actually types of capital is itself problematic. Arrow (2000) rejects the term on the grounds that social capital does not have the characteristics of capital, and suggests that it should be abandoned. He states that "capital" should have three aspects: extension in time, sacrifice of today's benefit for future returns, and alienability. He regards social networks as something built up for noneconomic reasons rather than for economic purposes. Solow (2000) is also negative about social capital, because capital should be the result of past investment flows, whereas social capital is not. Social capital, according to Solow, could simply be behavior patterns. To be capital, it should constitute a stock of production factors that would produce goods and services over a period of time. Solow also points out that behavior patterns may have not only positive impacts on economic performance but also negative impacts, and hence they cannot constitute capital in the same sense as physical capital. Although Arrow is

These stem from the context-specific nature of social capital and its complex theorization and operationalization.[5]

Putnam (2000) defines social capital as follows: "Social capital refers to connections among individuals—social networks and the norms of reciprocity (expectations from a community about the behavior of members) and trustworthiness that arise from them. . . . A society of many virtuous but isolated individuals is not necessarily rich in social capital." Here, Putnam points out three important elements of social capital: trustworthiness, norms, and networks (Durlauf and Fafchamps 2004).[6] This chapter uses the economic concept of stock to define social capital, following the argument of Fisher (1906), who uses the concept of stock and flow, with stock as capital (wealth) and flow as income (see also Morotomi 2010; 2003).

> The distinction between a fund and a flow has many applications in economic science. The most important application is to differentiate between capital and income. Capital is a fund and income a flow. This difference between capital and income is, however, not the only one. There is another important difference, namely, capital is wealth, and income is the service of wealth. We have therefore the following definitions: A stock of wealth existing at an instant of time is called capital. A flow of services through a period of time is called income (Fisher 1906).

Applying Fisher's concept of stock, social capital can be defined as "the stock of trustworthiness, norms, and networks." The amount of stock is not fixed. It can be increased or decreased as stock is added by policy intervention or destroyed by natural disasters. In many cases, natural disasters destroy social

---

critical of the concept, he admits that social capital could contribute to economic performance. Further, depending on the discipline, the meaning differs. In social sciences fields such as sociology and political science, social capital is generally referred to as norms, networks, and organizations. In economics, in addition to these aspects, there is a focus on its contribution to economic growth (macro) and improving market function (micro) (Serageldin and Grootaert 2000). Although there is debate among researchers about definitions, nobody rejects the idea that ingredients of social capital such as trustworthiness, networks, and norms are important (Solow 2000; Putnam 2001).

5. Despite its popularity, the concept of social capital is still controversial. For instance, Portes (2000) admits, in defending the usefulness of the concept, that: "this remarkable range of applications has been accompanied by a great deal of confusion concerning the actual meaning of social capital and growing controversy about its alleged effects." He classifies the issues surrounding social capital into two categories. One is its application to different types of problems; the other is theories involving different units of analysis.

6.The work by Putnam applies the economic concept of stock to the social capital of communities and nations, stressing the importance of the historical path or a legacy of long periods of historical development (Portes 2000). The concept of stock is very useful in defining social capital. I discuss this in a later section.

capital—for instance, by forcing people to leave the disaster-hit area. That is why it is very important to nurture social capital after natural disasters.

The Role of Social Capital after Natural Disasters

A social function consists of formal institutions, the market, and social capital (figure 12-7). Formal institutions and social capital are closely associated with each other. Formal institutions include political regimes, governments, court systems, rule of law, and bureaucracy (North 1990; Olson 1982).[7] Social capital, formal institutions, and markets interact and complement each other as components of social function. Social capital makes up the deficiencies in the market.[8] In the presence of market failures such as imperfect information and enforcement, externalities, free riders, the tragedy of the commons, and the prisoner's dilemma, social capital is one way to achieve Pareto efficiency (though not the only one) (Durlauf and Fafchamps 2004; Aldrich 2012). The role of social capital is to increase Pareto efficiency in the society, filling the gaps left by markets, as Durlauf and Fafchamps (2004) and Stiglitz (2000) discuss.

The appropriate balance among these three factors differs depending on social conditions, such as the level of development and the external shocks suffered.[9] After a disaster, it is challenging for any government (a part of a formal institution) to provide the required help. This is particularly true for developing countries, where resources and capacities are limited compared with developed countries. This is the same as the function of the market in developing countries. Due to various disruptions (for example, damages to offices and transportation) and a sudden spike in demand by disaster-affected people, the market cannot work properly and effectively in the initial emergency phase after a disaster, even in developed economies. Further, the poor are less able to afford market goods and services. On the other hand, building social capital requires time.

---

7. The institutional approach has been studied by North (1990), Aoki (2010), and Ostrom (2005), among others. Matsuoka (2009) compares the definitions of institutions made by these three authors and argues that their definitions were similar, since *institution* implies a variety of actors forming a society by interacting with each other through formal (legal) and informal (traditional rules and social norms) structures.

8. Social capital not only addresses market failure but also complements government functions (Durlauf and Fafchamps 2004). Coleman (1988) shows that voluntary participation in a PTA reduces and solves interpersonal conflicts, which cannot be resolved by state intervention. In terms of development, it has been suggested that social capital is especially important in the early stages. Once a sufficient level of general trust is generated, the importance of social capital decreases (North 2001; Durlauf and Fafchamps 2004). That is why even though the social capital of the United States had decreased, as Putnam (2000) finds, economic performance during the same period was not affected.

9. Serageldin and Grootaert (2000) argue that the appropriate level of social capital differs depending on country and period. This argument is in line with Stiglitz (2000).

Figure 12-7. *Three Components of Social Function*

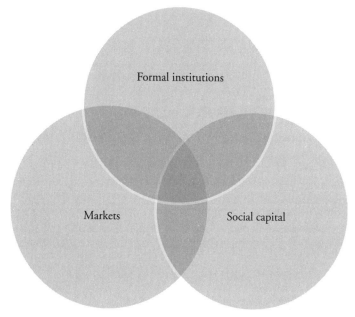

Source: Author.

The poor have an advantage because their opportunity cost is less than that of the rich to build social capital (Collier 1998).

Figure 12-8 shows how these three factors work before and after external shocks and throughout the recovery and reconstruction phases. The vertical axis shows the component proportion ratio of social capital. The upper end is the total social function a society needs from formal institutions, markets, and social capital. The horizontal axis shows time. From left to right it moves from the pre-disaster situation, through disaster, recovery, then reconstruction. The left side shows that, in normal conditions, the role of social capital compared with institutions and markets is relatively small. However, when disasters occur, relative to the emergency needs of society the role of formal institutions and markets is small. People rely on social capital in emergency situations. For instance, without information from neighbors, it is difficult for emergency workers to identify those who need immediate help, such as seniors and disabled people. In many cases, neighbors are the first to extend help to those people.

In the process of recovery and reconstruction, institutions and markets gradually start to function, complementing or replacing the role of social capital. For instance, in the early recovery phase, food and water (or any other necessary

Figure 12-8. *Component Proportion Ratio of Social Function*

Share

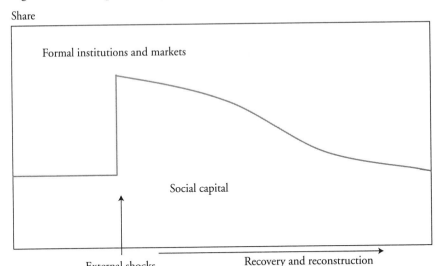

External shocks

Recovery and reconstruction

Time

Source: Author.

goods) need to be provided to victims by government or NGOs. However, the situation needs to return to normal in the end.

As Arnott and Stiglitz (1991) discuss, people have choices regarding insurance. One is market-based insurance and the other is social capital (nonmarket insurance), such as marriage (in which a husband and wife help each other). The cost of market-based insurance is less since private insurance companies can hedge their risks much better than families can. What then is the optimum for the economy? If nonmarket insurance crowds out market-based insurance, it is not optimal. It is not effective for risk sharing because it is provided on an individual basis. That is why Stiglitz (2000) states that, as an economy develops, its social capital must adapt, allowing the formal institutions of a market economy to replace informal arrangements. Stiglitz describes this as "an inverted U-shape relationship." Initially, economic development increases as social capital increases. In other words, social capital provides the conditions for development. After a certain level of development, the role of social capital decreases and the roles of the market and formal institutions increase in importance.

After natural disasters, very similar scenarios to the insurance case described above occur. Soon after a disaster, huge amounts of relief supplies and volunteers flow in. This quick response is very important, since it is difficult for governments and markets to respond to natural disasters and to provide the necessary

Table 12-1. *Roles of Social Capital in Disasters' Recovery Phase*

Broad mechanism	Recovery application
Informal insurance: Strong social capital provides information, knowledge, and access to members of the network.	Social resources serve as informal insurance and mutual assistance after a disaster.
Encourage collective action: Strong ties create trust among network members.	Strong social capital helps by overcoming collective action problems that stymie recovery and rehabilitation.
Encourage participation: Social capital builds new norms about compliance and participation.	Networks strengthen voices and decrease the probability of exit from neighborhood.

Source: Based on Aldrich 2012.

help efficiently. Informal assistance helps the affected society to recover its social function quickly. However, in the mid-to-long term, if this aid remains it could crowd out private sector activities and hamper healthy market recovery. As time goes by, the market needs to play its role in recovery, providing the necessary goods and job opportunities for the victims of disasters.

The most important point is that a larger role has to be played by social capital until disaster-affected societies fully recover (see figure 12-8). This is particularly true in developing countries, because markets and institutions usually do not function as effectively as in developed countries.

Social Capital in the Recovery Phase

Now let us consider the role of social capital in detail in a post-natural-disaster context. The previous discussion gave us a macroeconomic perspective. Now we will examine the mechanism from a microeconomic perspective. We start with the recovery phase and then move on to the reconstruction phase. There are three possible mechanisms through which social capital can achieve Pareto efficiency (table 12-1).

Social Capital as Informal Insurance

First of all, strong social capital provides information, knowledge, and access to members of the network, reducing asymmetry of information and enforcement. This becomes informal insurance for the local community. It is known that few households buy market-based insurance (Sawada and Shimizutani 2008) and that it is also difficult for governments to deal with the very first phase of disasters—the recovery phase. Further, in the context of developing countries, it is difficult for the poor to afford private insurance, so they need to depend on social capital.

Therefore, mutual help within communities after disaster is often critical in the recovery phase. This type of mutual help can include physical help (the sharing of tools, living space, and food), information sharing, and financial aid, among other things. Information sharing is important to help victims know where help is provided and to help government and NGOs reach vulnerable people. During the chaotic first phase, providing a match between the needy and the help that is on offer is often a very difficult task. Information provided by the informal social network in the area is often most useful in making the emergency rescue operation effective. In addition, for those who are forced to leave because of a disaster, information on how and where other community members have moved affects their decisions about whether to come back or whether to settle down in a new area.[10]

As box 12-1 shows, the very process of preparing a hazard map heightens the awareness of the community about possible disasters and about the weaknesses of the community to respond.

Collective Action as a Solution

Second, strong ties create trust among network members, making collective action possible and resolving coordination failures of economies with multiple Pareto-ranked equilibriums (avoiding free riders and the tragedy of the commons).[11] Collective action makes members able to use scarce resources more efficiently. Social capital encourages more people to participate in community actions. People's collective actions allow them to overcome difficulties that they could not address alone.

---

10. After the great Hanshin Awaji earthquake, the allocation of victims to temporary shelter in Kobe was random. Many old people lost ties (informal insurance) that had existed before—and eventually died alone ("lonely death," or *kodokushi*) in temporary shelters. In many cases, nobody knew of their deaths, and they were found months later.

11. As Putnam, Leonardi, and Nanetti (1993) discuss, social capital contributes to overcoming collective action problems, making it possible for communities or networks to choose a better option among the possible Pareto-ranked equilibriums. People who collaborate accomplish more, reducing the required inputs. In the context of a social dilemma or collective action, individuals tend to maximize short-term benefits, which render them worse off compared with the option of collaboration (Ostrom 2000). In other words, the issue of public good needs to be decided collectively rather than individually (Serageldin and Grootaert 2000). It is well known that uncoordinated or opportunistic behavior by economic agents will cause market failure. For instance, irrigation projects fail if there is no formal or informal means to impose norms regarding sharing the water (Ostrom 1995; Meinzen-Dick and others 1995). Social capital is the key to this problem. This can be achieved through such means as selective incentives (rewards), social pressure (criticism and ostracism), and surveillance (visible oversight of members) (Serageldin and Grootaert 2000; Dasgupta 1988; Aldrich 2012).

Box 12-1. *Case Studies from Pakistan and Central American Countries*

Rehabilitation and Reconstruction in Muzaffarabad City, Pakistan

Muzaffarabad, the political and commercial center of the Kashmir region, suffered devastating damage from the earthquake of October 8, 2005, that hit northern Pakistan. Located near the epicenter, the city received the most direct effect of the quake. The effect of the earthquake was augmented by the lack of disaster preparedness in Pakistan.

One of the three principles of the Japan International Cooperation Agency (JICA) is to support self-help, mutual help, and public help. In Pakistan, therefore, JICA built a system to organize community-based organizations to remove debris left by disasters and to monitor possible landslides, to warn people about them, and to evacuate people away from them. After the earthquake, a slope disaster-risk map was composed with the help of community members; the map showed the area of landslide and helped identify an evacuation route. JICA also rebuilt the Sathibagh government's girls' high school. It conducted classes on disaster preparedness and provided mental health care for students affected by the disaster.

Disaster Risk Management in Central America

Natural disasters such as hurricane, floods, earthquakes, and volcanic activities occur frequently in Central America. To respond to these disaster risks, the governments of six countries in the region—Costa Rica, El Salvador, Guatemala, Honduras, Nicaragua, and Panama—pledged to make a concerted effort to develop disaster-resilient societies and build a regional cooperation mechanism through the Center of Coordination for the Prevention of Natural Disasters in Central America (CEPREDENAC), a regional disaster coordinating organization.

JICA has been assisting regional cooperation through the center in developing disaster-resilient societies. JICA's Project on Capacity Development for Disaster Risk Management in Central America (known as BOSAI) aimed at reducing risks and damages caused by disasters by increasing the disaster management capacity of communities and local government. To achieve this, JICA conducted the following activities.

—Analyzed disaster risks in the selected pilot communities with the participation of those communities.

—Developed hazard maps.

—Developed community disaster management plans.

—Organized emergency response drills.

—Involved the disaster management teams of central and local governments in the activities described above, enhancing their capacity.

—Shared the knowledge gained from the aforementioned activities with the pilot communities, so as to enhance the disaster management capacity of the area.

This is critical in the recovery process. For instance, Nakagawa and Shaw (2004) studied the old town of Buji, Gujarat, in India, and the Mano area of Nagata ward, Kobe, in Japan after the earthquakes. They found that the work of NGOs was critical in connecting people to recovery efforts. They also report that the interaction between the official bureaucracy and local people was best catalyzed by NGOs or voluntary town organizations, and this fostered trust and facilitated a smoother recovery.

Participatory Networks and the Possibility of Community Members Exiting Their Neighborhoods

The case studied by Nakagawa and Shaw (2004) relates to the third mechanism as well, because a social network strengthens the voice of the community and links it to the government bureaucracy (complementing the work of government). In other words, social capital helps people participate in the community and remain in the community or return to it. This role is particularly important because after a disaster people leave the disaster-hit area. Social capital decreases the probability of residents leaving (or increases the probability of them coming back to) stricken neighborhoods.

For instance, the great East Japan earthquake caused the destruction of community (or social capital) on a huge scale in Tohoku. The tsunami after the earthquake hit the coastal region hard. Many people lost their families, relatives, and friends. In the tsunami-hit area, there was a question as to whether to rebuild the community in the same area, which might be hit by a tsunami in the future, or whether to rebuild it on higher ground, away from the original area. Views differed among community members. Some people insisted that they should go back to the original place to maintain their community. However, others were against this because it might result in further victims in the future. Almost two and half years after the earthquake, there are still many communities where opinions are divided about where to rebuild.

Furthermore, because of the time it has taken to make a decision, people have started to move away from shelters to rebuild their lives, getting jobs, buying houses, and entering schools in new places. This indirect impact slowly destroys communities. This situation is further complicated in Fukushima as a result of the nuclear power plant accident. People were forced to evacuate. Cities inside the evacuation zone have decamped to other cities, with all their administrative structures and work, since nobody has been allowed to stay. Hence, in Tohoku, the community has been destroyed on a huge scale as a result of the earthquake, tsunami, and the nuclear power plant accident. People are still flowing out of the area. That is why rebuilding social capital is important to make people stay or to come back.

Table 12-2. *Roles of Social Capital in Disasters' Reconstruction Phase*

Broad mechanism	*Reconstruction application*
Trade network rebuilding and expansion:	Strong social capital reduces transaction costs among neighbors and private sector activities.
Job creation, business rebuilding, and information sharing:	Social capital promotes job matching between employer and employee, reducing asymmetry of information.
	Social capital promotes knowledge transfer among networks (technology and business information) to make industrial clusters more competitive.
	Social capital provides access to distant markets.

Source: Author.

Social Capital in the Reconstruction Phase

Among the issues communities face in the reconstruction phase are the chronic problems that they faced before the disaster but that have been amplified by the disaster. As discussed before, jobs are key.[12] Jobs and population recovery are inseparable. These two cogs are especially important in the phase of reconstruction beyond recovery; without this mechanism, no economy will succeed in either recovery or reconstruction. In the reconstruction phase, the mechanisms by which social capital works are four causal relationships (table 12-2): transaction cost reduction, job matching, business information and technology transfer, and access to distant markets.

Trade Network Rebuilding and Expansion

The private sector is key to the reconstruction of economic activities after natural disasters. Especially important are small and medium-sized enterprises, including retail shops. Social capital plays an important role in revitalizing these private sector activities because it decreases transaction costs.[13] If people can trust their business counterparts, then they can avoid certain negotiations and paperwork. Through social capital people may not need contracts, for instance,

12. Putnam (2000) emphasizes that norms of reciprocity and trustworthiness are the key ingredients of economic growth and that social capital provides such norms to the society.
13. See Coase (1937). Transaction costs also include information costs (Stiglitz 2000).

in dealing with neighbors; without social capital, a contract is needed.[14] This effect of social capital promotes new businesses. In this way, social capital can address market failures by reducing transaction costs in private sector activities.[15]

Job Creation and Business Rebuilding through Information Sharing

As discussed, job creation is one of the big issues after natural disasters. In many cases, companies are forced to stop operation (or go bankrupt) due to damage caused by natural disasters, and many people lose their jobs. So in the mid-to-long term, people need decent jobs to rebuild their households. Therefore, job matching is an important function of social capital.[16] Asymmetry of information is common in labor markets. In this situation, it is difficult to match actual jobs with the labor available. For the employer, it is not easy to find somebody suitable through references, since it is difficult to get accurate information

14. Putnam (2001) finds a correlation between the declining trend in social capital and an increase in the number of lawyers in the United States. Fukuyama (2000) also points out that high social capital "reduces the transaction costs associated with the formal coordination mechanism like contracts, hierarchies, bureaucratic rules, and the like." This is also a point made by Arrow (1972), who states that social capital can promote investment, substituting for certain institutions, such as legal frameworks. Further, riskier projects can be resourced.

15. As repeated-games literature shows, cooperation becomes easier if there is the prospect of further interaction in the future (Abreu 1988; Fudenberg and Maskin 1986; Kreps and others 1982).

16. Take the example of imperfect information; one important role of social capital is to decrease the asymmetry of information, as Hayek (1945) and Stiglitz and Rothschild (1976) point out. As a result of such a market failure, agents will not be able to find each other efficiently. Social capital can address this market failure and improve social exchange through networks (Hayami 2009). As Serageldin and Grootaert (2000) note, the high performance of the East Asian "miracle" economies cannot be explained by factors that neoclassical economics emphasizes, such as investment in human and physical capital and technology. They argue that East Asian countries invested in social capital by creating an enabling environment for economic growth (such as institutional arrangements and organizational designs to enhance efficiency, to promote public–private partnerships, and to promote exchange of information). On the other hand, because of imperfect information, traditional societies with high social capital may hesitate to adopt unfamiliar and unconventional new technologies (Ostrom 2000). Hence it can be the case that the same social capital produces opposed results (Akerlof 1976). Stiglitz (2010, 2012), therefore, suggests that learning should be promoted through government intervention in the market. As Ostrom (2000) states, it is important for entrepreneurs to understand relevant factors of production and to relate these effectively. Those entrepreneurs try to establish networks of relationships to increase benefits. With regard to the issue of free riders, Akerlof and Kranton (2000) discuss the idea that group identity affects altruism; hence making group identity stronger is an efficient solution to free riders. This has been confirmed by much empirical research employing the trust game and the dictator game (for example, Fershtman and Gneezy 2001). The sense of community triggers behavior better aligned with the common good. Moreover, the norms developed in societies alter the actions and preferences of its members. The norm is an expectation placed on others regarding issues and responsibilities (such as walking patrols and traffic control in school zones by a parent-teacher association). That is why community and norm building is beneficial in preventing possible external shocks as well as in recovering from shocks.

on job applicants' capacities.[17] Put more simply, information in the form of personal recommendation addresses the asymmetry of information and catalyzes job matching.

Further, social capital also helps to rebuild industries promoting information sharing among entrepreneurs and within industrial clusters (Nam, Sonobe, and Otsuka 2009; Shimada 2013). For instance, Barr (2000) discusses a social network among entrepreneurs in Ghana that catalyzes information exchange on new technology.[18]

So far, throughout this section, we see how social capital works to foster recovery and reconstruction. But we need to ask, is social capital always good? The next section tackles this question.

Is Social Capital Always Good?

As Portes (2000) points out, social capital is not always beneficial to society. The same social capital that benefits members in privileging access to certain resources might exclude nonmembers from access (Portes 1998; Arrow 2000). Social networks are by nature exclusive to their members; otherwise they would not be social networks (Dasgupta 1999).[19]

Narayan (1999) provides a useful framework of analysis for understanding the negative externalities, categorizing social capital into two parts: bonding and bridging. His focus is on the social structure. As figure 12-9 shows, social capital can bond networks, which maintain solidarity within social groups, or it can bridge networks. One example of bonding is the family. It is possible to have high bonding social capital (by which members help each other) but a lack of bridging social capital (the exclusion of members of other social groups).

---

17. Studying the U.S. labor market, Granovetter (1974) finds that social networks raise the efficiency of the job-matching process and speed up the job search for workers.

18. The function of social capital in ethnic business enclaves, employing a co-ethnic labor force, has also been extensively studied (Portes 1998). These include Chinatown in New York (Zhou 1992), Little Havana in Miami (Portes 1987; Portes and Stepick 1993; Perez 1992), and Koreatown in Los Angeles (Light and Bonacich 1988; Nee and others 1994). Stone and others (1992) studied the garment industries in Brazil and Chile. They found that in Brazil the regulatory system, with inconsistent laws and very expensive courts, is too complex. Hence, garment entrepreneurs rely on informal credit information. Contracts are also insecure in Brazil; these circumstances hinder the expansion of small and medium-sized enterprises. The situation is different in Chile, where there is a relatively simple legal system and enforcement. They conclude that, if formal institutions do not work, then social capital works to complement them. Through these mechanisms social capital contributes to reconstruction.

19. According to Waldinger (1995), it is well known that the fire department of the city of New York) is dominated by Italian Americans, the diamond trade in New York is monopolized by Jews, and various sectors of Miami's economy are dominated by Cubans.

Figure 12-9. *Bonding and Bridging Social Capital*

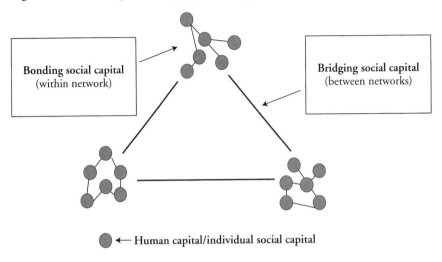

Source: Based on Aldrich (2012).

In many cases, external shocks, such as natural disasters, amplify existing chronic problems and inequalities in a community (Olson 1982; Aldrich and Crook 2008). Aldrich (2012) states that social capital is "a double-edged sword" or "Janus-faced." This is because there is a possibility that social bonding can halt the recovery effort if the nature of a network is exclusive (these groups include a caste, the Mafia, the Ku Klux Klan). Social capital can also restrict personal freedom or individual behavior (such as a woman in purdah in northern India; Narayan 1999). Thus strong ties often encourage young and independent-minded people to leave because they do not like to be regulated by others.[20] This is the classic dilemma, as Simmel (1903) discusses, between social norms (or control) and personal autonomy (or freedom). These negative points should be kept in mind, since we tend to call for more strong ties without being aware of their negative aspects.

In this regard, Granovetter (1973) points out the importance of the "strength of weak ties," by which he means loosely knit networks working apart from the ties of the immediate circle (like a small family) to serve as an informal employment referral system. His view is opposed to the orthodoxy that ties to the immediate circle are the most helpful in finding jobs. This view is also contrary to the argument of Lin, Ensel, and Vaughn (1981). Portes (1998) characterizes

20. Boissevain (1974) studied village life on the island of Malta and found that strong ties and the enforcement of norms reduced the privacy and autonomy of individuals.

their argument as the "strength of strong ties."[21] As we saw, social capital can work negatively, depending on the situation. Therefore, in the process of policy planning, it is important to recognize these negative aspects.

Empirical Findings.

The number of empirical studies on social capital and natural disasters is still small. There are some qualitative studies (Nakagawa and Shaw 2004; Shibanai 2007; Tatsuki 2005, 2007).[22] One of the most comprehensive studies of this field is Aldrich (2012). He quantitatively studied the postdisaster responses of four communities: Tamil Nadu, India, after the 2004 Indian Ocean tsunami; Tokyo following the 1923 earthquake; Kobe after the 1995 earthquake; and New Orleans after Katrina. He employed econometric analysis to study the impact of social capital for population growth and found that the amount of social capital (measured by the number of nonprofit organizations created per capita) most strongly determines recovery rates. This is an important study because he found how important social capital is in different places and in different historical times.

The case studies examined by Aldrich mainly deal with the recovery phase in our framework. Extending his framework, Shimada (2014) quantitatively examined the impact of social capital during the reconstruction phase, focusing on Kobe after the great Hanshin Awaji earthquake. The study finds that both bonding and bridging social capital are important factors for employment. Due

21. Burt also emphasizes weaker ties rather than dense networks, because dense networks simply convey general information among members (nothing new) and oppress the flow of information. He defines social capital as "friends, colleagues, and more general contacts through whom you receive opportunities to use your financial and human capital" (1992).

22. The city of Kobe formed the Social Capital Study Group in 2006, inviting social scientists as advisers. The group published a report just before the great East Japan earthquake. It also organized a workshop among stakeholders and studied the Mano area (a downtown section with a residential area and an artificial leather shoes industrial cluster) and the northern part of Noda in Kobe's Nagata ward. The report finds that the community was a catalyst between the city administration and residents, which is critical in the process of recovery. Further, it concludes that the community functioned well even before the earthquake and that people actively participated in the reconstruction process. The Study Group published a number of articles on social capital in the city of Kobe, such as Shibanai (2007) and Tatsuki (2005, 2007). The former uses elementary school areas as the unit for social capital, which seems to be a useful alternative to disaggregate prefectural data, since much of the community effort centers on elementary schools in Japan. The latter proposed the Seven Elements Model of life recovery for the Kobe earthquake. These seven elements are housing, social ties, townscape, physical/mental health, preparedness, economic/financial situation, and relation to government. Tatsuki (2005, 2007) finds that these seven critical elements accounted for nearly 60 percent of the life recovery variance. Nakagawa and Shaw (2004) also studied the Mano area and find that a community with social capital records the highest satisfaction rate for new town planning and has the speediest recovery rate.

to lack of data, quantitative studies are still scarce, but several research projects are ongoing in various countries, including developing countries such as Philippines. As natural disasters have been rapidly increasing, this in an important area of empirical research in the future to draw concrete policy implications.

Conclusion and Way Forward for International Communities

This chapter explains how social capital works with markets and institutions during recovery and reconstruction from natural disasters. Social capital is the driver to make a society resilient, complementing the work of institutions and markets, especially in developing countries. In ordinary circumstances, institutions and markets work very efficiently to provide social services. However, when external shocks hit societies, neither markets nor formal institutions can provide all the necessary help. People need to rely on social capital in emergency situations. Neighbors are usually the first to extend help. Social capital working together with other types of capital, such as physical capital and human capital, will enhance the social return on investment.

The stock of social capital can be added to or destroyed by internal or external forces. There are possibilities for promoting social capital by policy interventions. In this regard, this chapter introduces community-based recovery and reconstruction projects. The process of preparing hazard maps with the help of community members can be valuable in strengthening the awareness of people in the community about possible future disasters—not just to know the risks but also to realize the weaknesses of the community (such as senior citizens living in unsafe areas). A map will enable people to react quickly at the time of crisis.

As the frequency of disasters increases rapidly, it is urgent for the international community to build resilient societies and promote social capital and link it with other types of capital, such as infrastructure. In most cases, damage caused by natural disasters has a greater impact on people in developing countries than those in developed countries. Therefore, it is important for the international community to assist developing countries to build resilient societies. This is an important missing element in existing efforts to assist the world's poorest people and ultimately to end extreme poverty.

References

Abreu, Dilip. 1988. "On the Theory of Infinitely Repeated Games with Discounting." *Econometrica* 56, no. 2: 383–96.

Akerlof, G. A. 1976. "The Economics of Caste and of the Rat Race and Other Woeful Tales." *Quarterly Journal of Economics* 90, no. 4: 599–617.

Akerlof, G. A., and R. E. Kranton. 2000. "Economics and Identity. "*Quarterly Journal of Economics* 115, no. 3: 715–53.

Aldrich, D. P. 2012. *Building Resilience—Social Capital in Post-Disaster Recovery.* University of Chicago Press.

Aldrich, D. P., and K. Crook. 2008. "Strong Civil Society as a Double-Edged Sword: Sitting Trailers in Post-Katrina New Orleans." *Political Research Quarterly* 61, no. 3: 379–89.

Anthony, E. J. 1987. "Risk, Vulnerability, and Resilience." In *The Invulnerable* Child, edited by E. J. Anthony and C. J. Bertram. New York: Guilford.

Aoki, M. 2010. "Individual Social Capital, Social Networks, and Their Linkages to Economic Game." Paper prepared for the Annual World Bank Conference, Global Lessons from East Asia and the Global Financial Crisis. Washington: World Bank.

Arnott, Richard, and Joseph E. Stiglitz. 1991. "Moral Hazard and Nonmarket Institutions: Dysfunctional Crowding out of Peer Monitoring?" *American Economic Review* 81 (March): 179–90.

Arrow, Kenneth J. 1972. "Gifts and Exchanges." *Philosophy & Public Affairs* 1, no. 4: 343–62.

———. 2000. "Observations on Social Capital." In *Social Capital: A Multifaceted Perspective,* edited by Partha Dasgupta and Ismail Serageldin. Washington: World Bank.

Boissevain, Jeremy. 1974. *Friends of Friends: Networks, Manipulators, and Coalitions.* Oxford, UK: Basil Blackwell.

Bourdieu, P. 1986. "Forms of Capital." In *Handbook of Theory and Research for the Sociology of Education,* edited by John Richardson. Westport, Conn.: Greenwood.

Bourdieu, Pierre, and Loïc J. D. Wacquant. 1992. *An Invitation to Reflexive Sociology.* University of Chicago Press.

Burt, Ronald S. 1992. *Structural Holes: The Social Structure of Competition.* Harvard University Press.

Coase, Ronald H. 1937. "The Nature of the Firm." *Economica* 4, no. 16: 386–405.

Coleman, J. S. 1988. "Social Capital in the Creation of Human Capital." *American Journal of Sociology* 94: S95.

———. 1990. *Foundation of Social Theory.* Harvard University Press.

Collier, Paul. 1998. "Social Capital and Poverty." Social Capital Initiative Working Paper 4. Washington: World Bank.

Cutter, S., and C. Emrich. 2006. "Moral Hazard, Social Catastrophe: The Changing Face of Vulnerability along the Hurricane Coasts." *Annals of the American Academy of Political and Social Science* 604: 102–12.

Cutter, S., and C. Finch. 2008. "Temporal and Spatial Changes in Social Vulnerability to Natural Hazards." *Proceedings of the National Academy of Sciences* 105, no. 7: 2301–06.

Dacy, D., and H. Kunreuther. 1969. *The Economics of Natural Disasters: Implications for Federal Policy.* New York: Free Press.

Dasgupta, Partha. 1988. "Trust as a Commodity." In *Trust: Making and Breaking Cooperative Relations,* edited by Diego Gambetta. Oxford, UK: Basil Blackwell.

———. 1999. "Economic Development and the Idea of Social Capital." Cambridge, UK: Faculty of Economics, University of Cambridge.

Davis, D., and D. Weinstein. 2002. "Bones, Bombs, and Break Points: The Geography of Economic Activity." *American Economic Review* 92, no. 5: 1269–89.

Durlauf, Steven N., and M. Fafchamps. 2004. "Social Capital." Working Paper 10485. Cambridge, Mass.: National Bureau of Economic Research.

Edgington, D. 2010. *Reconstructing Kobe: The Geography of Crisis and Opportunity.* Toronto: UBC Press.

Fershtman, C., and U. Gneezy. 2001. "Discrimination in a Segmented Society: An Experimental Approach." *Quarterly Journal of Economics* 116, no. 1: 351–77.

Fisher, Irving. 1906. *The Nature of Capital and Income.* London: Macmillan.

Fudenberg, Drew, and Eric Maskin. 1986. "The Folk Theorem in Repeated Games with Discounting or with Incomplete Information." *Econometrica* 54, no. 3: 533–54.

Fukuyama, Francis. 1999. *The Great Disruption: Human Nature and the Reconstitution of Social Order.* New York: Free Press.

———. 2000. "Social Capital and Civil Society." Working Paper 00/74. Washington: International Monetary Fund.

Granovetter, M. 1973. "The Strength of Weak Ties." *American Journal of Sociology* 78, no. 6: 1360–80.

———. 1974. *Getting a Job: A Study of Contacts and Careers.* 2nd ed., 1995. University of Chicago Press.

Guillaumont, P. 2009. "An Economic Vulnerability Index: Its Design and Use for International Development Policy." *Oxford Development Studies* 37, no. 3: 193–228.

Hanifan, L. J. 1916. The Rural School Community Centre. *Annals of the American Academy of Political and Social Sciences* 67: 130–38.

Hayami, Y. 2009. "Social Capital, Human Capital, and the Community Mechanism: Toward a Conceptual Framework for Economists." *Journal of Development Studies* 45, no. 1: 96–123.

Hayashi, H. 2012. *Saigai kara Tachinaoru Chikara* [Resilience—power of recovery from disasters]. Kyoiku to Igaku. [Education and medical science].

Hayek, F. A. 1945. "The Use of Knowledge in Society." *American Economic Review* 35, no. 4: 519–30.

Horwich, G. 2000. "Economic Lessons of the Kobe Earthquake." *Economic Development and Cultural Change* 48, no. 3: 521–42.

JICA (Japan International Cooperation Agency). 2008a. *Community Disaster Management from the View Point of Capacity Development.* Tokyo.

———. 2008b. *Building Disaster Resilient Societies—JICA's Cooperation on Disaster Management.* Tokyo.

Kates, R., and D. Pijawka. 1977. "From Rubble to Monument: The Pace of Reconstruction." In *Reconstruction Following Disasters,* edited by J. E. Haas, R. Kates, and M. Bowden. MIT Press.

Katz, B. 2006. "The Material World: Concentrated Poverty in New Orleans and Other American Cities." *Chronicle of Higher Education,* August 1.

Kreps, David M., Paul Milgrom, John Roberts, and Robert Wilson. 1982. "Rational Cooperation in the Finitely Repeated Prisoners' Dilemma." *Journal of Economic Theory* 27, no. 2: 245–52.

Lam, Wai Fung. 1996. "Institutional Design of Public Agencies and Coproduction: A Study of Irrigation Associations in Taiwan." *World Development* 24, no. 6: 1039–54.

Light, Ivan Hubert, and Edna Bonacich. 1988. *Immigrant Entrepreneurs: Koreans in Los Angeles, 1965–1982.* University of California Press.

Lin, Nan, Walter M. Ensel, and John C. Vaughn. 1981. "Social Resources and Strength of Ties: Structural Factors in Occupational Status Attainment." *American Sociological Review* 46: 393–405.

Longstaff, Patricia H., Nicholas J. Armstrong, Keli A. Perrin, Whitney May Parker, and Matthew Hidek. 2010. "Community Resilience: A Function of Resources and Adaptability." INSCT White Paper.

Loury, Glenn C. 1977. "A Dynamic Theory of Racial Income Differences." In *Women, Minorities, and Employment Discrimination,* edited by P. A. Wallence and A. M. La Mond. Lexington, Mass.: Heath.

———. 1981. "Intergenerational Transfers and the Distribution of Earnings." *Econometrica*: 49, no. 4: 843–67.

Matsuoka, S. 2009. "Capacity Development and Institutional Change in International Development Cooperation." *Journal of Asia Pacific Studies* 12: 43–73.

McCreight, R. 2010. "Resilience as a Goal and Standard in Emergency Management." *Journal of Homeland Security and Emergency Management* 7, no. 1: 1–7.

MCEER (Multidisciplinary Center for Earthquake Engineering Research). 2006. *Resilience Framework*. State University of New York, Buffalo.

Meinzen-Dick, Ruth Suseela, Richard Reidinger, and Andrew Manzardo. 1995. "Participation in Irrigation." Environment Department Participation Series. Washington: World Bank.

Morotomi. T. 2003. *Kankyo* [Environment]. Tokyo: Iwanami.

———. 2010. *Chiiki Saisei no Shin Senryaku* [New strategies to revitalize local economy]. Tokyo: Chuko Shobo.

Nakagawa, Y., and R. Shaw. 2004. "Social Capital: A Missing Link to Disaster Recovery." *Journal of Mass Emergencies and Disasters* 22, no. 1: 5–34.

Nam, V. H., T. Sonobe, and K. Otsuka. 2009. "An Inquiry into the Transformation Process of Village-Based Industrial Clusters: The Case of an Iron and Steel Cluster in Northern Vietnam." *Journal of Comparative Economics* 37, no.4: 568–81.

Narayan, Deepa. 1999. *Bonds and Bridges: Social Capital and Poverty*. Washington: World Bank.

Nee, Victor, Jimy M. Sanders, and Scott Sernau. 1994. "Job Transitions in an Immigrant Metropolis: Ethnic Boundaries and the Mixed Economy." *American Sociological Review* 59, no. 6: 849–72.

Norman, G. 1971. "Vulnerability Research and the Issue of Primary Prevention." *American Journal of Orthopsychiatry* 41, no. 1: 101–16.

Norris, F., S. Stevens, B. Pfefferbaum, K. Wyche, and R. Pfefferbaum. 2008. "Community Resilience as a Metaphor, Theory, Set of Capacities and Strategies for Disaster Readiness." *American Journal of Community Psychology* 41: 127–50.

North, D. C. 1990. *Institutions, Institutional Change and Economic Performance*. Cambridge University Press.

———. 2001. "Comments." In *Communities and Markets in Economic Development*, edited by M. Aoki and Y. Hayami, pp. 403–08. Oxford University Press.

Okada, K. 2005. *Sigai Risk Management no Houhou-ron to Keizai Bunseki no Kosa* [Methodologies of disaster risk management and economic analysis]. In *Saigai no Keizai gaku* [Disaster economics], edited by A. Takagi and H. Tatano. Tokyo: Keiso.

Olson, Mancur. 1982. *The Rise and Decline of Nations: Economic Growth, Stagflation, and Social Rigidities*. Yale University Press.

Ostrom, Elinor. 1995. "Incentives, Rules of the Game, and Development." In *Annual Bank Conference on Development Economics 1995*, edited by M. Bruno and B. Pleskovic. Washington: World Bank.

———. 2000. "Social Capital: A Fad or a Fundamental Concept?" In *Social Capital: A Multifaceted Perspective,* edited by Partha Dasgupta and Ismail Serageldin. Washington: World Bank.

———. 2005. *Understanding Institutional Diversity.* Princeton University Press.

Perez, Lisandro. 1992. "Cuban Miami." In *Miami Now: Immigration, Ethnicity, and Social Change*, edited by Guillermo J. Grenier and Alex Stepick III. University Press of Florida.

Portes, Alejandro. 1998. "Social Capital: Its Origins and Applications in Modern Sociology." *Annual Review of Sociology* 24: 1–24.

————. 2000. "The Two Meanings of Social Capital." *Sociological Forum* 15, no. 1: 1–12.

Portes, Alejandro, and Alex Stepick. 1993. *City on the Edge: The Transformation of Miami*. University of California Press.

Putnam, Robert D. 1995. "Bowling Alone: America's Declining Social Capital." *Journal of Democracy* 6, no. 1: 65–78.

————. 2000. *Bowling Alone: The Collapse and Revival of American Community*. New York: Simon and Schuster.

————. 2001. "Social Capital: Measurement and Consequences." *Canadian Journal of Policy Research* 2 (Spring): 41–51.

Putnam, Robert D., Robert Leonardi, and Raffaella Y. Nanetti. 1993. *Making Democracy Work: Civic Traditions in Modern Italy*. Princeton University Press.

Rasmussen, T. N. 2004. "Macroeconomic Implications of Natural Disasters in the Caribbean." Working Paper 04/224. Washington: International Monetary Fund.

Sawada, Y., and S. Shimizutani. 2008. "How Do People Cope with Natural Disasters? Evidence from the Great Hanshin-Awaji (Kobe) Earthquake in 1995." *Journal of Money, Credit, and Banking* 40: 463–88.

Serageldin, Ismail, and Christiaan Grootaert. 2000. "Defining Social Capital: An Integrating View." In *Social Capital: A Multifaceted Perspective*, edited by Partha Dasgupta and Ismail Serageldin. Washington: World Bank.

Shibanai, Y. 2007. "Kobe shinai no social capital ni kansuru jissyo bunseki" [An empirical study of social capital in Kobe-city]. *Toshi Seisaku*, no.127.

Shimada, Go. 2013. "The Economic Implications of a Comprehensive Approach to Learning on Industrial Development (Policy and Managerial Capability Learning): A Case of Ethiopia." Discussion paper. Tokyo: Columbia University and JICA Research Institute (http://jica-ri.jica.go.jp/ja/publication/booksandreports/africa_task_force_meeting_jica_and_the_initiative_for_policy_dialoguecolumbia_university.html).

————. 2014. "A Quantitative Study of Social Capital in the Tertiary Sector of Kobe: Has Social Capital Promoted Economic Reconstruction since the Great Hanshin Awaji Earthquake?" Working Paper 68. Tokyo: JICA Research Institute.

Simmel, Georg. 1903. "The Metropolis and Mental Life." In *The Blackwell City Reader*, edited by Gary Bridge and Sophie Watson. Oxford University Press.

Solow, Robert M. 2000. "Notes on Social Capital and Economic Performance." In *Social Capital: A Multifaceted Perspective*, edited by P. Dasgupta and I. Serageldin. Washington: World Bank.

Steinberg, T. 2000. *Acts of God: The Unnatural History of Natural Disasters in America*. Oxford University Press.

Stiglitz, Joseph E. 2000. "Formal and Informal Institutions." In *Social Capital: A Multifaceted Perspective*, edited by P. Dasgupta and I. Serageldin. Washington: World Bank.

————. 2010. "Learning, Growth and Development." Lecture in honor of Sir Partha Dasgupta, presented at the World Bank's Annual Bank Conference of Development Economics, Stockholm.

————. 2012."Creating a Learning Society." Amartya Sen Lecture, London School of Economics and Political Science. London.

Stiglitz, Joseph E., and M. Rothschild. 1976. "Equilibrium in Competitive Insurance Markets: An Essay on the Economics of Imperfect Information." *Quarterly Journal of Economics* 90, no. 4: 629–49.

Stone, Andrew H. W., Brian Levy, and Ricardo Paredes. 1992. "Public Institutions and Private Transactions: The Legal and Regulatory Environment for Business Transactions in Brazil and Chile." Working Paper 891. Washington: World Bank.

Tatsuki, S. 2007. "Social Capital to Chiiki Zukuri." *Toshi Seisaku* 127.

Tatsuki, S., and others. 2005. "Long-Term Life Recovery Processes of the Survivors of the 1995 Kobe Earthquake: Causal Modeling Analysis of the Hyogo Prefecture Life Recovery Panel Survey Data." Paper presented at the first International Conference on Urban Disaster Reduction. Kobe, January 18–21.

Tocqueville, Alexis de. 1835. *Democracy in America.* University of Chicago Press. Reprinted 2000.

UNISDR (United Nations International Strategy for Disaster Reduction). 2005. *Hyogo Framework of Action 2005–2015: Building the Resilience of Nations and Communities to Disasters.* Geneva.

———. 2009. *Terminology on Disaster Risk Reduction.* Geneva.

———. 2012. "Making Cities Resilient." Geneva (www.unisdr.org/files/28240_rcreport. pdf).

UNU-EHS (United Nations University, Institute for Environment and Human Security). 2013. *The World Risk Report 2013.* Bonn.

Vale, L., and T. Campanella, eds. 2005. *The Resilient City: How Modern Cities Recover from Disaster.* Oxford University Press.

Waldinger, Roger. 1995. "The 'Other Side' of Embeddedness: A Case Study of the Interplay of Economy and Ethnicity." *Ethnic and Racial Studies* 18, no. 3: 555–80.

Weil, F. 2010. "The Rise of Community Engagement after Katrina." In *The New Orleans Index at Five.* Brookings Institution and Greater New Orleans Community Data Center.

World Bank. 2013. *World Development Report: Managing Risk for Development.* Washington.

Zhou, Min. 1992. *Chinatown: The Socioeconomic Potential of an Urban Enclave.* Temple University Press.

Contributors

Michael Carnahan, Department of Foreign Affairs and Trade, Government of Australia

Laurence Chandy, Brookings Institution

Raj M. Desai, Georgetown University and Brookings Institution

Shane Evans, Department of Foreign Affairs and Trade, Government of Australia

Akio Hosono, Japan International Cooperation Agency—Research Institute

Bruce Jones, Brookings Institution

Hiroshi Kato, Japan International Cooperation Agency

Homi Kharas, Brookings Institution

Marcus Manuel, Overseas Development Institute

John McArthur, Brookings Institution and UN Foundation

Alastair McKechnie, Overseas Development Institute and National Centre for Peace and Conflict Studies, University of Otago

Gary Milante, Stockholm International Peace Research Institute

Yoichi Mine, Japan International Cooperation Agency—Research Institute and Doshisha University

Ryutaro Murotani, Japan International Cooperation Agency

John Page, Brookings Institution

Go Shimada, University of Shizuoka, Japan International Cooperation Agency—Research Institute, Columbia University, and Waseda University

Stephen C. Smith, George Washington University and Brookings Institution

Index

Page numbers followed by *b, f, n,* or *t* refer to boxed text, figures, footnotes, or tables, respectively.